B 90

A History of the Oklahoma State University College of Veterinary Medicine

CENTENNIAL HISTORIES SERIES

Centennial Histories Series

Committee

W. David Baird
LeRoy H. Fischer
B. Curtis Hamm
Beulah Hirschlein
Harry Heath
Vernon Parcher

Murl Rogers
J. L. Sanderson
Warren Shull
Milton Usry
Odell Walker
Eric. I. Williams

Robert B. Kamm, Director
Ann Carlson, Editor

CENTENNIAL
1890 • 1990

A History of the Oklahoma State University College of Veterinary Medicine

by Eric I. Williams, F.R.C.V.S., M.S.

with contributions from
Dean Joseph W. Alexander, D.V.M., M.S.
Duane R. Peterson, D.V.M., M.S.
Sidney A. Ewing, D.V.M., M.S., Ph.D.
Dan E. Goodwin, D.V.M., Ph.D.

OKLAHOMA STATE UNIVERSITY / Stillwater

Published by Oklahoma State University,
Centennial Histories Series, Stillwater, Oklahoma 74078

Library of Congress Cataloging-in-Publication Data

Williams, Eric I., 1922-
  A history of the Oklahoma State University College of Veterinary Medicine.

  (Centennial histories series)
  Bibliography: p.
  Includes index.
  1. Oklahoma State University. College of Veterinary Medicine--History. 2. Veteri-
nary medicine--History. I. Oklahoma State University. College of Veterinary Medicine.
II. Title. III. Series. [DNLM: 1. Schools, Veterinary--history--Oklahoma.
SF 777 W722h]
SF756.36.0520358 1986   636'.007'1176634   86-28457
ISBN 0-914956-29-9

Contents

Foreword

A History of the Oklahoma State University College of Veterinary Medicine is the second volume of Oklahoma State University's Centennial Histories Series and the first volume to be published about academic units. The College of Veterinary Medicine is the youngest of OSU's eight colleges, and its history is within the memories of many. Following so soon after volume one in the series, *Historic Old Central*, it provides readers with some interesting contrasts. Among other considerations, *Historic Old Central* offers views and insights relative to nearly a century of happenings on the campus, while *Veterinary Medicine* speaks essentially to the last four decades of the university's first 100 years. Also, *Historic Old Central* is, in many ways, a history of the total university, while *Veterinary Medicine* concentrates on the growth and development of one college of the university.

The Oklahoma State University and the College of Veterinary Medicine are most fortunate in the selection of the author. Dr. Eric I. Williams brings to this history a deep love and commitment to his profession, a loyalty to his college and university, a zest and an enthusiasm for his work and his writing, and both sensitivity and excitement in relating the history of OSU's College of Veterinary Medicine. Punctuated throughout with anecdotes and firsthand observations, *A History of the College of Veterinary Medicine* "comes alive" for its readers.

The Centennial Histories Committee is grateful to all who have shared in the production of *A History of the College of Veterinary Medicine*. Special appreciation is expressed to Vice President Richard Poole, coordinator of OSU's overall Centennial observance, who originally conceived the idea of a Centennial Histories Project. He and President L. L. Boger have been most generous and supportive of the project. Dr. Ralph Hamilton and his staff (notably Gerald Eby and Edward Pharr) have assisted generously. Ann Carlson, as editor for the entire series, has brought keen insight to the project and has worked devotedly to assure high quality volumes.

Special appreciation is expressed to the two deans of the College of Veterinary Medicine who served during the time of preparation of the volume, Dr. Patrick M. Morgan and Dr. Joseph W. Alexander. Their interest, support and encouragement helped to make *A History of the Oklahoma State University College of Veterinary Medicine* a reality.

Robert B. Kamm, Director
Centennial Histories Project
President Emeritus
Oklahoma State University

November 1986

Preface

It is the spirit of the School of Veterinary Medicine to win in spite of the odds. When a spirit like that pervades, there is nothing which will stop our progress.

Dean Clarence H. McElroy

In order to appreciate the status of modern veterinary medicine and our College of Veterinary Medicine in particular, we journeyed back through the shelves of history to God's covenant with Noah to take care of the animals.

The healing arts were stymied for centuries by ignorance, superstition, religious, and philosophical beliefs. The renaissance of medical thought in the fifteenth and sixteenth centuries heralded an era of freedom of thought and innovation. Eventually the ravages of the cattle plagues and other diseases across Europe provided the impetus for the establishment of schools to train veterinarians.

It was a long time before the public became convinced of the need for qualified veterinarians in early America. The colonies were relatively free of disease, and there was still a widespread belief that disease was a punishment for sin. Eventually, private schools began to appear, but they were gradually forced out by more demanding educational standards established by the national government, states, and the veterinary profession.

A demand for "democracy's colleges" resulted in the establishment of land-grant schools. By the beginning of the present century, their influence was considerable. Oklahoma became the forty-sixth state of the Union, and Dr. L. L. Lewis emerged as the father of veterinary medicine in the state. A School of Veterinary Medicine was founded in 1913, but it survived only in name until the 1920s. Eventually it was established (or re-established) and opened in 1948.

As the history of the present college unfolds in the following chapters, it becomes increasingly evident that its survival through very hard times in the formative years was only made possible by the loyalty and hard work of a core of faculty and staff whose dedication far transcended their financial rewards. It is to their yeoman service and the diligent early students that this book is dedicated.

The preparation of this publication would not have been possible without the assistance of many colleagues. During the past four years, we have browsed through endless documents, newspaper clippings, and photos in libraries and archives.

Special recognition is due to our contributing authors: Dr. Duane R. Peterson, regents service professor of physiological sciences, for the history of the curriculum, which is included in many chapters; Dr. Sidney A. Ewing, professor of parasitology, microbiology and public health, for the beginning of the graduate program in Chapter 6; and Dr. Dan E. Goodwin, director of the Oklahoma Animal Disease Diagnostic Laboratory and professor of medicine and surgery, for the Oklahoma Animal Disease Diagnostic Laboratory in Chapter 13. More detailed information on these subjects are available in the college archives. Dean Joseph W. Alexander ''set the sail'' for the future with his euphoria in the final chapter.

I wish to thank Dr. Everett B. Miller, associate editor, American Veterinary Medical Association, and well-known veterinary medical historian for his guidance, encouragement, and several references in the literature and Dr. J. F. Smithcors, American Veterinary Publications, Inc., for advice and assistance.

I extend to our former dean, Dr. Patrick M. Morgan, my sincere thanks for assigning this monumental task to me. I accepted it as a great honor and challenge, though it was exceptionally frustrating at certain times! However, I have been blessed with exceptionally good and loyal assistance from Ann Henson, Susan Harris, and Denise Weaver, formerly in the Dean's Office; Marilyn Wilson, Dorothy Scarbrough, Verlynda Beane, Paula Craven, and Karen McCombs, in the Business Office; Jean Robbins and Wanda Maddux, Department of Veterinary Medicine and Surgery; Kathleen Purdum, Department of Veterinary Pathology; Susanne Spears, formerly college graphic artist; and Robert Slocum, college medical photographer.

Special thanks are extended to Mrs. Katherine McCollom, Stillwater; Dr. William E. Ryan, class of 1951; Mrs. Laverne Jones, college librarian, Mr. Warren Shull, member of the Centennial Histories Committee;

and Dean Joseph W. Alexander for reviewing the manuscript. Mrs. Charlotte Kincaide, coordinator of admissions and former English teacher, was our ever vigilant "eye" for proper grammar. I also cordially thank Mrs. Janet Peterson for information and photographs on Vetceteras; Mrs. Robin Nick and Sharon Fall for the history of the Auxiliary to the Student Chapter, AVMA; Karen Bratcher and Robert Norris, class of 1986, for much information on the Student Chapter, AVMA; and Meg Preston, executive director, Oklahoma Veterinary Medical Association. To our alumni and their spouses, far too numerous to record, I express our sincere appreciation for photos and interviews.

Invaluable research assistance was provided by the staff of the Oklahoma State University Library, OSU Personnel Services, the OSU Public Information Office, and *Daily O'Collegian.* It would have been impossible to prepare a historical document of this nature without the numerous articles and pictures from the *Stillwater NewsPress, Redskin,* and *Aesculapius.* Mrs. Laverne Jones, college librarian, and her staff deserve special credit for their hard work. Dr. Duane Peterson, who gave the first lecture on March 1, 1948, has been an "encyclopedia" of information on many critical issues.

It has been a real pleasure working with OSU President Emeritus Robert B. Kamm, director of the Centennial Histories Project, and Mrs. Ann Carlson, the ever vigilant and meticulous editor of this series who kept us all in line with a smile.

No words can adequately express my deep gratitude to my secretary, Marilyn French, for her loyalty, exceptional hard work, patience and humor in searching the archives and typing the manuscripts in between answering endless phone calls and many other assignments. Her contibutions must always remain an essential part of this book.

Finally, it is a source of great pleasure for me that the publication of this historical document coincides with the 25th anniversary of the arrival of my family from the hills and vales of Wales.

Eric I. Williams
Director of Student and
  Alumni Affairs
Professor of Medicine and Surgery

November 1, 1986

Veterinarian's Oath

Being admitted to the profession of veterinary medicine,

I solemnly swear to use my scientific knowledge and skills for the benefit of society through the protection of animal health, the relief of animal suffering, the conservation of livestock resources, the promotion of public health, and the advancement of medical knowledge.

I will practice my profession conscientiously, with dignity, and in keeping with the principles of veterinary medical ethics.

I accept as a lifelong obligation the continual improvement of my professional knowledge and competence.

Adopted by the AVMA House of Delegates, July 1969

A History of the
Oklahoma State University
College of Veterinary Medicine

1 The Covenant

But with thee will I establish my covenant; and thou shalt come into the ark, thou, and thy sons, and thy wife, and thy sons' wives with thee. And of every living thing of all flesh, two of every sort shalt thou bring into the ark, to keep them alive with thee; they shall be male and female.
Genesis 6:18,19

Ever since God's covenant with Noah, man has been charged with responsibility for the welfare of animals. Throughout the ages, this covenant has been honored; but the path to modern veterinary medicine was arduous and, for centuries, stymied by religious and philosophical beliefs.

Historical analysis reveals that the common belief that veterinary medicine evolved from human medicine is not true. It is a fact, however, that progress in both areas was impeded by the perpetuation of ignorance, born of exorcism.

The history of medicine is closely related to the evolution of a series of "man-animal" cultures. Shepherds began to acquire rudimentary medical skills around 9000 B.C. From their shepherding life emerged values, such as gentleness and caring, conducive to an interest in healing and acquiring the elementary skills of the healing art. Man came to view sky gods as superior gods envisaged in animal form, hence the origin of most signs of the zodiac.[1]

The bull-cow god-worshiping Egyptians, Canaanite-Phoenicians, and Babylonians gained ascendancy over the sheep people throughout the Middle East from about 4000 to 300 B.C. Established about 1850 B.C. before the introduction of the horse to Babylonia, the Code of Hammurabi laid down the first factual foundation for medicine and referred to "doctors of oxen and asses." Legal fees and malpractice penalties were set for these healers. For a successful major surgery on an ox or ass, the specialist received one sixth of the animal's value, and if it died, he paid the owner one fourth of its value.

In ancient Egypt, in addition to performing religious rites, the priests cared for their animals which were maintained in the temples as gods incarnate. Bulls and cows were the greatest and most ancient gods from which the pharaohs claimed their mythological descent. For a long period the horn of a bull remained a symbol of rulers and power throughout the area between the Tigris and Euphrates Rivers on the east and the Mediterranean on the west.

One of the oldest known medical texts was the Kahun papyrus of about 1900 B.C., a manual of veterinary medicine written by an Egyptian priest. It showed an almost entirely rational approach to medical problems, particularly in the field of surgery, based upon acute clinical observation and the development of sound empirical practice and procedure.[2]

The Hurrians, invaders from Asia, introduced the horse to Egypt. The horse became an important animal in the development of medicine and a symbol of wealth.

The first veterinarian whose name is recorded was Salihotra. Living in India in 1800 B.C., he wrote about horses and established high standards for veterinary practice. In 250 B.C. King Asoka ordered the erection of the first veterinary hospitals in India.

In ancient times there was a belief that animals were equal to man. Man's religious and philosophical beliefs about animals in relationship to himself had a profound bearing on his inability to make medical discoveries and progress beyond the demon and exorcist stage. The sanctity of both human and animal life precluded deliberate dissections or experiments designed solely to learn about bodily structure or processes. Hence, everything depended on observation.

During the thousand years before Christ, the center of civilization moved from Egypt to Greece. To be a Greek in the classical era was to be a part of a communion where man aspired to glory, reason, and beauty. Man's recognition of human superior spiritual status over animals evolved among seventh century B.C. Greeks. They became investigators and tried to explain bodily structure and function.

During this Golden Age of Greece, medicine began to sever its direct connection with religion and control by the priesthood. The greatest among the many city-states, Athens, was ruled by men who did not claim divinity. Aristotle,[3] the most comprehensive mind of antiquity who lived in the fourth century B.C., did not practice the art of healing but wrote at length about veterinary medicine and related aspects of animal biol-

4

PHARMACOPOEA **HAGANA.**

A frontispiece by David Coster created in 1738 depicts Aesculapius kneeling with his arms raised in prayer. He is looking at his father Apollo, driving his sun-chariot in the heavens. Chiron the Centaur, Aesculapius' teacher, is seen in the background.

ogy. The early Greek philosophers were pioneers of rational medicine. However, this did not exclude a parallel rise of magic-religious medicine in Greece. This centered around the Greek god Asklepios, later named Aesculapius by the Romans, who is closely associated with the development of Greek medicine.

Raised by Chiron the Centaur,[4] Aesculapius developed great powers of healing. Carrying a staff and accompanied by a sacred serpent, he symbolized hope and triumph over illness. Today the staff of Aesculapius symbolizes the art of healing.

Aesculapius
SYMBOL OF VETERINARY MEDICINE

The Caduceus, the first official symbol of the healing arts, was adopted by the U.S. Army Medical Department in 1902. It consists of two serpents entwined around the winged staff of Mercury, messenger of the gods. Mercury wore a winged cap and had wings on his feet which give him great speed as he conducted the souls of the dead across the Styx, the river which flows through Hades.

The Caduceus was also adopted as the official symbol of the American Veterinary Medical Association in 1921. At that time the association had a large number of members who had served in the Army and who were also looking for an emblem to display on their automobiles. Mercury was also the god of speed and the god of travelers, traders, and thieves. The fast driving veterinarian became a legend in rural practice. The emblem used for veterinarians usually had a V superimposed on the Caduceus.

On June 22, 1970, the American Veterinary Medical Association House of Delegates adopted the Aesculapius as a more appropriate official symbol of the veterinary profession. It depicts a staff with one serpent entwined and a large central V.

Aesculapius was the Roman mythological figure known as Asklepios to the Greeks. Asklepios was the Greek mythological son of Apollo, god of light, healing, and truth, and Coronis, a beautiful maiden.

Coronis did not care for Apollo's divine love and preferred a mere mortal. During her pregnancy she fell in love with Ischys. Apollo, appraised of her infidelity by a white raven (which later turned black), commanded Artemis, his twin sister, to kill Coronis. As Apollo watched the flames roaring up around the maiden who had been placed on the funeral pyre, he snatched the babe that was near birth away from her. Apollo took his son Asklepios to Chiron, the wise and kindly old Centaur, who reared him on goat's milk in a cave on Mount Pelion. Chiron's special medical skills were transmitted to Asklepios who became the Greek god of healing. He was the father of Hygieia, the goddess of health. Leaning on his staff with its entwining serpent, Asklepios revealed himself to every mortal who came to him in distress. Wherever he went, crowds gathered and he cured the sick.

When Asklepios brought a dead man back to life, he offended Hades, lord of the underworld. Hades killed him with a thunderbolt. After his death, Asklepios was represented holding a staff with a single snake wreathed around it. Because of Asklepios's healing power, the staff and serpent is known as the Aesculapian staff, a symbol of the healing art.

The serpent had become the symbol of the healing arts when Gilgamesh, legendary ruler of Uruk, set out in desperate search for the herb of life to free his people from sickness and death. Gilgamesh came to the "primal sea" and, weighted down with stones, sank into the dark waters and plucked the sacred herb from the sea bed. On his way home he left the herb on the bank while he bathed in cool water. A snake ate the herb. Immediately the snake cast off its skin and crawled away rejuvenated. So Gilgamesh lost the herb of life, and the gods condemned man to sickness and death. The snake, possessing the herb of life, became the symbol of healing.

In 1921, the American Veterinary Medical Association took the Caduceus, symbol of the medical profession, superimposed a V on it and adopted it as their official symbol. In 1970, however, the Aesculapius was adopted as a more suitable symbol for the veterinary profession.

As Aesculapius's influence spread far and wide, health resorts, controlled by priest-physicians and known as Asklepiads, sprang up along the Aegean to numerous islands. Into such a guild on the Island of Cos in the fifth century B.C. was born Hippocrates,[5] the "father of medicine." Practically nothing is known of his life, but many legends have sprung up about this great doctor and teacher. About two centuries later, the Greeks, who founded the Alexandrian library and set out to gather all the knowledge of the ancients in one place, found several writings of Hippocrates on medical matters. His approach to medicine dispelled the religious aspect of suffering and laid the foundation for the scientific study of disease. Clinical medicine thus had its inception.

In spite of this breakthrough in human medicine, there remained among many healers an antagonism to the practice of medicine on animals. In fact, it was believed that practicing animal medicine might be a degrading activity for the socially ambitious and wealth-seeking healers.

Eventually, the Greek world was replaced by the Roman Empire in the sixth century B.C. Throughout the new empire, indigenous healers possessed little more than folk knowledge and some Greek slaves possessed more medical knowledge than the Romans!

Rome managed for about six hundred years without physicians. Medical cults utilized religious rites, magic, and sacred animals, including dogs and snakes. The Romans left few monuments in the field of natural sciences, but at least they can be credited with the introduction of horseshoeing.

In the first century A.D., however, it was Cornelius Celsus, who documented the cardinal signs of inflammation: *rubor et tumor cum*

Chronology of Veterinary Medicine Through the Middle Ages

ANCIENT CIVILIZATIONS

B.C. 2200	[Babylonia]	Code of Hammurabi regulates veterinary fees.
B.C. 1900	[Egypt]	Papyrus of Kahun. Oldest veterinary prescriptions.
B.C. 1800	[India]	Salihotra. First veterinarian whose name is recorded; wrote on horses; high standards of practice.
B.C. 400	[Greece]	Hippocrates. Humoral pathology affects veterinary practice for more than 2,000 years.
B.C. 350	[Greece]	Aristotle's *History of Animals* contains references to animal disease.
B.C. 250	[India]	King Asoka orders erection of first veterinary hospitals.

ROMAN AND BYZANTINE PERIOD

B.C. 200	[Rome]	Cato's agricultural works show early veterinary practice to be crude—based on superstition.
B.C. 30	[Rome]	Virgil's *Georgics*. Good descriptions of animal plagues.
A.D. 70	[Rome]	Varro's agricultural treatise. Gives first indication of professional veterinary class; good on contagion.
A.D. 330	[Byzantium]	Apsyrtus, "father" of veterinary medicine. Hierocles, and other veterinarians, write *Hippiatrika,* first major work by professional veterinarians.
A.D. 450	[Rome]	Vegetius: *Books of the Veterinary Art;* an educated layman who decries low state of veterinary art. Book is the first important veterinary work printed (1528).

MIDDLE AGES

A.D. 500-1500	[Europe]	The age of Faith. Patron saints in veterinary medicine. Series of devastating animal plagues rage unchecked. Diminishing influence of veterinary medicine.
A.D. 900	[England]	Anglo-Saxon *Leech Book*. Includes animal leechcraft.
A.D. 1250	[Sicily]	Jordanus Ruffus: *Equine Medicine;* becomes "regenerator" of veterinary art in Europe.
A.D. 1350	[Italy]	Laurence Rusius: *Hippiatria*. Widely circulated in printed editions after 1530.
A.D. 1490	[Spain]	Short-lived veterinary schools established. Licensure required for practice.

From *Evolution of the Veterinary Art* (Kansas City: Veterinary Medicine Publishing Co., 1957), pp. xv-xvii, by kind permission of J. F. Smithcors, author.

calore et dolore, redness and swelling with heat and pain. They are as valid today as they were two thousand years ago. The eight books comprising his *De Medicina* were written in Latin. Because medical and scientific treatises of his time were written in Greek, his writings were not known until the Renaissance when reborn interest in the ancients led to their discovery by Pope Nicholas.

The other contributor of historical significance was Galen,[6] a Greek living in Rome in the second century A.D. Human dissection had been outlawed, so Galen was forced to work on animals. He became the first important researcher on physiological process and anatomy. Based on observations of a variety of animal species, he wrote *Dissections of the Dead and Dissections of the Living*. Galen's theological exposition of medicine proved to be an attractive dogma to the church in whose hands knowledge and learning, including that of medicine, became a monopoly. Medicine already had a "father" in Hippocrates; without Galen it might have died an orphan.[7]

Unfortunately, Galen's writings gave the impression that he was dealing with the human body which accounted for the scorn later heaped upon him for his apparent mistakes.

Virtually nothing new was learned in human or animal medicine following Galen's death in the third century until the ninth century A.D. reign of Harun-al-Rashid Abbasid, caliph of Baghdad and patron of arts and science. Because dissection of man was forbidden to Muslim healers, they continued the Alexandrian Greek tradition of comparative veterinary studies in the interest of human health. This era marked the emergence of specialist healers of horses. The Arabs were great horse lovers, and the royal stables had over twelve thousand horses.

In an attempt to salvage an empire, Roman government shifted eastward to Byzantium during the fourth century A.D., and thus Roman medicine became more Grecian in character. During this brief return to the glories of ancient Greece, the *Hippiatrika*, not only a veterinary classic, but one of the prized literary works of all time, appeared. Compiled on order of the tenth century Emperor Constantine Porphryrogenitus, it comprised the original communications of a large number of veterinary practitioners and contained the work of the fourth century Greek veterinarian Apsyrtus, now considered the "father of veterinary medicine." Byzantium was established as the birthplace of veterinary literature.

The *Hippiatrika* has never been published in English, but the works of the later Roman writer, Vegetius, were translated to English in 1748. He was a layman with an intense interest in the veterinary art. *Books of the Veterinary Art* was the first time that the term *veterinary* was used in a book title. The word *veterinary* comes from the Latin *veterinarius* meaning "beast of burden."[8]

Other than Vegetius's contributions in the sixth century A.D., veterinary medicine fell into a morass of ignorance and superstition in the first half of the millennium between the fall of Rome in 475 A.D. and the end of the Byzantine era in 1453 A.D. In these Dark Ages medicine entered a long period of bondage. Christian philosophy was adopted so literally that physicians were denied the right to heal. Incantations and fasting became pre-eminent. The ancient concept of disease as a punishment for mortal sin—a return to the cults of the temple healers of ancient Greece—was re-established. It was nearly a thousand years before a worthy name appeared on the veterinary horizon.

Even though the Greeks and the Romans stood on the threshold of the modern world, they did not "push the door open." The failure, or paralysis, was a social one. Science had failed to become a real force in the life of society; it was regarded as suitable study only for the elite. Ancient society was firmly entrenched in the thought that power could only be found in the muscles of slaves. Even Plato and Aristotle believed in this doctrine, and St. Augustine in the fourth century accepted slavery as the judgment of God on a world guilty of original sin. The labor of freemen was eventually morally ostracized. Nothing could help but a complete revolution which came with the barbarians from the north between the fifth and ninth centuries A.D.

By the ninth century, ancient slavery was gone. Social classes had been formed by the birthpangs of a new civilization built primarily on non-human power, namely, wind and water power. Benjamin Farrington, in his book *Greek Science,* stated that the technical revolution of the Middle Ages was necessary to prepare the soil of western Europe to receive the seed of Graeco-Roman science which could not grow on the stony ground of ancient slave society. He continued, "the technical device of printing was necessary to multiply and broadcast the seed before the ancient wisdom could raise a wholesome crop."[9]

It was not all "medical darkness." The first medical school in Europe was established in Salerno, near Naples, Italy, in the ninth century. The seeds for medical reform in the Renaissance were sown, and the school was separated from the church. Because papal edict forbade the dissection of the human body, the anatomy of the pig was taught as the best available substitute. The teaching was predominantly Greek, and an apparent conflict with Arabian medicine brought about the decline of the school in the thirteenth century.

The renaissance of medical thought during the fifteenth and sixteenth centuries was not merely a revival of classic culture already begun late in the Middle Ages, but the slow replacement of the depressing aura of the Dark Ages by the concepts of freedom of thought, human dignity, philosophy for the living, and a receptive attitude toward innovation. The Renaissance stimulated an appreciation of the beauty of the human body. Many great artists, such as Michaelangelo, Raphael, Dürer, and DaVinci, were anatomists, but Andreas Vesalius emerged as the foremost anatomist of all time. Vesalius' writing of *De Humani Corporis Fabrica* in the sixteenth century altered the Galenian concept of the structure of the human body. In spite of Christian repression of scientific

Chronology of Veterinary Medicine
In the Sixteenth and Seventeenth Centuries

SIXTEENTH CENTURY

A.D. 1522	[Spain]	Francisco de la Reyna: *Book of Veterinary*. Anticipates Harvey (1628) on circulation of blood.
A.D. 1523	[England]	John Fitzherbert: *Boke of Husbandrie*. Important agricultural work with much on animal disease.
A.D. 1528	[Switzerland]	Vegetius' work (as *Mulo-Medicina*) is first printed book on veterinary medicine.
A.D. 1565	[England]	Thomas Blundeville: *The Fower Chiefyst Offices Belonging to Horsemanshippe*. First major English veterinary work.
A.D. 1576	[England]	George Turberville: *The Arte of Venerie or Hunting*. First English work dealing with diseases of dogs.
A.D. 1587	[England]	Leonard Mascall: *Fyrst Booke of Cattell*. "Greatest rogue in veterinary history."
A.D. 1598	[Italy]	Carlo Ruini: *Anatomia del Cavallo*. First anatomy of the horse; marks beginning of veterinary science.

SEVENTEENTH CENTURY

A.D. 1610	[England]	Gervase Markham: *Markham's Maisterpeece*. This and numerous other worthless works are to be curse of veterinary medicine for two centuries.
A.D. 1639	[England]	Thomas de Grey: *The Compleat Horseman and Expert Ferrier*. Mentions hereditary diseases, first to give rationale for many practices common until recently, e.g., bleeding, purging.
A.D. 1664	[France]	Solleysel: *The Perfect Farrier*. Best veterinary work to date; good account of glanders.
A.D. 1673	[Ireland]	Michael Harward: *The Herdsman's Mate*. First account of intestinal surgery (cattle); antedates human practice.
A.D. 1683	[Scotland]	Andrew Snape: *The Anatomy of an Horse*. First in English; well written, but marred by theft of Ruini plates.

From *Evolution of the Veterinary Art* (Kansas City: Veterinary Medicine Publishing Co., 1957), pp. xv-xvii, by kind permission of J. F. Smithcors, author.

inquiry, this work and that of others led to experiments including those of William Harvey,[10] who described blood circulation.

Veterinary medicine, however, did not flourish. It was not until the end of the sixteenth century that Carlo Ruini wrote *Anatomy of the Horse, Diseases and Their Treatment*. A wealthy Italian nobleman and lawyer, Ruini is one of the most revered in the whole history of veterinary medicine and is credited with the founding of veterinary science separate from the art. It is a remarkable commentary on the state of veterinary medicine for a lawyer to produce the first scientific work!

Surgery also became popular and many advances were made during the Renaissance. Wars were frequent which encouraged the development of surgical approach to the treatment of injuries.[11] During this era, the Spaniards gave the most professional attention to the veterinary art. King Ferdinand and Queen Isabella fostered the establishment of veterinary schools and a system of examinations prior to licensure to practice. The Inquisition, however, put an end to this era and the schools were discontinued.

The cattle plague rinderpest, sweeping Europe repeatedly between 1711-1769 destroying more than 200 million animals, caused a historic turning point in veterinary medicine. Farmers appealed to saints as the protectors of animals, and the clergy preached about divine retribution. However, Pope Clement XI sent his personal physician, Giovanni Lancisi, to investigate and propose controls. He recommended the slaughter of diseased and exposed cattle. The outbreak was subdued within months in many areas of France, but elsewhere it continued to rage—causing untold misery in mass human starvation and more disease.

It is a paradox that a century which started without any veterinarians capable of coping with such an outbreak should become one of the most eventful in the history of veterinary medicine. The French, after losing nearly half their cattle in the first onset of the plague, spent a decade trying to cope with the fearsome disease. When the plague returned in 1750, government action was taken to make animal medicine a scientific profession. The world's first permanent veterinary college, École Vétérinaire de Lyon, opened in Lyons in 1762 with the veterinary practitioner and writer Claude Bourgelat as director. There was such an influx of students from all over Europe that a second college, École Vétérinaire d'Alfort, was established near Paris in 1765.

The need to train persons to manage the devastating diseases of cattle and other animals that were essential in the nation's transport, farm power, shoes and clothing, and food supply and to maintain the health of cavalry and artillery horses brought into existence more colleges for educating veterinarians. Schools were started in Vienna, Austria, in 1768 and Torino, Italy, in 1769. Before the end of the century, twenty veterinary schools had opened in a dozen European countries.

In the British Isles, the art of veterinary medicine had been practiced from the earliest time, veterinary practices having been recorded as early as 900 A.D. By the fourteenth century, practitioners were called "marshals," but practice fell into the hands of empirics known as "cow leeches" (quacks!), who handed down recipes from father to son, and farriers. The latter, who usually served an apprenticeship with their fathers, considered themselves far superior to the leeches. By the end of the eighteenth century, the practice was in disrepute. In 1788, a French veterinarian, Charles Vial de Saint Bel (also known as Sainbel), arrived

Statue of Claude Bourgelat stands on the campus of École Nationale Vétérinaire D'Alfort, near Paris, France. Bourgelat was the director of the first permanent veterinary college, established in Lyons, France. He later also established the college at Alfort.

to study the rural economy and to publish a proposal for establishing a veterinary college in Britain. Saint Bel's plan attracted the attention of Granville Penn, a relative of William Penn, who wrote, "the art requires to be recast not upon a basis of farriery—but on a basis of nature, reason, and wide observation. The name 'farrier' must not be mildly excised and cleaned but altogether expunged."[12]

The Agricultural Society of Odiham became interested and the Veterinary College of London was established in 1791. A staunch supporter was John Hunter, a surgeon who was made a vice president of the college. He had strong views on the need for sound veterinary education and deplored the fact that "the incompetence of persons to whom veterinary practice has been abandoned has drawn contempt upon the art, which should be second only to human medicine—it requires the sacrifice of as many years to make a skillful veterinarian as a skillful physician. The idea must be abandoned that anyone of ordinary capacity can acquire the veterinary art. The nation requires a veterinary school in which the structure and diseases of animals can be scientifically taught—when this is duly accomplished, men of liberal education will cease to look on veterinary medicine as a mean and degraded profession."[13]

Chronology of Veterinary Medicine
In the Eighteenth and Nineteenth Centuries

EIGHTEENTH CENTURY

A.D. 1711	[Italy]	Investigations of cattle plague (rinderpest) by Giovanni Lancisi, a physician, and in England (1714) by Thomas Bates, a surgeon, establish basis for control by slaughter, segregation and sanitation. Later disregard for sanitary police measures results in death of 200,000,000 cattle in Europe.
A.D. 1720	[England]	William Gibson: *The Farrier's New Guide.* First of a series of works by surgeon-farriers; advocates humane treatment of animals, rational medication, and attention by educated men.
A.D. 1761	[France]	Lyons Veterinary School (and Alfort, 1765) founded by Claude Bourgelat. Marks beginning of veterinary profession in contrast to farriery.
A.D. 1778	[Scotland]	James Clark: *Treatise on the Prevention of Disease.* Best work of century, makes Clark, a farrier, "father" of veterinary hygiene.
A.D. 1783	[England]	Francis Clater: *Every Man His Own Farrier.* Progenitor of countless later "horse-doctor" books.
A.D. 1791	[England]	London Veterinary College founded by a French veterinarian, Sainbel. Sets up three-year course covering all animals, but dies 1793. Edward Coleman, a surgeon, succeeds Sainbel, course is reduced to three months study of horse. Training remains inferior for half century.

EARLY NINETEENTH CENTURY

A.D. 1802	[England]	Delabere Blaine: *Outlines of the Veterinary Art.* First reasonably scientific exposition of veterinary medicine in English. *Canine Pathology* (1817) is first veterinary specialty.
A.D. 1823	[Scotland]	Edinburgh Veterinary College is founded on sound basis by William Dick, a farrier of unusual ability.
A.D. 1828	[England]	William Youatt and William Percivall establish the *Veterinarian,* the first English veterinary journal, which becomes a major factor in elevating the profession.
A.D. 1843	[England]	Major outbreaks of pleuropneumonia, foot-and-mouth disease, and rinderpest (1865) force reforms in veterinary education and governmental policies regarding control.
A.D. 1852	[England]	William Haycock advocates veterinary homeopathy as a protest against the violent practices of bleeding, purging, etc. His rational principles are followed by George Dadd, first outspoken advocate for veterinary reform in America.

From *Evolution of the Veterinary Art* (Kansas City: Veterinary Medicine Publishing Co., 1957), pp. xv-xvii, by kind permission of J. F. Smithcors, author.

Instruction started in January 1792 with four students and Saint Bel as professor. Unfortunately, Saint Bel died of glanders[14] in 1793. Hunter stepped in and arranged for his medical colleagues to take the veterinary students into their classes until a professor could be appointed. The successor to Saint Bel was Edward Coleman, a surgeon who knew very little of the veterinary art or about domestic animals. He acquired some knowledge of the horse and soon confined teaching solely to this species. Later when foreign livestock were admitted, they brought diseases to the herds and flocks, but there were no practitioners who could treat them. Even worse, Coleman persuaded the governing body to reduce the three years of training to a course of three to six months under the guise that every cavalry regiment might quickly need a veterinary surgeon. He "reigned" for forty-five years and the school fell into decline.

Meanwhile there were some exciting advances in medical science of considerable significance to the veterinary profession. Edward Jenner, English physician and a pupil of John Hunter, achieved a significant breakthrough in 1796 when he was able to inoculate an eight-year-old boy with matter from cowpox vesicles on the hands of a milkmaid. A few months later the boy was inoculated for small pox, but the disease did not follow. Jenner became the "father of vaccination."

William Dick established a rival veterinary school in 1823 in Edinburgh, Scotland, currently named the Royal (Dick) School of Veterinary Studies. The son of a farrier who continued his self-education and worked at his father's forge, Dick had received his diploma which was granted from the London School in 1818 after three months'study. He obtained the support of the Highland and Agricultural Society for a course of veterinary lectures. The lectures were such a success, the patrons encouraged him to establish the Edinburgh school, funds for which came from Dick's practice.

By the beginning of the nineteenth century, educational institutions for veterinary medicine were well established. Almost another full century would pass, however, before such progress would be made across the ocean in the United States.

Endnotes

1. Calvin W. Schwabe, *Cattle, Priests and Progress in Medicine* (Minneapolis: University of Minnesota Press, 1978), p. 10.

2. Many early historians regarded the medicine of ancient Egypt as largely magical or magico-religious. However, *Papyrus Edwin Smith* was discovered in 1862. Ancient Egyptian medicine is now regarded, despite the lack of sharp distinctions, as one in which magic, religion, and medicine proper had separated extremely early. In the transition of ancient Egyptian

medicine from magico-religious concepts to empirico-rational practice, there developed the term *whdw,* which represents an idea of great significance in the gropings of the mind of man towards a scientific theory of internal disease and rational therapy. The term refers to a substance adherent to the fecal content of the bowel, which, on absorption, was believed to cause coagulation and destruction of blood and to the eventual putrefaction of the body. Purges and enemas were used to clean the bowel, and blood letting was employed to rid any absorbed *whdw.* The concept was the basis for adopting embalming to prevent putrefaction and also influenced the medical thought of Aristotle and Hippocrates in the ensuing Greek civilization.

3. Aristotle (384-322 B.C.) was a Greek philosopher, scientist, tutor of Alexander the Great, "father of biological sciences," and founder of comparative anatomy.

4. A centaur, half-man and half horse, was generally a savage creature, but Chiron was known for his goodness, wisdom, and healing power.

5. Hippocrates (460-377 B.C.) was a Greek physician and is considered the founder of medicine. The Hippocratic Oath, administered to ancient physicians, is still in use. He is best known for his astute clinical description of disease.

6. Claudius Galen (129-200 A.D.) was born at Pergamus in Asia Minor which was famous for its Aesculapian Temple. He became a physician to the gladiators. At the age of 31, he went to Rome where he built a great reputation. However, his fellow practitioners disagreed with his medical philosophy and practice, and they forced him to leave in 166 A.D. In 168 A.D. he was summoned back by Emperors Marcus Aurelius and Versus because the plague was making rapid progress. At this time he began his medical writings in Greek which were voluminous. For nearly 1500 years his philosophy ruled the medical world. Much of what he wrote is inaccurate, but his thinking was fundamentally sound and showed startling anticipation of future discovery.

7. Hippocrates and Galen expounded the theory of the four humours. This theory states that the universe is made up of four elements—earth, air, water, fire. In the human body, these correspond to cold, dry, moist, and hot humours. When they are in balance the result is health. When one gets the upper hand, good regimen demands that its opposite be applied. Blood is hot and moist; phlegm is cold and moist; yellow bile is hot and dry; black bile is cold and dry. Humans are likely to show a balance towards one humour—they are sanguine, phlegmatic, choleric, or melancholy. Through them a person feels illness or enjoys health. When one of these elements is out of balance, the particular part of the body where it is supposed to balance becomes diseased.

8. The adjective *veterinary* was popularized by Frenchman Charles Vial de Saint Bel, whose plan for "An Institution to Cultivate and Teach Veterinary Medicine" developed into Britain's first veterinary school in London. Animal-doctoring was called "farriery" until this time, but the first diploma granted from the London school in 1794 described the holder as "qualified to practice the Veterinary Art."

9. Benjamin Farrington, *Greek Science* (Harmondsworth, Middlesex, England: Penguin Books Ltd., 1944), p. 308.

10. William Harvey (1578-1657) was an English physiologist. His *Essay on the Motion of the Heart and Blood in Animals* in 1628 is considered one of the most important books in the history of medicine. He refuted many of the misconceptions of Galen regarding the heart and blood circulation. Galen believed that the real work of the heart was done in diastole which was supposed to suck air from the lungs and that there were three different kinds of blood, each with its own mode of distribution.

11. In Britain the term *veterinary surgeon* was designated by the British Army's Board of General officers in 1796 to distinguish them from human surgeons and has remained ever since. In eighteenth century England, the surgeon was kept in an inferior position by the more powerful physician. Surgery was a trade rather than a profession and was associated with that of a barber; Iain Pattison, *The British Veterinary Profession 1791-1948,* (London: J. A. Allen and Co., Ltd., 1984), p. 1.

12. J. F. Smithcors, *Evolution of the Veterinary Art* (Kansas City: Veterinary Medicine Publishing Co., 1957), p. 305.

13. Smithcors, p. 306.

14. Glanders is a highly fatal, contagious disease of horses, mules, and donkeys caused by *Pfeifferella mallei* (now *Actinobacillus mallei*). It is transmissible to man.

2 Early American Era

Except for those few facets which are peculiarly American, however, the veterinary history of all time is at the same time the history of veterinary medicine in America. . . . The value of a knowledge of our own history should not be under-rated however—it is precisely those names, dates, and places which, perhaps even more than in the case of a general history, give meaning and vitality to our American heritage.

J. F. Smithcors

The establishment of veterinary colleges in Europe during the eighteenth century was stimulated by severe outbreaks of the cattle plague (rinderpest), glanders, strangles, anthrax, rabies, dog distemper, and other diseases. In addition, armies needed veterinary skills to ensure the proper care of their horses. In the United States during early settlement, there was no great demand for veterinary services. Thus, veterinary medicine was slow in developing.

The public was not convinced that qualified veterinarians were needed to supplant the hordes of cow doctors (leeches) and farriers, most of whom were incredibly ignorant, although a few persons with great insight had delineated the need. Graduates of European schools who had immigrated were few and not well prepared professionally. The colonies were relatively free from disease, and there was a widespread belief that disease was a punishment for sin. The decorative hex signs still found on Pennsylvania barns were originally protection against "witching." Many home-grown medical concoctions, touted secret Indian remedies, and the itinerant medicine peddler charmed a mint of money from a gullible community.[1]

The American Indians practiced their own brand of doctoring and had few domestic animals. Several attempts were made to introduce live-stock. The Spaniard Juan Ponce de León brought cattle into Florida in 1520, but apparently they all perished. The first horses landed in the same area in 1527, but most did not survive. The beginning of the six-teenth century saw a radical change when domestic animals were brought into Virginia, but the five thousand cattle that existed in 1627 were in constant danger of being captured or killed by Indians or being slaughtered for food. The Governor finally proclaimed that none could be killed without a permit.

The first reference to a veterinary service in America was made by the medical historian Blanton who described William Carter as an expert veterinarian or cow doctor who lived in James City in 1625. The Pil-grims imported cattle into the northeastern part of the country, while the Dutch brought domestic animals to New Amsterdam (New York) in 1625. Though most of the sheep introduced in the early century fell prey to wolves and dogs, the provident Puritans established town commons for grazing sheep under the watchful eye of flock masters and enacted laws regarding sheep-killing dogs.[2]

It is not surprising, therefore, in view of the lack of public interest, that the original colleges in this country were established as private insti-tutions, as was the case in Europe.

The first public figure to create an awareness of the need for a veteri-nary profession in America was Richard Peters, a prominent lawyer, patriot, and country gentleman, who became president of the Philadel-phia Society for Promoting Agriculture in 1805. A year later the society offered a gold medal for the best essay and plan for promoting veteri-nary knowledge and instruction. A paper entitled "On the Yellow Water of Horses," read by Peters in 1807, was probably the first full descrip-tion of any animal disease in America.[3]

Benjamin Rush, a prominent physician and signer of the Declara-tion of Independence, called for the establishment of veterinary schools in an address to medical students at the University of Pennsylvania on November 2, 1807. He stated, "I have lived to see the medical school of Philadelphia emerge from small beginnings, and gradually advance to its present flourishing condition; but I am not yet satisfied with its prosperity and fame, nor shall I be so, until I see the veterinary science taught in our university."[4] Rush also referred to the possible interrela-tionship of human and animal diseases and emphasized the advantages to medicine from the study of animal diseases.

George Dadd, a Massachusetts physician who developed an interest in animal disease and deplored phlebotomy (bleeding), wrote the *Mod-ern Horse Doctor* in 1854, and later, *American Cattle Doctor*.

In 1852 Robert Jennings made the first effort to organize a college

Milestones of the Nineteenth Century
In U.S. Veterinary History

1800	First graduate veterinarians from foreign colleges begin arriving in U.S.
1833	Hog cholera appears in Ohio, first recorded outbreak of this disease anywhere in the world.
1843	Pleuropneumonia imported with infected dairy cows decimates livestock in three epidemics over forty years.
1852	First U.S. veterinary college established in Philadelphia.
1861	Ontario Veterinary College established.
1863	United States Veterinary Medical Association—now American Veterinary Medical Association (AVMA)—established in New York by Alexandre Liautard.
1865	On December 18, law passed by Congress to prevent the spread of foreign animal diseases to the United States by restricting livestock importations.
1870	First known outbreak of foot-and-mouth disease in the U.S.
1879	Iowa State College establishes veterinary school at Ames—oldest existing veterinary college in U.S.
1883	On May 1, a Veterinary Division, directed by Dr. D. E. Salmon, established in the U.S. Department of Agriculture. On July 1, investigation of Texas (cattle tick) fever begun.
1884	Bureau of Animal Industry established within the U.S. Department of Agriculture to control epizootics (animal epidemics).
1890	Federal meat inspection established and placed under administration of Bureau of Animal Industry.
1892	Contagious pleuropneumonia wiped out, making the U.S. the first nation to eradicate the disease. First tuberculin test made in United States on Jersey herd in Pennsylvania, disclosing 30 reactors among 79 animals.
1893	Cattle tick fever research conducted by Drs. Fred L. Kilborne, Cooper Curtice, and Theobald Smith proves that insects may transmit infection between animals or from animals to man. This discovery laid the groundwork for Major Walter Reed's conquest of yellow fever.
1898	"Embalmed beef" scandals of Spanish-American War lead government to contract with veterinarians for food inspection to overcome special military problems of food transport and preservation under field conditions.

Prepared by the American Veterinary Medical Association

in Philadelphia. Similar colleges followed in New York in 1855 and in Boston in 1885. However, in spite of the support of the newly founded United States Veterinary Medical Association in New York in 1863, these schools failed. Led by the Frenchman, Dr. Alexandre Liautard, most of the faculty of the New York College of Veterinary Surgeons, New York City, removed themselves and established the American Veterinary College. Founded in New York City in 1875, this school is regarded as the first successful veterinary medical school in the United States.[5]

Approximately forty privately-owned, independent veterinary colleges were established between 1852 and 1913. Pressure was great to shorten the curriculum, admit ill-prepared candidates, graduate large numbers regardless of qualifications, and even sell diplomas. Financial backers wanted their money's worth and more! The curriculum was limited to two sessions of four months each, a length of time which probably exhausted the knowledge of the teachers! Students accompanied their professors on calls in their private practices.

According to Walter L. Williams, an early veterinarian and professor at Cornell University, "the early veterinary colleges of America were launched on tempestuous seas, some of them were soon hopelessly wrecked, others led a precarious existence for a time, only to decline and later perish, while a few continue to exist; but some of these are wanting in prosperity, vigour, or efficiency."[6]

Private colleges were gradually forced out by advancing educational standards established by state and national governments and by the profession itself. The increasing recognition of the need for research in addition to teaching also contributed to their demise; fees could not be raised enough to support both programs. A sharp decline in the horse population drastically reduced income from private practice. The last private school in the United States closed in 1927. However, the private schools had served a good purpose in providing practitioners at a time when they were badly needed.[7]

There was a good deal of dissatisfaction in the second quarter of the nineteenth century with traditional liberal-arts colleges in America. President Francis Wayland of Brown University "asserted in 1850 that the United States had 120 colleges, 47 law schools, 42 theological seminaries, and yet not a single institution designed to furnish the agriculturist, the manufacturer, the mechanic, or the merchant with the education that will prepare him for the profession to which his life is to be devoted."[8] As late as 1862, there were only six "higher" schools in the whole country purporting to deal with these utilitarian fields.

Individual states did not possess sufficient resources to push for educational developments of this type; hence, a number of enthusiasts launched a movement for federal support. By the 1840s the so-called farmers' vote in America was becoming increasingly self-conscious politically. There was more grass-roots support for the program of "vote yourself a farm" at this time than for special training in how to till such farms. Nevertheless, some farm organizations came to regard agricultural education as at least a partial cure for the farmer's economic ills. In the 1850s, the agitation of a gradually expanding agricultural press and by various local and national agricultural societies built up a body of opinion which demanded the establishment of what were called "democracy's colleges."

The result was the introduction, in 1857, of a bill in Congress by Justin Morrill calling for federal aid to agricultural and mechanical colleges. Sectional differences prevented final approval until 1862; then, with the southern delegations absent due to the Civil War, Congress passed the Morrill Act, and President Lincoln signed it.

The act granted large tracts of federal land to states willing to establish agricultural and mechanical colleges, but none of the grant was to be used for construction of buildings. In 1890, the second Morrill Act provided for annual federal expenditures to the land-grant colleges. This was the beginning of the "matching dollars" concept.

The land-grant colleges fostered the emancipation of American higher education from a purely classical, formalistic tradition. Applied science and the mechanical arts were given a recognized place in the American college curriculum.

In 1862 Congress also created the U.S. Department of Agriculture because "national assistance for agriculture also provided avenues for national assistance to the livestock industry and all of the animal and veterinary sciences."[9] These federal programs influenced the early orientation of veterinary medicine toward agriculture.

Dr. James Law, a graduate of the Edinburgh Veterinary School, Scotland, was recruited in 1868 by President Andrew D. White to initiate instruction in veterinary science at Cornell University. Described as one of the "men of great talent who rise above the norm of life to impart knowledge, works and deeds which profoundly influence the subsequent course of history,"[10] Dr. Law's vision and wisdom contributed enormously to the course of veterinary medicine in this country. Dr. Law established a four-year course leading to a B.V.Sc. degree; an additional two post-graduate years, plus a thesis, were required for the D.V.M. degree. Dr. Daniel Salmon was awarded the D.V.M. degree in 1876, the first to be conferred by any university in the United States.

In the developing eastern port cities, demand for food, including meat, increased. However, the supply of meat was in jeopardy because of the feared cattle plague, contagious bovine pleuropneumonia. The disease was introduced in 1845 to the United States by a cow which was purchased by a Brooklyn, New York, dairyman from a British ship and spread rapidly among the previously unexposed cattle population of the eastern seaboard. In 1880 European nations restricted cattle importation from the United States. This crisis contributed to the action of Congress to establish the Bureau of Animal Industry within the Department of Agriculture in 1884. This agency's drastic policy of isolating and exterminating all afflicted livestock resulted in the eradication of contagious bovine pleuropneumonia in 1894. Dr. Daniel E. Salmon, the first director of the bureau, and his staff helped to elevate the status of the veterinary profession to a level of respectability hitherto unknown.[11]

Within the general provisions of the Morrill Act, the first state veterinary school was founded in 1879. Originally named the Iowa State Col-

In 1876 Dr. Daniel E. Salmon received the first D.V.M. degree to be conferred in the United States. He later became the first director of the Bureau of Animal Industry.

lege Veterinary Division, it is known today as Iowa State University College of Veterinary Medicine.

In his dissertation, "A Historical Study of the Oklahoma Agricultural Experiment Station," Francis R. Gilmore stated, "The early experimentation and treatises of individual landowners and the successful efforts of agricultural societies in the nineteenth century stimulated the demand for practical answers to agricultural problems."[12] By 1887, twenty-eight states were conducting research in a formal manner, and it had become evident that state land-grant colleges would be excellent locations for research stations.

It was due to the efforts of their representatives to secure federal aid for research that the Hatch Act was passed.[13] It provided that "there shall be established under the direction of the colleges or agricultural department of colleges in each state or territory established or which may hereafter be established . . . a department to be known and designated as an 'agricultural experiment station.'"[14] The Smith-Lever Act in 1914 provided similar funds for university extension and the Smith-Hughes Act in 1917 for vocational education.

The experiment station became a very important link in the triad of teaching, research, and extension. The whole character of the colleges was changed with the development of research programs. The faculty could transmit directly to the farmer and members of the public new knowledge which later became organized extension programs.

Toward the close of the nineteenth century, veterinarians were emerging at the college level. They separated themselves from self-educated practitioners and physicians who had been mainly involved with horses. In 1887 the United States Veterinary Medical Association changed its bylaws on new-member qualifications. An applicant was required to furnish evidence that he was a graduate of a recognized veterinary or medical school. This caused some confusion. In 1889 there was another change which became effective January 1, 1893. In addition to an applicant proving that he was a graduate of a regularly organized and recognized veterinary school, the school had to have a veterinary curriculum of at least three years and a faculty of at least four instructors who were veterinarians.[15]

The War Department required its cavalry regimental veterinary surgeons to be graduates of established and reputable veterinary schools or colleges. Soon afterwards, applicants seeking examination by the U.S. Civil Service Commission for employment with the Bureau of Animal Industry were also required to be graduates.[16]

The century had also seen great strides in medical and veterinary medical science.[17] However, the biggest influence on veterinary education was the introduction of veterinary practice laws in the states as a result of state veterinary medical associations working with state legislators. State board examinations emerged and public veterinary education was well established.

Such was the scene when Oklahoma Agricultural and Mechanical College (now Oklahoma State University) was founded in 1890 in the midst of a serious agricultural depression and the emergence of the horseless carriage.[18]

Endnotes

1. J. F. Smithcors, *The Veterinarian in America, 1625-1975* (Santa Barbara, CA: American Veterinary Publications, Inc., 1975), p. 25.

2. Smithcors, pp. 22, 25.

3. Smithcors, pp. 50-51.

4. Smithcors, p. 53.

5. Everett B. Miller, "Private Veterinary Colleges in the United States, 1852-1927," *Journal of the American Veterinary Medical Association,* vol. 178 (15 March 1981), pp. 583-585.

6. W. L. Williams, "Veterinary Education in America," *Veterinary Journal,* vol. 62 (November 1906), p. 668.

7. The Ontario Veterinary College in Canada, established by Andrew Smith in 1862, survived and attracted large numbers of students from the United States. When it became a part

of the University of Toronto in 1919, the school had over three thousand graduates. The college was moved to Guelph, Ontario, in 1922 and in 1965 became a part of the University of Guelph.

8. John S. Brubacher and Willis Rudy, *Higher Education in Transition: A History of American Colleges and Universities, 1636-1976,* 3rd edition (New York: Harper and Row, 1976), p. 62.

9. B. W. Bierer, *A Short History of Veterinary Medicine in America* (East Lansing: Michigan State University Press, 1955), p. 36.

10. Ellis P. Leonard, *A Cornell Heritage: Veterinary Medicine 1868-1908,* with a foreword by Edward C. Melby (Ithaca: New York State College of Veterinary Medicine, 1979), p. xi.

11. Larry Marks, *100 Years of Animal Health, 1884-1984* (Washington, DC: U.S. Government Printing Office, 1984).

12. Francis Richard Gilmore, "A Historical Study of the Oklahoma Agricultural Experiment Station" (Doctor of Education Dissertation, Oklahoma State University, 1967), p. 2.

13. Gilmore, p. 5.

14. United States Congress, *Statutes At Large of the United States of America, From December 1885 to March 1887, and Recent Treaties, Postal Conventions, and Executive Proclamations,* vol. 24 (Washington, DC: Government Printing Office, 1887), p. 440.

15. Everett B. Miller, "Nonacademic Influences on Education of the Veterinarian in the United States, 1887-1921," *Journal of the American Veterinary Medical Association,* vol. 175, no. 10 (15 November 1979), p. 1107.

16. Miller, "Nonacademic Influences on Education of the Veterinarian in the United States, 1887-1921," p. 1107.

17. Frenchman Louis Pasteur (1822-1895) established the validity of the germ theory of disease. He discovered that fermentation was the result of minute organisms and that food products could be sterilized by a pasteurization process of controlled heat treatments. He also isolated the anthrax bacillus and developed the Pasteur vaccine for rabies.

   A German, Rudolf Virchow (1821-1902), accepted the prevailing idea that all living creatures are composed of living cells. He established that cells arise only from pre-existent cells and that disease was produced by disturbances in the structure and function of the body cells. The dominant figure in European medicine in the second half of the nineteenth century, Virchow is known as the "father of pathology."

   Frenchman Claude Bernard (1813-1878), one of the greatest of the great nineteenth-century physiologists and teachers, demonstrated the functions of the pancreas and glycogenic function of the liver which threw light on the cause of diabetes. He also discovered the vasomotor system.

   A German bacteriologist Robert Koch (1843-1910) obtained a pure culture of the bacillus of anthrax in 1876 and a method of preventive inoculation seven years later. In 1882 he isolated the bacillus of tuberculosis and developed tuberculin which was erroneously claimed as a possible cure. Although disclaimed fiercely by veterinarians, he maintained that tuberculosis of man and cattle is not the same disease. Nevertheless, he was one of the greatest bacteriologists ever known. Koch's phenomenon is the basis of the tuberculin test while Koch's postulates established the specificity of microorganisms in an infectious disease.

18. Scotsman John Boyd Dunlop (1840-1921) graduated from the veterinary college, Edinburgh, in 1859, and settled in a veterinary practice in Belfast, Ireland. In 1887 he constructed a pneumatic tire for his son's tricycle. It paved the way for the development of the automobile.

3 New School On the Prairie

It is only by a perceptive awareness of the heritage of the past that the veterinarian of today can fully arm himself to cope with the problems of tomorrow.

J. F. Smithcors

All of present-day Oklahoma, except the Panhandle, was part of the Louisiana Purchase secured by the United States from France in 1803. Land in Oklahoma had been given to various Indian tribes in exchange for their land in the more populous eastern part of the United States. After the Civil War, some Indian holdings were ceded back to the United States government. These lands were unsettled; occupied only by cattlemen and railroad workers, they became known as "Unassigned Lands." President Benjamin Harrison issued a proclamation opening the first land for settlement on April 22, 1889. Over the next few years, the remaining area would also be opened.

The Agricultural and Mechanical College of the Territory of Oklahoma and the Agricultural Experiment Station connected with it were established by the First Legislative Assembly, the act taking effect December 25, 1890. The Oklahoma Assembly had accepted the responsibility for implementing the Morrill Act but had not designated the exact location for the institution. Towns in Payne County were eager to capture the site of the college, and a mighty struggle between Stillwater and Perkins ensued. Stillwater was awarded the school and the research station provided the citizens of the town would furnish eighty acres and put up $10,000 to erect a building.[1]

The college opened on December 14, 1891, with classes held in the

Congregational Church. Old Central,[2] the main college building on campus, was not occupied for regular work until September 1894.

Admission to the institution was granted to all citizens of Oklahoma between the ages of fourteen and thirty years, who passed a satisfactory examination in reading, arithmetic, geography, English grammar, and United States history and who were known to possess good moral character.

There was no entrance, tuition, or incidental fee, but students were required to pay a part of the cost of material and apparatus used or destroyed in their work in the laboratories. Students not fully prepared for admission to the freshman class could be admitted to the preparatory department.

Veterinary science was required during the winter term of the senior year according to the *1891-1892 Announcement*. The forenoon work also included stock breeding, geology and metallurgy, and criticism.

In June 1896, the Agricultural and Mechanical Board of Regents appointed Dr. L. L. Lewis to the position of professor of veterinary science effective July 1. The spring term of the junior year curriculum in 1896-97 included comparative anatomy and veterinary science.[3]

In the following academic year of 1897-98, Dr. Lewis was listed as professor of physiology and zoology and also of veterinary science. He gave classes in physiology, zoology, comparative anatomy, animal physiology, materia medica and therapeutics, and veterinary medicine. Veterinary medicine was described as a course of study with "lectures on the most important contagious and infectious diseases, the relation of bacteria to the various diseases, and the best means of applying disinfectants."[4]

Dr. Lewis continued to teach a wide range of subjects for the next decade. The course in veterinary science was "intended more especially for students of agriculture, and is planned with the idea of giving thorough and practical information regarding the diseases of domestic animals."[5]

Dr. Lewis was obviously a very remarkable person.[6] In addition to all his teaching assignments, he found time to study some of the veterinary problems characteristic of the southwest. Hitherto, research had been devoted mainly to horticulture, agronomy, and some entomology. As territorial veterinarian, Dr. Lewis expanded his duties. He investigated glanders and anthrax. His research brought wider contact with livestock producers.

The Board of Regents, meeting in December 1897, authorized the research station to undertake an extended series of experiments on the prevention of Texas fever. In the 1890s it had been proved that ticks spread Texas fever and dipping cattle to kill the carrier ticks would eliminate the disease. The research station built a dipping vat at Noble, Oklahoma Territory, in the summer of 1898 where 240 cattle were dipped with insecticide. Dr. Lewis conducted dipping experiments with extra dynamo oil containing sulfur.[7]

In 1899 a reorganization of the research station occurred. Dr. Lewis, the station veterinarian, in addition to being professor of veterinary science, was also professor of zoology. Research projects by the veterinarian included the bacteriology of milk and for the first time some research on horse diseases.

In 1901 Dr. Lewis moved his office from Old Central into the new library building, which later became known as Williams Hall. He continued his work on the parasites of domestic animals and poultry and published his results in an experiment station bulletin. He also investigated the effect of loco plant on animals.[8]

The following year Dr. Lewis distributed a vaccine against blackleg in cattle, selling the vaccinating outfit and information to stockmen for $4.50. In 1902, 123,620 doses were distributed to 1,552 animal owners. The serum was prepared in one of the rooms in the Library that was used by both the zoology and veterinary medicine departments as a laboratory for experiment station work. When the use of federal Hatch funds for producing vaccine was discontinued, the legislature appropriated $2,500 for the continuation of the project.[9]

As early as 1900, Dr. L. L. Lewis, in collaboration with the experiment station, began preparing a vaccine to be used against blackleg. Vaccination outfits were provided to livestock owners by the experiment station for a fee of $4.50. An illustration of the equipment and directions were published in *Oklahoma Experiment Station Bulletin Number 57*.

Research was now directed toward hog cholera, bacterial analysis of drinking water, and sheep and cattle dips. A tuberculin test of the college herd revealed only two reactors.

Veterinary medical education had survived the serious economic depression of the 1890s, and emerging graduates were better prepared for professional practice. By the turn of the century, there were sixteen schools of veterinary medicine in the United States, half being privately owned. At this time and after the closure of the Harvard University Veterinary Department, the United States Veterinary Medical Association renewed its efforts to obtain improvement in the colleges. The association's long-standing Committee on Intelligence and Education was given a new responsibility to take a leadership role in elevating the standards of veterinary medical education.[10]

In 1898 the name of the United States Veterinary Medical Association was changed to the American Veterinary Medical Association. In 1906 on-site inspection of the schools was undertaken by members designated by the president of the American Veterinary Medical Association. The accreditation of United States veterinary medical institutions started—free from state or federal government control.

More and more veterinarians were needed by the federal government. Laws passed in 1891 and 1895 provided for both antemortem and post-mortem veterinary inspection of animals slaughtered for foreign and interstate trade. The laws were inadequate concerning slaughter house sanitation and meat products preparation. Much was to be desired in the working conditions. When Upton Sinclair revealed these conditions

In 1912, Dr. L. L. Lewis, professor of physiology, zoology, and veterinary science, teaches physiology in Williams Hall.

in his novel *The Jungle* in 1906, the public became outraged and demanded that the average consumer should have clean and safe meat. The U.S. Congress responded with the Meat Inspection Act of 1906.[11]

When Oklahoma became a state in 1907, the college was placed under the supervision of the Oklahoma State Board of Agriculture and suffered because of the alleged corruption of officials. However, research continued and veterinary scientists concentrated on the effect of feeds on breeding animals and artificial insemination in hogs. The state legislature appropriated $6,000 toward the supply of hog cholera serum to farmers, and 34,000 hogs were inoculated.

In 1913 the Board of Agriculture was recalled by popular vote, and the research station got into difficulties with the U.S. Department of Agriculture over inefficient accounting procedures. Federal funds were withheld for nine months. On August 7, 1914, an extensive fire in Morrill Hall, the main administrative building on campus at the time, destroyed the building and the entire research station property of bulletins, library, and official materials.

However, veterinary scientists continued research on hog cholera and blackleg, saving livestock owners from substantial economic loss. The passage of the Smith-Lever Act in 1914 paved the way for the college extension service. Practical information on subjects relating to agriculture and home economics could be disseminated in cooperation with the U.S. Department of Agriculture.[12]

Dr. Lewis, who had labored with only one assistant, was joined in 1909 by an enterprising young man from near Tulsa who would have a major role in the veterinary profession in Oklahoma. He was Clarence H. McElroy, but it would be another ten years before he became a veterinarian!

The name of the department was changed to zoology and veterinary medicine. The *1910-11 Announcement* stated, "The equipment consists of twenty-two Zeiss and Leitz microscopes with oil immersion lenses, microtomes, dissecting instruments and cameras. The department is also well supplied with dissectable models of various animals, including an Azoux model of the horse, skeletons and charts for lecture room work."[13] Veterinary medicine classes were still designed for students in animal husbandry.

There was a growing feeling that more graduates should be practicing in the state. Kansas in 1905 and Colorado in 1907 had already established veterinary colleges. Dr. L. L. Lewis and his staff, joined by other veterinarians in the state, set about to organize a School of Veterinary Medicine at Oklahoma A. and M. College in 1912.

Classes started in the fall of 1913 with Dr. L. L. Lewis as dean, assisted by C. H. McElroy, L. B. Ritter, W. P. Shuler, and R. O. Whittenton. The new school had the same staff as the Department of Zoology and Bacteriology in the School of Science and Literature. Dr. Lewis was dean of both schools. The entire work of the School of Veterinary Medicine was confined to one department called the Department of Veterinary Medicine.

Recognizing the importance of the livestock industry in the state, Oklahoma A. and M. College provided a thorough and well balanced course which, when completed, would result in the Doctor of Veterinary Medicine degree. Entrance requirements were the completion of a four-year high school course and completion of the freshman year of college. A good general education was stressed in addition to the specialized work offered in veterinary medicine. Students were encouraged that job opportunities existed in private practice, in civil service with the Department of Agriculture, and in state veterinary, municipal, and army services.

Dr. Lewis persuaded Clarence McElroy to become a veterinarian. He left during the 1914-15 year to pursue his studies at St. Joseph Veterinary College in Missouri and received the D.V.M. degree in 1919 and then returned to Oklahoma A. and M. College.

In April 1917, the United States entered World War I. The call up of young men threatened to empty the colleges, but the army's combined programs for the health professions enabled veterinary students to enlist in the Reserve Corps and remain in college until graduation.

By 1919-20 Dean Lewis and Dr. McElroy had been joined by Assistant Professor H. W. Orr. The School of Veterinary Medicine had only three faculty members—Lewis, McElroy, and Orr—and all three would eventually serve as dean![14]

Financial problems and politics continued to plague the new school. Because of a deadlock between the two political parties, the Oklahoma Legislature adjourned in the spring of 1921 without providing an appropriation for the college. President Cantwell asked the staff to remain at their posts and not be too discouraged!

An Extraordinary Session of the Eighth Legislature, April 25-May 21, appropriated funds for the college and the experiment station, but the station staff members were grossly overburdened with teaching assignments due to the interference of the dean of agriculture. Only seven publications were produced during the year.[15]

The death of Dr. L. L. Lewis in September 1922 was a profound loss to the college and station. He had served his profession and community far beyond the call of duty. For many years he *was* the profession. Undoubtedly he stands today as the "father of veterinary medicine in Oklahoma."

The *Oklahoma A. and M. College Announcement* stated, "The last two years' work in veterinary medicine will not be given in 1919-20."[16] However, the school continued, at least on paper, until the 1926-27 aca-

Early in the history of Oklahoma A. and M. College, short courses became an integral part of education. Available to everyone, these courses offered practical instruction in agriculture and related areas. Dr. L. L. Lewis conducts a clinic outside the Veterinary Hospital.

demic year, whereupon, without any fanfare or official announcement, it ceased to exist. There are no known graduates of the school. The full curriculum was never taught beyond the second year, even though the *Announcement* had carried full information about a wide range of courses being offered by the school each year since 1913.

It is difficult to explain why there were no graduates. The school had been established in an era of considerable progress in veterinary medical education. The Oklahoma Veterinary Medical Association had been founded in 1905, and the State Board of Veterinary Medical Examiners was established in 1913. The American Veterinary Medical Association endorsement was given to any college that maintained a three-year curriculum and had four veterinarians on the staff. In 1916, the U.S. Congress had made the Veterinary Corps a component of the U.S. Army Medical Department, thus giving the profession a medical assignment distinct from the hitherto purely agricultural orientation. Undoubtedly, wider horizons were developing for graduating veterinarians. Perhaps the last two years of the curriculum were never offered due to a lack of funds being appropriated by the State Department of Agriculture to provide clinical instructors, facilities, and equipment.

Following the demise of the School of Veterinary Medicine in 1926, the Department of Veterinary Medicine was incorporated into the Department of Bacteriology, Physiology and Veterinary Science in the School of Science and Literature with Dr. C. H. McElroy as head. The depart-

Lowery Layman Lewis, D.V.M., M.S.
1869-1922

Born in Newport, Eastern Tennessee, on September 3, 1869, Dr. Lewis moved with his family to Texas when he was ten years old. He attended Texas A. and M. College and did postgraduate work there in 1893, receiving the M.S. degree in 1894. He received the D.V.M. degree from Iowa State College Veterinary Division in 1896 and then came to Oklahoma A. and M. College as professor of veterinary medicine and territorial veterinarian. His professional advancement was rapid due to his virile personality and his technical knowledge. He married Georgina Holt on September 30, 1903. They had two children, Samuel Lee and Ruth. Dr. Lewis died at his home in Stillwater on Tuesday, September 2, 1922.

Dr. Lewis was one of the greatest educators and the father of veterinary medicine in Oklahoma. He conducted extensive research programs and was a pioneer of artificial insemination in pigs and horses. At the time of his death, he was professor of veterinary medicine, professor of zoology, experiment station bacteriologist and veterinarian, dean of the School of Veterinary Medicine, dean of the School of Science and Literature, and dean of the faculty of Oklahoma A. and M. College. The latter title was created for him. He served as acting president of A. and M. College from June 1, 1914, to June 30, 1915. He was by far the oldest member of the faculty in point of service and title.

The Oklahoma A. and M. football stadium was named Lewis Field in his

honor. An avid supporter of athletic events, especially track, he was the only faculty member at Oklahoma A. and M. College in the early 1900s who knew how to play football. He coached a group of enthusiastic students who named their playing field which was located in front of Crutchfield Hall for him.

Many honors were conferred upon Dr. Lewis, but few were more fitting than the dedication of the first A. and M. College yearbook, the *1910 Redskin*. The senior class stated that "no more worthy person could have been selected upon whom to confer this parting tribute of respect and affection than good old Doc Lew."

ment still occupied quarters on the second floor of the old library building, which was now called Biology. Three veterinary science courses were offered.

Anatomy and physiology was a three-hour course with laboratory offered during the first semester. Required of animal husbandry students, it was a study of some of the practical points of the anatomy of domesticated animals with a consideration of the functions of the important systems of the animal body.

Animal diseases was a second semester course with special consideration given to farm sanitation and first aid to animals. A three-hour course, it had prerequisites of bacteriology and veterinary science.

Poultry diseases was also a second semester course of two hours. Required of poultry husbandry students with a prerequisite of bacteriology, it covered common diseases of poultry with special emphasis on the prevention of diseases and the principles of sanitation.[17]

The physiology section of the department confined its curriculum to the human subject, but it was taught by "Mr. Orr" (Dr. H. W. Orr), veterinarian. The departmental faculty also included Professor C. H. McElroy, Associate Professor E. E. Harnden, and Instructors G. C. Hassler and R. M. Northup. In 1929 Dr. Lewis H. Moe, a 1927 graduate of Ohio State University, joined the department as an assistant professor.

The introduction of a course in anatomy and physiology of the animal body taught by "Mr. Orr" was the only significant change in curriculum until 1935 when the Biological Sciences Group was established. This group included the Department of Bacteriology, Physiology and Veterinary Science; Department of Botany and Plant Pathology; and the Department of Zoology.

Professor McElroy was named chairman of the group. A pre-professional program was initiated in the newly established School of Arts and Sciences which had replaced the School of Science and Literature. The program was confined to pre-nursing, pre-medical, and pre-dental studies.

Dr. Harry Orr, professor of physiology, described the scene in March 1934 to Dr. C. H. McElroy: "The section of Veterinary Medicine is doing splendid work. Doctor Moe, who is largely responsible for the work in this section, is very devoted to his tasks, and has proved very satisfactory. His program for the control of disease in the college livestock is excellent, especially in view of a lack of cooperation in some instances. This section also is in serious need of an additional staff member,—a number of instruments, an instrument case, and a new emergency bag."[18]

Veterinarians in Oklahoma had continued to encourage the upgrading of the profession through the Oklahoma Veterinary Medical Association and the State Board of Veterinary Medical Examiners. The annual Conference for Veterinarians, first held in May of 1926, continued to be

Early records indicate a veterinary and zoology laboratory was housed in a frame structure near the present day Morrill Hall in the 1890s. That building was probably razed or moved prior to 1905, as often was done in the early days. The building shown above, located near present-day Cordell Hall in a complex of agriculture buildings, was known as the Veterinary Hospital. It was possibly the third veterinary structure.

sponsored annually by the college. Some persons felt the need to establish (or re-establish!) a veterinary school at Oklahoma A. and M. College, while others were strongly opposed to the idea. It was a time of severe depression in the state that had borne the brunt of the Dust Bowl in the 1930s.

The practice of veterinary medicine still depended on "art" more than "science" with copper sulfate, epsom salts, sodium iodide, and pine tar being the most commonly used therapeutic agents! However, an exciting new era appeared with the introduction of sulfonamides, and very soon a whole new world of medical therapy centered on the use of antibiotics. Although Sir Alexander Fleming had discovered penicillin in 1928, it was not until 1939 that it was isolated, purified, and produced on a large scale in the United States. World War II accelerated the production of antibiotics and brought tremendous strides in medical science.

Nationally the number of students entering veterinary colleges was low, marking a period of low enrollment after World War I which lasted well into the third decade. The number of schools had decreased to about twelve. There were some changes in the education of veterinarians. "Starting with the 1919-1920 academic year, veterinary colleges approved as new member sources for American Veterinary Medical Association membership were required to admit only persons having at least four years' high school."[19]

At the annual meeting of the Oklahoma Veterinary Medical Association held in Oklahoma City in 1935, Dr. R. S. Mackellar, president of the association, called on his colleagues to "focus on veterinary consciousness" and to try "to make America veterinary minded."[20] In the same era, Dr. C. H. Fauks, editor of the *Oklahoma Veterinarian*, urged his colleagues to up-grade the profession, adding "the sad truth is that with all our vaunted knowledge of science we have neglected to learn something equally important as far as public relations and esteem is concerned, namely, how to conduct ourselves like professional people; . . . [veterinarians cannot] be looked upon as professional men as long as we are so careless in our dress and personal habits in public."[21]

Veterinary medicine in Oklahoma continued in a state of depression. In 1942-43 recognition was given for the first time to pre-veterinary work as indicated in the *College Announcement*, "Students who later plan to take up the study of Veterinary Medicine can spend one full year here, completing their pre-veterinary course."[22]

Although it was twenty-six years before a School of Veterinary Medicine would be re-established, it was during this era, however, that Oklahoma A. and M. College emerged as the leading institution in research on anaplasmosis in cattle. The disease was diagnosed in Oklahoma for the first time in 1927 by Dr. George W. Stiles, an animal scientist from the U.S. Department of Agriculture who was cooperating with researchers at Oklahoma A. and M. College. The following year, anaplasmosis research formally began. It was found that blood from affected animals made healthy animals sick with the disease and that many recovered animals became carriers. The researchers identified the "microparasite," as they described it, in the blood of anaplasmosis-infected animals. Later they found that the disease could be transmitted by dehorning, vaccination, and castration, unless the utensils were thoroughly cleaned and sterilized between each animal.[23]

World War II was coming to an end and the veterinary profession was about to embark on its most exciting era in history.

Endnotes

1. Robert A. Martin, compiler, *The Statutes of Oklahoma, 1890* (Guthrie, OK: State Capital Printing Company, 1891), p. 82.

2. A separate book in the Centennial Histories Series, *Historic Old Central* by Dr. LeRoy H. Fischer, deals with the establishment of the school and the first academic building on campus.

3. *Oklahoma A & M College Mirror*, 15 June 1896, p. 7; *Announcement for 1896-97 of the Oklahoma Agricultural and Mechanical College*, p. 5.

4. *Oklahoma Agricultural and Mechanical College and Agricultural Experiment Station Annual Announcement of College 1897-8 and Report of Director of Station for Fiscal Year Ending June 30, 1897,* p. 13.

5. *Oklahoma Agricultural and Mechanical College Annual Catalog, 1900-01 with Announcements for 1901-02,* p. 41.

6. "Doc Lew" was one of the first promoters of athletic programs at Oklahoma A. and M. College. His contributions in that area are described in another book of the Centennial Histories Series, *Intercollegiate Athletics* by Doris Dellinger.

7. *Oklahoma A & M College Mirror,* 15 December 1897, p. 6; Francis Richard Gilmore, "A Historical Study of the Oklahoma Agricultural Experiment Station" (Doctor of Education Dissertation, Oklahoma State University, 1967), pp. 59-60.

8. L. L. Lewis, "Common Parasites of Domestic Animals," *Oklahoma Agricultural Experiment Station Bulletin,* no. 53 (June 1902).

9. *Oklahoma Agricultural Experiment Station Eleventh Annual Report 1901-1902,* p. 16.

10. Everett B. Miller, "Nonacademic Influences on Education of the Veterinarian in the United States, 1887-1921," *Journal of the American Veterinary Association,* vol. 175, no. 10 (15 November 1979), pp. 1107-1108.

11. The public uproar resulted in a Congressional hearing. The blame for the poor conditions in the plants was placed on the Bureau of Animal Industry and its director, Dr. Daniel Salmon, was forced to resign. However, only seventeen of forty-six plants were under federal inspection. Sinclair described conditions not under the control of the bureau and wrongly implicated the BAI and discredited one of the greatest veterinarians in history.

12. United States Congress, *The Statutes at Large of the United States of America from March 1913 to March 1915,* Part 1, vol. 38 (Washington, DC: no publisher, 1915), pp. 373-374.

13. *Oklahoma Agricultural and Mechanical College Twentieth Annual Catalog 1910-1911 with Announcements for 1911-1912,* p. 97.

14. *Twenty-Ninth Annual Catalog 1919-1920 with Announcements for 1920-1921,* p. 150.

15. Gilmore, pp. 134-135.

16. *Twenty-Ninth Annual Catalog 1919-1920 with Announcements for 1920-21,* p. 150.

17. *Thirty-Sixth General Catalog 1926-1927, Announcements 1927-1928,* pp. 169-170, 172.

18. Dr. H. W. Orr to Dean C. H. McElroy, 21 March 1934, Archives, College of Veterinary Medicine.

19. Miller, p. 1109.

20. J. F. Smithcors, *The American Veterinary Profession* (Ames: Iowa State University Press, 1963), p. 594.

21. C. H. Fauks, "Editorially Speaking—Is Our House in Order," *Oklahoma Veterinarian,* vol. 2, no. 4 (December 1955), p. 2.

22. *Bulletin Oklahoma Agricultural and Mechanical College General Catalog Issue 1942-43, Announcements 1943-44,* p. 115.

23. "Chronological History of Anaplasmosis Research at OSU Shows Varied Experiences," *Oklahoma Veterinarian,* vol. 12, no. 3 (Fall 1965), pp. 8-9.

4 The School is Resurrected

'Tis the set of the sail that decides the goal and not the storms of life.
Ella Wheeler Wilcox

The end of World War II brought a new era to Oklahoma A. and M. College. The Oklahoma State Board of Agriculture was replaced in 1944 as the governing body of Oklahoma A. and M. College. A constitutional amendment established the Board of Regents for Oklahoma A. and M. College and all agricultural and mechanical colleges maintained by the state. In 1945 the Oklahoma Veterinary Research Institute was established to research animal diseases and parasites. A branch of Oklahoma A. and M. College, the institute worked in close cooperation with the experiment station.

Student enrollment increased dramatically, and many veterans were interested in animal science. Dr. Henry G. Bennett, college president, was a master politician who was keenly interested in broadening the educational scope of the college. Dr. Bennett took advantage of the influx of agricultural students and decided it was time to establish a School of Veterinary Medicine. At that time there were only two veterinary medical colleges in the South: Alabama Polytechnic Institute at Auburn and Texas A. and M. College at College Station.

Oklahoma veterinarians contributed enormously in convincing people of the need for a school of veterinary medicine. One afternoon a group of prominent cattlemen "pounded on President Bennett's desk demanding a veterinary school."[1] They emphasized that such a school could make a major contribution toward research into animal disease,

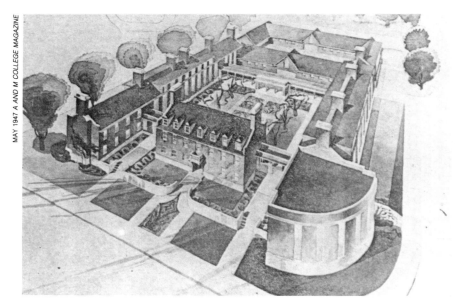

Plans in 1947 included this architects' drawing of the proposed new building to house the School of Veterinary Medicine.

especially cattle, the second largest industry in the state. A growing need for more veterinarians existed so that eradication programs for tuberculosis, brucellosis, and hog cholera could be implemented.[2]

Dr. Bennett ordered the organization of the school in 1945 to prepare for admission of the first class in September 1947. Bennett promised the staff that he would provide adequate space for the school by the time the first class started.

Dr. Bennett remarked in an interview in May 1947 that the Veterinary Medicine Division in this college "answers one of the foremost educational needs in the progressive post-war college program" planned by Oklahoma A. and M. College.[3] He stated the blueprints called for 6,825 feet in the animal anatomy building. Some 275 applications were already on file from students seeking admission. There was general agreement that enrollment be limited, provisionally, to sixty students. The estimated cost to the state of $1,000 per year for each veterinary student was considered conservative. Over $1.5 million would be invested in the physical plant. However, the original architects' drawing of the proposed building bears little resemblance to the present structure. The annual operation would require about $275,000, with another $200,000 for equipment and supplies. The value of the school to the livestock industry and to its future in Oklahoma would be inestimable; death losses of cattle, sheep, and swine in 1946 were over $5.5 million.

Dr. Clarence H. McElroy was appointed acting dean of the new school. "Dean Mac," as he was affectionately called, had already served in several administrative capacities, including acting president. His enthusiasm and drive brought the dream of many to a reality.

President Bennett and Dean McElroy traveled widely to stimulate support for the school. Eventually they succeeded. The *Third Biennial Report of the Oklahoma State Regents for Higher Education, Period Ending June 30, 1946*, stated, "On the basis of information from the Oklahoma A. and M. College, Stillwater, and after consultation with the governing board and administrative officers of that institution, the Oklahoma State Regents for Higher Education have encouraged the expansion of instruction in veterinary science as a function of the A. and M. College. . . . This function will probably need to be served in Oklahoma due to the place of the live stock industry in the economy of our people."[4] The Oklahoma State Regents for Higher Education had been established by the state legislature in 1941 to coordinate curriculum and recommend budgets for all institutions of higher learning within the state.

Dr. McElroy set out, frantically, to assemble equipment and supplies for the start of classes, planned hopefully for January 1948. He located several steel-topped dissecting tables and rushed an order for thirty microscopes and, of course, barrels and barrels of formaldehyde (a scarce commodity in those days) for the anatomy laboratory. Next, there was the major problem of obtaining a suitable building to hold classes. Eventually, a World War II army building, temporary frame #9 (TF-9), was located in Texas City, Texas, but shipment of this building was delayed because it had a refrigerator. The hut had been commandeered and set up as a temporary morgue for fifty unidentified bodies after a disastrous fertilizer explosion.

Dr. Raymond Henry, Pawnee, recalled that he was enrolled in some agriculture classes during the 1948 spring semester. One morning in the middle of his animal science lecture, Dr. Glen Bratcher received a message and announced, "Will all students who are enrolled in veterinary medicine report to Dean Mac's office to pick up your packets because veterinary school is going to start next Monday." Dr. Henry remarked that "we all got up and left right then. We had to drop all the courses we had taken since January."[5]

The selection of the first class was by individual interview, recommendations, and a good pre-veterinary scholastic record. Early plans had envisioned sixty students, but by this time plans were to admit forty-eight students. Thirty-one were enrolled. Dr. Henry recalled the selection committee consisted of Dean Mac, Dr. Orr, and Dr. Moe, who were looking for an agriculture background! He received a postcard a week later stating that he had been selected![6]

On Monday morning, March 1, 1948, the School of Veterinary Medicine, the seventeenth in the United States, opened, with Dr. Clarence H. McElroy as acting dean. He became dean of the school on September 1, 1948. His office was in 310 Life Sciences (now known as Life Sciences East). For the first time since 1926, the college catalog listed the School of Veterinary Medicine and described "a four-year professional course designed to meet the demands of modern veterinary education" leading to the degree of Doctor of Veterinary Medicine. Among the opportunities for veterinarians, it reported that, in general, salaries were at a high level and the work interesting. "The opportunity for rendering a useful service to humanity is limited only by the capacities of the individuals engaged therein."[7]

Dean McElroy was on hand to welcome the first class on that historic morning. He knew most of the students already because he had enlisted them as volunteers to macerate some bones in a little pre-fab hut in order to be ready for laboratory instruction.

Dr. Duane Peterson, who gave the first lecture, was younger than some of the students! He came on February 1 and had only one month to get ready. In fact, his appointment and that of Dr. Donald Trotter, who was named head of anatomy, were not confirmed by the Board of Regents until April.

Dean C. H. McElroy *(far right)* and Dr. Duane Peterson *(left of the dean)* examine a carcass in histology lab during the summer of 1948. Two courses, histology and anatomy, composed the course work for the first year of study, held from March through August of 1948. The Azoux model of the horse, bought by Dr. L. L. Lewis in 1899 for $940, appears in the top right corner of the picture.

King Gibson, Tom Ritchie, Sam Best, Jack Ambrose, Jack Bostwick, and Weldon Glenn head for home after seven hours of work. During the first year of 1948, class and laboratory were both held in the TF-9 building shown in the background. A "lean to" attached to the front of the building was a dormitory for two students who looked after the property.

The curriculum and schedule for the first class was quite simple. From March 1 to August 15, 1948, two subjects dominated the curriculum. Gross anatomy was taught every morning from 7:00 a.m. until noon by Dr. Peterson, and histology was taught every afternoon from 1:00 until about 5:30 by Dr. Trotter. A portion of Wednesday's time, however, was reserved during March and April so students could complete a restricted number of other subjects.

Dr. James Tucker, who was working on a master's degree and ended up with three degrees paid for by the G.I. bill, still has a vivid memory of the grueling first year.[8] Another student, Dr. William Ryan, recalled, "We studied until two or three in the morning just to keep up, and it was not unusual for students to visit each other in the wee hours of the night to pick each other's brains or learn new tricks of study."[9] Air conditioning did not exist in the classrooms, and there was only a two-week break before starting the sophomore year.

The intensive class schedule and the hot weather sometimes caused friction among the students, ending at one time in a fight over histology slides which were rather scarce! Basically, however, a great sense of "camaraderie" existed in the class. Being mostly ex-servicemen, the students knew that team work was basic to survival. The following year Ray Henry was burned very badly while working on the homecoming float. During the time he was in the hospital, from October until

Christmas, his classmates took a tape recorder ("As big as a desk"!) to all the classes, and Dean McElroy's secretary transcribed the lectures. Students and instructors also helped pay his bills. Another student, Mark Wilson, was also hurt in the accident and was hospitalized for three weeks.

The anatomy and histology laboratories and lectures were all held in TF-9. In addition to classwork, the students were given pages and pages of Greek and Latin prefixes and suffixes as extra learning material. Pop quizzes lasted an hour. Students always knew when to expect them because the door was locked and they had to stand in line until the quiz material was ready. So-called "hour examinations" usually lasted three times that long. At the end of the first semester the grades in anatomy were one A, six Bs, eighteen Cs, four Ds, and two Fs. Of the thirty-one students who started together in the first class, only twenty-six graduated. No wonder a faculty member regularly admonished the freshmen at orientation to look at the classmate on either side because at least one of them would not be present next year!

The students in the first and subsequent three or four classes were veterans who were well disciplined and eager to learn. Some enterprising students raised chickens and pigs to help their food budget, while one kept a cow which he milked every morning before going to class. Undoubtedly their positive attitude and a dedicated faculty contributed enormously to the survival of a school which started with an unrealistic budget, second-hand equipment, hand-made tables, and quonset huts.

Blazing a trail unequaled by members of other campus organizations in either fire or stamina, the first veterinary class organized the Oklahoma A. and M. Student Veterinary Society in March of 1948. They fostered a more professional atmosphere, outlook, and relationship among student members of the school. When the school received provisional accreditation in 1951, the organization received official affiliation to become the Oklahoma Student Chapter of the American Veterinary Medical Association (sometimes referred to as the Junior Chapter, American Veterinary Medical Association).

As members of the chapter, individuals were eligible to receive gold keys and certificates of membership and to subscribe to the official veterinary journals. Members in good standing for two or more years could, upon graduation, apply for membership in the American Veterinary Medical Association without payment of membership fees. Currently four years in good standing are required.

When the second class started in September 1948, the chapter plunged into the swim of things and set about building a float for the homecoming parade. Designed by William Ryan, it had a huge dinosaur that moved its legs, neck, and head. Judged to be the best one of

Dr. Duane Peterson, Dr. D. M. Trotter, Dr. J. W. Wolfe, Dean McElroy, Dr. Wendell Krull, Dr. E. E. Harnden *(left to right)* gather in Dean McElroy's office on the third floor of Life Sciences in April of 1951.

all, "it helped to put our school on the map." The school's float entry soon became a major attraction in homecoming parades. Through the years, the originality of the float and the ever present little trailer amused most onlookers but raised some eyebrows.[10]

In November 1949, the students launched another project, the *Veterinary Bulletin,* a quarterly newsletter to "carry future and past events of the veterinary profession in Oklahoma and surrounding areas. Its scope includes personals, news of epidemics, disease outbreaks, births, deaths, research in the area, or any other pertinent items of news value to veterinarians in the state."[11] The first editors were Austin W. Weedn and Leonard Carpenter, both of the class of 1951. Dean McElroy's message to his fellow veterinarians in the first issue stated: "The school is now in the third year, with all the classes well filled and the students are doing their part, not only to do good work, but to aid in every way possible to make the school a real entity on the campus. The faculty likewise is industriously and diligently working to bring up their various departments to recognition and acceptable standing."[12]

In January 1950 the title was changed to *Oklahoma Veterinary Bulletin.* An important link between the school, the alumni, and the state, it was discontinued in 1957 when the students voted to publish the *Caduceus,* an annual yearbook. The *Oklahoma Veterinarian,* established in 1954 as the official publication of the Oklahoma Veterinary Medical

Association, took over the function of the student bulletin. For several years students contributed to a special section entitled "College Gleanings."

Another example of student enterprise was the first annual "Veterinary Smoker" held on May 4, 1950, in the animal science arena. Over five hundred people attended, including nearly fifty veterinarians and their wives. Ray Wilcox from Weleetka, class of 1952, was in charge of the program. The smokers were held in May for several years in conjunction with the Conference for Veterinarians and were moved to the school auditorium when it was completed.[13]

The student chapter soon became very active in the college intramural sports program. During the 1950-51 academic year, the All Sports Club-Dorm Trophy found a permanent home in the veterinary school's trophy case. In 1954-55 the chapter entered ten sports events. They placed third or above in nine of these events and fourth in the other to out-class completely all of the other twenty-one participants. Their athletic activities have blossomed throughout the years.[14]

The student wives organized an auxiliary to the student chapter in the fall of 1950. They adopted the motto, "through promoting good fellowship among ourselves we assist in promoting the interests of the veterinary profession." At that time, the official name was Women's Auxiliary to the Student Chapter, American Veterinary Medical Associ-

COURTESY MRS. JANET PETERSON

The faculty wives, known as Vetceteras, always provided support for activities of the school. A highlight of the social calendar in the early years was the faculty wives entertaining the wives of senior students. Mrs. McElroy, Mrs. Harnden, Mrs. Gerald Goetsch, and Mrs. Janet Peterson stand in back of some of the wives of senior students at the home of Mrs. Harnden in the early 1950s.

ation, denoting an organization for females only. Twenty-five years later the organization included all student spouses. During that same year, Mr. Marvin Murphy became an active member and consequently served as vice president and alternate delegate to the national convention in 1976. Membership in the auxiliary has continued to grow with student enrollment rising from twenty in 1950 to thirty-five in 1985-86.

The auxiliary has a number of annual projects, a "Howdy Party" in honor of the spouses, Halloween Carnival, bake sales, preparing articles for the Marketplace of States at the annual convention, pet shows, and a number of community projects. They prepared and distributed a college directory, to which Stillwater businessman Mr. Claude Bradshaw added financial support. The auxiliary has provided light refreshments following student chapter meetings on Thursday evenings for many years.

The student chapter has remained a very active, vigorous organization. Chapter meetings featured outstanding speakers and the students initiated the Christmas party, picnic, and an end-of-year dance. Who better than Professor Newton Tennille to play the role of Santa Claus which he did with gusto for many years?

The school was organized into four departments: Department of Veterinary Anatomy, teaching the horse as the pattern animal; Department of Veterinary Pathology, including histology, embryology, and food hygiene and inspection; the Department of Clinics and Surgery, including an ambulatory service; and the Department of Veterinary Medicine, offering the study of infectious and non-infectious diseases. Physiology, microbiology, and parasitology were taught by instructors in the School of Arts and Sciences, housed on the third and fourth floors of Life Sciences.

The sequencing of courses within the curriculum of the School of Veterinary Medicine was not precise in those early days because it was sometimes necessary or expedient to delay scheduling a particular course until a new faculty specialist was appointed.

In the 1950s the curricula were remarkably similar among the various colleges of veterinary medicine. Dr. Paul Barto and Dr. Duane Peterson compiled the data of the credit and contact hours taught in the various subjects in veterinary medical colleges. Each subject was allotted as much time as the average time spent by the other colleges. Although this assured the time allotted to each subject was competitive with other colleges, it did tend to add a few extra credit and contact hours to the total curriculum.

The curriculum overload was somewhat compensated by the phasing out of required animal production courses. The courses in animal husbandry, dairy husbandry, and farm poultry (three credit hours each) were taught by the respective departments in the College of Agriculture.

The essential aspects of these three courses and limited information concerning pet animals were concentrated into one three-credit-hour course called veterinary zootechnics offered by the veterinary school.

The above realignment of the so-called agricultural introductory courses also opened the door for the introduction of a limited amount of new "ologies." Dr. Newton Tennille had recognized a need for more student involvement and training in radiology. The curriculum and scheduling committee added a one-credit-hour radiology course to the curriculum, initiated during the spring semester of 1954 for third-year students.

Because the new veterinary medicine building was still under construction, the small animal clinic was located on the fourth floor of Life Sciences. Some of the patients were pigs, sheep, and goats. It was not unusual for the "academic peace" to be disturbed by a squealing pig or a skunk being transported on the elevator!

Clinics were held from 9:00 a.m. until noon daily except Sunday with classroom teaching in the afternoons. Clinical experience in the large animal section was provided through the ambulatory service which had been operated by the veterinary science staff for many years. Students went on calls with Dr. Frank R. Knotts who had established a practice in Stillwater and was also an assistant professor of clinics and surgery. As a part-time employee, he was paid to take two students on his calls during each clinic period (three hours each morning). He was credited by the students with a terrific sense of humor, but it was a hair-raising experience riding with him! Dr. William Ryan, class of 1951, recalled that Dr. Knotts drove along the country lanes at 70 m.p.h. often singing "Nearer My God to Thee," while the students held on grimly and felt that they were indeed getting close to the Pearly Gates![15]

Practical experience was sometimes gained firsthand. Early in the spring of 1952, several students were given permission to leave campus to aid in controlling the newly discovered anthrax epidemic in northeast Stephens County. The 12-mile danger area had been placed under quarantine by Dr. R. H. Ricks, head of the State Board of Agriculture's veterinary division. Over fifty cattle and pigs had died from this oldest and deadliest disease of livestock.

The class of 1952, admitted in the fall of 1948, had completed nearly two years of professional training when parts of the new building became available. The "north wing" comprised an auditorium with direct access from outside, the large animal stalls, and treatment area. The "south wing" had mainly food animal and a few isolation stalls.

Access to the classrooms (201, 202, and 203) and the library was by stairs leading from the radiology area adjacent to the auditorium. On the third floor was the "crow's nest," home for several students for many years. In return for free "board and lodging" the students were respon-

The first new building for the College of Veterinary Medicine (as viewed from the south) was constructed in 1949. The auditorium, with direct access from the outside, is in the lower right foreground. Classrooms are on the upper floor. The large animal treatment and surgery area are on the left.

sible for certain departmental assignments, answering telephone calls on evenings and weekends, and admitting or discharging clinical cases after hours, in collaboration with the clinicians on emergency duty. Each student was also provided a rope which was to be his fire escape! It was an exceptionally rewarding extra clinical experience for the students.

The office area and small animal wing had not been built so part of the south wing was used as temporary faculty offices. One Saturday noon a clinician locked his "office" with a chain and padlock and went home. Unknowingly, he had locked the department secretary inside! She was rescued a few hours later by a clinician on emergency duty.

The small animal clinic and kennels were also in the south wing, a section built for swine and sheep. The large animal treatment area was a "catch all" for equipment and surgical operations that were performed in the lower part of the auditorium. The school was already gaining recognition as a vital force in the treatment and prevention of animal diseases.

Success of the new school would be, to a large degree, determined by the school's ability to secure accreditation. The faculty was keenly aware of this situation. In November 1950, the veterinary medicine faculty members sent Dean McElroy a letter expressing grave concern about the plight of the school. They urged the formulation of a general policy for the school, explanation of the allocation and distribution of the budget, appointment of committees, and closer cooperation between

For many years, student clinical rotations included a week in the pharmacy. Ed Blevins (class of 1952), Chris Burnett (class of 1952), R. J. Brown (former student), and Sam Best (class of 1951) work in the drug room located in the southeast corner of the large animal treatment area.

the Veterinary Research Institute and the school with the dean as director so that faculty members could do both teaching and research. The letter ended, "We will cooperate to the fullest extent of our ability to help achieve satisfactory solutions to the problems of the school. Accreditation is our immediate goal. The establishment of a modern institution of learning respected by students, faculty members, and members of our profession is our ultimate aim."[16]

Early in the century, the Bureau of Animal Industry, which later became the Bureau of Veterinary Medicine and then the Center for Veterinary Medicine, had established a committee on veterinary education to visit schools to ensure that they were of the necessary caliber to qualify students for federal appointments. This committee visited the school on February 5-6, 1951. In its report in April, the committee recommended that the school be accredited with the understanding that the building program would be completed as planned and "that a much closer working relationship than now exists will be worked out between the staffs of the School of Veterinary Medicine and the Veterinary Research Institute."[17] The committee maintained that the normal growth of the school and its standing in the field of veterinary education would be seriously retarded unless research and teaching were closely coordinated.

The report also stated, "Graduates of your school will be eligible to participate in civil service examinations for employment as veterinarians by the federal government and also will be qualified to take the federal accredited veterinarian examinations given to practicing veterinarians for participation in official animal disease control and eradication programs."[18] Dean McElroy explained that recognition would place the school on an equal basis with the other U.S. accredited schools of veterinary medicine. In 1952 the federal government recognized the American Veterinary Medical Association as the official accreditation body.[19]

Later in the spring, the education committee of the American Veterinary Medical Association also visited the school. They made some recommendations that were more or less "musts" for the year 1951-52, and the school was placed on public probation for one year. Their report suggested the following improvements: a better trained staff in the clinic, especially in the surgery for large animals; a radiologist and pharmacist for dispensary; greater volume of clinic accessions; more equipment such as swine operating tables; completion of the building plans; acceptable facilities for autopsy; integration of the veterinary teaching and research services; less complicated pre-veterinary admissions requirements; combination of the two departments now known as veterinary clinic and surgery and veterinary medicine into a single department; and combination of diagnostic laboratory and pathology department. The school received annual provisional accreditation for many years.

Following its official recognition by the American Veterinary Medical Association in 1951, students contrived initiation procedures (better described as "antics") for the freshman pledges. Each one had to carry a polished white bone and obtain the signature of every instructor in the School of Veterinary Medicine. The pledges held daily meetings on the Student Union veranda at 12:30 p.m. where the initiation committee checked their progress and asked some tough questions, such as, "Can you recite completely and accurately the veterinarian's code [oath]?" or "Give me a complete description of this bone."

The "excuse" for this rather bizarre procedure was that it enabled the students to get acquainted with their professors. However, the initiates had the last say and established a tradition of dunking the entire initiation committee in Theta Pond after initiation week was over! The practice was discontinued in the late sixties.

On May 28, 1951, the first graduating class of twenty-six students walked proudly across the platform during commencement exercises to receive their academic hoods and the degree of Doctor of Veterinary Medicine. The ceremony was held in the Field House, more affectionately known as Gallagher Hall. President Bennett was so proud of the first class, he arranged for them to be seated in the front row.

The first class didn't have to worry about taking National Board

Centennial Histories Series

Dr. Henry Bennett, president of Oklahoma A. and M. College, valued the creation of the School of Veterinary Medicine as one of the most important post-war programs of the college.

Examinations because they had not been adopted by the Oklahoma State Board of Veterinary Medical Examiners. The first National Board Examination in Oklahoma was not given until June 1956. However, they were required to take the State Board Examination in order to be licensed in Oklahoma.

Before the school opened in 1948, the administration had promised financial and other necessary support. Proponents of the school envisioned the development of a physical plant and faculty that would place Oklahoma as a leader in veterinary medical education. However, these great expectations did not come to pass for many years. Not more than $160,000 was spent in any one of the first four calendar years.

In the summer of 1951, Dean McElroy attempted to summarize the needs of the school for the next year in a report to President Bennett. A salary budget in the region of $163,810 was needed, but due to the curtailment of appropriations, the budget had been cut to $119,410. No salaries could be increased to compare with similar positions in other schools of veterinary medicine. Dr. R. L. Butler, who was considered one of the best small animal clinicians in the Middle West, had already left. Dean McElroy maintained that "permanency in staff is essential to a professional school. This budget practically ruins the School of Veterinary Medicine." The dean went on to express his concern that the maintenance budget would be cut in half. His final paragraph is especially noteworthy: "Keep in mind that one either has a school that is accredited or no school at all. It is about the same category as the Medical School at the University [University of Oklahoma]. Our graduates must be acceptable to the American Veterinary Medical Association and to the Bureau of Animal Industry."[20]

The school and the community were shocked in disbelief when, in December 1951, President Henry Bennett, along with his wife and two aides, were killed in a plane crash near Tehran, Iran. Dr. Bennett, who had been president since 1928, had great aspirations for the school which he considered of vital importance to the state of Oklahoma. Dr. Bennett, who had served Oklahoma A. and M. College longer than any other president, had been appointed by President Harry Truman to served as head of the Technical Cooperative Administration. The administration was also known as the Point Four Program because it was the fourth point mentioned in President Truman's inaugural address. The entire world mourned his death.

Because of Dr. Bennett's increasing involvement in international education, he had been granted a leave of absence in 1950, and the Board of Regents had named Dr. Oliver Willham, a vice president, to act in Dr. Bennett's absence. Dr. Willham, a graduate of Oklahoma A. and M. College in the field of agriculture, was named president the month following Dr. Bennett's untimely death.

Some administrative changes occurred in the early fifties. The Department of Clinics and Surgery presented courses in the diagnosis and treatment of surgical and clinical cases and was also responsible for operating the hospital and the ambulatory clinic. Dr. Lewis Moe was the department head. The Department of Veterinary Medicine with Dr. J. Wiley Wolfe as head was a separate unit and offered courses in infectious and non-infectious diseases of large and small animals and poultry, along with therapeutics. During the 1952-53 academic year, the two departments were joined to become the Department of Veterinary Medicine and Surgery with Dr. J. Wiley Wolfe as head. Dr. Moe took over the ambulatory clinic.

In 1952 the Oklahoma A. and M. College administration separated veterinary parasitology from the Department of Zoology. Dr. Wendell Krull, who was previous head of zoology, became head of the Department of Veterinary Parasitology in the School of Veterinary Medicine.

When it became necessary to teach bacteriology to the veterinary medicine students who were now in the second year of the curriculum in 1949-50, veterinary bacteriology was established as a department, jointly administered by the new school and the School of Arts and Sciences. Dr. Edward E. Harnden, a 1915 Colorado State University graduate who had joined the faculty in 1923, became head. For many years he and Dr. McElroy were the only teachers of bacteriology. Dr. Harnden was a very quiet, dedicated man, caring greatly for his students

Clarence Hamilton McElroy, D.V.M.
1886-1970

Dr. Clarence H. McElroy (affectionately known as Dean Mac) was born on March 26, 1886. He attended grade school in Tulsa. He enrolled for the fall semester of 1900 in the college preparatory school at Oklahoma A. and M. College. Money was scarce so he worked as a janitor in Old Central for ten cents an hour and his "room" was a bed in the attic of the building. He recalled, "My board and room cost $2.50 a week. One year I spent only $90!" He went on to study general science and received his B.S. degree in June 1906.

Dean Mac returned to the ranch for a while and then worked at a store in Jennings for one and a half years. However, on February 1, 1909, he returned to Oklahoma A. and M. College as an assistant to Dr. L. L. Lewis, head of the Department of Zoology and Veterinary Medicine. He was urged by Dr. Lewis to become a veterinarian and entered the St. Joseph Veterinary College, Missouri, where he received the D.V.M. degree in 1919.

Dr. McElroy returned to Stillwater and became an assistant professor in the School of Veterinary Medicine. He became dean of the School of Science and Literature in 1925, as well as professor of veterinary medicine and bacteriology. In 1935 he became chairman of the Biological Sciences Group which was established in the School of Science and Literature. He was dean of men from 1928 until 1947, a position he often referred to as "Dean of Wild Life"! He served for many years on the Athletic Cabinet and was acting president of Oklahoma A. and M. College for several months in 1928.

Dean Mac became dean of the

COURTESY MRS. ANN TRIBBEY

School of Veterinary Medicine until he retired in 1953. At the 89th American Veterinary Medical Association Convention in Atlanta in July 1969, Dean McElroy was installed as honorary vice president.

Dr. McElroy was active in civic and church life. He served as president of the Stillwater Lions Club and the Chamber of Commerce. He was a member of the First Christian Church, YMCA, Masonic Lodge, and Isaak Walton League. He was a charter member of Sigma Nu fraternity and a member of Phi Kappa Phi, Phi Sigma, Ittanaha Club, Blue Key, Grange, Xi Mu, Phi Eta Sigma, and Ruf Nex. He died at Stillwater Municipal Hospital on March 7, 1970.

The Dean Clarence H. McElroy Award was established in 1954 and is presented annually to the outstanding senior student.

who regarded him as a very conscientious and able teacher. He was one of the nation's leading authorities on poultry diseases. Dr. Louie Stratton, class of 1955, recalled that when Dr. Harnden was hospitalized due to a "break-down of old typhoid lesions," the students formed a blood bank for him. They traveled to the hospital in Oklahoma City and among them gave 148 pints of blood.[21]

When Dr. Harnden retired in 1953, Dr. Lynn Gee became head of the department, re-named the Department of Bacteriology. Staff and funds at this time were extremely scarce so Dr. George Short volunteered to teach bacteriology. Dr. Short, who had left his practice in El Dorado, Kansas, in 1950 and joined the Department of Veterinary Pathology, had to work Saturdays and Sundays preparing culture media for the laboratory class. He recalled doing autopsies in a wooden shack behind the anatomy building. One day an autopsy revealed that the animal had died of anthrax. It was loaded onto a truck, taken up by elevator to the third floor of the Life Sciences, and burned in the incinerator. He commented, "That took all day. The next day we received notice not to do it again. The only reason we did it in the first place was that there wasn't anything else to do with it."[22]

Dr. Short, who left in 1955, reflected in his advancing years that "Oklahoma State can pride itself on having turned out some of the finest practitioners that I have seen, considering the primitive conditions that existed there. They had to be quite innovative which led to a pragmatic approach to veterinary medicine that put them in good stead when they graduated and set up practice."[23]

In addition to being responsible for courses in histology, embryology, and food hygiene, the Department of Veterinary Pathology provided service courses for students in the Division of Agriculture and maintained a diagnostic laboratory, which provided services for practitioners and the livestock industry. Dr. D. M. Trotter, who was head of the Department of Veterinary Anatomy when the school opened in 1948, became head of the Department of Veterinary Pathology in the fall of 1948. Dr. Duane Peterson then became head of anatomy. In the mid 1950s, courses in histology and embryology were transferred to the Department of Veterinary Anatomy, and food hygiene was transferred to the Department of Veterinary Parasitology and Public Health.

The Department of Veterinary Pathology was housed in a temporary frame building with 1,386 square feet of floor space for instruction, 240 for office space, and approximately 1,500 square feet for a diagnostic laboratory, microtechniques laboratory, and storage space. Later on the office was moved to the hay loft above the south wing. Dr. A. L. Malle joined the pathology staff in 1953. Dr. Malle had been in practice in Iowa for several years and was mayor of the town of Pierson when he left. He was a colorful individual who spiced his lectures on poultry pathology with a lot of philosophy and economics of practice. He described the pathology facilities: "We had a little red tar paper shack and we would run back and forth up and down those outside steps on the end of the south wing to do necropsies. We had no hot water."[24]

Dr. Trotter left in 1953, eventually returning to his alma mater, the College of Veterinary Medicine, Kansas State University, where he later served as dean for many years. Dr. Duane Peterson took on the added duty of acting head of the Department of Veterinary Pathology.

In spite of the lack of facilities and resources there were some interesting highlights in the early 1950 era. The Conference for Veterinarians, which continued to be held each spring since 1926, created much interest and good relations with practitioners. The first closed circuit TV presentation was given at one of the meetings. WKY Channel 4 in Oklahoma City, the first TV station in the state, brought their big mobile unit to the school in 1953 and trained the students to run the cameras. The surgical demonstrations, performed in the large animal treatment area, were televised to the auditorium so that everyone could watch the techniques up close. This first telecast by any veterinary school was a huge success.

Dean Clarence H. McElroy retired on June 30, 1953. The young lad who joined Dr. L. L. Lewis as an assistant in bacteriology in 1909 became a legend in his time, beloved and respected by members of both the academic and social community. The student chapter presented "Dean Mac" with a gold watch and established the Dr. Clarence H. McElroy Award.

The award is made annually[25] to the outstanding senior student selected by a ballot of the faculty members and his/her classmates on the basis of scholarship, character, and professional ability. The original award was an engraved bronze plaque, and the recipient's name was also engraved on a larger plaque displayed in the veterinary medicine lobby. The first recipient was Paul Edmundson from Shawnee, class of 1954. Later the award consisted of a certificate and a $50 honorarium. This has been increased to $500 by a recent endowment from the Austin Weedn Foundation in honor of Dr. Duane Peterson.

The school, founded "on a shoestring," had established itself. The future of the school, however, was still in the balance and unpredictable. It was only because of the dedication of a loyal faculty and staff and conscientious students, who labored and studied in extremely inadequate, probably precarious, facilities that an outstanding academic institution finally emerged.

Endnotes

1. Dr. C. K. Whitehair to Dr. E. I. Williams, February 1986, Archives, College of Veterinary Medicine.

2. Whitehair to Williams.

3. Austin W. Weedn, "A. & M.'s Newest School," *Oklahoma A. and M. College Magazine,* vol. 21, no. 7 (March 1950), p. 12.

4. Oklahoma State Regents for Higher Education, *Third Biennial Report of the Oklahoma State Regents for Higher Education, Period Ending June 30, 1946,* pp. 41-42, Archives, College of Veterinary Medicine.

5. Author interview with Dr. Raymond E. Henry, 15 August 1984, Archives, College of Veterinary Medicine.

6. Henry interview.

7. *Bulletin Oklahoma A. and M. College General Catalog Issue, 1948-49, Announcements 1949-50,* p. 228.

8. Author interview with Dr. James O. Tucker, 25 May 1983, Archives, College of Veterinary Medicine.

9. Author's personal communication with Dr. William Ryan, July 1986.

10. Ryan communication; In acknowledgement of the homecoming float, C. H. McElroy, Dean, School of Veterinary Medicine, wrote the following letter to the attention of Sam H. Best, President, Student Veterinary Medical Society:
    "Dear Boys:
    "I want to hasten to congratulate you on the success of your float. You deserved to win and I appreciate the fact that you did win and received such nice recognition.
    "Please accept our congratulations and in closing, will repeat that it is the spirit of the School of Veterinary Medicine to win in spite of odds. When a spirit like that pervades, there is nothing which will stop our progress."
    C. H. McElroy to Sam H. Best, 25 October 1948, Archives, School of Veterinary Medicine.

11. "Veterinary Bulletin's Scope and Purpose," *Veterinary Bulletin,* vol. 1, no. 1 (November 1949), p. 6.

12. "Letter from Dean McElroy," *Veterinary Bulletin,* vol. 1, no. 1 (November 1949), p. 1.

13. "Veterinary Smoker Success," *Oklahoma Veterinary Bulletin,* vol. 1, no. 4 (May 1950), p. 3.

14. *1957 Caduceus,* College of Veterinary Medicine Yearbook.

15. Ryan communication.

16. School of Veterinary Medicine Faculty to Dean C. H. McElroy, 11 November 1950, Archives, College of Veterinary Medicine.

17. B. T. Simms, Chief of Bureau, to Dr. C. H. McElroy, 6 March 1951, Archives, College of Veterinary Medicine.

18. "U.S. Accredits VM School," *A. and M. College News,* vol. 4, no. 1 (15 April 1951), p. 1, Scrapbook, Archives, College of Veterinary Medicine.

19. "U.S. Accredits VM School," p. 1.

20. Dean C. H. McElroy to Dr. Henry Bennett, Archives, College of Veterinary Medicine.

21. Author interview with Dr. Louie G. Stratton, 4 June 1984, Archives, College of Veterinary Medicine.

22. Dr. George Short, tape recording to Dr. Eric I. Williams, May 1984, Archives, College of Veterinary Medicine.

23. Short recording.

24. Author interview with Dr. Albert Malle, 7 January 1983, Archives, College of Veterinary Medicine.

25. A complete listing of the McElroy Award recipients is in the Appendix.

5 Dr. Orr Takes Over the Reins

He applied his heart unto wisdom and his years were full of the fruit of God.

Rev. William Haig

Dean McElroy was succeeded by Dr. Harry W. Orr who took over the mantle of leadership on July 1, 1953, at a very precarious time in the school's history. Dr. Orr, who had joined the faculty of Oklahoma A. and M. in 1919, was well acquainted with the problems of the new school and the need to firmly and permanently establish the school.

Dean Orr set about the monumental task of acquiring desperately needed new buildings with the same vigor he had shown in the classroom. Just prior to his appointment as dean, he focused on the critical situations involving the Department of Medicine and Surgery and the Department of Pathology in a letter to J. L. Sanderson, chairman of the space committee at Oklahoma A. and M. College.

He described the current situation: "At the present time the staff of the Department of Medicine and Surgery has offices in the isolation stalls of the veterinary hospital. In addition to the fact that these stalls are badly needed by the hospital, they are highly unsatisfactory as offices. In the winter it is impossible to keep them warm enough for anything approaching comfort and during the summer they become unbearably hot. These stalls are so crowded that they are highly inefficient and trying to work under such conditions has kept the morale of the staff at a low ebb. I sincerely wish that your committee could devise some way of relieving this situation, for it has contributed to a considerable extent to the all too frequent changes in staff of the Department of Medicine and Surgery. The space needed for offices for the staff and for a business office for the Clinic and Hospital would be about 3000 sq. ft. Inasmuch as it appears that an additional unit could not possibly be added to the present building and be ready for use in less than four years, it is imperative that something be done to take care of the requirements of the School of Veterinary Medicine in the interim.

"The Department of Pathology also is in critical shape for lack of space. At the present time part of the department is housed in the hay mow of the hospital and part in TF-9 which is a considerable distance away. The movement of staff, materials, and equipment between the two places results in a considerable loss of time, efficiency and tempers. I am wondering if it might be possible to convert the northwest building of the South Village into a suitable place to house the Department of Pathology at a minimum expense to the College.

"I am particularly anxious to make the changes outlined above in the near future for it would help a great deal as far as the attitude and morale of the staff is concerned. But even more important, the Committee on Accreditation of the A.V.M.A. will be on the campus in October and I am very anxious to make these provisions for the School of Veterinary Medicine before they arrive. They have been quite critical of our arrangement in their past inspections but have given us three years to correct it. The committee was promised when they were here for inspection in 1952 that by this year we would either have the present building in the process of being completed or we would provide temporary accommodations which would be reasonably satisfactory until the permanent building was built."[1]

Because Dr. Orr had served the A. and M. College in various capacities and had been located in Life Sciences along with other disciplines, he was well aware of the considerable ill feeling toward the budding School of Veterinary Medicine by members of other departments who felt that some of their funds, limited as they were, had been "drained away" to help establish the school. It was thus Dr. Orr's objective to work with the university administrators and the legislature to obtain separate funding for the school. By the creation of a new "line item" in the budget for the School of Veterinary Medicine, it was hoped that appropriations for the school might increase.

Dean Orr's efforts to achieve this and other goals were hampered when he suffered a heart attack in September 1954. For several weeks he worked from his home.

On November 19, 1954, Dean Orr reminded Dr. M. A. Nash, chancellor, State Regents for Higher Education, of the need for better facilities. He said, "The School of Veterinary Medicine could contribute a great deal more to the welfare of all Oklahomans if it were supplied with adequate facilities. At the present time the critical need of the school

Mrs. Ruth Orr *(standing),* wife of Dean Harry Orr continues the tradition of faculty wives entertaining the student wives.

is a physical plant in which to carry on the numerous activities and services that the people of Oklahoma and the students expect from their veterinary medical school.''[2]

Dr. Orr went on to describe the seriousness of the current situation: ''Doctor Bennett promised the staff that he would provide adequate space for the operation of the school by the time the first class was started. His plan for a building did not go through as he expected and as a result two departments were housed in a small, entirely inadequate frame building which was obtained from the army. This building is frightfully hot in summer, cold and drafty in winter, and constitutes a serious fire hazard. If it should catch on fire, more than $75,000 worth of equipment would be lost. In addition, a histological and pathological slide library of enormous value would be destroyed. It would take years to replace it in part only, for some of the preparations could not be duplicated. Although the two departments were promised adequate permanent quarters not later than 1949 or 1950, they are still trying to operate in the army building. A great deal of money has been spent to keep the plumbing, heating system, and the refrigeration machines in a state of repair; the situation is getting worse month by month. We have lost several highly competent professors from the departments housed in the building simply because of the conditions under which they had to work, and our physical setup in general is hampering us seriously in securing competent men; they simply will not accept positions with this physical situation.

"Plans for a building to house the School of Veterinary Medicine were developed by the architects in 1946-47 and the animal hospital wing (north wing) was built in 1949-50. This building must serve for the medicine and surgery departments and for the hospital clinics and their staffs. There is not a single office or laboratory in the structure. It has been necessary to convert several animal stalls into offices and laboratories. Two laboratories and three offices are located in the hay mow which is extremely hot in summer, cannot be properly heated in winter, and has no windows. The secretaries and technicians must be sent home on some days in the winter because of the cold and there are few days when the temperature is really comfortable.

"There are only five faculty members in the entire School of Veterinary Medicine who have private offices and two of these offices are located in the temporary frame army building mentioned above."[3]

Dean Orr described the difficulties that existed because the school was located in three different buildings (TF-9, north wing, and pathology diagnostic laboratory) and then, he continued, "This letter does not begin to tell you the full story. We were given probationary accreditation in 1951 upon the expressed promise of Doctor Bennett that the school would be in its new building by the 1952-53 school year. Funds were not appropriated by the 1951 legislature and the accrediting agency is becoming hard to handle. It has consented to leave everything status quo until after the next legislature meets. If funds are not appropriated for the completion of the building next spring I am sure that we shall find ourselves in a most embarrassing situation. Therefore I am petitioning you and the Board to assist us in every way that you deem advisable to secure the necessary appropriation from the next legislature for the remainder of the building."[4]

There was light on the horizon! In 1954 Oklahoma voters approved $15 million in bonds. Of these funds, Oklahoma A. and M. College was granted $3,475,000 by the State Regents for Higher Education in January 1955 for capital improvements. Funds were designated for a new chemistry and physics building. President Oliver Willham stated at that time, "Our second greatest need is to add another unit to our veterinary medicine building. Much of this instruction is in temporary quarters spread over the campus."[5]

The O'Collegian focused on veterinary medicine, stating, "What the general student body does not know so much about are the needs of the School of Veterinary Medicine. Since it has so few students, and is largely located apart from the main area of the campus, not much is known about it by the average Aggie." It went on to praise the allocation of funds to the school.[6]

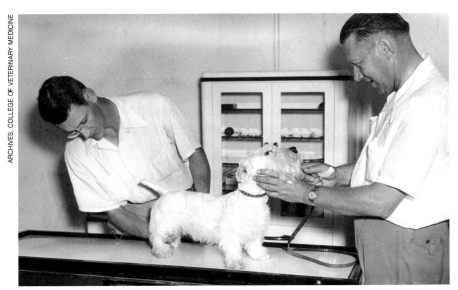

Dr. William O'Mara *(right)* examines a patient owned by Mr. Henry Iba, renowned A. and M. basketball coach, in the small animal clinic that was located in the old south wing.

In January 1955, Governor Raymond Gary outlined details of his $170 million budget for the next two years. Oklahoma A. and M. College had requested $6,631,324 for each year, including $321,370 yearly for the School of Veterinary Medicine. This appears to be the first reference to a "line item" for the school in the state budget.[7]

Although not a total solution to the facilities problem, in 1955 the Department of Medicine and Surgery found a new home! They moved out of their offices in the stalls to a brand new building which was located adjacent to the south wing. It became known officially as the Annex, and in those days it was almost akin to a palace! It was meant to be a temporary building, but it was not built that way. Not even the most violent electric storm could sweep it away to answer the prayers for a better building in later years! So it became the temporary home of the small animal clinic and the "permanent" home for the large animal clinicians (until 1981!). The first clinical research project was housed in the Annex, and a telephone exchange for the school was installed there.

An optimistic report by the Oklahoma Veterinary Medical Association's Committee on Education, published in the *Oklahoma Veterinarian* in June 1955, may have been influenced by these developments. It described the school as well staffed, with an operating budget for 1954-55 that was 25 percent greater than for 1953-54. It reported that the administration was asking for a 25 percent increase for the next year, which did not include the $10,000 that was spent on books and periodicals annually since the library budget came from other sources. The 1954-55 school year started with an enrollment of 140 students with 97 Oklahoma residents, 17 contract non-residents, and 26 other non-residents. The class of 42 first-year students had been selected from 113 applicants. The ages of the 1953 graduating class of 34 ranged from 23 to 36 years with an average age of 29 1/2 years.[8]

In spite of the improving, but still limited facilities, the school was acquiring a favorable reputation and 30 percent of the students were from other states. The Southern Regional Education Board had been established in 1949 as an outgrowth of an earlier Southern Governors Conference to design a program to avoid the costly duplication of veterinary medical education facilities and improve the quality of staff and students. At that time there were only five veterinary medical colleges in the south, and these would serve as regional training institutions for all the southern states.

Each veterinary school signed contracts to admit a quota of qualified students from other southern states. Students were required to secure admission and pay tuition but no out-of-state fee. The contracting state would pay a flat fee of $1,000 per year to the institution for reserving the space. This was raised to $1,500 in 1958 and $1,800 in 1968.

On February 8, 1948, Oklahoma Governor Roy J. Turner signed a compact to accept a certain number of applicants for admission in the beginning class each September. For the immediate future, the agreed allocation to Oklahoma A. and M. College was ten applicants comprised of seven from Arkansas and three from Louisiana.

In 1956 the regional contract was amended to provide a quota for entering students of veterinary medicine from the state of Texas. Although not specifically stated in the contract or amendment, it was made clear that Texas wished to have admissions limited to women! Since at that time Texas A and M College did not admit women students, it was amended in 1960 to admit four Texas females and in 1961 to five (in all classes).

A similar agreement was signed with the University of Nebraska in September 1957. The University of Nebraska agreed to pay $600 per semester for Nebraska students in lieu of the ordinary non-resident differential fee.

Oklahoma A. and M. College also admitted a limited number of students from other states that did not have a veterinary medical school such as Rhode Island, Massachusetts, and Wisconsin. These students paid out-of-state fees. Beginning with the class admitted in 1961 this policy was discontinued and admission was restricted to students from Oklahoma and contract states.

Between 1949 and 1970, Oklahoma provided 697 spaces and received

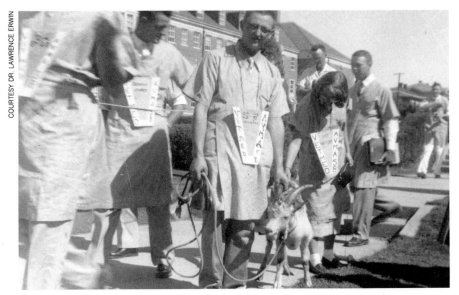

Freshmen students parade on campus in the fall of 1954 as part of the AVMA student pledge exercises. A student who could not answer a pledge question would be responsible for the goat and take it to class that day.

$1,040,850 from contracting states. The program was terminated in 1974.

Graduates and faculty were becoming involved on the international level. In 1950 Dr. Henry Bennett, then president of Oklahoma A. and M. College, had discussed with Emperor Haile Selassie and other Ethiopian officials the possibility of the college providing technical assistance under the Technical Cooperation Administration. In 1952 such an agreement was finally reached.

Although the School of Veterinary Medicine was not directly involved, Dr. Clifton Murphy, a large animal clinician, and Dr. Kenneth Keahey, a recent graduate, left for Ethiopia in June 1954. Involvement in Ethiopia would continue until 1968.

President Oliver Willham stated that their appointment was for a two-year period to set up a program of vaccination for cattle against rinderpest which was a serious problem to the cattle industry. Their work entailed visiting each of the eleven provinces of Ethiopia once a year where they instructed local teams on vaccination procedures. They traveled mainly by jeep, but in some areas they had to use donkeys or mules.

Dr. Murphy also taught students at Addis Ababa University College, and both Dr. Murphy and Dr. Keahey helped establish and operate the Animal Disease Control Center, working out of Addis Ababa. It provided interim facilities for agricultural and animal disease research while the physical plant of the Imperial Ethiopian College of Agriculture was being constructed.

Dr. Murphy returned to the United States in 1956. Dr. Keahey became head of the Animal Science Department when the Imperial Ethiopian College of Agriculture of Alemaya was opened in 1956. In 1957 he was appointed dean, and in 1959 he served as acting president of the Imperial Ethiopian College. Dr. Keahey left in 1960 to become a post-doctoral fellow at Michigan State University.

Dr. Delbert Whitenack went to Ethiopia a month after Dr. Murphy and Dr. Keahey and served as a science teacher in Jimma for two years, then moved to the college in Alemaya for the next four years. He believed that teaching young people was Oklahoma State University's greatest accomplishment there. Several students went for advanced studies in the United States and Europe. Since Dr. Whitenack was not a veterinarian (at that time), he was more involved with the production side of the animal industry. Dr. Whitenack and others became convinced that selective breeding of native cattle was needed and eventually developed a quality beef cattle herd at the Agriculture Research Station, Alemaya. He returned to Oklahoma State University in 1960 where he received the D.V.M. degree in 1965.

Dr. Anton Kammerlocher received the D.V.M. degree from Oklahoma State University in 1957. He joined the U.S. Air Force and was stationed in the Azores where he assisted in organizing a dairy cooperative to increase milk production and processing in the Angra do Heroismo district. He was honored by the civil governor of the district for his efforts. When Dr. Keahey and Dr. Whitenack returned to the United States in 1960, Kammerlocher was appointed to succeed them. He recalled that President Oliver Willham "recruited me to go to Ethiopia because I had already had overseas experience and was instrumental in developing a food production and distribution system which enabled their products to be approved by the world market."[9]

Dr. Kammerlocher served as a veterinarian on the staff of the Imperial Ethiopian College of Agriculture at Alemaya and lived on the college campus. He taught several courses to Ethiopian students who were hungry for knowledge and studied hard. Dr. Kammerlocher also took care of the Emperor's animals that were kept in several palace grounds. They included forty-two dogs, the Emperor's horses, a pet lion which rode on his Rolls Royce, and other wild animals. He recalls operating on the U.S. Ambassador's dog on the kitchen table. The two Marine guards who were supposed to assist him passed out! His experience with food distribution was a great asset in his teaching assignments. Dr. Kammerlocher's first class in parasitology had seven outstanding students who went on to receive Ph.D. degrees in various countries and later returned to play major roles in disease control, particularly rinderpest. Within

Harry William Orr, D.V.M., M.S.
1896-1956

Harry William Orr was born in Mystic, Iowa, on August 9, 1896. He received the D.V.M. degree from Iowa State College in 1918 and served as a second lieutenant in the Army during World War I. In 1919, he joined Dr. L. L. Lewis in the original School of Veterinary Medicine as an assistant professor of veterinary science. Following the official demise of the school in the 1920s, Dr. Orr taught physiology courses to pre-medical students in the Department of Bacteriology, Physiology, and Veterinary Science. He also taught human anatomy, animal, and poultry disease courses.

Dr. Orr received the M.S. degree from Iowa State College in 1930. In 1948 Dr. Orr became head of the Department of Physiology and Pharmacology, housed in Life Sciences. On the retirement of Dr. C. H. McElroy, he was named dean of the School of Veterinary Medicine on July 1, 1953.

Dr. Orr was a delightful conversationalist, a colorful and demanding lecturer, and an impressive public speaker. He was magnificently supported by his wife Ruth, a very gracious and beautiful lady.

Dr. Orr was a member of the American Veterinary Medical Association, Oklahoma Veterinary Medical Association, New York Academy of Science, Oklahoma Academy of Science, American Association for the Advancement of Science, and the American Society of Veterinary Physiologists and Pharmacologists. He served as president and long-time member of the Oklahoma Board of Examiners in the Basic Sciences. In 1952 he attended the Second International Congress of Physiology and Pathology in Copenhagen. His fraternal membership included AF and AM blue lodge, Consistory, Phi Kappa Phi, Phi Eta Sigma, Phi Sigma, and Kappa Sigma. He was given the Silver Beaver Award for fifteen years service to the Boy Scouts.

Dr. Orr died at his home on Saturday morning, January 14, 1956. Funeral services were held at the First Presbyterian Church, Stillwater, on Monday, January 16, with interment in Fairlawn Cemetery. His pastor, the Rev. William Haig of the First Presbyterian Church, stated in his eulogy, "The man whose memory we honor today applied his heart unto wisdom and his years were full of the fruit of God."

The Dean Harry W. Orr Award was presented for the first time in 1958. The award has been made annually to a third-year veterinary medicine student who has demonstrated high academic achievement and unusual professional growth in pre-clinical training.

seven years the cattle population increased from fifteen million to thirty million.

When Dr. Kammerlocher left Ethiopia in 1963, he was succeeded by Dr. Martin Frey, who had received the D.V.M. degree from Kansas State University in 1956 and had joined the Department of Veterinary Anatomy at OSU in 1961. In Ethiopia, Dr. Frey taught anatomy, physiology, parasitology, and veterinary hygiene, which were required courses for students in the Department of Animal Science at Alemaya, and took care of the college herds. In June 1964 he travelled to Greece where he married Dr. Demarious Keller, who received her D.V.M. degree from OSU in 1963. They spent another year in Ethiopia with Dr. Demarious Frey assisting her husband with the college herd. Also, she took care of the Emperor's forty-two Arabian horses at the military academy in exchange for horseback riding privileges.

Dr. Bruce Stringer, class of 1963, was the last graduate of the OSU College of Veterinary Medicine to serve in Ethiopia. From 1965 until 1968 he taught several courses in the animal science department in Alemaya and traveled extensively to promote disease control programs. Dr. Stringer was instrumental in establishing a zoological garden. This venture was strongly supported by the Emperor who was greatly fascinated by animals. Dr. Stringer accepted an appointment at the Albuquerque Zoo in New Mexico on his return to the United States.[10]

While faculty and graduates of the College of Veterinary Medicine were blazing new educational frontiers in Ethiopia, students in the class of 1955 were establishing new precedents for the college. The class of 1955 was unique; one of its members was June Iben, the first woman to receive the D.V.M. degree from Oklahoma A. and M. College. She began as a chemistry major at Allegheny College in Meadville, Pennsylvania, because her father forbade her to take anything leading to veterinary medicine. ("In those days you did as you were told!") Later she went to work for a small animal practitioner and finally overcame her father's objection. She set about completing pre-veterinary courses, but the schools of veterinary medicine were reluctant to interview a woman for admittance. One school told her that even if she qualified for admission there would have to be two female students because they only took women in groups of two!

June moved to Union, Kentucky, and did research on blood grouping in horses. She applied to Oklahoma A. and M. College and recalled, "I vividly remember the day the acceptance letter came. I couldn't believe, after all these years, it was really true and I fear I drove most of my friends crazy by having them read and re-read the letter to verify its contents"! At school some opposition was encountered from some classmates and some faculty. "I worked hard, had a sense of humor and rolled with the punches. After all, I was not only a woman but a damn

Veterinary Medicine was not always a subject suitable for study by young ladies, but
in 1955, June Iben from Union, Kentucky,
became the first female graduate of the
School of Veterinary Medicine. In future
years, the number of women graduates
would steadily increase.

Yankee to boot! I was lucky that fellow Yankee, John King, teased me
a lot and broke the ice for the rest of the class"! She was also invited
to join the ladies' auxiliary.[11]

An exchange picnic with the student chapter at Kansas State University was started early in the 1950s. The afternoon "get together" started
with a softball game followed by a a tug-of-war contest, barbecue and
later a dance. This very popular event was hosted by the two schools
alternately for many years. Due to increasing costs of travel and considerable apathy, it was discontinued in 1977.

The class of 1955 was the first to have a uniform-looking class photo.
It was so "uniform" that they all ended up being photographed wear-
ing the same tie and jacket, except June Iben! They also fought to be
the first class to wear proper D.V.M. graduating gowns. Leo Ford, a member of the class, led the request to obtain the proper D.V.M. gowns with
the gray paneling. Former classes used robes with black paneling.

On a different note, the Oklahoma Board of Veterinary Medical
Examiners tried to get legislation to enable it to institute injunction action
against flagrant violators of the state law governing the practice of medicine and surgery, but it failed dismally. However, at about the same time,
House Bill No. 831, known as the Barbers' Bill, passed empowering the
Board of Barbers' Examiners to institute "injunction action" in courts
of competent jurisdiction in the state of Oklahoma when necessary to
enforce established minimum rates. An editorial in the June 1955 issue
of the *Oklahoma Veterinarian* concluded, "Whatever the answer, it is
high time we take 'stock' of ourselves, both individually and collectively,
to learn why we don't 'click' like the barbers do."[12]

Dr. Leslie McDonald came to the School of Veterinary Medicine in 1954 and assumed the headship of the Department of Physiology and Pharmacology.

The Department of Physiology and Pharmacology did not have a department head following Dr. Orr's appointment as dean until February 1954 when Dr. Leslie E. McDonald assumed these duties. A stern and demanding leader, Dr. McDonald contributed enormously to the development of the physical facilities and research. Although some faculty were angered by his "supposedly" high salary, others felt his appointment was necessary to help establish the graduate program which was just starting.[13]

Dr. Andrew W. Monlux was appointed head of the Department of Veterinary Pathology (including histology), effective January 1, 1956. He was formerly with the United States Department of Agriculture Research Service in Denver, Colorado.

Dean Orr appointed Dr. Peterson, Dr. Walter Rice, and Dr. Robert Rubin to the school building committee. Their main task was to work with the college architects to "iron out the bugs" from the proposed plans for the new wing before presenting them to the Board of Regents for approval. Dr. Peterson served as chairman. An L-shaped two-story addition with one arm extending south 220 feet and the other arm extending west 172 feet was proposed.

Included in the 36,150 square feet of floor space would be the small animal clinic, faculty offices, and the anatomy laboratory and preparation rooms on the ground floor. The dean's office and the pathology and parasitology departments would be on the second floor. The Department

Dr. Andrew Monlux *(left)* was head of the Department of Veterinary Pathology from 1956 to 1972. Between 1972 and 1979, Dr. Monlux and Dr. Jeffie Roszel *(right)* established the nation's second animal tumor registry; the research was sponsored by the National Cancer Institute.

of Physiology and Pharmacology remained in Life Sciences for several years.

The school suffered a severe loss when Dean Orr died suddenly of a heart attack at his home on Saturday morning, January 14, 1956, at the age of fifty-nine. Although he had served as dean for only thirty months, he had spent almost forty years influencing education at Oklahoma A. and M. College.

Dr. A. E. Darlow, dean of the School of Agriculture and vice president of Oklahoma A. and M. College, expressed the sentiments of many: "The college and its school of veterinary medicine have suffered a most serious loss in the untimely death of Dean Orr. His eminence as a scholar, his competence as an administrator, and his stature as a man have endowed his school and the college with a rich inheritance. It is our conviction this endowment will be a permanent one."[14]

Dr. Duane R. Peterson was appointed acting dean by the Board of Regents on February 6, 1956.

The years under Dean Orr had been productive ones. Progress had been made in creating a separate budget. A new building, although a "temporary" one, had been obtained, and plans had begun for a more permanent building solution. The first graduate degree in the veterinary medicine program was granted in 1956. The school had reached another landmark in the quest for academic excellence.

Endnotes

1. Dr. Harry Orr to J. L. Sanderson, 22 June 1953, Archives, College of Veterinary Medicine.
2. Dr. Harry Orr to Dr. M. A. Nash, 19 November 1954, Archives, College of Veterinary Medicine.
3. Orr to Nash.
4. Orr to Nash.
5. Newspaper clipping from Scrapbook, Archives, College of Veterinary Medicine.
6. Newspaper clipping from Scrapbook, Archives, College of Veterinary Medicine.
7. Newspaper clipping from Scrapbook, Archives, College of Veterinary Medicine.
8. "Committee on Education, 1954 Report—Oklahoma Veterinary Medical Association," *Oklahoma Veterinarian,* vol. 2, no. 1 (March 1955), p. 12.
9. Author's personal communication with Dr. Anton Kammerlocher, June 1983.
10. Jerry Leon Gill, *The Great Adventure: Oklahoma State University and International Education* (Stillwater: Oklahoma State University Press, 1978), pp. 9-66.
11. Dr. June Iben, tape recording to Eric I. Williams, June 1984, Archives, College of Veterinary Medicine.
12. C. H. Fauks, "Editorially Speaking of Barbers and Veterinarians," *Oklahoma Veterinarian,* vol. 2, no. 2 (June 1955), p. 2.
13. Author's personal communication with Dr. C. K. Whitehair, 1986.
14. *Stillwater NewsPress,* 15 January 1956, p. 1. Also in Scrapbook, Archives, College of Veterinary Medicine.

6 Graduate Education Begins

*The past cannot be separated from the present without grievous loss.
The present without its past is insipid and meaningless; the past without
the present is obscure.*

George Sarton

When E. R. Beilfuss was granted a doctorate in parasitology in 1957 under the direction of Dr. Wendell H. Krull, it marked the first Ph.D. degree bestowed in the College of Veterinary Medicine; the first master of science had been granted to G. A. Stover, a student of Dr. W. S. Newcomer, in 1956. These two events represented tangible evidence that a milestone reached in 1954—approval of a program of graduate study in veterinary medical science—was bearing fruit.

The successful establishment of a modest graduate program in the early 1950s was a key factor in strengthening the fledgling School of Veterinary Medicine. Not only did the program help provide a new generation of veterinary medical scientists, its very existence helped attract faculty and enhanced the scholarly atmosphere in which students wishing to become veterinarians were taught.

Aside from his success as a teacher and researcher in parasitology— and quite apart from his role as an academic department head—Dr. Wendell H. Krull made lasting contributions to the college and university in his successful effort to develop a graduate program through the basic science departments of the new School of Veterinary Medicine. He foresaw the need for graduate education in its own right, and he saw it as a mechanism for strengthening the professional curriculum designed to produce veterinarians.

In the spring of 1947, Dr. Krull, while serving as a teacher of parasitology and as head of two academic departments at Colorado A. and M. College in Fort Collins, became interested in the emerging school of veterinary medicine at Stillwater and contacted C. H. McElroy, who was the acting dean. Dr. Krull already had some fifteen years of teaching and research experience in universities and had worked for eleven years in full-time research for the Zoological Division of the United States Department of Agriculture's Bureau of Animal Industry, a forerunner of today's Agricultural Research Service.

Although Dean McElroy responded to Dr. Krull's inquiry in March, the future for the proposed school was still uncertain. It was October 1947 before Dean McElroy wrote to Dr. Krull and invited him to make formal application for employment. The school was assured. Dean McElroy indicated that the students for the first veterinary medical class were already selected, taking pre-veterinary courses, and would begin the professional curriculum in the spring semester of 1948.[1]

Dr. Krull applied in October and provided supporting documentation regarding his qualifications for teaching veterinary parasitology. Effective September 1, 1948, Dr. Krull became associate head and professor in the Department of Zoology and professor and head in the Department of Parasitology.[2]

The precedent for heading two academic departments at Colorado A. and M. was used to justify the same arrangement at Oklahoma A. and M. Apparently it was necessary that Dr. Krull assume a dual administrative role in order to justify offering him adequate salary to insure that he would leave Ft. Collins for Stillwater. The plan, adopted in the spring 1948, was for him to serve as associate head of zoology for one year and to become head in 1949, when Professor R. O. Whittenton retired after long service as zoology department head.[3]

Dr. Krull's interest in academic matters affecting the developing college, including concern about graduate education, was obvious even before his appointment. In a letter to Dean McElroy dated June 9, 1948, he raised a question of opportunity for students to pursue graduate work through the zoology department. After he agreed to accept the position, Dr. Krull forwarded much of his personal collection of scientific journals, parasitologic specimens and other teaching materials to the school; he also requested that certain references be added to the library—references that would be of use both in teaching professional students and in developing graduate education.[4]

When the newly authorized school was having some difficulty in getting established during 1947 and 1948, Dr. Krull expressed concern about the academic health of the institution and its standing in the veterinary medical profession. He had consulted with a veterinary medical leader from Colorado A. and M. regarding the requirements for accredi-

In 1954 Dr. Wendell Krull was receiving international attention for his work with *Dicrocoelium dendriticum*, the lancet fluke of sheep. A member of the faculty from 1948-1964 and again in 1969, Dr. Krull was chairman of the committee that developed the proposal for a graduate program.

tation by the American Veterinary Medical Association. In a letter to Dean McElroy in April 1948, he stressed the need for clinics to be set up by the time the first class was started.[5]

Dr. Krull went on to say later in the letter: "With the investment that Oklahoma is putting into a veterinary school, I cannot help but believe that it *is* [Krull's emphasis] being created with the advice of the committee in the AVMA. It certainly was done with regards to building plans." Dr. Krull held his completed letter overnight, apparently pondered his concerns, and then added a postscript: "I should like to have positive statements indicating that requirements will be met for accreditation and that I am hired to teach parasitology to veterinary students and that I am free to do research to further this end."[6]

To those who would come to know Dr. Krull in Oklahoma and to appreciate his philosophy and ideals, it is not surprising that his major concerns about joining Oklahoma A. and M. had to do with the academic health of the emerging school. He did not seem to be as concerned about the physical plant, apparently believing that particular aspect of development was under control if not less critical to a successful start. From the outset he was concerned about graduate education and about opportunities for research around which graduate education could develop.

Oklahoma A. and M. officials were pleased to attract a scientist of

Dr. Krull's stature and his impact on the developing school proved to be enormous. There were no textbooks available from which to teach veterinary parasitology. Therefore, Dr. Krull revised his class notes and requested that they be prepared for distribution to the students.[7]

Dr. Krull was chairman of a committee of three (with Dr. W. S. Newcomer and Dr. C. K. Whitehair) that developed a proposal to the Graduate Council of the Graduate School of Oklahoma A. and M. College. The committee reported to Dean H. W. Orr, who in turn endorsed the proposal for consideration by the Graduate Council. It was approved in 1954, six years after classes began for veterinary medical students. The proposal ran to more than eighty typewritten pages including the curricula vitae of faculty who were qualified to teach potential graduate courses.[8]

Justification for establishing the program, as stated in the document, included the following critical section: "Little coordinated or declared effort and interest has ever been made to prepare personnel for research and teaching in veterinary schools. The lack of knowledge concerning many diseases of domestic livestock is actually critical in some respects because of this gross short-sightedness, because better remuneration and facilities in other positions have depleted the research personnel, and because the excessive public demands for practitioners have taken the potential supply. Surveys and observations of trained individuals with perspective show that veterinary schools are woefully inadequate in their graduate programs."[9]

Dr. Krull and his colleagues were well aware of the critical situation that had developed in the post-World War II boom times when, in the span of only a few years, seven new schools to educate veterinarians had developed in the United States. Academically well qualified faculty were in short supply and too few schools were engaged in developing new teachers or researchers. Key members of the faculty recognized that the Oklahoma A. and M. veterinary school could not gain academic respectability nor discharge its responsibilities to the scientific community without having a graduate program in addition to the professional curriculum. Dr. Krull and his committee captured that concern and argued effectively for mounting the effort.

The committee's report further stated that "the training of a scientist requires many years of schooling in formal courses and years in experience and, consequently, cannot be supplied on an emergency basis. This condition will be corrected only with the introduction of a well-supported graduate program to stimulate specialists and scholars who are willing to use their ability to produce and assemble accurate information without unusual financial gain. Graduate students also enhance and stimulate an undergraduate teaching program. The gravity of the situation as far as teaching personnel is concerned is also intensified because of the ever increasing demand made on the schools by the national accrediting agencies." Their plea for approval continued, "The effects should finally manifest themselves in a more competent and devoted staff; an improved teaching and scholarly research program; and the economic and social betterment of the state and nation."[10]

The committee was persuasive. The quality of the document detailing justification and outlining faculty resources was excellent and would serve as a model to be followed even in the 1980s. The committee members were clearly farsighted in their view of the potential and need for future development of graduate education and in the importance of faculty control of the program. On the final page of the document they recommended "that advanced degrees be administered in the School of Veterinary Medicine, with specialization in subject matter divisions, such as physiology, parasitology, or others. Graduate study divisions will be initiated currently in physiology and parasitology, and others will be added as soon as adequacies in staff, facilities and courses permit. The number of graduate students any department can accept is limited because of space and facilities. Consequently, acceptance of a qualified applicant must rest finally with the departments involved."[11]

Two departments, physiology and parasitology, were approved by the Graduate Council and immediately began offering graduate study. (Specialization in veterinary microbiology and public health were added to the area of parasitology beginning in 1971.) At a later time the pathology program was approved for graduate study and the first M.S. was granted in 1962.

Dr. Krull became well known for his teaching style and for his enthusiasm as a classroom teacher. He was exceedingly demanding, but students responded positively for the decade and a half that he was to teach in the new school. Dr. Krull was renowned for his demands in the classroom and expectations as an academic administrator, but the personal standards of excellence, obvious in his own work coupled with an infectious enthusiasm for veterinary parasitology, made his exacting expectations acceptable to those around him in veterinary medicine. S. A. Ewing, a new faculty member and graduate student in 1960, was addressed by a faculty wife upon first meeting as follows: "So you are the new guy in Parasitology! You will have a grey beard down to here [signalling the waist] before you get a Ph.D. from that man." In fact it did take a while![12]

The committee report on the development of the graduate program in veterinary medical science reveals a statement of attitude toward the student's responsibility for his own development. A section headed Philosophy of Graduate Degrees states: "It is assumed that the candidate for the degree of doctor of philosophy is a molded individual who has an appreciation and working knowledge of the scientific method and who has most of his basic informational subjects and training prepara-

Wendell Henry Krull, A.B., M.S., Ph.D., D.V.M., D.Sc.
1897-1971

Born December 8, 1897, at Tripoli, Iowa, Wendell H. Krull was the son of William and Theresa Schuknecht Krull. After serving in the U.S. Navy from 1917-20, he earned college degrees at Upper Iowa University (A.B., 1921), University of Iowa (M.S., 1924), University of Michigan (Ph.D., 1931), and Colorado State University (D.V.M., 1945). He taught zoology at North Central College (Naperville, Illinois), Kansas Wesleyan (Salina, Kansas), and Elmhurst College (Elmhurst, Illinois) from 1924-28. He married Nellie Godard in 1927 at Salina.

He served in various capacities in several locations with the United States Department of Agriculture from 1931-42. He began his study of veterinary medicine at Auburn University while teaching veterinary parasitology in the professional curriculum. Later, he transferred to Colorado State where he taught parasitology while completing requirements for the D.V.M. degree. He served as head of zoology and as parasitologist for the Experiment Station at Colorado State from 1945-48. At Oklahoma State University he served as associate head and then head of zoology and head of veterinary parasitology. In the summers 1951-54 he was senior research fellow at Cornell University where he discovered the life cycle of *Dicrocoelium dendriticum,* a liver fluke of sheep.

Upper Iowa University in Fayette, his alma mater, awarded Dr. Krull an honorary Doctor of Science degree in 1954. The school was justifiably proud of his scientific achievements, and UIU's president cited many of Dr. Krull's accomplishments and "outstanding record in the field of science."

Dr. Krull was recognized in 1962 by the College of Veterinary Medicine student body through dedication of the yearbook, the *Caduceus.*

ARCHIVES, COLLEGE OF VETERINARY MEDICINE

In 1963 Norden Laboratories, Lincoln, Nebraska, initiated its program for recognizing outstanding teaching in veterinary medicine. Dr. Krull became the first recipient.

After retirement from Oklahoma State he was associated with the Animal Medical Center in New York City (1964-65) and Kansas State University (1965-68). In the fall of 1969, Dr. Krull came back to Oklahoma State University to teach veterinary parasitology. He died on August 29, 1971.

Dr. Krull published more than eighty-five scientific papers. He made important contributions to the scientific knowledge concerning virtually every parasitic flatworm that affects meat-producing domestic animals in North America. Miriam Rothschild, herself an internationally acclaimed authority on parasitologic topics, considers Dr. Krull to be among America's most brilliant parasitologists, "monstrously under-rated and inexplicably disregarded."

tion behind him. He should be capable of determining and acquiring the supplemental informational subjects that are necessary. He should be given academic freedom in the realm of his research and the preparation of his thesis. He should be made to shoulder the responsibility of producing and made to justify his acts and procedures for the scientific approach. He should be queried and advised when necessary, but encouraged to do everything himself in connection with the gathering and processing of data and the final preparation of an acceptable thesis."[13] This philosophy, molded by Dr. Krull, later received national attention through publication in the *Biologist*, the official organ of Phi Sigma Biological Society.[14]

In spite of the emphasis on self sufficiency, Dr. Krull refused to accept more than a few graduate students at a time believing that to do so would be unfair given his teaching obligations in the professional curriculum. In fact he personally directed only seven successful candidates in the ten-year period that elapsed between approval of the graduate program and his retirement. Among his students were only two American-trained veterinarians who earned Ph.D. degrees. Ironically, both of those individuals (E. D. Besch and S. A. Ewing) later became deans of veterinary medical colleges (at Louisiana State University and the University of Minnesota) and their direct contributions to the discipline of parasitology were accordingly curtailed. Dr. Besch, who replaced Dr. Krull as department head, left Oklahoma State in 1968 to assume his deanship, and Dr. Ewing replaced Dr. Besch.

After forced retirement, Dr. Krull left Stillwater in 1964 and later retired to Sun City, Arizona. The Board of Regents permitted Dr. Krull to be employed on a part-time basis in the fall of 1969. Unfortunately, he was forced to return to Arizona for medical reasons shortly thereafter. He died two years later.

Many friends and former students spontaneously made contributions in his memory. These funds, together with others provided by his widow, Nellie Godard Krull, were used to establish the "Wendell H. Krull Parasitology Prize." Recipients are selected by faculty members in parasitology based upon the criteria of academic achievement, evidence of specific interest in parasitology, and general standards of excellence.[15]

The earnings from the investment capital have outgrown the expenditures, and it is anticipated that at some future time it will be possible to provide a stipend for a graduate student who is specializing in parasitology. It would be fitting, indeed, for the man who played such a central role in developing graduate education in veterinary medical science to have his name connected perpetually to graduate study in parasitology.

After almost three decades, to mid-1985, 61 degrees (42 M.S. and

19 Ph.D.) were granted in the area of parasitology (including veterinary microbiology and public health). In the area of physiology 116 degrees (74 M.S. and 42 Ph.D.) were granted. A total of 27 degrees were granted in pathology, 6 of them doctorates.

The figures cited with respect to numbers of graduate degrees granted are rather modest, approximately 300 in thirty years, slightly less than one-fourth of them doctorates. Nevertheless, the three graduate programs have been widely recognized and have produced a reasonable share of scientists who have made significant contributions to veterinary medicine and, more generally, to biological sciences.[16]

Endnotes

1. C. H. McElroy to W. H. Krull, 18 October 1947, Personnel file of Wendell Krull, Business Office, College of Veterinary Medicine.

2. W. H. Krull to C. H. McElroy, 21 October 1947, Personnel file of Wendell Krull, Business Office, College of Veterinary Medicine.

3. R. O. Whittenton, S. Scroggs, and C. H. McElroy to W. H. Krull, 2 June 1948, Personnel file of Wendell Krull, Business Office, College of Veterinary Medicine.

4. W. H. Krull to C. H. McElroy, 9 June 1948, Personnel file of Wendell Krull, Business Office, College of Veterinary Medicine; W. H. Krull to C. H. McElroy, 22 June 1948, Personnel file of Wendell Krull, Business Office, College of Veterinary Medicine.

5. W. H. Krull to C. H. McElroy, 12 April 1948, Personnel file of Wendell Krull, Business Office, College of Veterinary Medicine.

6. Krull to McElroy, 12 April 1948.

7. Krull to McElroy, 22 June 1948.

8. C. K. Whitehair, W. S. Newcomer, and W. H. Krull, chairman, "A Proposal to the Graduate Council, Graduate School, Oklahoma Agricultural and Mechanical College: A Program for Advanced Degrees in Veterinary Medical Science in the School of Veterinary Medicine" (Stillwater, Oklahoma, 1954), pp. 3-4, Archives, College of Veterinary Medicine.

9. Whitehair and others, pp. 3-4.

10. Whitehair and others, pp. 4-5.

11. Whitehair and others, p. 84.

12. Author's personal communication with S. A. Ewing, April 1986.

13. Whitehair and others, pp. 7-8.

14. W. H. Krull, "Philosophy of Graduate Degrees," *Biologist,* vol. 39 (1956-57), pp. 40-41.

15. Aside from a cash award derived from interest income earned by the original capital, names of recipients are inscribed on a plaque that has special significance. Krull was an avid woodworker and skilled craftsman who made most of the furniture for his home. When he left Stillwater in 1964 to work at the Animal Medical Center in New York City, he gave fellow faculty member and former student, Roger Panciera, some fine pieces of solid mahogany and black walnut lumber. Panciera, himself a superb woodcraftsman, still had some of the wood more than a decade later, and he constructed the handsome plaque. The plaque is displayed in the College of Veterinary Medicine as a permanent record of "Wendell H. Krull Parasitology Prize" winners.

16. A list of students who have earned doctoral degrees, together with dissertation titles, can be found in the Appendix.

7 The School Becomes a College

It is better to light one candle than to curse the darkness.
Old Chinese Proverb

Dr. Glenn C. Holm, dean of agriculture and director of the experiment station at North Dakota State College at Fargo, was appointed dean of the school effective October 1, 1956. The selection of the dean was rather different in those days. One of the department heads at the time recalls a meeting which took place between Dr. A. E. Darlow, dean of the School of Agriculture and vice president in charge of agricultural sciences, and the school's department heads following the death of Dr. Orr. Dr. Darlow was asked if he would like to receive some nominations, whereupon he very abruptly informed the group that they were not necessary. The dean was selected by the university administration. Apparently, it caused some uneasiness between the dean, his department heads, and the faculty for some time.

Shortly after Dean Holm took up his office on the third floor of Life Sciences, it became evident that he would be in command. Mrs. Lois Greiner (affectionately known as "Mrs. G.") had been in the dean's office since 1955. Many years later she recalled, "I felt he was one of the best administrators I had ever met. He knew how to delegate authority, and he impressed on me that when you have to make a decision, don't dilly dally; do it. Another of his best qualities was dealing with his department heads as individuals. He was more concerned with their own individual budgets. There were those who probably didn't fight hard enough for their departments, and others were constantly out for everything they could get!"[1]

Mrs. "G," Lois Greiner, was a familiar face in the dean's office. In 1967 she was named OSU Secretary of the Year.

Dean Holm was a strict disciplinarian. From the beginning he promoted (even demanded) professionalism in the faculty and students. Mrs. Greiner recalls, "If they didn't come dressed properly or looking like they should or representing what he thought they should, they were nicely told in a way that they knew. That was the greatest thing he did for them."[2]

During the nine months that Dr. Duane Peterson served as interim dean, plans for construction of the new wing had continued. Although the original bids exceeded the budget, Phil Wilber, the college architect, reported that a revision in the plans involving ceramic and glazed tile finish could trim the estimated cost to within the $550,000 budget allocation. The Board of Regents approved the contract for $550,000 with the Manhattan Construction Company on December 1, 1956, and the way was cleared for the much awaited construction of the L-shaped two-story addition.[3]

Included in the 36,150 square feet floor space were the small animal clinic, faculty offices, and the anatomy laboratory and preparation rooms on the ground floor. The dean's office and the pathology and parasitology departments were on the second floor. The Department of Physiology and Pharmacology would remain in Life Sciences for several more years.

In 1956, the Pitman-Moore Awards for Research Proposals were established. Dr. Newton Tennille believed that his students would learn more from preparing research proposals than term papers. In addition they would become acquainted with research work, veterinary medical literature, and scientific writing. He approached several pharmaceutical companies to give cash awards for the best papers. The Pitman-Moore Company accepted his invitation, and awards of $100, $50, and $25 were presented to three third-year students in the radiology class. Dr. George Burch, director of veterinary research for Pitman-Moore, was the enthusiastic coordinator of the project, and he visited the school to present the awards. Papers were judged independently by selected faculty members from the school and other institutions.

The awards presentation became a highlight of the school calendar. It was truly the "Dr. Newton B. Tennille Show." Held in the veterinary medicine auditorium in the morning, Dr. Tennille supervised and planned every detail, including the lunch which followed. It was always a real treat to hear Dr. Burch's address. He was truly a dynamic Christian gentleman, always immaculately dressed, complete with a bow tie. With emphasis on people, he expounded with great fervor on the importance of integrity, good public relations, and a dedication to one's profession and community. Even though the awards program was discontinued in 1972, Dr. Burch continued to visit the school almost annually to speak to the freshman class and the student chapter until his retirement in 1982.

COURTESY DR. NEWTON TENNILLE

The Pitman-Moore Awards for Research Proposals began in 1956 to improve students' proficiency in writing research proposals. Dr. George Burch, director of veterinary research for Pitman-Moore; Dean Glenn Holm; Dr. Louis Hawkins, director of the Agricultural Experiment Station; Lloyd C. Weldon, award recipient; Dr. Newton Tennille; Joe B. Jolliffe, award recipient; and George A. Lestor, award recipient, pose after the 1957 award ceremony.

His motivation and enthusiasm were a welcome break from the awesome first-year curriculum!

The year 1957 was packed with excitement. Finally, in the spring of 1957, along with the redbuds, the dogwoods, and the daffodils emerging in all their splendor, came the thrilling sounds of construction.

Work had begun finally on the new wing which created a "spring fever" of a different kind—euphoria at the thought of a new office (or an office for the first time!), a modern small animal clinic, laboratories and equipment, even a place to shower! Faculty, students, and staff could hardly wait for the finishing touches.

In May, Representative Jim Arrington, Stillwater, introduced a bill to change the name of Oklahoma A. and M. College to Oklahoma State University. The Senate Education Committee added "of Agriculture and Applied Science." The attorney for the college, John Monk, who drafted the amendment, felt that the more lengthy title would better meet the corporate implications and protect the bonds involved in the name change by maintaining some designation of the college's function in agriculture and engineering. The name was shortened to Oklahoma State University in 1980.

After clearing its final legislative hurdle with a vote of 103-7, Governor Raymond Gary signed the bill on Wednesday, May 15, 1957. The Board of Regents gave approval at their meeting in July. Thus Oklahoma Agricultural and Mechanical College officially became the Oklahoma State University of Agriculture and Applied Science on July 1, 1957.

President Oliver S. Willham commented, "The faculty and administration are pleased and grateful for this action by Governor Gary and the 26th session of the Legislature."[4] Mr. Edwin Roberts, Cushing, president of the Alumni Association, pointed out that "we have felt for many years that a new name, befitting the size and scope of the institution, should be selected. Our institution is a true university offering training in many colleges and divisions, in addition to the agriculture and mechanical courses."[5]

At the same time, the School of Veterinary Medicine, Oklahoma A. and M. College, became the College of Veterinary Medicine, Oklahoma State University.

Also in 1957 a grant of $5,400 was received from the Mark L. Morris Foundation to extend radiological research. The grant was the result of the development of new techniques for making X rays of dogs with diseased kidneys by Gus Thornton, a senior student from Bartlesville. The previous year he had used a $1,000 grant from the same foundation to conduct preliminary studies. Dean Holm stated that it was one of the more important grants for clinical medicine research that had been received by the school.

By 1957 the school was becoming established as a viable institution

The middle wing of the Veterinary Medicine building is finally under construction in 1957. At the far left, the construction attaches to the auditorium of the existing building. The Annex, a temporary building which survived much longer than anticipated, can be seen at the far left. Dr. Roger Panciera stands at the far right.

on campus. There were thirty-five faculty members and six departments. Word was getting out that the courses were tough, the instructors very demanding, and the dean "ruled the roost."

It appears that throughout its short, precarious history, the students had asserted themselves as a group on campus. Due to the dedication and persistence of students active in the Student Government Association and especially Anton Kammerlocher, class of 1957, individual class pictures of the veterinary medicine students appeared in a special section of the 1956 Redskin, the A. and M. College yearbook. In the past they were scattered throughout the academic class groups.

Enterprising students initiated the publication of the school's own yearbook. Entitled Caduceus, the first issue was published by the graduating class of 1957. It was a great success and its publication has been eagerly awaited every spring. The name was changed to Aesculapius in 1973. Each yearbook is dedicated to a faculty or staff member by the senior class.[6]

Anton Kammerlocher from Moreland served as president of the Student Senate during his junior year, 1955-56. He was the first student to run "unaffiliated" and win. He also directed the final drafting of a much needed new constitution and by-laws for the student association which included "legalizing" student walkouts after winning important athletic events! (This has since been discontinued).

There was also romance in the air, and another first for the young school. Leon Self from Albion and Betty Benton from Odessa, Texas, were married during their junior year. According to the groom, "We met while dissecting on opposite sides of a horse in a class here last year!"[7] It appears they were still in honeymoon mood when they graduated in the spring of 1957.

The Conference for Veterinarians, started in 1926, had become established as a very important event in the school calendar. So much building activity was going on in 1957 that the conference was not held, but in May 1958, over two hundred attended the meeting with speakers from five states. Closed circuit television demonstrations of surgical techniques in large and small animals, radiology, and clinical laboratory procedures were featured. The keynote speaker was Dr. W. W. Armistead, president of the American Veterinary Medical Association, who forecast a bright future for veterinary medicine and predicted the veterinary medical profession would not be left behind in a cloud of rocket smoke in the space age.[8]

With the influx of several new faculty members, the course contents and approaches to teaching changed considerably. There were few restraints in a new college for making changes, and the college was not encumbered with some of the traditions that were entrenched in old established colleges. In Dr. Newton Tennille's laboratory course in sur-

The annual "Smoker," often held during the Conference for Veterinarians, continues during the mid-1950s. A time of entertainment by the students, it was later replaced by the senior skit.

Centennial Histories Series

gical exercises, students were given an unusual and demanding opportunity to practice their surgical skills.

In earlier years, Dr. Henry Featherly of the Department of Botany taught a one-credit-hour course in poisonous plants to the veterinary medical students. Dr. Peterson had suggested that a D.V.M. needed to know more about plants in addition to poisonous plants because it was the more common agronomic plants that, through mismanagement, were causing the overwhelming percentage of economic losses in livestock production. The curriculum and scheduling committee agreed and authorized a two-credit-hour fall semester course and a one-credit-hour spring semester course in medicinal and poisonous plants. Dr. Peterson taught these courses for the first time in the 1954-55 school year, but in 1958 the name veterinary agronomics and poisonous plants was introduced. This curricular subject and its approach to soil-plant-animal interrelationships was unique among the colleges of veterinary medicine.

By December of 1958, the building was ready for the "big move" which was executed with a minimum of fanfare or whoop-to-do! Everyone was elated to have most of the college under one roof for the first time. Thirty percent of the 36,000 square feet in the new wing was given over to public service. One of the most important services was the free diagnosis provided farmers and ranchers who brought in dead and ailing animals from herds all over the state. Dean Holm stressed the importance of the small animal clinic which was the very best in equipment and arrangement. "We're not going to turn out a half-trained veterinarian (only large animal). People have more pets now because they have more leisure time. Somebody's got to be able to take care of these animals."[9] The new building would also be a great asset for veterinary research.

The winter of 1959 proved to be a period of great adjustment. A new building at last, but as so often happens, there were teething problems. One morning the small animal staff found that there had been a leak in the steam pipe which caused extensive dripping from the ceilings of their offices and the clinic. One clinician remembers it was like a shower of light rain. However, this was a minor setback and everything was back on track very soon.

In 1959 the U.S. Atomic Energy Commission gave the college a grant of $23,185 to improve student training in the use of radioactive isotopes in veterinary medicine. The equipment was to be housed in laboratories in the college and in Life Sciences.

The end of the 1958-59 academic year saw the introduction of an event which proved to be the highlight in the college calendar for many years. The first Annual Awards Banquet was held in the Student Union Ballroom in May 1959. According to the 1960 yearbook, "The banquet has been the outgrowth of the feeling of some far-sighted people that the traditional awards night program did not adequately honor the graduating seniors and other outstanding students in the veterinary college. . . . there was no formal program except fine food, presentation of awards, and close fellowship which is a symbol of the veterinary college student body and faculty fellowship. The overall feeling was that the campus and state-wide prestige of the Oklahoma State University Veterinary College had been enhanced."[10] The master of ceremonies was Dr. James B. Corcoran. Awards presented included the Dean McElroy, Dean Orr, Who's Who, National Life, Merck, and the American Veterinary Medical Association Auxiliary. The twenty-three senior wives received PHT (putting hubby through) certificates.

The decade of the fifties, the first full decade in the school's history, had unveiled many trials and tribulations. The end also marked the end of the "water follies" whereby faculty and students had a water hose battle before graduation. It appears that a student really "blew it" when he poured a large can of water over a stall partition on a "fellow student" who turned out to be the head of clinics![11]

The college had, indeed, come a long way since its beginning, just over ten years prior—with 255 graduates located in 37 states and overseas.

The decade of the sixties opened with a commitment to develop what was already a viable institution into a recognized center of veterinary medicine. Dean Holm had established himself as a resolute leader with a clear vision of the needs of this young college. There was also far more interest in veterinary medicine as a profession and requests for admission were pouring in almost daily. Research was becoming a major factor in college activities.

Above all, there was a need for more and better physical facilities. The Department of Physiology and Pharmacology was still housed in Life Sciences. Bacteriology was also taught as a service course through the College of Arts and Sciences. There was thus an urgent need to complete the final part of the "E" of the original building proposal when the school was established. A major breakthrough was on the horizon.

On Saturday, December 17, 1960, OSU President Oliver Willham announced that Oklahoma had been offered an opportunity to become an important center for national research in animal health. He stated, "The National Institutes of Health (NIH) have singled out Oklahoma State as the most logical educational institution to provide a new and unusual service for our country."[12] Dr. Francis L. Schmedl, chief of the Health Research Facilities Division of the National Institutes of Health in Washington, D.C., had formally notified the university that this branch of the U.S. Public Health Service was recommending that a facilities grant of $855,945 be awarded to the College of Veterinary Medicine to be used for veterinary medical and nutrition research facilities. It would be the biggest single federal grant ever approved for a college of veterinary medicine.

The project had been considered carefully by the NIH national advisory council, a council composed of deans of medicine, veterinary medicine, and basic science. Dean Holm stated, "This facility would be constructed for an entirely new venture . . . in veterinary medical and basic animal nutrition research."[13]

In order for the facilities grant to become a reality, Congress would have to appropriate the funds for the grant in the National Institutes of Health budget, and the Oklahoma legislature would have to appropriate the funds to match the federal grant. Both legislative bodies would convene again in January 1961.

Research fostered by the Veterinary Research Institute and the Agricultural Experiment Station had provided a firm foundation. The college was attracting more graduate students—a major factor in the quest for the new facility which had to be justified on a research and graduate training basis. Dr. Leslie McDonald had already laid the groundwork for the Department of Physiology and Pharmacology to be in a position for the college to qualify for a major grant.

The real challenge in securing the facilities grant was to present the application in such a way as to comply with the NIH regulations regarding its use only for research and graduate training and still provide some much needed undergraduate teaching laboratories. It was also hoped that the Department of Physiology and Pharmacology would acquire a new home.[14]

Oklahoma voters had approved a state building bond issue in 1960 from which funds were authorized during the 1961 session of the legislature. Oklahoma State University was allocated $8.1 million by the State Regents for Higher Education. Seven million went to the university in general and the College of Veterinary Medicine received $400,000 toward the construction of a south wing. These bond funds were in addition to $996,000 approved by the house appropriation committee in May 1961. Dean Holm anxiously waited for Congress to fund the $855,000 grant already approved by the NIH Research. This was received in November 1961.[15]

The stage was set for another major leap forward in the college building program.

In 1961 there was also progress in obtaining grants for basic research and study fellowships from other sources. Dr. Bertis L. Glenn was awarded a National Science Foundation (NSF) faculty fellowship for advanced study towards a Ph.D. in pathology at the University of Oklahoma Medical School, while Dr. John H. Venable received a NSF fellowship to study for the Ph.D. degree in electron microscopy and histochemistry at Harvard Medical School in Boston.

In September a $60,889 two-year grant to the college by the National Institutes of Health was announced. The grant was made to determine the spleen's influence on disease susceptibility in livestock by studying its action in bovine anaplasmosis. Dr. E. Wynn Jones would be the principal investigator.

The Student Chapter, American Veterinary Medical Association, Student Loan Fund was also established in April 1961. For some time, the chapter had organized a blood donor drive to assist the city hospital (now Stillwater Medical Center). The funds received from this drive provided the basis for the student loan fund. Over the years the fund has provided emergency, short-term loans to financially needy students.

At a later date, other student loan funds were established in the dean's office. Donations were given in memory of Dr. Bill M. Carnes of Muskogee by his family in 1973 and in memory of Teresa D. Williams, who died on February 20, 1972, while she was a second-year student. Donations were also made in honor of Dr. A. L. Malle when he retired in 1981, as well as contributions in memory of Mrs. Addie Stratton in 1983.

The class of 1961 had one last fling before facing the national board examinations. They traveled by bus to Indianapolis, Indiana, as guests of Pitman-Moore, Inc., and Eli Lilly. During their visit they toured Pitman-Moore's pharmaceutical plant, research farm, and biological production plant, followed by a tour of Eli Lilly's research farm and several production plants.

This annual highlight continued for many years. Originally only for the students, the companies changed their policies in the late sixties to include student spouses, and in 1975 the trip became a junior, instead of a senior, class project. When Pitman-Moore, Inc., became part of the Johnson and Johnson Company and moved to New Jersey, the itinerary was changed to include The Upjohn Company in Kalamazoo, Michigan. In the mid-1970s, the Eli Lilly Company decided to discontinue tours for all veterinary colleges.

Students now made alternate plans for their trip to Kalamazoo, breaking their journey in St. Louis overnight, and visiting the zoo or the famous Clydesdale stables. On the return journey they also stayed a night in St. Louis and visited the Ralston Purina Research Center at Grey Summit, Missouri, the following morning.

By 1961, over two-thirds of the college's three hundred graduates were employed in Oklahoma and adjoining states and about one-half of them in Oklahoma. Dean Holm emphasized that "the training of competent professional people to serve livestock and pet owners and to supply personnel for the many programs and agencies requiring veterinary medical skills is our primary objective. Two additional activities—research and public service—are also important areas of our educational program."[16] He stated that there was an increase in specialized practice

Dr. Doyne Hamm explains the use of radioisotopes to a group of visitors at the first Open House held in 1962.

across the state, especially in small animals.

The spring of 1962 marked the beginning of Open House. Organized by the student chapter, the first Open House was an overwhelming success. In spite of inclement weather, over 1,500 people attended the event held on Saturday, April 28, from 10:00 a.m. to 5:00 p.m. All six college departments put on elaborate displays and demonstrations. Tours were conducted by the students, explaining the role of the veterinarian in the care of farm animals, poultry, and pets. Several programs dealt with public health, research, and teaching methods. Surgical demonstrations and treatment were featured in the large and small animal clinics. A frequent comment by the visitors was "we didn't realize the amount of work and training that a veterinary student is subject to." Chairman Don Roach, junior student, stated, "With such fine cooperation between faculty and students, we can look forward to an even better open house next year."[17]

The second Open House was held on April 27, 1963. Lieutenant Governor Leo Winters was the guest speaker at the official opening ceremony in the veterinary medicine auditorium. The first veterinary medicine queen, Miss Deanna King from Stillwater, a junior student in the College of Education, performed the ribbon cutting. New features were a cutting horse demonstration, a sheep dog gathering and penning a flock, and display of several unusual breeds of dogs.

In the fall 1963, the student chapter voted to hold Open House bien-

Janet Grantham, the first female graduate from Oklahoma, receives the American Veterinary Medical Association Auxiliary Award from Mrs. Jewell Holm. Mrs. Edwin Fisher, Dr. A. E. Darlow, and Dr. Robert MacVicar view the presentation.

nially in the future. The event, widely recognized as a major factor in promoting the professional image of veterinary medicine as well as attracting youngsters to an exciting career, has continued as such ever since.

Also, in the spring of 1962, Janet Yvonne Grantham from Gage became the first Oklahoma woman to receive the D.V.M. degree from Oklahoma State University. There were three girls in her freshman class, but before long she was the only one! This did not bother her, because "I was an only child and I was often the only girl in some pre-vet classes."[18] She married a Stillwater area farmer and they returned to the dairy farm in Gage where she grew up. She practiced part-time from her home and raised five sons.

The class of 1962 also distinguished itself by leading the nation in the National Board Examinations with six students, Doyne Hamm, David Mitchell, Edward Schenk, Truman Hudson, Nicholas Nail, and Lewis Nightengale, gaining top marks in various categories.

The college received a well-deserved boost when the Arkansas Veterinary Medical Association established a $300 annual cash scholarship program for deserving Arkansas students in the college in 1962. Dr. Thayer D. Hendrickson, executive director of the association, stated, "This new annual award from our association is in recognition of the high quality of education we believe our native sons are receiving from your college."[19] The scholarship program was also dedicated to the memory of Dr. Orval Meinecke, Hot Springs, Arkansas. When the program came into full operation, three students selected from the second-, third-, and fourth-year classes received $100 each. Doyne Hamm, a fourth-year student from Mount Judea, Arkansas, was the first recipient. He had attained membership on the President's Honor Roll (4.00 grade point average) for seven consecutive semesters.

In May 1963 the Department of Physiology and Pharmacology was selected for the nation's first grant in support of post-doctoral study towards the Ph.D. degree in physiology by holders of the D.V.M. degree. The grant of $200,000 for a five-year period was awarded by the National Institutes of Health.

Dr. L. E. McDonald, department head, indicated that plans called for three trainees in the program and that each would receive a yearly stipend during the three to four years required to earn the Ph.D. degree. The grant also provided for additional technical and non-technical help as well as a yearly budget for research equipment and supplies needed in the project. Dr. Dennis Goetsch was appointed director of the program. The nine areas of study included cellular, invertebrate and ruminal physiology, metabolism, endocrinology, neurophysiology, pharmacology, reproduction, and toxicology—but where was the new building to house all these exciting developments?

Dean Glenn Holm administers the Veterinarian's Oath to the class of 1963 during the Annual Awards Banquet. In later years, the oath became a part of the college's Convocation.

In May 1963 bids were received from eight contractors for the construction of this third wing, referred to as the research unit or the final section of the originally conceived "E" shaped building, on the south and west side. The contract was awarded to W. R. Grimshaw and Co., Tulsa, for $1,233,643.00 on May 14, with construction to commence within 15 days with completion within 365 days. The plans for this and previous buildings were prepared by Hudgins, Thompson, Ball & Associates, Oklahoma City. Construction moved along well but was not completed within the original 365 days agreement.

The extra space and modern teaching equipment would enable the college to increase the student class size. For the entering class of 48 students in 1964, Dean Holm stated that 1578 inquiries and 423 actual application requests had been received. This surge in interest in a career in veterinary medicine was maintained well into the next decade. The February 1, 1964, edition of the *Daily Oklahoman* carried an editorial entitled, "Veterinary Medicine's Role" which stated, "Although its role in protecting public health and aiding our economy surpasses the ordinary conception, veterinary medicine has not received all the attention it should."[20] The editorial went on to describe the profession's vital importance in animal and human health.

Each class has its own particular character, and each had individuals who stood out academically or as unique personalities. The class of 1964 was no exception, for who could ever forget Tran-Quang Minh, the dynamic, multi-talented, dapper student from South Vietnam, who became the first American-trained Vietnamese veterinarian. He was in much demand as an after dinner speaker because of his bluntness, tempered with dry humor. His remark at a civic club meeting had great historical significance. He felt if there was a time to draw a line against communism, it was in the rice fields of Vietnam. He received a standing ovation following his acceptance speech on receiving the Auxiliary Award at the Annual Awards Banquet. In the same class Janice M. Smith from Denton, Texas, was named the outstanding woman veterinary graduate in the United States for 1964.

All was not quiet on the campus though. Dr. Wendell Krull had a written agreement with Dean Holm to teach at Oklahoma State University until he reached seventy years of age.[21] A system-wide change in regulations adopted by the Board of Regents in academic year 1963-64, however, resulted in his forced retirement on June 30, 1964. When the information became public that Dr. Krull would be forced to retire, 165 of the 167 students then enrolled in the College of Veterinary Medicine petitioned the Board of Regents to reconsider their requirement for mandatory retirement. Indeed, the Board of Regents heard the students out and even commended them for their "courteous and persuasive presentation," but they did not relent.[22] The local newspapers were filled with letters of entreaty and sometimes indignation.

Fortunately for all concerned, the Board of Regents of Oklahoma State University and A. and M. Colleges permitted Dr. Krull to be employed on a part-time basis in the fall of 1969, five years after his forced retirement. He came back to Stillwater to teach parasitology in the department he had founded and headed. This temporary arrangement made it possible to accommodate a shift in curriculum which required that two courses ordinarily taught in sequential semesters be taught simultaneously. The parasitology faculty was at an all-time low in terms of available personnel in 1968-69, and the quality of the teaching program would have suffered without Dr. Krull's help.

Dr. Everett D. Besch was appointed to succeed Dr. Krull as head of the Department of Veterinary Parasitology, effective July 1. A 1954 graduate of Texas A. and M. College, Dr. Besch had joined the department in 1956.

The American Veterinary Medical Association Council on Education recommended in its report of January 1963 that the Department of Parasitology and the teaching of veterinary bacteriology should be consolidated. A satisfactorily equipped teaching laboratory was available for microbiology, and thus, the teaching program should be transferred to the veterinary medicine building to enhance liaison between the laboratory services and the clinics.

Dean Holm followed up this recommendation in a letter to President Oliver Willham on February 22, 1964: "With the appointment of Dr. E. D. Besch as Head of Veterinary Parasitology, it would be natural to make a transition on July 1, 1964." Dr. Besch, who was trained in veterinary public health, would head up a combined department. Dean Holm continued, "Some adjustment must be made if we hope to receive full accreditation."[23]

Thus was established the Department of Veterinary Parasitology and Public Health. Dr. Paul Barto, who had remained in Life Sciences in the Department of Microbiology, moved his office to Veterinary Medicine.

There were also changes in the Department of Medicine and Surgery. The clinical physical facilities were as antiquated as ever with little progress being made for improvement. There were no summer classes and students were employed to assist the clinicians. In spite of the sweltering heat, the ever present battery of flies, and the constant danger of physical harm due to the totally inadequate equipment, the summer periods were enjoyable, productive, and exciting. The day was never made unless some bull or wild cow off the range had broken loose, resulting in a mad chase through the neighborhood yards! Clinicians became remarkably good athletes and adept at jumping over walls—sometimes helped along by a ferocious animal! There were also some embarrassing moments such as for the lady pharmacist who encountered a mean cow in the hallway. She ran for her life to the men's room and landed in the lap of a clinician! It was, nevertheless, a time for much clinical instruction on almost a one-to-one basis and there was always the opportunity to try new techniques and tackle the "impossible."

Such a case was presented during the early summer of 1964. A registered milking shorthorn cow with a huge udder was brought to the clinic. Two clinicians set about the task of removing it. The operation lasted over four hours in sweltering heat. The removed organ weighed 115 pounds. The cow made an excellent recovery, and produced a bull calf which was named "Lestwill" in honor of the clinicians! She produced a set of twins the following year.

Completion of the new wing was accepted by the university on September 14, 1964. The total cost of the building and equipment was about $1,850,000, which included the $855,945 grant, of which $55,945 was not received until July 1964, for the purchase of moveable research equipment. An allocation of $200,000 was received from state building bond funds and the remainder from a special state appropriation referred to earlier.

The 68,000 square feet "L" shaped building provided a major increase in laboratory space for physiology and pharmacology classes and research, experimental surgery, and animal nutrition research. The latter occupied the western part of the new building and was administered by the animal husbandry (later named animal science) department with Dr. Allen Tillman as research leader. Dr. E. Wynn Jones became director of clinical research which had excellent facilities and equipment in the new wing. There was no grand opening of the new area, but it was the highlight of the next college Open House in 1965.

The Department of Physiology and Pharmacology finally moved out of Life Sciences and joined the rest of the College of Veterinary Medicine in January 1965. Several of the faculty members retained joint appointments in the department and in the College of Arts and Sciences. Because of these modern facilities and a competent faculty, the department was able to apply for more research grants. Regarded as one of the best in the nation, the department was comprised of five D.V.M.s with Ph.D.s in their specialty. They represented considerable strength in endocrinology and reproductive physiology (Drs. S. Newcomer, L. McDonald, G. Stabenfeldt, M. Morrissette, and L. Ewing), research in neurophysiology and neuroanatomy (Dr. J. Breazile), biochemistry, metabolism, and toxicology (Drs. D. Goetsch and P. Cardeilhac), cell physiology (Dr. C. Beames), and gastroenterology (Dr. T. Staley).

Dr. L. E. McDonald, the department head, was now a member of the physiology fellowships review panel of the National Institutes of Health. He was one of six scientists across the country appointed in 1964 to this

U.S. Public Health Service public advisory committee.

Very soon all the laboratories were "buzzing" with exciting research projects supported by National Institutes of Health and National Science Foundation grants totaling over $600,000.

Meanwhile there was little progress made in obtaining much needed clinicians in the Department of Medicine and Surgery. A small group of loyal, hard working clinicians were put to a severe test in June of 1965. For one month, Dr. Lester Johnson was solely in charge of the large animal clinic, Dr. Ernest Benner took care of the university herds, and Dr. Lewis Moe ran the ambulatory clinic. Dr. Eric Williams, a bovine practitioner at heart and soul, was assigned to take care of the small animal clinic along with four upcoming senior students! It was a summer to remember, with four consecutive weeks of emergency duty as well.

July 1, Dr. Eugene M. Jones became head of the small animal clinic. He was a very successful small animal practitioner who had built a modern, well-equipped hospital in Midwest City, one of the first in Oklahoma. He had delivered guest lectures to the senior class for several years previously.

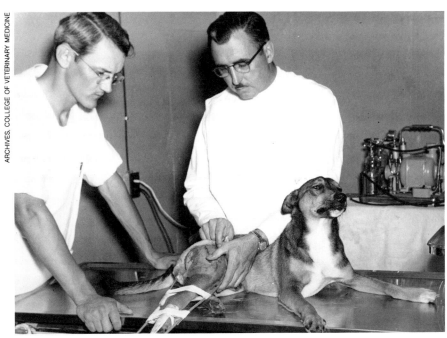

Dr. Walter Rice examines a dog with a Thomas splint following bone fracture repair while Don Roach, class of 1963, observes.

Dr. Walter Rice, who joined the department in 1949 after a period of practice in Canada, left in the fall of 1965 to enter small animal practice in Oklahoma City. Dr. Rice had been named assistant director of clinics in charge of the large animal hospital service in January 1952. In May 1952 he became associate director of clinics in charge of the small animal section. He had the reputation of being a very dedicated clinician with an excellent rapport with his clients.

Thus ended the first half of the sixties, a golden era in teaching and research. A new period of international service was about to begin.

Endnotes

1. Author interview with Mrs. Lois Greiner, 9 December 1982, Archives, College of Veterinary Medicine.

2. Greiner interview.

3. Board of Regents minutes, 1 December 1956, p. 18, Special Collections, Edmon Low Library, Oklahoma State University.

4. Oklahoma State University *Daily O'Collegian,* 17 May 1957, p. 1.

5. *Daily O'Collegian,* 17 May 1957, pp. 1, 6.

6. Persons to whom the yearbook has been dedicated are listed in the Appendix.

7. *Stillwater NewsPress,* 16 May 1956, Scrapbook, Archives, College of Veterinary Medicine.

8. Newspaper clipping, 6 May 1958, Scrapbook, Archives, College of Veterinary Medicine.

9. *Stillwater NewsPress,* 26 December 1958, Scrapbook, Archives, College of Veterinary Medicine.

10. *1960 Caduceus,* College of Veterinary Medicine Yearbook.

11. Author's personal communication with Dr. Lawrence Erwin, 1985.

12. Oklahoma City *Daily Oklahoman,* 18 December 1960, p. A13, Scrapbook, Archives, College of Veterinary Medicine.

13. *Tulsa Sunday World,* 18 December 1960, Scrapbook, Archives, College of Veterinary Medicine.

14. Author interview with Dr. Leslie E. McDonald, 29 July 1985, Archives, College of Veterinary Medicine.

15. *Daily O'Collegian,* 25 October 1961, Scrapbook, Archives, College of Veterinary Medicine.

16. *Tulsa World,* 28 January 1961, Scrapbook, Archives, College of Veterinary Medicine.

17. Newspaper clipping, Scrapbook, Archives, College of Veterinary Medicine.

18. Author's personal communication with Dr. Janet Grantham, 1985.

19. Newspaper clipping, Scrapbook, Archives, College of Veterinary Medicine.

20. *Daily Oklahoman,* 1 February 1964, p. 10.

21. G. C. Holm to O. S. Willham, 14 June 1962, Personnel file of Dr. Wendell Krull, Business Office, College of Veterinary Medicine.

22. W. R. Williams to B. J. McDougal, 13 April 1964, Personnel file of Dr. Wendell Krull, Business Office, College of Veterinary Medicine.

23. G. C. Holm to Oliver Willham, 22 February 1964, Archives, College of Veterinary Medicine.

8 Veterinary Research

In the field of observations, chance favors only the prepared mind.
Louis Pasteur

Research in the College of Veterinary Medicine has the stated mission to expand medical knowledge of animals, including its relationship to the health and welfare of mankind. The veterinary profession is directly concerned with the health care of food producing animals, small and large companion animals, disease regulation, food inspection and more. Research focuses on the application of biological systems and organisms to technical and industrial processes.

The pioneer of veterinary medical research in Oklahoma was Dr. L. L. Lewis. His many contributions during territorial and early statehood days were outstanding.[1] As the new School of Veterinary Medicine became well established, Oklahoma State University would again emerge as a leader in veterinary medical research.[2]

Although there was a decade of relative inactivity in animal research related to veterinary medicine following Dr. Lewis's death in 1922, researchers continued experimentation on anaplasmosis. Early in the 1930 decade after researchers proved experimentally that flies carried and transmitted anaplasmosis from animal to animal, they began studying the role of ticks as intermediate hosts. A few years later, the first attempt to make a vaccine was begun. A vaccine made from spleen material from a sick animal was prepared but proved unsuccessful.

Later in the decade researchers found that ticks could carry and transmit the anaplasmal organism from any stage of their life cycle. During this time an anaplasmosis laboratory was constructed at Oklahoma A. and M. College. Dr. Lewis Moe, who had joined the veterinary science department in 1929, was one of the leaders in the evaluation of drugs in anaplasmosis control at that time.

A major milestone in veterinary research was reached in 1945 when the Oklahoma Veterinary Research Institute was established with laboratories on the main campus and a large barn on the college farm just west of campus. Members of the Osage County Cattlemen's Association had spearheaded a state-wide drive to convince the Oklahoma Legislature to appropriate $100,000 for livestock disease research. Dr. Herman Farley, D.V.M., was director of the institute that placed emphasis on animal diseases and internal parasites.[3]

In addition, the institute had a field laboratory in Pawhuska, which included a ranch of approximately 1000 acres equipped with all facilities for handling cattle, a 35-acre central corral area with an isolation barn, a fully-equipped laboratory, and office space. Ira O. Kliewer was the laboratory technician starting in 1946, and he was joined a year later by Dr. Charles C. Pearson. Research on anaplasmosis, which was causing over one million dollars loss to the Oklahoma cattle industry annually, was greatly expanded. Researchers also conducted a survey of the gastrointestinal tracts of deer brought to them by hunters, and work was begun on pink eye (infectious bovine keratitis) in cattle.[4]

Between 1946 and 1948 seven types of vaccine were prepared and tested with one of blood tissue origin apparently having some protective effect. Later, twenty drugs were tested and two showed curative value 85 percent of the time, but the recovered animals remained carriers and therefore a source of infection for other cattle.

In 1949, Dr. William E. Brock joined the research team, and emphasis now focused on finding an effective test with practical application for anaplasmosis control. A test for detecting carrier animals was successfully developed and became widely used on commercial herds. Carrier animals, detected by the test, were found to be cleared by two new antibiotics, Aureomycin and Terramycin, but animals were susceptible to re-infection. Later it was found that anaplasmosis could be prevented by feeding these antibiotics to cattle.

Toward the end of the 1950 decade, efforts were intensified to find an effective preventive vaccine for the disease. This opened the door to an exciting discovery. A modification of the same substances used to test for anaplasmosis was tried in vaccine form with encouraging results. In the early 1960s, it was tested in small doses, and an agreement was reached with Fort Dodge Laboratories in Fort Dodge, Iowa, to supply the final stages of the development and testing of the vaccine. Forty cattle at the Pawhuska research station were inoculated. Shortly afterwards a large scale field test was done on two hundred cattle at the

Dr. C. C. Pearson, Mr. Fred G. Drummond, and Dr. Herman Farley tour the ranch at the research station southeast of Pawhuska.

Joe Soderstrom ranch near Pawhuska.

At a special meeting of the Osage County Cattlemen's Association at the research station on Thursday, June 17, 1965, Dean Glenn Holm announced the development of the world's first successful vaccine for anaplasmosis, the culmination of continuous research for thirty-seven years by scientists at Oklahoma State University. The vaccine would be manufactured by Fort Dodge Laboratories under the registered name of Anaplaz.® Starting in the fall, it would be distributed through veterinarians. Fort Dodge Laboratories agreed to pay Oklahoma State University, the patent holder, royalty equal to five percent of the net sale of the vaccine for ten years. Dr. Brock, Dr. Pearson, and Mr. Kliewer, in return for relinquishing all of their inventor rights, shared on an equal basis, fifteen percent of the gross revenue from the vaccine, also for ten years.

Dr. E. R. Walker, who started his practice in Pawhuska in 1945, recalled, "I remember . . . when the cattlemen came back from the open house at the research laboratory on June 17, 1965. I thought, at first, word had been announced that the banker had retired everyone's note! For the cattlemen, this was a great breakthrough, both financially and materially. For the veterinarian, it meant a tool that will greatly improve his proficiency and his professional status in his community."[5] It was estimated to save the state over $7 million in cattle losses annually. Dr. Brock, Dr. Pearson, and Mr. Kliewer were named 1965 Men of the Year

Olin Kliewer works on the complement fixation test for anaplasmosis at the Pawhuska Station.

in Oklahoma Agriculture by the *Progressive Farmer*.[6]

In 1965 when Dr. W. E. Brock went to Guatemala, he initiated research on anaplasmosis, a major cattle disease in Central America, at University of San Carlos. Research focused, in addition, on developing a test for another disease, babesiosis, that results in anemia in cattle and is also transmitted by ticks.

Since bovine red blood cells were used in the preparation of the vaccine developed at the Pawhuska station, the vaccine sometimes resulted in the undesirable side effect of severe anemia in the calves from cattle with certain blood types. Research at OSU was directed toward studying the influence of the spleen in anaplasmosis, growing the causal organism on artificial media, and preparing the vaccine from a tissue culture. Attempts were also made to purify the vaccine to preclude these side effects.

Eventually, attention was directed towards locating *Anaplasma marginale*, the causal organism, in a tick that transmits the disease. Dr. Katherine Kocan and entomologist Dr. Jakie Hair set about this task and were later joined by Dr. S. A. Ewing and Dr. S. J. Barron. They dissected literally hundreds of ticks which were known to transmit the disease. Different tick tissues were ground up and injected into test animals to ascertain which tissue proved to be the most effective in transmitting the disease. Once the inoculated animals had contracted anaplasmosis,

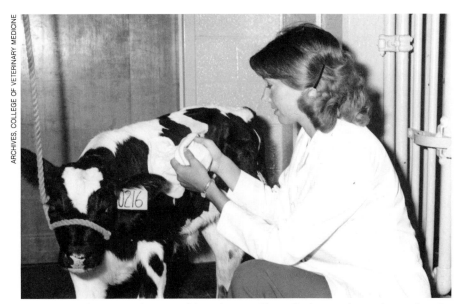

Dr. Katherine Kocan examines one of the calves used in continuing anaplasmosis experiments.

the research workers searched for and found the causal organism in the particular tissue causing the disease. They used several approaches to confirm the identity of the organisms with light and electron microscopy.

In 1979 researchers proved the existence of *Anaplasma marginale* in ticks. Though research on the disease had been conducted for over fifty years, it was the first time the organism had been demonstrated in an intermediate host. Since that time, the OSU researchers have documented most of the organism's complex developmental cycle in ticks. In the fall of 1982, this exciting work brought Dr. F. T. Potgieter to work with Dr. Kocan whose research was gaining world-wide recognition. Dr. Potgieter, a research scientist at the Veterinary Research Institute, Onderstepoort, Republic of South Africa, has authored many publications on bovine babesiosis and anaplasmosis. Investigators are now concentrating on understanding the stage of the organism when it is transmitted from ticks to cattle so that a vaccine can be prepared against the transmitted stage.

In December of 1984, Dr. Katherine Kocan, a shining light in anaplasmosis research, took her talents to distant shores when she became a visiting scientist at the International Laboratory for Research on Animal Diseases in Nairobi, Kenya, and later she visited the famous Veterinary Research Institute in Onderstepoort, South Africa, to present some seminars. It would be the first of several visits to Africa. Meanwhile, her husband Dr. Alan Kocan spent his sabbatical leave studying the diseases of wildlife there.

Experimental approaches used with *Anaplasma marginale* in ticks have been employed to identify another disease-producing organism, *Cowdria ruminantium*, also found in ticks. *Cowdria ruminantium* causes heartwater disease in cattle. The disease occurs throughout Africa and has been recently discovered in the Caribbean, posing a threat to cattle in the United States. In research conducted cooperatively with investigators in Kenya, Zimbabwe and the Republic of South Africa, *Cowdria* has also been found in its tick vector by the use of light and electron microscopies. Most recently, the transmitting stage of *Cowdria* has been found to develop in tick salivary glands. A vaccine prepared against this stage would prevent infection of cattle with this organism.

Research on another tick-borne disease was initiated in 1978 by Dr. Bertis Glenn, Dr. Alan Kocan, and Dr. Katherine Kocan. A blood parasite of domestic cats had been recently reported to be 100 percent fatal to domestic cats. Field studies conducted by Dr. Glenn and Dr. Alan Kocan revealed that wild bobcats were the natural carriers of this parasite. Further studies by these researchers with the cooperation of Dr. Jakie Hair and graduate student Ed Blouin confirmed the association between the bobcats and domestic cats and identified the tick vector for this parasite.

Other exciting research projects were initiated during an earlier era. In 1947 Dr. C. Kenneth Whitehair, a young Kansas State University graduate, came south from Wisconsin at the request of Dr. A. E. Darlow, dean of agriculture, to establish a herd of "disease free" pigs, research malnutrition in cattle, and teach basic and advanced nutrition. In 1950 an experiment was started in which baby pigs were taken by cesarean operation, raised, and maintained in an environment entirely isolated from other swine-raising operations. The study was designed to observe the possibilities of eliminating a digestive disturbance in the young pigs that had existed in the parent stock and also to study the nutritive requirements of pigs raised in this manner. The pigs reached maturity, reproduced, and lactated in a normal manner. Infectious diseases in swine herds could be eliminated by this procedure, but artificially raising baby pigs for commercial pork production was not economically feasible at that time.

In 1953 Dr. Whitehair's main assignment was to "get research going in veterinary medicine with funds provided from the Agricultural Experiment Station."[7] Dr. Whitehair was given the unofficial title of director of research. The Veterinary Research Institute became a component of the School of Veterinary Medicine on September 1, 1953. As individual departments implemented their own research, Dr. Whitehair's work diminished. He left in 1955 to work at the Rowett Research Institute in

Aberdeen, Scotland, later returning to Michigan State University.

Motivated by requests from general practitioners for an effective technique for regional anesthesia of the bovine eye and its adjacent tissue, Dr. Duane R. Peterson developed a procedure which addressed the relevant aspects of the six cranial nerves that are involved. Before this time there had been several reports of death due to the commonly used deep infiltrative procedures that involved the subarachnoid space surrounding the optic nerve. The new technique was universally accepted as the "Peterson eye block."

In the early 1960s several outbreaks of acute pulmonary emphysema occurred in cattle in southeastern Oklahoma. As the result of his field investigations, Dr. Peterson discovered that it was due to a garden mint, *Perilla frutescens*, that had been introduced from Vietnam and spread from the farmsteads to the flood plains.

Clinical research in the late fifties and early sixties was directed towards developing general anesthesia techniques in horses to ensure rapid, safe, and smooth induction without excitement and with a minimum of restraint. Intravenous barbiturates were used for this purpose, using a rapid induction technique. Research by Dr. E. Wynn Jones and his staff then focused on inhalation anesthesia which eventually resulted in the development of the first suitable and efficient anesthetic machine

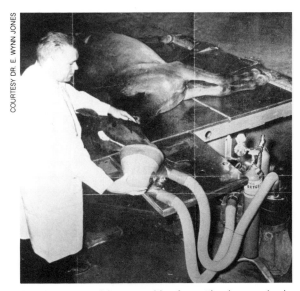

COURTESY DR. E. WYNN JONES

The first successful gas machine for putting large animals to sleep in preparation for surgery was perfected by Dr. E. Wynn Jones. This United Press International photograph received national exposure by Timely Events.

using endotracheoscopy. There was also a study of tranquilizers in domestic animals.

Another research project was a study of porcine malignant hyperthermia, an abnormal response to anesthetic agents occurring in some pigs. Certain breeds, including Poland China, Landrace, Pietrain, and Yorkshire, are particularly susceptible. Because of a similar condition in man, porcine malignant hyperthermia provides a suitable model for investigating cause and diagnostic procedures, assessing the potential of certain drugs, and determining safe and dangerous anesthetics.

In the same era veterinary research embarked upon an exciting venture with the production of germ free (gnotobiotic) pigs. These pigs were delivered by cesarean section at 112-114 days of gestation under strictly aseptic conditions. After delivery they were transferred to stainless steel rearing isolators where they were maintained in a germ free environment for the duration of experiments. As a result of this work, Dr. T. E. Staley and his co-workers were able to describe, for the first time, the ultrastructure of the intestinal epithelium of the newborn pig, changes associated with absorption of colostral proteins, and the penetration of *E. coli* into the intestinal lining. *E. coli* is a common cause of diarrhea in both animals and man. They also conducted similar studies on calves.

In 1962 in the course of a study of canine babesiosis, a blood disease

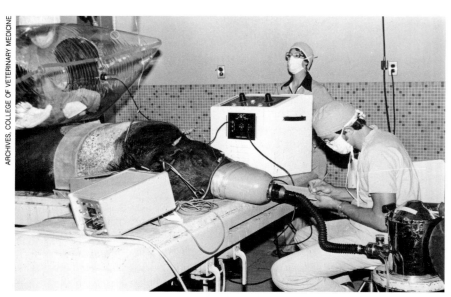

Germ-free (gnotobiotic) pigs were delivered by cesarean section and maintained in a germ-free environment for the duration of the experiment.

in dogs, scientists at Oklahoma State University discovered a foreign particle in the white blood cells. Dr. Sidney Ewing later determined that the particle was actually *Ehrlichia*, probably *E. canis*. Dr. Ewing's investigations led to the discovery that the dogs were actually infected with two parasites, one a protozoan that parasitized red blood cells and the other a rickettsia that lived in white blood cells. It was the first recognition of *Ehrlichia* in the United States and only the second in the Western Hemisphere. Work by Dr. Ewing and Dr. Ralph Buckner describing the two diseases and development of treatment for ehrlichiosis proved to be useful in the next two decades because *Ehrlichia* infections were soon recognized to occur throughout the United States. Furthermore, military scientists working with guard dogs during the Vietnam War consulted with Dr. Ewing and Dr. Roger Panciera about a mysterious disease they were seeing in the Orient; it, too, proved to be ehrlichiosis but was often referred to in the literature as tropical canine pancytopenia. Aside from studies on *Babesia* and *Ehrlichia*, Dr. Ewing and Dr. John Venable investigated another hematozoan parasite of dogs, *Haemobartonella canis*, and were able to show its relationship to the host cell by electron microscopy.

Interest in blood diseases extended beyond research on anaplasmosis, babesiosis, haemobartonellosis, ehrlichiosis, and cytauxzoonosis. Dr. Brock and Dr. Buckner worked with a team of scientists from the University of Oklahoma Medical School on hemophilia. The research leader at the medical school was Dr. James W. Hampton. The studies were focused on blood clotting mechanisms.

A hemophilic beagle colony was established in the spring of 1964 for the purpose of collaborative coagulation research with the University of Oklahoma School of Medicine. Prior to this time in 1961, Dr. Brock obtained a male, "Buster," from a practicing veterinarian in Duncan. A suitable beagle bitch was also obtained and the first litter of five puppies was whelped in the fall of 1963. A second litter followed in the spring of 1964, and in November the National Institutes of Health awarded Dr. Brock a grant to establish the animal colony for research on blood clotting.

The hemophilic colony grew steadily for many years. Over 400 puppies were whelped in the colony providing stable animal models for many research groups in the United States and France. Through cooperation with investigators in California and Canada, the colony maintained three lines of hemophilic beagles, each with a different type of coagulation defect.

Cooperative studies between the University of Oklahoma School of Medicine and the OSU College of Veterinary Medicine included spleen transplants, trials in the treatment of hemophilia, and coagulation changes associated with the contraceptive pill. Several others were

Dr. William E. Brock and Dr. Ralph Buckner examine Charley, a hemophilic patient, in 1969. The hemophilic beagle colony established in 1964 provided stable animal models for many research groups in the United States and Canada.

related to immunological changes associated with hemophilia.

The colony was unique in that, while spontaneous hemorrhage occurred, it was not a daily episode in spite of the vigorous activity of the dogs. Bleeding was generally manifested as a subcutaneous swelling anywhere on the animal's body, enlarged muscle, limping, or abdominal pain. Correct treatment for hemophilic dogs was established using a ryo-precipitate made from plasma of normal dogs in the coagulation laboratory of the College of Veterinary Medicine.

The colony later became the only established resource colony in the country with partial support from the National Institutes of Health. It was disbanded in 1977 due to the non-renewal of the grant. Over a period of fourteen years, $840,000 in grants had been received. New information on the processes involved in the clotting of blood was revealed that would be of benefit to man and animal.[8]

Commencing in 1966, Dr. Bertis Glenn was the principal investigator in a study on porphyria, a substance in the blood that results from a red blood cell metabolic defect. Research was funded by a National Institutes of Health grant of $127,000. The study of feline and bovine porphyria involved the development and supervision of a porphyric cat colony, development of a porphyric cattle herd, and genetic studies and biochemical characterization of feline and bovine porphyria.

Dr. Stanley Newcomer, a member of the Department of Physiology for over thirty years, conducted extensive research on thyroid function in birds. He was able to prove that diurnal rhythms of thyroid hormones and thyroid function occurred. Levels of concentration of both substances, thyroxine and tri-iodo thyronine, exhibited a wave form pattern. The peak of the former began occurring about 7:00 a.m. and the latter around 4:15 p.m. His research was supported by the National Science Foundation as well as the U.S. National Academy of Science. In its exchange program for cooperative research, the Hungarian Academy of Science sponsored four visits by Dr. Newcomer to the University of Veterinary Science in Budapest. He was presented the Hutyra Medal by the rector of the university in 1981.

In 1969 research began on bovine respiratory disease, a major problem to cattle owners in the state. It was a joint project between the college and veterinarians in the feedlot area of Oklahoma and the Texas Panhandle. The initial goals were to isolate and identify the agents causing the respiratory diseases of cattle, and to establish the relationship of the agents to the normal respiratory flora of feedlot cattle. The project leaders were Dr. Roger J. Panciera, Dr. Richard E. Corstvet, and Dr. Harold Rinker, class of 1958. Initially, research was focused on thromboembolic meningoencephalomyelitis. Later, as a result of preliminary work, pasteurella, a major cause of shipping fever, became the primary focus of study.

When Dr. Helen Jordan joined the faculty in 1969, she continued her work as a clinical parasitologist, studying a wide variety of helminths, including many trematodes. She has contributed significantly to the study of gastrointestinal parasitisms, especially in cattle, sheep, and swine and enhanced her standing nationally with work on ostertagiasis and published strategies for corrective/control programs for parasitism in domestic animals. She has also published studies dealing with parasites of companion animals and exotic species including certain endangered ones living at the Oklahoma City Zoo.

Studies began in the mid-1970s to evaluate the effectiveness of laboratory-produced pasteurella vaccines. Attempts to develop a model of shipping fever that would serve for well controlled experimental studies led, in 1979, to an intrapulmonic injection method to produce experimental pasteurella pneumonia. Much needed serologic methods were developed for identifying antibodies to components of the organism that appear to be highly important in disease production. Using the various experimental methods developed, it has been shown that under experimental conditions cattle can be effectively protected against pasteurella pneumonia. Currently, researchers are attempting to identify and engineer genetically the production of those antigens to create an effective and safe vaccine that will prevent shipping fever.

Other significant research accomplishments included work on previously undescribed syndromes such as the first report on hairy vetch plant poisoning in cattle, cryptosporidial fungal infection in a calf, early contributions on cantharidin poisoning in horses due to a blister beetle contained in the hay, and major contributions to the literature on oak poisoning in cattle.

Between 1972 and 1979 the college received a grant of $821,000 from the National Cancer Institute to establish the nation's second animal tumor registry as part of the research on cancer. Practicing veterinarians in the Tulsa area were requested to collect and submit for study all tissue and cytology specimens from suspected tumors in dogs and cats brought to them. The Tulsa area was selected because of its distribution of approximately forty-six veterinary hospitals and the sparse human population that made it a geographical area with a relatively concentrated and isolated dog and cat pet population. Dr. Andrew W. Monlux was the project's principal investigator with Dr. Jeffie Roszel as the co-principal investigator of the registry.

Material from this project has been used in teaching veterinary students, pathology residents, and graduate students at OSU. Presentations based upon the results obtained from this study have been given at veterinary schools in the United States and Canada, scientific meetings for veterinarians, and other meetings concerned with comparison of tumors from animals and man in the United States and Europe. The registry furnished material for numerous scientific publications on the pathology, cytology, and epidemiology of animal tumors.

In 1973 Dr. G. Pat Mayer continued his research on hypocalcemia (parturient paresis or milk fever) in dairy cattle and the role of calcitonin, a parathyroid hormone, and vitamin D in calcium metabolism. He and his co-workers also focused on the restriction of dietary calcium during gestation as a preventive measure for this metabolic disorder.

Dr. Charlotte L. Ownby, Department of Physiological Sciences, and Dr. George V. Odell, Department of Biochemistry, were investigators of a research project actually begun in 1976 on myotoxic protein found in the venom of the prairie rattlesnake. Myotoxin a, the first myotoxin isolated from rattlesnake venom, was shown to cause a specific destruction of skeletal muscle cells when injected intramuscularly into white mice. In 1977 Dr. Odell isolated myotoxin a and subsequently produced an antiserum.

These studies have shown that it is possible to produce anti-serum of a purified myotoxin which has outstanding ability to neutralize the myotoxic effects of the crude rattlesnake venom. This anti-myotoxin serum is superior to the commercially available anti-venom in its ability to prevent the myotoxic action of the venom. Additionally, when the anti-myotoxin serum is added to the commercial anti-venom, there is a vast improvement in neutralization of the myotoxic and lethal activities of the venom with no reduction in the neutralization of the hemorrhagic activity. Thus the research represents a new approach to improving the overall treatment of snake venom-induced death of tissues.

Beginning in 1976, Dr. Alan Kocan established a research program on parasitic and infectious diseases of wild animals. These studies, funded primarily by the Oklahoma Department of Wildlife Conservation through the Federal Aid to Wildlife Restoration Program, led to a clearer understanding of the role of wild animals as a reservoir for such diseases as bluetongue virus, epizootic hemorrhagic disease, and parasitic nematodes. With the assistance of Dr. Thomas Thedford and Dr. Selwyn Barron, additional advances were made in the understanding of the effects of clinical immobilizing drugs on blood values in deer and elk, as well as the identification of numerous parasitic disease agents of wild animals.

In the fall of 1981, at the request of cattlemen in his congressional district, U.S. Congressman Wes Watkins assembled leaders from Oklahoma State University and state and federal agencies, to discuss brucellosis problems in Oklahoma. As a result of this meeting, the Kerr Foundation sponsored a national brucellosis conference at Poteau, Oklahoma, in the spring of 1982. For two days the participants focused on programs to facilitate the final elimination of brucellosis from the United States. The disease causes abortion in cattle and undulant fever in humans.

The conference recommended that basic research be increased to study *Brucella abortus* and biological responses to invasion by the organism. The field testing and demonstration station should research and demonstrate improved vaccination methods. It was further recommended that a brucellosis task force testify before congressional appropriations committees on the need for additional federal appropriations to eliminate brucellosis from the United States. Dr. Lloyd Faulkner, director of veterinary research at Oklahoma State University, was chairman of the task force of veterinarians and cattlemen. The same year, the Kerr Foundation entered into a cooperative agreement with the College of Veterinary Medicine and the Agricultural Research Service of the U.S. Department of Agriculture to study brucellosis.

The Livestock Health Research Center was established in Hugo. Dr. Anthony W. Confer, Department of Veterinary Pathology, who was trained in immunopathology, assembled an interdisciplinary research team to work in cooperation with brucellosis researchers at the USDA National Animal Disease Center in Ames, Iowa, to test improved vaccines at the Hugo center. The team would also study genetic engineering of subunit brucella antigens for vaccine development and the production of antibodies for improved diagnostics. The Oklahoma State team included scientists in the College of Veterinary Medicine and in

James Horne, vice president for agriculture for the Kerr Foundation, speaks at the dedication of the Livestock Health Research Center in Hugo in June of 1983. Congressman Wes Watkins *(seated)* encouraged a meeting of state and federal experts in 1981 to discuss the brucellosis problem. The Hugo center would be used to test improved vaccines.

biochemistry, zoology, botany, and microbiology. It led to the formation of the OSU Biotechnologies Program and the University Center for Molecular Genetics.

The Hugo center is an isolated, five-acre enclosure with a barn and cattle working facilities. Research began with the purchase of local yearling heifers that were selected from herds without a history of brucellosis and that tested negative on a blood test. The study confirmed other findings that the possibilities of reactions following vaccination are greatly diminished with the new dosage. In continued testing after six months, all cattle eventually tested negative. When the cattle were between four and five months pregnant, they were divided into two sections and infected with live Brucella organisms. One section received a heavy amount greatly exceeding the normally exposed dose; the other section received a field-level amount. There were also non-vaccinated controls. Cattle receiving a heavy amount incurred a high abortion rate, but for those in the field-level group, the vaccine performed very well.

Other research projects undertaken have included the study of stomach and intestinal parasites, transport mechanisms of the intestine of the roundworm *Ascaris suum*, Klebsiella bacterial infection of the uterus in mares, wildlife research, male reproduction, toxic plants of Oklahoma, and neurology. Researchers developed a surgical procedure for the production of a monogastric calf whereby food would pass from the

Dr. Everett Besch *(right)* works in February 1960 as an assistant professor and a graduate student in parasitology under Dr. Wendell Krull. Dr. Besch later succeeded Dr. Krull as head of the department and eventually became the dean of Louisiana State University's School of Veterinary Medicine.

esophagus directly to the fourth or "true" stomach.

What of the future? Dean Joseph W. Alexander brought a new commitment to research in the college in 1985. A report submitted to the American Veterinary Medical Association Council on Education on November 18, 1985, by Dean Alexander and OSU President L. L. Boger stated, "The current administration is working toward the recruitment of outstanding scientists who have the potential of making significant contributions to the college research mission. All faculty are encouraged to be creative and to share their knowledge with the profession through publications. If the college is to continue to grow, especially in the area of research, additional sources of funding must be identified. The college is committed to increasing its efforts in research and creative activities.

"Funding for research increased 24 percent from $1,078,587 in 1984 to $1,339,598 in 1985. State dollars for research were increased 17 percent from $571,524 in 1984 to $668,741 in 1985. Federal grants increased 58 percent from $357,459 in 1984 to $565,625 in 1985."[9]

The College of Veterinary Medicine and the OSU Agricultural Experiment Station will focus future research in the exciting and challenging area of biotechnology which promises to revolutionize agricultural production. Reducing losses from animal disease will contribute directly to Oklahoma's economy. Building a capacity for biotechnological research is necessary in order to compete successfully for federal and industrial research grants and to stimulate the growth of animal agri-business in Oklahoma.[10]

The college has strong programs in bovine respiratory disease, brucel-losis, and anaplasmosis. Future research in these and other areas will center around the biology of interleukins and lymphokines, which are the cellular products of the host in response to invading pathogens.[11]

Let the clarion call of this great new era echo all around our state and the world!

Endnotes

1. Early research activities in veterinary medicine at Oklahoma A. and M. College are dis-cussed in Chapter 3.

2. Complete acknowledgement of the contributions of researchers at Oklahoma State University in the field of veterinary medicine is far beyond the scope of this history. A separate sec-tion in the Bibliography, however, lists both selected references used in the preparation of this chapter and other research undertaken by members of the College of Veterinary Medicine.

3. *Oklahoma Agricultural Experiment Station Biennial Report 1946-48, Part 1, July 1, 1946, to June 30, 1948*, p. 43.

4. Author's personal communication with I. O. Kliewer, 1986.

5. E. L. Walker, "I Remember When. . .," *Oklahoma Veterinarian* vol. 12, no. 3 (Fall 1965), p. 5.

6. "New Anaplasmosis Vaccine Developed by Researchers at Oklahoma Agricultural Research Station," *Oklahoma Veterinarian,* vol. 12, no. 3 (Fall 1965), p. 2.

7. Author's personal communication with Dr. C. K. Whitehair, 1986.

8. Author's personal communication with Dr. Ralph Buckner, 1986.

9. College of Veterinary Medicine, "Report to the AVMA Council on Education, November 18, 1985," Archives, College of Veterinary Medicine.

10. Research in the College of Veterinary Medicine, included as Appendix 7 of the "Report to the AVMA Council on Education, November 18, 1985," Archives, College of Veterinary Medicine.

11. "Report of the Committee on Biotechnology (Dr. R. W. Fulton, A. W. Confer, B. A. Lessley, and G. L. Morgan) to Dean Alexander, January 31, 1986," Archives, College of Veteri-nary Medicine.

9 Central American Adventure

We must embark on a bold new program for making the benefits of our scientific advances available for the improvement and growth of under-developed areas.

President Harry S. Truman, Inaugural Address

In mid 1965 the College of Veterinary Medicine embarked on a new venture in international programs. Over the next seven years Oklahoma State University would participate in a program with the U.S. Agency for International Development to provide for training of veterinarians in Central America. It proved to be a highly successful and rewarding experience for all concerned.

Oklahoma State University's outstanding contribution to the development of education and food production in Ethiopia in 1952-68 placed it among the pioneers of international programs. It emerged in the late 1950s as a versatile institution ready to extend its expertise to other developing countries.

Dr. Glenn C. Holm, dean since 1956, had a great interest in international programs and had been actively involved in selecting graduates from the school to serve in Ethiopia. About this time there was a strong movement to establish a Common Market in Central America and Panama along the lines of the European Common Market. This unifying of common interest also led to the formation, in 1962, of the Consejo Superior Universidad de Centro America (Superior Council of the Universities of Central America) by the presidents of the national universities of Guatemala, El Salvador, Honduras, Nicaragua, Costa Rica, and Panama to unify their higher education programs.

In November 1962, Dr. Francisco R. Rodas, dean of the veterinary school at University of San Carlos, attended a talk given by Dean Glenn Holm on regional education based on the Southern Regional Education Board program, at the IV Pan American Veterinary Medical Congress in Mexico City. Dr. Rodas and Dr. Jorge Arias de Blois, president of the University of San Carlos, then presented the concept of regional education to the superior council. The council designated the College of Veterinary Medicine and Animal Husbandry of San Carlos University as the Central American training center for veterinary medicine. This regional school for Central America would admit students from the other Central American universities following two years of basic studies in any of them.

The college had been established in 1957; three veterinarians had graduated in 1962. At that time, Guatemala had only four general practitioners available to the livestock industry of approximately 2,000,000 cattle, 750,000 sheep, 500,000 swine, and 250,000 horses.

Early in 1963, the president and Dean Rodas requested that Oklahoma State University conduct a feasibility study of a cooperative program between the two universities designed to strengthen instruction and research in veterinary medicine and animal husbandry at the University of San Carlos. On February 28, 1963, Dean Glenn Holm, Dr. Louis Hawkins, director, OSU Agricultural Experiment Station, and Dr. Randall Jones, dean of resident instruction in agriculture, visited the University of San Carlos to conduct the study. Three areas were highlighted for improvement in the overall regional school program, namely instruction, research, and control of animal diseases with special emphasis on anaplasmosis and other causes of cattle mortality. The study, which was funded by the Rockefeller Foundation, lasted until March 11. In July, the feasibility report was submitted to the Agency for International Development by Oklahoma State University.

The feasibility study stated the main objectives of the program were to strengthen the instruction at San Carlos and increase the number of graduates who could fill positions in the fields of veterinary medicine, or do effective work in extension education and other areas under the Ministry of Agriculture. More effective teachers were needed at the university and secondary school levels. Additional objectives were to develop a strong program of research and strengthen the instruction program in veterinary medicine to serve better the countries of Central America.

The study team determined that excellent opportunities existed for cooperation between the University of San Carlos and Oklahoma State University in college-level instruction and research, but supporting agencies outside of the two universities would be required to provide financial support. Research under such a cooperative program, particularly as related to control and eradication of diseases and parasites of animals and plants, could be highly valuable to Oklahoma and other areas of the United States.

A contract for $227,000 between the Agency for International Development and Oklahoma State University was signed on June 23, 1965. Dean Holm attended the signing ceremony in Washington, D.C. President Oliver Willham had already signed for OSU in his office on June 19, 1965. Senator Fred Harris and Congressman Tom Steed also attended the ceremony.[1]

Because Dean Holm became convinced during his visit to Central America that one of the most important contributions the college could make would be in anaplasmosis research, he insisted that the chief of party for the program possessed expertise in this area. Such a person was Dr. William E. Brock who had developed the first effective vaccine for anaplasmosis in cattle.

Dr. Brock assumed his duties in Guatemala City in the summer of 1965. One of the most pressing needs was the revision and updating of the veterinary medicine curriculum. Dr. Duane Peterson, chairman of the OSU College of Veterinary Medicine curriculum and scheduling committee, spent a few weeks at the school in October 1965, interviewing faculty members and studying the curriculum. He found that each faculty of the university established its own course of study with review and approval by the administration of the university. Each faculty also prepared its own schedule of classes and its opening and closing dates. The administration had the authority to establish uniform degree requirements and to modify the course offerings of the various faculties but never exercised this authority. Dr. Peterson developed a four-year program on the lines of the OSU College of Veterinary Medicine curriculum which was adopted by the University of San Carlos.

During the first year of the contract, there were eleven students in the senior class who were studying under the combined animal science and veterinary medicine degree program. Because of the policy of accepting all who applied for admission, there was traditionally a very high dropout rate during the first year.

Dr. Brock set about establishing administrative procedures and personnel for the operation of the contract. He also led the development of an animal disease research program that taught an informal course in experimental design to faculty and students. Ongoing research in anaplasmosis and babesiosis were used as examples. Research projects in these major diseases were developed that resulted in three published research papers.

An important part of the contract was to familiarize the faculty of the San Carlos school with OSU teaching and research methods in order to broaden their horizons and stimulate professional interest. Beginning

Three men served as chief of party in Guatemala: Dr. Theodore S. Eliot Jr., Dr. Paul B. Barto, and Dr. William E. Brock.

in the fall of 1965, ten faculty members spent from two weeks to eight months at OSU working on a one-to-one basis with the College of Veterinary Medicine faculty. It became evident that arrangements were needed for longer periods of training and to work toward advanced degrees. This was accomplished when University of San Carlos faculty members began pursuing studies at OSU and other academic institutions in the United States and other countries.

During the fall semester 1965 and the following spring, several OSU faculty members made hectic efforts to become proficient in conversational Spanish—with an Oklahoma or other accent! Dr. Dennis Goetsch was the first to venture forth, at the dean's request (or was it command?). He spent two weeks in May 1966 visiting the physiology department at the University of San Carlos. He arrived in the middle of a student strike! In his report, Dr. Goetsch emphasized that "student influence on administration and faculty at San Carlos University must be minimized or improvement of the university as a whole will be extremely low, if not impossible."[2] This sentiment was later reiterated by several other visiting faculty members.

Dr. Lester Johnson, Department of Medicine and Surgery, arrived a few weeks later to spend two months with the clinical faculty, most of whom worked on a part-time basis and conducted private practice in addition to their teaching duties. Dr. Johnson delivered numerous lectures on large animal diseases and demonstrated a variety of surgical operations. His vast clinical knowledge, outstanding lecturing ability, and congenial personality contributed enormously toward the future success of the program. He highlighted the need for more and better equipment and permanent clinical buildings.

Following his two-year term as chief of party, 1965-67, Dr. Brock returned to Oklahoma State University. He had accomplished the very difficult task of implementing the program in spite of all the bureaucratic and language obstacles. Oklahoma State University had again embarked on a successful international program.

Dr. Brock was awarded the honorary degree of "Doctor Honoris Causa" by University of San Carlos for his outstanding services. This is the highest honor bestowed by the university, one that only ten people have received since 1675. The award was presented before the full convocation of the university and attended by U.S. Ambassador John Gordon Mein.

Several OSU faculty members spent varying periods at University of San Carlos during the following years. As the contract extended beyond the original two-year period, it became obvious that the San Carlos faculty could derive enormous benefit from the expertise of the visiting faculty. Probably the most productive, and undoubtedly the most exciting, were the short courses that were presented in the various coun-

Dr. William E. Brock *(center right)* receives the honorary degree of Doctor Honoris Causa from University of San Carlos in Guatemala by Edwardo Vasquez Martinez, rector of the University of San Carlos. Dr. Victor Orrellano, dean of the College of Veterinary Medicine and Animal Husbandry, is present on the left.

tries. During the summer of 1968, a team of clinicians and animal scientists from both universities presented seminars to veterinarians and cattle owners in Guatemala, El Salvador, and Honduras. The visit to Honduras was unforgettable! The group was confronted by the local police for using a government vehicle after 6:00 p.m. Only fast talking by the shrewd and affable coordinator, Dr. Francisco Rodas, saved the visitors a trip to the local "carcel" (jail!).

On a more pleasant note was the short course at the Pan American Agricultural Institute in Zanoramo, Honduras. Following a hair-raising drive over very rugged country, Dr. Allen Tillman, Dr. Milton Wells, Dr. Eric Williams, and Dr. Paul Barto, along with faculty members from the University of San Carlos, descended on a beautiful campus that was kept in immaculate condition under the stern leadership of a dour Scot principal. Here the highlight was a demonstration of a bovine cesarean operation in the standing position—such feats were unheard of in this hinterland. The live, red bull was immediately and suitably named after the performing clinician!

The flight out of Honduras from Tegucigalpa was also memorable! After taxiing halfway down the runway, the plane returned to the terminal whereupon an "engineer" came aboard with a screwdriver and a pair of pliers to correct some problem at the back of the plane. He soon left and so did the plane to a safe destination in Guatemala. This and

COURTESY DR. ERIC WILLIAMS

El Rojo was delivered by caesarean section at the Pan American College of Agriculture at Zanorama, Honduras, by Oklahoma State University veterinary faculty.

other incidents had created a motto, "Stay home and live," among Central Americans.

In the summer of 1969 another series of short courses were presented in Nicaragua and Costa Rica. Following a colorful opening ceremony in Nicaragua, Dr. Ernesto Villagran, San Carlos, and Dr. Eric Williams performed a rumenotomy under a tree on the outskirts of Managua, the capital city.

In view of the satisfactory progress during the first two years, the contract was extended for a three-year term, 1967-70. Dr. Paul Barto, Department of Veterinary Parasitology, Microbiology and Public Health, succeeded Dr. Brock as chief of party on September 1, 1967. Dr. Barto was responsible for planning short courses for veterinarians and cattlemen in Guatemala City and in all the Central American countries. He also taught a poultry disease course to two classes of veterinary medicine students.

In his 1967-68 annual report, Dr. Barto stated that monies were provided to purchase clinical equipment and library books and to support research projects. A major addition was a Jeep Wagoneer for the ambulatory clinic. Twelve students had received their degrees in veterinary medicine. The following year, twenty-two students completed their degree requirements. During the same year, work began on the anaplasmosis-babesiosis research project, a cooperative effort between the two universities. Dr. Barto also reported that the Regional Veterinary School had received a farm of approximately 160 hectares from the Guatemalan government to teach and demonstrate proper livestock production.

During the 1968-69 academic year, the Regional School of Veterinary Medicine and Animal Science was reorganized to consist of two schools: Escuela de Medicina Veterinaria y Zootecnia (School of Veterinary Medicine and Animal Science) and Escuela de Zootecnia (School of Animal Science). The School of Basic Studies had been abolished following a student strike. The two-year basic studies program was transferred to the schools of their intended specialty. The Regional Veterinary School was now responsible for enrolling pre-veterinary students and shared the teaching assignments with the other health profession schools. It also administered the newly adopted animal science degree program. The degree of Doctor of Veterinary Medicine and Animal Husbandry was granted after six years, including two years of pre-veterinary studies (formerly basic studies) and four years of veterinary training. A degree was granted after five years of study—two years pre-animal science (formerly basic studies) and three years in the animal science curriculum. Approximately 250 students enrolled—125 in basic studies courses, 88 in the School of Veterinary Medicine and Animal Science, and 13 in the School of Animal Science.

The last chief of party was Dr. Theodore S. Eliot Jr., who had joined the small animal section of the Department of Medicine and Surgery in 1967 after eleven years in private practice. Dr. Eliot concentrated his efforts on the final planning and supervision of a much needed clinic facility at University of San Carlos which included the only modern small animal surgery unit in Central America. He and San Carlos clinicians returning from Oklahoma State University completely redesigned the old clinic building.

The College of Veterinary Medicine's adventure in international programs was a great success. The program of short-term exchange of professors on a person-to-person basis worked very well. Language did not appear to be a large handicap in this non-formal situation due to the personal relationship and the work's scientific nature. The technical and professional assistance offered in Guatemala by OSU personnel covered a very wide range. They provided guidance in research, individual course preparation, curriculum design, and even architectural assistance in the preparation of the plans for the Veterinary Hospital. The final report emphasized the need of the Regional School to continue to develop the education of the faculty. The experience for the College of Veterinary Medicine in Guatemala was such a good one that the possibility of a continuing relationship remains open.

Endnotes

1. Contract between the United States of America and Oklahoma State University, 1965, can be found in Archives, College of Veterinary Medicine.
2. *Final Report Contract No. LA-282 Between the Agency for International Development and the Oklahoma State University, 1965-1971, for Assistance to the Regional College of Veterinary Medicine and Animal Science at San Carlos University, Guatemala,* September 1972, Archives, College of Veterinary Medicine.

10 New Curriculum Emerges

Personally, I have always felt that the best doctor in the world is the veterinarian. He can't ask his patients what is the matter. . . he's just got to know.

Will Rogers

While important advances were being made in Central America, other significant changes were occurring in Stillwater. Involvement of the faculty in state and national veterinary events was increasing.

Dean Glenn Holm was elected to the American Veterinary Medical Association's Council on Education in 1965. Dr. Andrew Monlux, head of the Department of Veterinary Pathology, along with his brother, Dr. William Monlux, Ames, Iowa, both of whom are internationally recognized pathologists, completely revised, updated, and enlarged their original textbook, *Principles of Veterinary Pathology.*

Dr. Lewis H. Moe retired on July 1, 1966, and joined the Veterinary Division of the State Department of Agriculture as a state field veterinarian. He had served Oklahoma State University with dignity, hard work, and true professionalism for thirty-eight years. As one of the original, hard working clinicians, Dr. Moe had helped steer the new school through very difficult and precarious times.

The golden anniversary meeting of the Southern Veterinary Medical Association was held at the Skirvin Hotel, Oklahoma City, on October 23-26, 1966. It was the first time for the convention to be held in Oklahoma. Dean Holm was the program chairman for that meeting and was also elected to the Board of Directors. The program chairman was Dr. J. Wiley Wolfe, and several OSU faculty members presented papers.[1]

Dr. Lewis Moe reminds students Ron Ford, Steve Holmes, and Don Arrington not to forget what he told them about copper sulfate as a veterinary remedy.

Dr. Eugene M. Jones was installed as president of the Oklahoma Veterinary Medical Association at the 52nd annual meeting which was held in Oklahoma City in January 1967. Dr. Eric Williams became editor of the *Oklahoma Veterinarian* in the spring. In 1969, "for the fun of it," Dr. Williams would later become editor of a national journal the *Bovine Practitioner*, the official journal of the American Association of Bovine Practitioners.

The Seventeenth Annual Southwestern Conference on Diseases in Nature Transmissible to Man was held at Oklahoma State University on May 18-19, 1967. The conference was sponsored by the College of Veterinary Medicine, Oklahoma State University, Oklahoma State Department of Health, and the Oklahoma Veterinary Medical Association. The keynote speaker was Dr. James H. Steele, chief, Veterinary Public Health, National Communicable Disease Center, Atlanta, Georgia. The program coordinator was Dr. Everett Besch.

In 1967 the Executive Board of the American Veterinary Medical Association Auxiliary created the Outstanding Senior Wife Award to be presented to the outstanding spouse of every local student chapter. In 1974, to honor Mrs. Lillie Grossman, the name of the award was changed to the Lillie Grossman Outstanding Senior Spouse Award. A charter member and past president of the national auxiliary, Mrs. Grossman is the wife of Dr. J. D. Grossman who was a faculty member at Ohio

State University. This award was first presented at the Annual Awards Banquet in 1968.[2]

U.S. Congressman Tom Steed of the Fourth Oklahoma District was the co-sponsor along with Representative Jed Johnson, Sixth District, of the Veterinary Medical School Construction Bill which was introduced in the spring of 1966 in the interest of better health and safer food supply for the nation. At a hearing held by the Public Health Subcommittee of the House Interstate Commerce Committee, with Congressman John Jarman of the Fifth District presiding, Representative Steed stated, ''We now have 24,000 veterinarians in the United States. Experts have shown that this number is already inadequate to protect our farm and domestic animals and do the vital research work needed to combat animal diseases and prevent their spreading to humans. With only eighteen veterinarian schools in the nation, we will have a shortage of more than 5,000 veterinarians in twenty years even below the existing inadequate ratio, unless expansion is possible.''[3] He urged the extension to veterinary medical schools and their students the same federal support that was already available to medical, dental, and other fields.

The bill was reported favorably to the House and it cleared its final hurdle when the Senate receded from its position on two amendments. The bill was supported by the Oklahoma Cattlemen's Association and the Oklahoma Veterinary Medical Association. Dean Holm testified before the House and the Senate as an expert witness. The Veterinary Education Facilities Act of 1966 was passed on the last day of the 89th Congress in October. It provided funds for expanding and remodeling teaching facilities for existing colleges and for the establishment of new ones. New and expanded space would be funded on a ratio of two federal to one state dollar and remodeling on a 1-1 basis. The act required colleges to increase the beginning class size by 50 percent.

The Health Professions Student Loan Program had been established in 1963 to provide loans to medical students. However, it was not available to veterinary medical students. The Veterinary Medical Education Act of 1966 extended eligibility to schools and students of veterinary medicine for participation in the Health Professions Student Loan Program. The Allied Health Professional Personnel Training Act of 1966 further amended the loan program.

Each participating institution was required to deposit and maintain in its loan fund an amount from other sources equal to at least one-ninth of the federal contribution (or, to state it in another way, an amount equal to at least one-tenth of the total working capital in its loan fund).

The maximum amount available to an individual borrower in an academic year or its equivalent was $2,000. In cases, however, where students were required to attend school for longer than the traditional nine-month academic year, students could borrow a maximum of twelve-

Fourth District Congressman Tom Steed holds a plaque for distinguished service presented to him by the American Veterinary Medical Association. Congressman Steed sponsored legislation to improve veterinary education.

ninths of $2,000 or $2,666 for the period.

Soon after Dean Holm began his tenure in 1956, Dr. Duane Peterson discussed with him a rather comprehensive proposal for curriculum and scheduling change. The most salient aspect of this plan was to integrate the clinical part of the D.V.M. program with an academic calendar. It did not seem in the best interest of the college's fiscal policy to hire several students to help operate the clinic during the summer without any clinical credit hours being awarded. Dean Holm expressed a real interest in the proposal, but more pressing issues of the college needed attention so he suggested a delay. He was a perspicacious administrator who did not want to deal with an issue that might be quite controversial at a time when he was just beginning to establish his administration.

In 1964, however, Dean Glenn Holm appointed an all-college committee to review the four-year veterinary medicine curriculum and to make recommendations to the Veterinary Administrative Council. This enormous task was undertaken with much enthusiasm, philosophizing, and the usual academic pontification, under the astute leadership of Dr. Peterson who now and forever more earned the auspicious and revered title of "Dr. Curriculum." Other members of the committee were Dr. Paul Barto, Dr. Everett Besch, Dr. E. Wynn Jones, Dr. Roger Panciera, and Dr. George Stabenfeldt. Dean Holm's charge to the committee was to consider, to develop further, and to refine the proposal that Dr. Peterson had previously discussed with the dean during the late 1950s.

The committee spent approximately three years addressing the various issues of the proposed curriculum and schedule and how it would impact the research and service assignments of the faculty. Prolonged discussion and debate on each aspect of the program resulted. The committee did spend some time ascertaining what some of the other colleges were doing with their clinical program, but the main thrust was to develop a new curriculum that would have the committee's stamp of creativity.

The committee recommended a year-round academic program in clinics. Since 38 percent of clinical cases were presented during the long summer vacation and fall or spring breaks when students were away from the campus, too much time was spent trying to adjust the case load to the times when students were in clinics. Clinicians had to deal with a very uneven number of students. During the summer they had no students. In the fall they had forty-eight fourth-year students while in the spring they had ninety-six third-year and fourth-year students. In the spring each clinician might have as many as eighteen students and that made it very difficult for anyone to instruct in a clinical case mode. Thus it was not surprising to find two horseshoe games going on almost continuously during the afternoons of the spring semester. The committee facetiously suggested that at least one-credit hour of clinics should be in horseshoe throwing.

A year-round calendar for fourth-year students would result in a more efficient use of the clinical facilities and a more uniform and desirable ratio of students to faculty and staff. An increased number of cases would be brought into the teaching program, and there would be a more direct study of the seasonal aspects of disease. The proposal allowed for certain free periods that could increase student enrichment experiences in such areas as teaching assistantships, research technicians, or other specialized activities.

The adoption of a preceptorship program, although not an obligatory part of the overall program, was strongly recommended by the committee. The program by which students would spend time gaining clinical experience with a practicing veterinarian would provide more association with the common disease problems and would complement association with the more complicated referral problems and chronic cases. The number of cases involved in the training program as well as the number of clinicians providing clinical instruction would increase. Students would become acquainted with "fee-for-service" type practices, not subsidized by the state, and thus give insights to the economic aspect of conducting a practice and the importance of offering prompt and efficient public service. It would enhance the student's ability to determine the particular area of veterinary medicine the student may wish to serve subsequent to graduation.

Since the proposed third- and fourth-year program would involve a calendar that would be different from that of the rest of the university proper, approval from the college administration was required. Dean

Holm convinced the administration that because veterinary medicine was a professional college, it needed to operate under a different calendar with special considerations not afforded to the other colleges. The higher administrative officials were quite receptive to the general concept of the proposal.

The committee's final report was presented to the dean on June 28, 1966. After consideration by the Veterinary Administrative Council, it was presented to the college faculty at a meeting on Thursday, July 7. They voted overwhelmingly to recommend the adoption of the report and implement its recommendations. Before the new curriculum and schedule could be implemented, Dean Holm indicated that it must be reviewed by the American Veterinary Medical Association Council on Education, approved by the vice president for academic affairs, endorsed by the Academic Standards Committee of the Faculty Council, and approved by the State Regents for Higher Education. Dean Holm targeted January 1967 as the date to get the above approvals.

On June 30, 1966, Dr. Oliver S. Willham retired as president of Oklahoma State University. He was succeeded by Dr. Robert B. Kamm, who was currently serving as vice president for academic affairs. Prior to that time, Dr. Kamm had served as dean of College of Arts and Science since 1958 when he had come to OSU from Texas A. and M. University where he had been dean of the Basic Division and of Student Affairs.

The proposed changes in curriculum were not implemented until the 1968-69 academic year. The college departed from the standard university calendar starting with the spring semester, third-year class. The senior year was changed to alternating six-week sessions for an entire year. A special week was introduced at mid-semester during the spring and fall when the class schedules for the third-and fourth-year students were re-arranged to include conferences on specialty areas, such as neurology and ophthalmology, by guest lecturers.

Monday morning, April 17, 1967, was not unusual, but before the day was over everyone was caught by surprise when Dean Glenn Holm announced that he had resigned, effective June 30, to accept a federal foreign aid post in India.

Dean Holm joined the U.S. Agency for International Development as agricultural education adviser for India. It was the second highest assignment ever given an OSU official in the foreign technical assistance programs being outranked only by Dr. Henry Bennett's position as the first administrator of the Technical Cooperative Administration, the forerunner to the Agency for International Development. It was a logical move for a man with such proven international vision. Dr. Holm helped to coordinate educational programs of major universities in India and those of six American land-grant universities in operation there. Later, he held a similar position in El Salvador, Central America.

Glenn Carlos Holm, D.V.M., M.S.
1909-1982

Glenn C. Holm was born and raised on a 240-acre irrigated farm near Shelley, Idaho, on December 17, 1909. He received the B.S. degree in 1932 and the M.S. degree in agriculture in 1933 from the University of Idaho. In 1936 he received the D.V.M. degree from Iowa State University. He and the former Jewell Leighton were married on September 5, 1933, in Caldwell, Idaho.

COURTESY MRS. JEWELL HOLM

Dr. Holm practiced at Rexburg, Idaho, for two years and then joined the Veterinary Science Department at the University of Idaho in 1938 where he taught anatomy and bacteriology. He became associate director of the Experiment Station in 1946 and left in 1949 to join the faculty at North Dakota State University as professor of veterinary science and bacteriology. He became dean of the School of Agriculture and director of the Experiment Station in 1953. He was a member of several organizations and honor societies and published over seventy papers on bacteriology and pathology.

Dr. Holm became dean of the School of Veterinary Medicine, Oklahoma A. and M. College on October 1, 1956. He assumed the title of assistant director of the Agricultural Experiment Station on March 1, 1957. Dr. Holm was particularly interested in selection methods for professional students. He was the driving force in negotiating the Agency for International Development contract between Oklahoma State University and University of San Carlos, Guatemala. Dr. Holm was a member of the American Veterinary Medical Association, Oklahoma Veterinary Medical Association, Intermountain Veterinary Medical Association, Association of State Universities and Land Grant Colleges Commission on Health Science Education, and served as vice president of the Southern Veterinary Medical Association.

Dr. Holm resigned his position as dean of the college effective June 30, 1967, to accept a federal aid post in India as agricultural education adviser under the U.S. Agency for International Development. Later, he held a similar position in El Salvador. In 1976 he was awarded the American Veterinary Medical Association XII International Veterinary Congress Award for outstanding international service to the veterinary profession. In the same year he was named Idaho Veterinarian of the Year. The University of Idaho named the veterinary medicine building the Glenn C. Holm Veterinary Medicine Building. In 1977 he was awarded the honorary Doctor of Science degree from the University of Idaho and was a consultant in establishing the Oregon-Washington-Idaho veterinary college.

Dr. Holm died on Sunday, November 7, 1982, at his home in Blackfoot, Idaho, at the age of 72.

OSU President Robert B. Kamm stated, "We regret very much to lose such an able person as Dean Holm. Under his direction our College of Veterinary Medicine has made tremendous contributions through its growing number of graduates, its research, and public service programs during the past eleven years. It is a distinct honor for Dean Holm to be chosen by our nation for such a major leadership role in India's educational system."[4]

Dr. J. Wiley Wolfe was appointed acting dean by the OSU Board of Regents, effective July 1, 1967. Dr. Lester Johnson became acting head, Department of Medicine and Surgery and director of the Large and Small Animal Clinics.

During his eleven years as dean of the college, Dean Holm presented diplomas to eleven classes and 407 graduates. He gave credit for OSU's strong veterinary medicine program to his staff and students. He was very proud of the curriculum changes and felt, "This is a big compliment to our faculty committee which was not satisfied just to keep abreast of needs, but wanted to be out in front. The greatest thrill for me has been the constantly improving quality of the veterinary medicine students and the kind of citizens they become as they graduate and begin their practice. They are truly professional men and women."[5]

Dean Holm's many accomplishments for the college will always rank high in the annals of history. He was a strict disciplinarian who demanded the extra mile from all around him. It is hard to imagine on reflection that he and his secretary, Lois Greiner, could handle so much paper work and endless other demands with very little extra help for so many years. He worked diligently to acquire the funds to complete two major building programs, the middle and the south wings of the college. Dean Holm's decisions were not always popular ones. He employed a key-person concept, in vogue at the time, that resulted in larger salaries for certain faculty that were "indispensable" to the college. Dean Holm had the wisdom, however, to realize that, having reached and probably surpassed the goals of his administration, it was prudent to move on to wider pastures and an exciting new endeavor.

Endnotes

1. "What is SVMA?" *Oklahoma Veterinarian*, vol. 13, no. 3 (Fall 1966), p. 2.

2. A list of the recipients may be found in the Appendix.

3. *Stillwater NewsPress*, 25 April 1966, Scrapbook, Archives, College of Veterinary Medicine.

4. *Stillwater NewsPress*, 18 April 1967, p. 9, Scrapbook, Archives, College of Veterinary Medicine.

5. *Stillwater NewsPress*, 18 April 1967, p. 9, Scrapbook, Archives, College of Veterinary Medicine.

11 The Tempest Blows Over

*Only the union of medicine and surgery constitutes the complete doc-
tor. The doctor who lacks knowledge of one of these branches is like
a bird with only one wing.*

Sushruta

Campus life throughout the nation was undergoing considerable
change on the east and west coasts. Finally it reached mid-America.
What seemed to have started with the appearance of the "Beatles," an
English rock music group, created such a sensation that life was never
to be the same again. These four "mopheads" introduced long hair. Gone
was the trim, flat-top haircut. The traditional social structure that had
existed in earlier years was changing. Before the end of the decade, many
of the nation's campuses literally fell apart.

The main trigger for the unrest was the "undeclared," unpopular
war that was waging in Vietnam. During the spring and summer of 1967,
civil disobedience became widespread. However, to their eternal credit,
cooler and wiser heads prevailed in many land-grant institutions. Blessed
with good leadership and a solid core of law abiding citizens, Oklahoma
State University had very little unrest.

Radicals and anti-establishment speakers were the center of heated
debates on whether they should be allowed on campus. Oklahoma State
University developed a speakers' policy which helped to avoid a major
turmoil.

Longer hair styles and the casual dress had come to stay. No more
white shirts and ties in the classroom! A Veterinary Administrative Council member remarked that too many jeans were being worn in the class-

room! Student chapter meetings on alternate Thursday evenings had been occasions for which to dress up and were often followed by a night on the town. Alas, that also changed and on came the jeans, shorts, sandals, tee shirts, or whatever was different!

Much of academic life went on as usual. Research activities continued on a brisk note. Dr. E. W. Jones received two grants totaling $211,000 from the Department of Health, Education and Welfare Public Health Service to continue the study of natural resistance to disease.

An Anaplasmosis Research Workers Meeting was held at Oklahoma State University on February 26-27, 1968, which was followed by the Fifth National Anaplasmosis Conference on February 28-29. Representatives from sixteen states and four foreign countries attended the meetings in which several faculty members from the OSU College of Veterinary Medicine presented papers.

Dr. Everett Besch left in April 1968 to become dean of the new veterinary medical school at Louisiana State University. He was succeeded as head of the Department of Veterinary Parasitology and Public Health on September 1 by Dr. Sidney A. Ewing. Dr. Derek Tavernor, Royal Veterinary College, London, joined the clinical research section as a visiting research professor working on anesthesia.

Meanwhile, a search committee for a new dean had been hard at work. Dr. Karl R. Reinhard was appointed by the Board of Regents effective April 1, 1968. Dr. Reinhard had an impressive administrative record. He was described by a colleague: "The intervening years in the Public Health Service have thrust him into the panoply of political and scientific leaders who have determined the academic and research course for post-war America."[1]

Dr. Reinhard assumed his duties with much enthusiasm and expectation. He showed a lot of interest in student affairs and in faculty academic enrichment programs. The new era was off to a good start. Dean Reinhard completely refurbished a room on the mezzanine to provide a much needed college conference area that was appropriately named the McElroy Room.

In November 1968 representatives from the American Veterinary Medical Association Council on Education visited the college. This was the first visit since 1962 when the college had been placed on conditional accreditation. The council's report to the university administration, presented in January 1969, recommended that fiscal support of the college should be increased in proportion to its special needs rather than in accordance with formulas based on student enrollments and that the state regents should initiate a thorough study to ascertain the value of the college to the state of Oklahoma. The council congratulated all faculty members responsible for the newly initiated professional curriculum. They were impressed by the appearance and morale of the students and

Dr. Sidney A. Ewing joined the faculty in 1960 and became one of the first Ph.D. recipients under the new graduate program in the College of Veterinary Medicine. From 1972-78 he was dean of the College of Veterinary Medicine at the University of Minnesota, and then he returned to Oklahoma State University.

their loyalty to the college, and they applauded the recent appointment of a student-faculty committee and the initiation of a program in veterinary medical extension.

The council made several other recommendations and placed the college on confidential probation, formerly known as conditional accreditation. If evidence of satisfactory progress toward implementing each of the recommendations were presented to the council by December 1, 1969, the classification would be reconsidered.[2]

A letter from Dr. Ronald J. Kolar, American Veterinary Medical Association director, Department of Education and Licensure, to Dean Reinhard on February 17, 1969, explained that the college was still accredited and would be treated as such. He promised the probationary status of the college would never be made public. Somehow the council's report was leaked to the press and quite a furor resulted.

The report was interpreted by the general public as an indication of possible closure of the college. Also, there was considerable concern among the students that a non-accreditation status would prevent them from being eligible to take national and state board examinations. However, the college was not in such a serious predicament. It was accredited, but certain conditions needed to be met before full accreditation could be achieved. Although accreditation status reflected the perennial problems of the lack of physical facilities and adequate funding, graduates of the program were highly regarded and in much demand.

At the Oklahoma Veterinary Medical Association Convention, held in Tulsa on February 2-4, Dr. Duane Peterson was installed as president for 1969-70. He became actively involved in promoting changes in the Oklahoma Veterinary Practice Act that would be in the best interest of the veterinary profession. The act, a code of professional conduct under the jurisdiction of the State Board of Veterinary Medical Examiners, the sole licensing authority, was under review by the state legislature. The revised act was signed into law by Governor David Hall on May 4, 1971.

Interest in international programs continued. Dr. John H. Venable from the Department of Physiological Sciences spent three months in Bangalore, India, in 1969. A member of the class of 1953, he served as a consultant in anatomy under the University of Tennessee's U.S. Agency for International Development contract at Mysore University of Agricultural Sciences. He participated in a one-week seminar on general research methods in agriculture with representatives from several agricultural universities from southern India. He was a member of a review team of the research projects at Mysore and held a short course three mornings a week for the faculty in anatomy, discussing histological techniques in anatomical research. Dr. Venable reviewed the syllabi of the anatomy courses and started two junior faculty members on research projects on the reproductive system of water buffalo.

The spring of 1969 was clouded with increasing rumblings of a serious difference between the dean and his departmental administrators. The dean's plan for reorganization of the college departments was seen as being too ambitious and overburdened with hierarchy for a college that had to survive on a very limited budget. It had become evident for several months that there was a totally different dynasty emerging which would eventually end unhappily. A serious division among the faculty developed, and several left for other institutions. The most severely affected was the Department of Physiological Sciences which lost seven faculty members. The department had built up a tremendous national reputation and received high praise in the American Veterinary Medical Association Council on Education's recent report. The department's former high stature would be difficult to regain.

Continuous efforts to solve the constant and ever increasing financial problems included a meeting between top OSU administrators and the college faculty. Finally on Memorial Day, 1969, President Kamm met with the faculty and announced that the dean had resigned.

The crucial problem facing the university administration following Dean Reinhard's resignation was the selection of an acting dean. There were very few faculty members who had not taken sides during the unfortunate happenings of the past year. However, Dr. William E. Brock was

Karl R. Reinhard, D.V.M., Ph.D.

Dr. Karl R. Reinhard was born at Coplay, Pennsylvania, in 1916. He received the M.S. degree from Pennsylvania State College (now University) in 1940, the D.V.M. degree from Cornell University in 1949, and the Ph.D. degree from Cornell University in 1950.

Dr. Reinhard was an assistant in animal pathology research, Department of Animal Pathology, Pennsylvania State College, 1939 to 1941, when he enlisted in the U.S. Army and was in charge of field sanitation and clinical laboratory, 28th Surgical (Field) Hospital, 1941-42. Later, as a warrant officer, he was a bacteriologist in the 3rd Medical Field Laboratory. He served in the southwest Pacific area, Australia, New Guinea, and the Philippines. Dr. Reinhard married the former Janet E. Correll in 1945. They have two sons and a daughter. He was a professor of bacteriology, Department of Animal Pathology, Kentucky Agricultural Experiment Station, Lexington, 1950-51.

In 1951 Dr. Reinhard was appointed a veterinary officer in the United States Public Health Service. His duties included head, Leptospirosis Unit, Rocky Mountain Laboratory, 1951-54; chief, Infectious Disease Program, Arctic Health Research Center, 1954-60; executive secretary General Medicine Study Section RGRB, Division of Research Grants, NIH, 1960-63; deputy chief, Research Grants Review Branch, Division of Research Grants, NIH, 1963; assistant to the chief, Division of Research Grants, NIH, 1963-67, and chief, Program Evaluation, Division of Indian Health, U. S. Public Health Service, 1967-68. He was dean of the College of Veterinary Medicine at Oklahoma State University, 1968-69. He returned to the U.S. Public Service in Arizona after his deanship.

Dr. Reinhard was a member of Phi Kappa Phi, Sigma Xi, Phi Zeta, American Society for Microbiology, American Public Health Association, Association of Military Surgeons of the U.S., and the AVMA. He was an adult adviser in youth activities, particularly the Boy Scouts.

Dr. Reinhard's scientific interests were animal and human infectious diseases, and environmental factors in epizootology and epidemiology; scientific research management and government-university relationships in science administration. He published numerous papers on these subjects.

one individual who was never prone to extracurricular activities in such a situation.

Dr. Brock had no aspirations for the high office, but in the interest of the college he accepted President Kamm's invitation to become acting dean effective June 1.

In order to obtain an outside opinion of the facilities and operation of the college, President Kamm invited Dr. William Armistead, dean of the College of Veterinary Medicine, Michigan State University, to visit the campus in June 1969 and advise him on the present state of the college. Following up on the Council on Education's recommendation, Dr. Kamm had already requested the State Board of Regents for Higher Education to make a study of the College of Veterinary Medicine and establish guidelines for the further development of veterinary medical education. The study commenced in September 1969. A plan of procedure was adopted, to be implemented by their research staff in collaboration with an advisory committee from Oklahoma State University and a consultant recommended by the American Veterinary Medical Association Council on Education.[3]

Dean Brock forwarded a progress report to the American Veterinary Medical Association Council on Education in November 1969 as had been requested in the report following their visit of November 1968. He discussed each of the council's recommendations. Regarding internal communications he stated, "Administration in the college has been reestablished as a function primarily of the department heads." The faculty had organized itself under a charter "to provide a forum for discussion of common problems and to develop a consensus of opinion that can be expressed to the administration." Dean Brock revealed that the average salary in all ranks of the college faculty was above the average for American colleges.[4]

Dean Brock indicated that during the past year the third floor of the north wing ("crow's nest," a home for students) had been remodeled to provide six additional offices containing 1,360 net square feet of floor space for the Department of Parasitology and Public Health and provided information on proposed building programs which would be in three phases. He also stated the new curriculum was being evaluated and steps initiated to obtain a diagnostic laboratory.

The search committee for a new dean had been working diligently. Late in the fall they recommended that Dr. W. E. Brock be appointed. His appointment was approved by the Board of Regents during their meeting on January 9, 1970.

Because of their concern about the rising cost of veterinary medical education and their loyalty to their alma mater, Dr. Robert D. Perkins, Dr. William C. Randle, and Dr. Truman L. Hudson founded the Stephens County Veterinary Students Scholarship Trust on January 3, 1970, to grant financial aid to deserving students engaged in the study of veterinary medicine. This dedicated group of veterinarians in southern Oklahoma were joined later by Dr. Robert M. Cross, Dr. J. Keith Flanagan, Dr. Lyndon Graf, Dr. John D. Minson, and Dr. Terry Wood. Participating veterinary clinics located in Stephens County would not charge a fee for euthanasia of animals but instead would advise clients that they could make a voluntary contribution to the trust. To date (1985) the trustees have contributed over $10,000 to students in financial need.

The public relations committee of the student chapter started a program of professional promotion in 1970. This included a slide and film series and the sponsoring of monthly pet clinics to teach proper management, care, and handling of pets. The clinics were conducted by third- and fourth-year students in association with local practitioners and college clinicians. Students visited civic and youth clubs to present film and slide programs. Articles on pet care and general health problems were prepared for the news media.

A new decade is often heralded by a quest for new and exciting horizons. It is also a time for soul searching on where we are and where we are heading. Such was the case at Oklahoma State University. President Robert Kamm felt that the university, on the threshold of the seventies, was experiencing dynamic but solid change! Computers and closed circuit television had taken their places beside blackboards and laboratory tables. A university needs a passion for human betterment and a persistent faith in the potential and power of the human mind to solve problems and to accomplish that which is good and noble.

The adopted theme for the seventies was "Quest for Academic Excellence." There was a major change in teaching methods with the establishment of the OSU Institute for Effective Teaching. Each college was encouraged to set up its own learning resources center where students and faculty could review in-depth presentations on a wide range of subjects on tape and/or slides at their own pace.

The college received a grant from the Department of Health, Education, and Welfare in the amount of $102,000 on July 1, 1970. The funds enabled the establishment of a learning resources center at the college and the purchase of audiovisual equipment. There was a lot of institutional emphasis on the use of closed circuit television for teaching purposes. The State Board of Regents for Higher Education established an educational television network.

The Oklahoma State University Veterinary Medical Alumni Association held its first meeting during the Oklahoma Veterinary Medical Association convention in Oklahoma City on February 9, 1970. Dr. Edwin D. Fisher of Winfield, Kansas, class of 1963, was elected president; Dr. Joe Smith of North Little Rock, class of 1967, was elected vice president; and Dr. Dan E. Goodwin of Stillwater, class of 1955, was elected secretary. All were elected by a mail ballot earlier, coordinated by Dr. A. L. Malle, extension veterinarian. It was the consensus of those present that the association should exist as a loosely-knit group, allied with the College of Veterinary Medicine and concerned primarily with the development of school pride and spirit. They felt there was no need for either a constitution or dues.[5]

The long awaited report requested by the State Regents for Higher Education was published in September 1970. It stated that the college had limited resources relative to the broad mission normally undertaken by veterinary colleges. The college had failed to develop communication, cooperation, and coordination between its departments and other OSU academic units enabling it to use resources in an efficient manner. A disparity existed between the need for veterinary medical personnel in Oklahoma and the kind and number of students being trained. A budgeting procedure programmed in terms of the mission to be accomplished was lacking. Inadequate facilities due to improper design, lack of comprehensive planning, and poor utilization permeated the entire college.[6]

The report included some nineteen recommendations including those related to the functions and goals of the college, administrative considerations, educational programs, enrollment and degrees, faculty needs, facility requirements, and financial needs. The Board of Regents was encouraged to develop a statement of functions of the college and adopt the American Veterinary Medical Association Council on Education's standards. The report recommended increased cooperation regarding instruction, research, and the utilization of space and equipment, the addition of instruction in laboratory animal care, and the establishment of a centralized data collection and reporting operation and a learning resources center. The curriculum should continue to be reviewed and updated; residency, internship, and continuing education programs strengthened and bachelor level training for veterinary technicians added. There were several recommendations to improve research opportunities, teaching load, and salaries for the faculty.

The report called for facilities expansion with top priority to be given to the construction of a teaching hospital, renovation of present facilities and the acquisition of new equipment, and the construction of a diagnostic laboratory. The State Regents for Higher Education were encouraged to follow-up on the recommendations to ensure their fulfillment.

Enrollment in the entering freshman class in 1969-70 was forty-eight students and had been likewise for four years. The study by the State Regents for Higher Education reported that about two-thirds of the graduates left the state. In order to meet the need for veterinary professionals in the future, the report recommended that more Oklahoma and minority

Dr. E. W. Tucker, president of the American Veterinary Medical Association, "greets" one of the displays in the anatomy section of Open House. He is accompanied by Dr. Bill Clay *(left)* and John B. Renfro, 1971 president of the Student Chapter, American Veterinary Medical Association.

students should be admitted, but the size of the class should not be increased.

Under the Public Health Service Act 1970, National Institutes of Health, health manpower capitation grants were made available to health profession colleges. One provision was that in order to receive a grant, the number of first-year students enrolled on October 12, 1972, and October 15 of each succeeding year had to exceed the number enrolled in October 1970 by 10 percent, if not more than 100, or by 5 percent, or ten students, whichever was greater, if more than 100.

The enrollment in 1971 was increased by five students in order to obtain this formula grant, and to 60 students in 1972. A total of $102,000 in grant funds were received. Dean Brock obtained the approval of the State Regents for Higher Education for this increase and subsequent increases. These increases were not unexpected; the curriculum changes adopted by the faculty in 1966 called for seventy-two students per class, provided space and funds would be available.

The pain and frustration of implementing the complex and innovative curriculum and schedule (especially its clinical phase) characterized the 1970s. When Dean Holm resigned, administrative leadership was lost in the implementation process. The new curriculum and schedule did not receive sufficient administrative support and guidance to deal with the problems. Committee members changed frequently.

Initially the fourth-year calendar of the new schedule was divided into six eight-week periods with the class sectioned, two one-week special weeks with the entire class present, and vacation during Thanksgiving and Christmas. In the mid-70s the sectioned activities were changed to eight six-week periods. The sectioned activities of the class of 1972 were scheduled from March 10, 1971, to March 9, 1972, but it was soon learned that the students lacked sufficient medicine and disease courses to fulfill adequately their preceptorship and clinic missions. In addition, the calendar called for all the fourth-year students to be on campus for the last eight weeks in a concentrated lecture series, much of it in public health, meat inspection, and departmental conference courses. This turned out to be a disaster. After going through the clinical and the preceptorship programs, the students did not accept the challenge of disciplining themselves to the lecture and conference courses.

The committee adjusted this type of calendar for the 1973 class by limiting the lecture and conference courses to the last four weeks before graduation. Motivation of fourth- year students during this last month continued to be a problem; at the end of the decade sectioned activity was scheduled to run from May 1 through the following month of April.

A great deal of experimentation in the daily scheduling of the clinic program as to an afternoon as compared to a morning activity or certain combinations of both occurred. The lecture courses were adjusted almost yearly. By 1975, there was a major scheduling change. Regular clinic hours had been 1:00-5:00 p.m., Monday through Friday. Now clinics were from 7:30 a.m. to 12:30 p.m. Lecture classes were held in the afternoon. The classroom sleep factor increased considerably! Limited changes in the preclinical program were made to adjust the overall program.

In the late sixties colleges on campus had progressed with plans to eliminate Saturday classes. Until this time, faculty, staff, and students reported for work and classes on Saturday morning. The College of Veterinary Medicine reacted to this process. By 1970 there were no Saturday classes in the non-clinic courses, but the Saturday morning clinic classes continued to meet until 1975. A restricted number of Saturday lectures in nutrition for third-year students continued to be scheduled until the late seventies, but these were linked to continuing education programs.

A feature of the new curriculum was the introduction of Special Week, a time when intensive courses by well-known, off campus speakers would be offered. These in-depth lectures on various specialties were scheduled during the spring and fall semesters. Topics for the 1971 sessions were neurology and ophthalmology.

Dr. Duane Peterson, the "father" of the new curriculum, became a regents service professor in 1971. Appointment to this position is given to administrators who have rendered meritorious service to the university over many years and desire to be relieved of administrative duties and return to resident instruction, extension, or research positions. He would continue to devote countless hours on the schedule for the new curriculum in addition to the teaching of veterinary anatomy. Dr. Peterson was named OSU Teacher of the Year for 1971 at the OSU Alumni Banquet in May.

In an effort to improve the administrative structure of the college, the Department of Anatomy was amalgamated with the Department of Physiology and Pharmacology. Dr. John Venable was appointed head of the new Department of Physiological Sciences, effective January 1, 1971. Dr. Sidney Ewing had served as acting head of the physiology department since Dr. McDonald left in September 1969.

In May 1971, Dr. Eric Williams, who had represented the college on the OSU Faculty Council since 1969, became chairman for 1971-72. He was elected vice-chairman in 1970. It was the first time for a representative from veterinary medicine to serve in the highest elected office at OSU. It was also the first time for the designation "chairman" to be applied to the office under the revised by-laws. Hitherto, the president of the university was the chairman, and the faculty officer was vice-chairman.

Another important landmark was established when the OSU faculty officers met for lunch with their counterparts from the University of Oklahoma Faculty Senate to discuss mutual problems in higher education. It was the "inauguration" of regular once-a-semester meetings which have been held ever since. A few years later, former officers of the OSU Faculty Council initiated a luncheon meeting once a semester with the current officers at OSU. The group came to be known as the House of Lords!

There have been times throughout the annals of history when the ravages of a new and deadly disease have threatened man and beast. In 1971 an outbreak of Venezuelan equine encephalomyelitis was reported in Texas. More than 94 percent of the horses in nineteen states, totaling over 2.8 million, were vaccinated at government expense. Ninety-nine percent (227,054) of the horse population in Oklahoma were vaccinated between July 21 and August 30, 1971. No cases of the disease occurred in Oklahoma. There were no further confirmed cases in the United States, but the disease did strike areas of northwestern Mexico during the summer and early fall of 1972.[7]

A year later, there would be great joy and relief for the Oklahoma livestock industry. After years of constant vigil and extensive vaccination programs that had begun under Dr. L. L. Lewis and Dr. C. H. McElroy, the state was declared to be free of hog cholera.

In the fall of 1971 Dr. Jonathan D. Friend, Department of Veterinary Anatomy, accepted an invitation from Dr. D. M. Trotter, dean of the College of Veterinary Medicine, Kansas State University, to undertake a teaching assignment at the College of Veterinary Medicine, Ahmadu Bello University, near Zaria, Nigeria, Africa. The college was established in 1964. The college was sponsored by the U.S. International Agricultural Programs and administered through the Kansas State University College of Veterinary Medicine.

For the first three months of 1971, Dr. Friend taught gross anatomy to the first-year veterinary medicine students and applied anatomy to third-year students. Dr. Friend recently recalled the curriculum was very similar to that in the United States, but the European system of external examiners was used. The students, the majority of whom were from Nigeria and the remainder from other African nations, were eager to learn with most of them more than appreciative of the help they received from visiting professors. Nigeria's heterogenous population had over 240 distinct languages, but English was the official language.[8]

The quest for academic excellence continued. A faculty workshop to examine the terminal behavioral objectives for the graduating veterinary student was organized by the college committee on educational innovation with Dr. Billy Ward as chairman. Four student class representatives also attended the workshop held at Western Hills Lodge on November 21-22, 1971. The college faculty had already participated in workshops for effective teaching sponsored by OSU.

After several months of discussion, the Veterinary Council approved the designation of a pass-fail grading system for clinic courses effective January 1, 1972. Outstanding students were to receive a ''Certificate of Distinction in Clinic Performance'' at the Annual Awards Banquet. On January 1, 1984, a pass-fail grading policy was extended to special conference courses.[9]

The American Veterinary Medical Association Council on Education returned on November 15-17, 1971. Visits are usually made every five years, but if a new dean takes over or if there are serious academic problems, visits may be more frequent.

The AVMA Council on Education report, received in February 1972, showed remarkable agreement with the deficiencies noted in the recent State Regents for Higher Education study. Both reports placed top priority on the need for a teaching hospital. The Council on Education report also mentioned a lack of faculty and staff, lack of laboratory animal medicine teaching program, lack of support for extension and continuing education, lack of a diagnostic laboratory, and lack of sufficient number of books added yearly to the library. The college was continued on confidential probation status.

On a lighter note, it was reported at a veterinary council meeting that the contract for exterminating work was successful—goodbye cockroaches for now—but not for long!

At the Annual Awards Banquet on April 29, 1972, President Kamm announced the establishment of the Dr. J. Wiley and Virginia C. Wolfe Trust Fund. The fund would provide grants for professional development to faculty members in the College of Veterinary Medicine who had served the college for at least three years and for whom no alternate funds were available. Mrs. Wolfe had conceived the idea of the trust fund several years earlier during a trip to Europe.

Another highlight of the awards banquet was the presentation of the first Barber and Lundberg Award to a third-year student. The student was selected for outstanding leadership, scholarship, and clinical ability. Dr. L. B. Barber, a veterinarian, and Mr. Ellis Lundberg established a pharmaceutical company in Oklahoma City. The award was renamed the L. B. Barber and F. Ellis Lundberg Memorial Award in 1974.

There was a major change in the college structure on July 1, 1972, involving Dr. Tennille and Dr. Wolfe who had been "pillars" of strength throughout the young college's evolution.

Dr. Newton B. Tennille, who had long reigned over his dynasty in radiology and student surgery, was given medical disability leave. Under the dour physical facade of a man who "roared" his message across the classroom, there was a professional who cared a lot for his students.

Dr. J. Wiley Wolfe and President Robert B. Kamm review the details of the Dr. J. Wiley and Virginia C. Wolfe Trust Fund established in 1972.

Dr. J. Wiley Wolfe relinquished his position as head, Department of Medicine and Surgery, and assumed duties as the first class scheduling officer. He also directed the preceptorship program. Dr. Lester Johnson became acting head of the department.

The task ahead was clear. Studies by the American Veterinary Medical Association Council on Education and the State Regents for Higher Education would provide the road map for the future. Dean Brock and his colleagues set about the monumental task of obtaining much needed facilities, extra faculty and staff, and better appropriations from the state legislature. The fruits of their hard work would soon be harvested.

Endnotes

1. Dr. G. Poppenseik to President R. B. Kamm, 1968, Archives, College of Veterinary Medicine.

2. "American Veterinary Medical Association Council on Education Report, January 1969," Archives, College of Veterinary Medicine.

3. The committee consisted of Vice President J. H. Boggs, Dean W. E. Brock, Dr. John Venable, and Dr. William R. Pritchard, dean, School of Veterinary Medicine, University of California, Davis.

4. "Report to Council on Education, American Veterinary Medical Association, from College of Veterinary Medicine, Oklahoma State University, November 1969," Archives, College of Veterinary Medicine.

5. Dan E. Goodwin, "A Letter to the Alumni," *Oklahoma Veterinarian,* vol. 22, no. 2 (April 1970), p. 30.

6. *Study of the College of Veterinary Medicine, Oklahoma State University,* prepared by Larry K. Hayes (Oklahoma City: Oklahoma State Regents for Higher Education, September 1970).

7. "Venezuelan Equine Encephalomyelitis," *Oklahoma Veterinarian,* vol. 25, no. 3 (July 1973), pp. 10-11.

8. Author's personal communication with Dr. J. D. Friend, 1985.

9. Veterinary Administrative Council Minutes, September 15, 1971, Archives, College of Veterinary Medicine.

12 Great Expectations

Climb every mountain, ford every stream, follow every rainbow, till you find your dream.

Sound of Music

The year 1972 became a great landmark for veterinarians worldwide. James Alfred Wight, a veterinarian practicing in the Yorkshire dales of England, published his first book, *All Creatures Great and Small,* in the United States. In a simple, direct, and engaging manner, under the pen name of James Herriot, he wrote a brilliant, honest, lucid, day-by-day-and-night exposition of the triumphs and despairing moments of veterinary practice in the early 1940s. His writings touched the hearts of animal lovers everywhere. Almost every youngster wanted to be a veterinarian, and applications for admission to veterinary schools soared. Dr. Wight wrote other books which also became best sellers.[1]

When the 1972 fall semester opened, some much needed improvements had already taken place and others would follow. The new learning resources center was well equipped and now even carpeted. It had 1,100 feet of space for ten audiovisual carrels and two conference rooms. The auditorium had undergone a complete facelift—out went the chairs on the cement floors and in came the carpet and 270 new permanently mounted seats (now the students could sleep in comfort!). A modern and sophisticated audiovisual system was installed with a back-lighted projection screen and booth which could be operated from the podium. TV monitors were installed which could relay audio-video material from the learning resources center upstairs or from the university television center. The north wing, comprising the auditorium, northwest classroom, and the histology/pathology laboratory were air-conditioned. The remodeling also provided space for a student lounge and new student chapter office.

This plush facility was a far cry from the early days when surgery classes were held in the auditorium. There was also a more timely, nostalgic note—no longer would "Luminous Lizzie," in all her splendor, be brought into the classroom for a live demonstration during lectures on bovine gastroenterology! "Luminous Lizzie," and likewise her predecessor "Daffodil," named after the national flower of Wales, was a Guernsey cow with her left side painted to delineate the topographical anatomy of the chest, diaphragm, and fore-stomach. Her successor is used for teaching clinical techniques.

A large area of the basement was not completed when the southwest wing was built in the mid-sixties. In the fall of 1972 and the following spring, an additional 7,000 square feet of space was provided and assigned to the Department of Parasitology and Public Health.

The urgent need for safer and better equipped facilities in the large animal clinic was now reaching almost a panic stage. It was, therefore, decided to design a cattle handling facility with 1,600 square feet of floor space and an attached, covered holding and recovery pens area. A plan for a very practical, safe unit was prepared with special attention to the easy removal of dead animals by an overhead mechanical hydraulic sys-

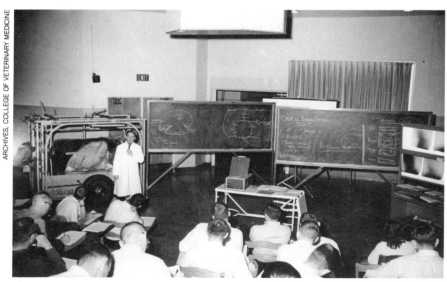

In 1972 the auditorium was renovated, and lectures on the bovine digestive tract given by Dr. Eric Williams and his assistant "Luminous Lizzie," a Guernsey cow, became a part of the history of the sixties.

tem. The cost was estimated at about $100,000. Insufficient funds were available and, unfortunately, the decision was made to build only half of it. A treatment area, small pharmacy/laboratory, equipment storage room, and a seminar room would cost about $40,000. Eventually, enough money was "scraped together" to add the covered holding and recovery pens.

The original well-planned design with the two sections on the same ground level was scrapped. A new committee and a different builder went to work. The end result was that in the interest of expediency, and due to great pressure from higher authorities to provide some sort of improved facilities, the college ended up with a totally inadequate split-level cattle facility to the chagrin of the clinicians who had spent hours designing a safe and practical building. At that time, however, the chances of obtaining a modern teaching hospital were extremely remote. The cattle facility did serve a good purpose for many years and is now used as a clinical techniques teaching and research unit.

Personnel were also changing. Dr. Andrew Monlux gave up his administrative duties as head of the Department of Pathology on October 1, 1972, in order to devote more time to teaching and cancer research. In recognition of his excellent research activities, he was appointed a regents professor by the Board of Regents. He was succeeded as acting head by Dr. James B. Corcoran, a long-time member of the department. On July 1, 1975, Dr. David C. Dodd became the head of the Department of Veterinary Pathology. A native of Australia, he had received the B.V.Sc. from the University of Sydney and had been a professor of pathology and head of the section of large animal pathology at the School of Veterinary Medicine, University of Pennsylvania, before coming to OSU.

Dr. Sidney A. Ewing left to become dean of the College of Veterinary Medicine, University of Minnesota, effective December 1972. Dr. Helen Jordan became the acting head of the Department of Parasitology and Public Health. Dr. Merwin L. Frey became head in the fall of 1973. A 1956 Kansas State University graduate, he was a professor at the Veterinary Medical Research Institute, Iowa State University, where he conducted research on respiratory diseases in cattle and poultry. In September 1975 the name of the department changed to the Department of Veterinary Parasitology, Microbiology and Public Health.

Dr. Eric Williams was appointed to replace Dr. J. Wiley Wolfe, who would be retiring soon as the scheduling officer. He moved into the dean's office on a part-time basis so that he could still continue to teach in the large animal clinic. He often remarked, "When I get enough of the 'bull' upstairs, I can go back to the bulls downstairs!"

Dr. J. Wiley Wolfe served as program chairman for the 55th Annual Meeting of the Southern Veterinary Medical Association held in Tulsa

Dr. David C. Dodd, a native of Australia, became head of the Department of Veterinary Pathology in 1975.

in October 1972. It was only the second time the meeting had been held in Oklahoma.

Dr. Lester Johnson became interim head, Department of Medicine and Surgery when Dr. J. Wiley Wolfe stepped down in 1972. When Dr. Johnson announced that he would not be a candidate for the position, a nationwide search was conducted. In February 1974 the Board of Regents appointed Dr. Fayne H. Oberst as head of the department and director of clinics effective July 1. Dr. Oberst graduated from Kansas State University in 1943. He held teaching assignments there and at the University of Missouri, and most recently was chairman of the Department of Large Animal Surgery and Medicine at Michigan State University.

In the fall of 1972 a special "people emphasis" program, underscoring the importance of each individual person on campus, was initiated on the campus of Oklahoma State University. In a memorandum to the faculty and staff, President Kamm expressed his hope that everyone at OSU—students, faculty, and staff—would join hands in a project called "Emphasis '72-'73—PEOPLE."

When Dean Brock prepared a progress report for the American Veterinary Medical Association Council on Education in October, he covered the budget, personnel, students, curriculum, and physical facilities. Many changes were taking place. From fiscal year 1972 to 1973, the teaching hospital budget had been increased by about $60,000 and the library was allocated $10,000 additional funds. College staffing had increased from 58 to 64.

After several weeks of study by various departments and committees, the Veterinary Council approved a revision of the "Mission, Goals, and Objectives" of the college. The mission stated: "In support of the mission of Oklahoma State University, the mission of the College of Veterinary Medicine is to preserve and transmit the art and science of veterinary medicine; to discover and examine critically medical knowledge of animals, including that related to the health and welfare of human beings."[2]

Between 1969 and 1970, the U.S. Department of Health, Education and Welfare had charged that ten states, including Oklahoma, were operating segregated systems of higher education in violation of Title VI of the Civil Rights Act of 1964. The chancellor and State Regents for Higher Education denied this allegation. In 1970, a class action lawsuit was filed on behalf of Kenneth Adams, a Mississippi school child, and other minority children seeking denial of federal education money to states practicing discrimination in their educational institutions. Judge Pratt of the U.S. District Court for the District of Columbia ruled in Adams' favor, and Oklahoma became one of six "Adams" case states.

After an unsuccessful appeal of Judge Pratt's ruling and rejection of earlier desegregation plans, Oklahoma submitted in 1978 a five-year plan

Dr. Fayne H. Oberst became head of the Department of Medicine and Surgery and director of clinics in 1974. He retired in 1984.

for desegregation that was acceptable to the U.S. Department of Health and Human Services and the U.S. District Court.

In 1973 at Oklahoma State University, Dr. Pauline Kopecky was appointed director of affirmative action with responsibility directly to the president of the university. The dean of each college appointed a coordinator of affirmative action with responsibility for monitoring and assisting in implementation of equal opportunity/affirmative action practices. Dr. Eric Williams was the first coordinator of affirmative action for the College of Veterinary Medicine. He was succeeded in 1979 by Dr. Don Holmes.

The College of Veterinary Medicine has attained its goals for employment of racial minorities and females. Dr. Helen E. Jordan, a native of Virginia and a graduate of the University of Georgia, had joined the Department of Veterinary Parasitology and Public Health in September 1969. She became the first female tenured professor at the college.

The college has been less successful in the recruitment of racial minorities, particularly black students. Despite earnest recruitment by many individuals and the availability of financial incentives for minority students, only three black students have graduated from the College of Veterinary Medicine, and only one black student was enrolled in the D.V.M. program. As part of the effort to attract minority students, a veterinarian in Oklahoma City, Dr. George Cooper, was employed to visit

1980 AESCULAPIUS

Dr. Helen Jordan, who had joined the Department of Veterinary Parasitology and Public Health in 1969, became the first female tenured professor in the College of Veterinary Medicine.

Oklahoma high schools with large minority student enrollment to speak on career opportunities in veterinary medicine. Later, Dr. Frank Roberts, class of 1982, became the minority recruiter.

When Oklahoma's five-year plan expired in 1983, it was replaced by an amended state plan that focused heavily on professional schools. Added inducements in the form of fee waivers and professional study grants for minority student enrollment in professional schools were provided.

Throughout much of the period in which affirmative action policies were being implemented, the College of Veterinary Medicine was fortunate to have Dr. John Montgomery serve as a member of the Board of Regents. Appointed for an eight-year term in 1975, Dr. Montgomery provided guidance, encouragement and an occasional nudge as the college recognized and acted on its social responsibility under affirmative action. Dr. Montgomery had been in general practice in Poteau since 1951.

March 1, 1973, marked the twenty-fifth anniversary of the college, and the highlight of the Open House was a special presentation to Dr. Duane Peterson who gave the first lecture on that memorable morning in 1948. The seventh biennial Open House, held for the first time on Sunday afternoon as well as Saturday, attracted over 2,500 visitors.

By 1972, in keeping with the recommendations made by the State Regents for Higher Education Study of the College of Veterinary Medicine, the college accepted applications only from Oklahoma residents and from North Carolina, West Virginia, Louisiana, Arkansas, and Nebraska.

The State Regents for Higher Education had recommended a more realistic funding for out-of-state students that would include the full cost of the student's education. The contract fee was calculated by dividing the allocation to the college by the number of Oklahoma residents enrolled as veterinary medical students. In accordance with this new policy, the cost for out-of-state students in the fall of 1973 would be $7,340 per student each year.

The cost for contract states, however, had been set by the Southern Regional Education Board at $4,500 per student each year. The Southern Regional Education Board requested delay in the implementation of this policy until 1976. Dean Brock stated that such a delay would destroy the orderly development of proper financing for the college, so OSU withdrew from the board. Thus a program which had prospered for over twenty years was terminated in 1974. The college continued to negotiate contracts directly with individual states at the higher rate.[3]

Homecoming 1973 brought in several alumni and their families for the college reception sponsored by the student auxiliary after the parade. True to form, the much awaited college float was eventually finished

Dr. Duane R. Peterson, who gave the first lecture in the College of Veterinary Medicine, displays a plaque that was presented to him during the 25th anniversary. Also attending the celebration are Mr. Ronald Wallis, president of the Student Chapter, American Veterinary Medical Association; Dean W. E. Brock; Mr. Robert Smith, chairman of the Board of Regents; Robert B. Kamm, president of OSU; Harry Camp, congressman; and Mr. Bill Schaeffer.

at daybreak and went on to win first prize. The theme for 1973 was "Cowboys Make It Happen." The student float for 1974 would not be so fortunate. As the float took to the road at the crack of dawn, it looked as if it had been entered in a regatta! Due to atrocious weather conditions, the parade was cancelled for only the second time in history.

The college was also gaining an excellent reputation for the quality of its instructors and the ever-increasing exciting new procedures that were being performed in the clinics. Because of a strong economy, pet owners were prepared to seek the best available health care.

Over 200 horse owners, breeders, and veterinarians attended the equine management course on November 16-17 which was sponsored by the college, OSU extension, and Oklahoma horse associations. Mr. Jack Anderson, Broken Arrow, presented a check for $1,250, on behalf of himself and Mr. and Mrs. George F. Martin, to initiate the Bent Arrow Ranch Scholarship which would provide one year's tuition for one third-year and one fourth-year student interested in equine practice.

Dr. Jimmie U. Baldwin, class of 1969, also established a scholarship in 1973 in appreciation for his college education. It has been presented each year to a third-year student with selection based on horsemanship and interest in equine practice.

In the College of Veterinary Medicine, the "Venable Plan" was finally adopted after much discussion by several committees and the Veterinary

Dr. John H. Venable became head of the Department of Physiological Sciences, a new department created from a merger of the Department of Anatomy and the Department of Physiology and Pharmacology in January 1971. Dr. Venable conducted extensive research on the development and growth of skeletal muscle by use of the electron microscope.

Council. It was a combined program whereby honor students could achieve an undergraduate, graduate, and veterinary medicine degree within seven years. Approved by the Veterinary Administrative Council on February 12, 1974, the plan seeks to identify and provide special advisement to students who have research potential and allow them to plan their curricula with courses of maximum benefit to the three degrees pursued.

A major relief for freshman students followed the decision to move biochemistry (not exactly a pet subject, except by those "pure of left cerebral hemisphere!"), and some of the microbiology courses into the pre-veterinary curriculum—much to the consternation of those who would have to face this "massive hurdle of the mind" much earlier. Course evaluations were introduced across campus.

The image of the College of Veterinary Medicine, especially from the physical plant aspect, had been of much concern to the Oklahoma Veterinary Medical Association Auxiliary for some time. Eventually they decided to do something about the main lobby. They obtained the services of an interior decorator and an architect. Unfortunately, most of their funds were used in the preliminaries so their great intentions fell through. However, the senior wives gave a frosted plate glass door panel with an Aesculapius at the east entrance to the lobby.

In order to obtain better information about the employment market for veterinarians in Oklahoma and surrounding areas, a questionnaire survey of the 1974 graduating class was conducted one week before graduation by Dr. Bill R. Clay, Department of Physiological Sciences and faculty advisor to the student chapter. It requested information about acquisition of the employment and a description of the new position. The results indicated that, after actively seeking employment for nine months prior to graduation, the majority had acquired their positions by January of their senior year. Most learned of their ultimate place of employment through one of several sources at the College of Veterinary Medicine. The results showed that about 80 percent entered practice, with two-thirds selecting mixed practices. The remaining students entered the military, graduate school, an internship, or other positions. About half of the graduates remained in Oklahoma.[4]

A survey conducted the previous year in 1973 by the Department of Veterinary Parasitology and Public Health had shown that approximately 78 percent of those who graduated between 1961 and 1971 remained in practice. About one-half were still in mixed practice and approximately 40 percent in small animal practice, with the remainder in large animal or other practices. Less than half began their employment in Oklahoma (25 percent were out-of-state students) and several went to the military and advanced education assignments.[5]

Commencement at OSU in May 1974 was a memorable and unique occasion. For the first time the commencement address was given by the President of the United States. On a gorgeous Saturday evening, President Richard Nixon landed by helicopter on the football practice field and proceeded to Lewis Field to join a large crowd of faculty, graduating seniors, families, and friends.

Dr. Thomas R. Thedford, Department of Medicine and Surgery, large animal section, spent a two-year assignment working through Oklahoma State University on a contract with Colorado State University and the Agency for International Development starting in June 1974. He was assigned to the Faculty of Veterinary Medicine at the University of Nairobi in Kenya, Africa. As section leader for the field service unit and a visiting associate professor of medicine and surgery, his responsibilities included the coordination of the field services unit which consisted of three other clinicians and three vehicles. They developed a broad-based clinical training program from this unit since 95 percent of all large animal clinical material was seen in the field. Dr. Thedford also taught a course on infectious diseases of food animals and on clinical pharmacology to the veterinary students and designed and taught a veterinary science course for agriculture students. Dr. Thedford returned to Oklahoma State University in 1976.[6]

Considerable consternation followed the tentative diagnosis of anthrax in a cow brought in for a post-mortem examination in July. Three cows had died suddenly on a ranch in Caddo County. Cultures of blood and spleen were confirmed to be positive for *Bacillus anthracis*. The first outbreak involving more than one animal to occur in Oklahoma since 1952, it was an excellent teaching experience for students and faculty, and a terse reminder that anthrax should always be considered in a case of sudden death.

When Dr. Lewis H. Moe passed away in 1970, a memorial fund was established in appreciation of his long and dedicated service to the profession. On October 3, 1974, the Dr. Lewis H. Moe Lecture Series was inaugurated. The first lecture was presented by Dr. Clifton A. Baile, Applebrook Research Center, West Chester, Pennsylvania, entitled "The Nature of Control Systems of Feed Intake." The Damon Foundation was the co-sponsor for this lecture. The second Lewis H. Moe Lecture was given by Dr. Hilary Koprowski, director of the Wistar Institute, Philadelphia, in March 1975. His subject was "Rabies" on which he was a world authority. The series has now become a highlight in the college calendar and is presented during the spring semester.

The Family Education Rights and Privacy Act of 1974, commonly referred to as the Buckley Amendment, guaranteed rights of privacy to students concerning information about their educational progress as well as other personal information contained in university records. Faculty members thus had a legal obligation to maintain the privacy of student records. Grades could no longer be posted publicly unless the instructor decided to do so on a code system. This amendment had a distinct effect relative to the files of students applying for admission to the college. They were henceforth not available for inspection, other than by the instructors, to anyone including political moguls without the student's written permission.

The college hierarchy, in their infinite wisdom, started the new year by adopting a new title because "Veterinary Council" lacked specificity. This organization composed of department heads and, from time to time, other key administrative personnel was renamed "Administrative Council" and under formal conditions where clarification was needed, it would be stated as the "Veterinary Administrative Council."

Dr. Lester Johnson was installed president of the Oklahoma Veterinary Medical Association at the 60th Annual Convention which was held at the Camelot Inn, Tulsa, on February 8-11, 1975.

The ever-mounting cost of textbooks and surgical instruments resulted in the establishment in April 1975 of OVES (Oklahoma Veterinary Educational Supply, Inc.), a not-for-profit corporation. Lawrence P. Ruhr, class of 1976, became the first president; David C. Zoltner, class of 1976, secretary; and Dr. Thomas C. Randolph, faculty adviser. The students launched their own off-campus bookstore, including surgical instruments, which proved of great benefit to the students and an indirect source of financial support for the student chapter.

Discontent had been growing over the years with the format of commencement exercises. There was a loss of identity for the individual student and the whole affair had become a "five ring circus." The College of Engineering had already initiated its own ceremony in addition to the all-university affair. Finally the College of Veterinary Medicine was permitted to plan its own, so, on the Saturday afternoon of May 10, in the beautiful setting of the Seretean Center for the Performing Arts surrounded by abundant fragrant honeysuckle, the first annual college convocation was held. Family and friends of the class of 1975 joined the faculty to honor the graduates.

To the stirring strains of the famous triumphal march from the opera *Aida*, Dean William E. Brock, Vice President James H. Boggs, and twenty-seven members of the veterinary medicine faculty in academic regalia, filed into the theater followed by the honorees. Dr. Brock gave the salutatory address.

A reception hosted by the Vetceteras, the organization for spouses of faculty members of the College of Veterinary Medicine, immediately afterwards was a delightful contribution to a truly memorable occasion with a lot of class.

As the class of 1975 graduated, a furor erupted with the announcement of the new freshman class. Certain lawmakers whose favorite "local boy" had not been admitted expressed much displeasure. Dean Brock and a faculty colleague journeyed to the state capitol to face a shower of abuse from leading legislators. As a result, the college was commanded to accept five more students, including the one at the center of the furor. Hence, the class size increased to sixty-five. The scope of the college admissions committee was broadened to include practicing veterinarians. Such action prevented the introduction of a bill in the next session of the legislature regarding the membership of the admissions committee.[7]

The State Regents for Higher Education approved a cut from 25 percent to 10 percent of out-of-state students to be admitted. The beginning class of 1976 had six such students. Pre-veterinary medicine academic requirements are always under constant review. In 1975 the State Regents also approved an increase in the minimum grade point average for future applicants from 2.5 to 2.8 in the required subjects.

For several months, the college administration, along with all the other colleges, had been gathering information for a visit of representatives from the North Central Association for Colleges and Universities for the ten-year accreditation review in August.

The North Central Association for Colleges and Universities was formed in 1895 at Northwestern University by thirty-six school, college, and university administrators from seven midwestern states. The constitution of the association stated that the North Central Association's object would be to establish close relations between the colleges and secondary schools of the region.

Within a very short time, the desire to improve articulation between secondary schools and colleges led to extensive examination of the quality of education at both levels; and that led to the accreditation of secondary schools and, later, colleges and universities.

Today, the association serves colleges and schools in nineteen states—Arizona, Arkansas, Colorado, Illinois, Indiana, Iowa, Kansas, Michigan, Minnesota, Missouri, Nebraska, New Mexico, North Dakota, Ohio, Oklahoma, South Dakota, West Virginia, Wisconsin, and Wyoming—and the American dependents' schools operated overseas for the children of American military and civilian personnel.

The college self study report prepared for the North Central Association highlighted program priorities developed on the basis of the degrees awarded and the people served by them. Programs to receive additional resources were the professional (D.V.M.) degree, research, and residency. Programs to receive the same level of support were the graduate degree, service teaching, extension and continuing education, and faculty development. Programs to be allocated less or phased out were the intern and diagnostic service.[8]

The OSU Office of Academic Affairs commented on the report: "It may be said, in looking at the program, that the college is not proposing any unusual change in the next few years, as one gets the idea that the program priorities in the college are such that only small reallocation of resources may be expected in any of these areas. This may well be the direction which the college should follow, however, it would appear . . . that a more positive statement concerning whether significant change is envisioned should be made." The statement went on: "One of the big problems. . . is the recruitment and retention of a good faculty in this college."[9]

The report of the North Central Association, received a few months later, contained an evaluation of the College of Veterinary Medicine and stated: "This college has a unique history. It was initiated with partial facilities and only the nucleus of a faculty. There was an understood commitment for a subsequent phased construction program and the acquisition of full staffing required for a complete and fully accredited institution. Failure to fulfill these commitments has meant operating with a very small faculty in improvised and unsuitable quarters. The faculty does not include the specialists required by an acceptable educational program. The salary level is at about the mean of the veterinary colleges in the nation. Quality faculty members have been regularly recruited away by other institutions. The faculty/student ratio is close to the average for U.S. vet schools, however.

"The completion of the Diagnostic Laboratory and the apparent funding for the construction of a modern clinic building is a major accomplishment. The stage is now set for a realization of the long awaited potential of the college. The remaining critical and key requirement is the establishment of a salary scale adequate to attract and retain a quality faculty. Since the College does not have a long and prestigious history, it must be prepared either to pay top salaries or compromise with mediocre personnel. The University administration can be most supportive by understanding that in veterinary medical education salaries are high in comparison to most disciplines and that the training and salaries will most closely parallel those of faculties in colleges of human medicine."[10]

Dedication of the Oklahoma Animal Disease Diagnostic Laboratory on a glorious Saturday morning, October 18, 1975, was a milestone for veterinary science in Oklahoma and the College of Veterinary Medicine. The college and university hardly had time to rest from the celebration. The entire university, in tune with the whole nation, was getting geared up for a huge birthday that would last a year long—1976.

Endnotes

1. James Herriot's other books were *All Things Bright and Beautiful* (1973), *All Things Wise and Wonderful* (1976), *The Lord God Made Them All* (1981), *James Herriot's Yorkshire* (1979), and *The Best of James Herriot* (1982).

2. "Mission, Goals, and Objectives: College of Veterinary Medicine, Oklahoma State University," 18 April 1973; revised 6 November 1973, Archives, College of Veterinary Medicine.

3. Comprehensive Health Manpower Training Act of 1971 (P.L.92-157); Edwin C. Godbold, Southern Regional Education Board to Dr. James J. Hudson, University of Arkansas, August 1973, with copies to Dean Brock and Vice President Boggs, OSU, Correspondence File, Admissions Files, Office of Coordinator of Admissions, College of Veterinary Medicine.

4. B. R. Clay, "A Profile of New Position Acquisitions by the 1974 Graduating Class College of Veterinary Medicine, Oklahoma State University," *Oklahoma Veterinarian,* vol. 26, no. 4 (October 1974), pp. 149-151.

5. "Data Collected from Graduates of the Oklahoma State University College of Veterinary Medicine, Department of Veterinary Parasitology and Public Health," *Oklahoma Veterinarian,* vol. 25, no. 2 (April 1973), p. 35.

6. Author's personal communication with Dr. Thomas R. Thedford, 1985.

7. Veterinary Administrative Council Minutes, 18 November 1975, Archives, College of Veterinary Medicine.

8. "College of Veterinary Medicine: Self Study 1975," Archives, College of Veterinary Medicine.

9. "College of Veterinary Medicine: Self Study 1975."

10. "Report of a Visit to Oklahoma State University, Stillwater, Oklahoma. April 5, 6, 7, 1976, for the Commission on Institutions of Higher Education of the North Central Association of Colleges and Schools," Archives, College of Veterinary Medicine.

13 Oklahoma Animal Disease Diagnostic Laboratory

Those who practice the art and science of medicine, whether in connection with the higher or lower animals, are undoubtedly all agreed that the most difficult problem encountered is that of diagnosis.
Dr. Hamilton Kirk

The need for diagnostic help that led settlers at the turn of the century to request assistance from Oklahoma Agricultural and Mechanical College was the same need that led to the establishment of the Oklahoma Animal Disease Diagnostic Laboratory at Oklahoma State University in 1976.

The roots of veterinary medicine in Oklahoma are intertwined with those of Oklahoma A. and M. College. Dr. Lowery L. Lewis, a veterinarian, was appointed to the college staff in 1896. In addition to his teaching, Dr. Lewis found time to study some of the veterinary problems characteristic of the Southwest and especially of the territories.[1]

In the fall of 1923, the zoology section of the Department of Bacteriology and Zoology was given the status of an independent department, and the bacteriology section became the Department of Bacteriology and Veterinary Medicine. Diagnostic services provided by the department were outlined in a report of activities for the four-year period of July 1, 1928, to June 30, 1932. During that time, almost 14,000 services were provided.[2]

There were six staff members in the Department of Bacteriology and Veterinary Medicine in 1932, four of whom had duties in Dr. L. H. Moe's "diagnosis" laboratory. An important function of the veterinary diagnosis laboratory was to provide diagnostic assistance also for human medical problems. Records for the 1934 calendar year show that the laboratory conducted 3580 veterinary tests and 1313 human tests. A summary of the work done in the laboratory during the calendar year 1944 disclosed that veterinary tests had increased to 11,657 (most of the increase was in serology) and that human tests had declined to 226.[3]

With the establishment of the School of Veterinary Medicine in 1948, the potential grew for higher quality diagnostic services. A small frame building covered with tar paper served as the necropsy room for the new school. It was located on an elevated concrete slab immediately south of the west wing of the original veterinary hospital. The south end of the hayloft portion of the west wing of the hospital served as a hematology, clinical pathology, and microbiology laboratory. The fragrant smell of new hay offset the foul odors of some of the laboratory specimens.

A 1950-51 bulletin of the school contained a section entitled "The Veterinary Diagnostic Laboratory." Dr. Charlie Barron was identified as head and Dr. George Short as associate professor in the laboratory which was described as "a service department set up to aid the veterinary profession and the poultry industry of the state in diagnosing diseases. This department is also prepared to aid livestock owners from all sections of the state where veterinary service is not readily available."[4] The laboratory was staffed with a full-time graduate veterinarian assisted by a poultry pathologist and a bacteriologist. Instruction in poultry pathology was offered to veterinary and agriculture students.

The need for diagnostic service increased in Oklahoma as graduates of the veterinary college established practices throughout the state. Although diagnostic laboratory facilities were greatly improved in 1958 and 1964 when the physical plant of the school was expanded, there were still shortages in staff and in funding for maintenance. Having received complaints from persons off-campus, President Oliver Willham sent a letter in 1966 to Dr. A. W. Monlux, head of the Department of Veterinary Pathology, expressing concern about tardy diagnostic services and the need for improvement.[5]

Dr. A. W. Monlux recounted problems of staff and maintenance fund shortages in 1967 to OSU President Robert Kamm: "When I was appointed by Dean Orr in 1956 as head of pathology, the staff of the Department of Veterinary Pathology was increased by one veterinarian and one technician to satisfy the criticism of livestock owners and veterinarians that satisfactory diagnostic service was not being provided. Unfortunately, at this date, and over 11 years later, no further increase in staff or maintenance has been provided."[6]

In 1969, the responsibility for providing diagnostic microbiology service was transferred from the Department of Pathology to the Department of Parasitology and Public Health. The added responsibility was not accompanied by additional funds, and as a consequence the depart-

Diagnostic laboratory facilities at Oklahoma Agricultural and Mechanical College are limited in 1956 to the necropsy building *(figure A)* with laboratory support services located in the south end of the hayloft above the large animal clinic *(figure B)*.

ment absorbed the new activity in its budget for teaching and research.[7]

The veterinary diagnostic services available at Oklahoma State University were usually provided as a sideline by persons whose major responsibilities were teaching and research. This led to frequent complaints from veterinarians and livestock producers that diagnostic service was not accorded the importance that it deserved. It was also apparent in the 1960s that diagnostic service was more than just conducting necropsy examinations; it involved new, sophisticated, and demanding laboratory tests that the College of Veterinary Medicine could not provide at the expense of its teaching and research budget. Thus, the stage was set for a campaign to obtain support to establish a diagnostic laboratory that would provide a full range of modern diagnostic services for Oklahomans. The campaign would be based on a promise to provide service that was accessible and accountable.

In October 1967, the building and facilities committee of the College of Veterinary Medicine sent a letter to Dr. J. Wiley Wolfe, acting dean of the college, regarding a proposal for the establishment of a separate diagnostic facility on the OSU campus near the College of Veterinary Medicine to provide adequate and quality diagnostic service to the livestock industry and veterinary medical practitioners of the state of Oklahoma.[8]

An early supporter of the effort to establish a full-service diagnostic laboratory at OSU was Mr. Fred D. Lowe, a rancher from McAlester. As chairman of the Legislative Committee of the Pittsburg County Cattlemen's Association, Mr. Lowe sought support from Mr. Lewis Munn, president of the Oklahoma Farm Bureau. State Senator Gene Stipe served as the coordinator of the campaign.[9] Mr. Lowe explained to U.S. Congressman Carl Albert in 1968 that the Pittsburgh County Cattlemen's Association was requesting the 1969 Oklahoma legislature to appropriate funds for a livestock diagnostic center in Stillwater and inquired "if it might be possible to get the federal government to participate in the establishment of such a center."[10]

When Dr. Karl Reinhard was appointed dean of the College of Veterinary Medicine in 1968, he joined the effort to establish a diagnostic laboratory at OSU. He sought a commitment of support and dedication of land from the university.[11]

President Kamm concurred "that the concept of a diagnostic laboratory was a sound one and that the teaching and research efforts of the university would receive beneficial side effects from our having such a laboratory in operation. However, I feel that the funds for the construction and a continuing obligation for the operation of a diagnostic laboratory should come from non-higher education funds. This might easily be accomplished through the State Department of Agriculture. I should like, therefore, for you to make it quite clear in discussing this project that the university expects the operation to be a service operation and that funds from non-higher educational sources would be provided for both capital and operational purposes from non-educational areas. In connection with a dedication of land for this purpose, I would, of course, commit the university to such a dedication."[12]

Dean Reinhard collaborated with Mr. James Ballinger, president of the State Board of Agriculture, and Dr. J. H. Brashear, state veterinarian, in planning for a laboratory.[13]

Senator Gene Stipe introduced Senate Bill 123 in the Oklahoma legislature on January 21, 1969, calling for the appropriation of 2.5 million dollars to the State Regents for Higher Education to be used for constructing, furnishing, and equipping a building at OSU to provide an animal diagnostic center for the veterinary college. The bill did not become law.[14]

Efforts to build a laboratory continued in the fall of 1969. Dr. W. E. Brock had succeeded Dr. Reinhard as dean of the college. A planning committee was formed to spearhead the drive for a veterinary diagnostic laboratory. The committee proposed that a sum of money be appropriated to the Department of Agriculture which would let a contract to the College of Veterinary Medicine to hire architects and a director. A detailed budget for $50,500.00 was prepared at that time.[15]

Support from Herb Karner, farm editor of the *Tulsa World*, was productive. On November 17, 1970, Representative J. D. Witt from Vinita introduced House Bills 1001 and 1002 to a legislative committee to appropriate money in order to make detailed plans for a laboratory. Oklahoma State University had tentatively designated a site for the facility directly north of the Veterinary Medicine Building on Farm Road. The Oklahoma Cattlemen's Association passed a resolution at their annual convention in Tulsa on December 4, 1970, strongly supporting the need for a state veterinary diagnostic laboratory for Oklahoma.

Events occurred in 1971 that would finally provide the push needed to bring the laboratory into being. David Hall was sworn in as Governor in January 1971; he had campaigned on a platform that called for the establishment of the laboratory. Billy Ray Gowdy, a strong advocate of the laboratory, was appointed president of the State Board of Agriculture. Representative J. D. Witt's legislative efforts bore fruit in House Bill 1148 which appropriated $25,000 to the State Department of Agriculture for contracting with Oklahoma State University to take such steps as necessary for the detailed planning of an animal disease diagnostic laboratory.[16]

In November 1971, Dr. Dan Goodwin was appointed director with his major responsibilities to provide leadership in planning for building, equipping, and operating the laboratory and to present these plans to the Oklahoma Department of Agriculture and Oklahoma Legislature. The director's administrative responsibility was to the dean of the College of Veterinary Medicine, thence to the OSU vice president for extension, and thence to the OSU president.[17]

Vice President J. C. Evans recommended the prompt organization of a board of advisors to facilitate planning for the laboratory and continuing support. Various animal industry and related organizations were asked to name advisors to serve on the board which met for the first time in February 1972. For the first three years of its existence the board met several times each year. After establishment of the laboratory in 1976, it continues to meet annually to provide guidance and support. Throughout its existence, the board has articulated the strong message that SERVICE must be the laboratory's mission.

Mr. Charles Sanders, associate university architect, was chosen by the university to prepare an initial design for the diagnostic laboratory. Mr. Sanders and Dr. Goodwin organized visits to several successful diagnostic laboratory operations in the United States. Strengths and weaknesses in each laboratory were identified with the goal of incorporating the strengths and avoiding the weaknesses in the Oklahoma laboratory.[18]

Dean Brock appointed a faculty ad hoc committee on the diagnostic laboratory. Dr. A. W. Monlux was named chairman. The committee met several times during 1972 to review the building plans and staffing of the laboratory. In an April 17, 1972, memorandum, Dean Brock asked the committee to make recommendations on developing relationships between the college and the diagnostic laboratory. The committee recommended on May 15, 1972, that professional staff be afforded faculty status, subject to problems related to tenure, an important factor in recruiting a high quality professional staff.[19]

The committee also recommended that the director should receive joint appointment to the faculty, be a voting member of the Veterinary Administrative Council, and be administratively comparable to the position of director of research. Laboratory staff should also be able to participate in academic activities that would not interfere with their service obligations. The Department of Pathology should be responsible for necropsy service at the college.[20]

The schematic design of the building was completed by Mr. Sanders in late spring 1972. The estimated cost of construction was $1,786,912.50. Dr. Goodwin estimated that approximately $300,000 worth of movable equipment would be required to make the laboratory functional, requiring a total of about $2 million. These estimates were discussed and approved at a meeting of the Board of Advisors on May 26, 1972.[21]

Efforts were exerted toward the generation of additional finances for the laboratory; $25,000 would not go very far toward building a $2,000,000 laboratory. In the next fiscal year, the legislature appropriated $51,000 in additional planning money. The following fiscal year, $50,000 was appropriated. The chief justification for the laboratory rested on economic and public health benefits for Oklahoma; the laboratory would reduce the state's $123 million annual loss to diseases and the potential for transmission of animal disease to humans. Articles supporting the laboratory were published in the *Oklahoma Veterinarian* and the *Oklahoma Cowman*.[22]

During the summer of 1972, four consultants visited Stillwater to review the laboratory plans during the design development phase. Numerous changes in the design were made as a result of these visits.

Because the benefits of the laboratory promised to extend beyond Oklahoma's borders, the Board of Advisors, some legislators, Governor Hall, and other supporters recommended that efforts be made to secure federal assistance. Accordingly, Gary Dage, deputy commissioner of the State Department of Agriculture, Walter Woolley, member of the Board of Advisors, and Dr. Dan Goodwin traveled to Washington, D.C., on September 13 and 14, 1972, to seek help from Speaker Carl Albert, Congressmen Steed, Belcher, Camp, and Edmondson, and Senators Harris and Bellmon. The Washington delegation seemed optimistic that matching federal funds of one million dollars could be obtained for the two million dollar laboratory. An article was prepared that called for federal support for a laboratory in Oklahoma to serve diagnostic and research needs in the southern plains feeding areas of Oklahoma, Texas, New Mexico, Kansas, and Nebraska.[23]

Good news came from the Oklahoma Wheat Growers Association meeting in Enid on December 5, 1972! Governor David Hall, in a speech to the farmers and ranchers gathered there, announced that $1 million of the federal revenue sharing money received by Oklahoma would be spent the following year on an animal diagnostic center to be built in Stillwater. Governor Hall said: "We believe it is vital to our livestock industry, to cattle that feed on our winter wheat, to family pets in Oklahoma, and to the general health of Oklahoma. The need was dramatized during the Venezuela equine encephalomyelitis outbreak."[24]

The Board of Advisors met on January 19, 1973, and discussed proposed funding. Representative Witt and Gary Dage, deputy commissioner of agriculture, were present at the meeting. Concern was expressed that aggressive efforts at that time to obtain federal funds, which were in short supply, might jeopardize the chances to obtain state funds which were closer to reality. It was agreed without dissent, that supporters needed to devote full efforts toward securing the million dollar appropriation from the legislature as Governor Hall recommended and after this was achieved, to look again at the possibility of federal participation to obtain the needed additional million dollars.[25]

The recommendations of the board were fulfilled during the late winter and spring of 1973. News items supporting the laboratory appeared in many state newspapers and journals. Support came also from Governor Hall, Senator Jim Hamilton, Speaker Bill Willis, Representative J. D. Witt, Mr. Billy Ray Gowdy, Senator Bob Murphy, Representative Dan Draper, and countless other individuals and groups to assure that the legislature would appropriate $1 million dollars for construction purposes to the State Regents for Higher Education with the stipulation that the accomplishment of the project was to be coordinated with the State Department of Agriculture. For the fiscal year 1973-74, $50,000 would be appropriated to the State Department of Agriculture to be contracted to the College of Veterinary Medicine for the purpose of developing comprehensive plans for building and operating the diagnostic laboratory. A supplement appropriation for the laboratory for the fiscal year 1972-73 of $26,000, would be made to the State Department of Agriculture for architectural fees.[26]

These successes were tempered by sad news. Representative Witt died on May 23. His sound counsel and effective advocacy for the laboratory were sorely missed.

The architectural firm of Jones, Hester, Bates and Riek completed the drawings and specifications for the laboratory in the spring of 1974. With the million dollar appropriation in hand, bids were invited for the project with the understanding that the shell could be built for that amount and that the remainder of the project would be bid as a delayed alternate to be enacted at the time the needed second million dollars became available. Bids were opened from eight general contractors on May 16, 1974. The high bid was $2,081,500; the low bid was $1,945,686. Because acceptance of the low bid would not leave sufficient funds for needed movable equipment, a large alternate—the isolation building— was dropped, and the low bid then came to $1,692,500. The contract was awarded to the Flintco Corporation of Tulsa and plans were made for a groundbreaking ceremony.

The ceremony was conducted on May 31, 1974, in the steer shed pasture immediately across Farm Road north of the College of Veterinary Medicine. Seated on the speaker's platform were Governor Hall, members of the Board of Regents, members of the Board of Agriculture, members of the Oklahoma legislature, OSU administrative officials, members of the laboratory's Board of Advisors, and the building architects.[27]

Billy Ray Gowdy, president of the Board of Agriculture, served as master of ceremonies. He introduced distinguished guests and noted that the laboratory would serve as a strong ally of Oklahoma veterinarians and animal owners. He paid special tribute to the late Representative J. D. Witt for his vision and hard work.

Speakers included Governor Hall; Burke Healey, chairman, Board

OKLAHOMA ANIMAL DIAGNOSTIC DISEASE LABORATORY

The groundbreaking ceremony on May 31, 1974, is a momentous occasion for all supporters of the Oklahoma Animal Diagnostic Disease Laboratory.

of Regents; Senator Robert Murphy; and President Kamm. Twelve shovels were thrust into the grass covered pasture where cattle had recently grazed, an appropriate beginning for the construction of a laboratory dedicated to serving Oklahoma's vital animal resources. Formal construction got underway soon after the groundbreaking ceremony.

The campaign for the second million dollars continued with the same enthusiasm and effectiveness. Governor Hall said in his January 9, 1974, budget message to the Oklahoma legislature: "Our health also is affected by our environment and the health of our animals. For that reason—and to strengthen our greatest industry, agriculture—we are proposing an additional one million dollar appropriation to complete construction and equipping of the new Animal Diagnostic Center at Stillwater. It will serve our cattlemen, farmers and pet owners."[28]

The 1974 legislature appropriated the requested money, and the completion of the building and the acquisition of equipment were assured. The Merrick Foundation of Ardmore made a generous contribution that would aid in the purchase of special equipment. The Board of Regents authorized the construction of the isolation building in 1977.

In the meantime, recruitment of personnel was proceeding, and plans for operation were being developed. Laboratory operations would be guided by a memorandum of understanding between the Oklahoma State Board of Agriculture and the Board of Regents. The memorandum provided needed assurance to the laboratory's supporters that its service mission would be respected and upheld.[29]

The new laboratory building was dedicated October 18, 1975. Bob Barr, who had succeeded Billy Ray Gowdy as president of the State Board of Agriculture, served as master of ceremonies. Mr. Barr's skill as a diplomat was demonstrated earlier when he resolved differences between the Senate and the House of Representatives. The Senate had adopted legislation to name the diagnostic laboratory after Fred Lowe; the House had adopted a bill to name it after their late colleague, J. D. Witt. Mr. Barr was able to reach agreement with legislative leaders that would name the laboratory "Oklahoma Animal Disease Diagnostic Laboratory." Suitably inscribed bronze plaques honoring both Fred D. Lowe and J. D. Witt were unveiled during the dedication ceremony. They are prominently displayed in the entry foyer of the laboratory.[30]

Although the laboratory was now officially dedicated, it would not be ready for occupancy until the contractor finished the building in January 1976. The doors were opened for business on January 26, 1976, with a professional staff consisting of Dr. Dan E. Goodwin, director; Dr. E. L. Stair, chief pathologist and assistant director; Dr. D. L. Whitenack, pathologist; Dr. Leon Potgieter, virologist; and Dr. Rebecca Morton, bacteriologist. Dr. W. C. Edwards, toxicologist, would join the staff in February 1977 to oversee the toxicology section.

Dedication ceremony for the Oklahoma Animal Diagnostic Disease Laboratory is held on October 18, 1975. Dr. Dan Goodwin, Mrs. J. D. Witt from Vinita, Bob Barr, president of the State Board of Agriculture, and Mr. and Mrs. Fred Lowe from McAlester are present for the unveiling of plaques during the ceremony in honor of the late J. D. Witt and Mr. Fred Lowe.

The professional staff has been remarkably stable. All of the original staff members continue to serve in 1986 except for virologist Leon Potgieter who was succeeded in 1978 by Dr. Anthony Castro. Dr. Charles Baldwin succeeded Dr. Castro in 1985. Two pathologists, Dr. B. J. Johnson and Dr. Ray Ely, have been added to the staff.

The first request for diagnostic assistance (Case 000001) came from Mr. Dale Barrington of Hulbert, Oklahoma, who was referred to the laboratory by Dr. Sam Crosby of Tahlequah. Of 250 pigs in Mr. Barrington's operation, 60 were sick and 2 had died. Four sick pigs were submitted. Laboratory findings were atrophic rhinitis, pneumonia, and eperythrozoonosis. The hundred thousandth request for diagnostic assistance (Case 100,000) came from Dr. Jim Shipman of Claremore on March 12, 1985.

During the first year of operation, the legislature transferred funding of the laboratory from the Oklahoma Department of Agriculture to the College of Veterinary Medicine.[31] The laboratory's original supporters, who had worked so hard for a service-oriented laboratory, feared this transfer meant that the laboratory would be taken over for teaching and research with service only a sideline. However, in June 1976, the State Regents for Higher Education developed a statement of functions for the laboratory that strengthened and clearly defined its service mission. The statement designated the laboratory as a public service agency whose primary mission is to: "Render service to veterinarians and animal owners in Oklahoma and through such service to carry out three objectives, namely to make an economic contribution to the State of Oklahoma, to reduce human disease attributable to animals, and to provide support for the College of Veterinary Medicine, insofar as the service mission is not thereby reduced."[32]

Approximately 90 percent of the laboratory's work load is directly related to service, with the remaining 10 percent given to the college teaching and research programs. The State Regents for Higher Education reconfirmed the laboratory's mission of service in a 1983 study of its programs and needs and stated that the laboratory is "well-organized, responsibly managed, and is rendering a valuable service to farmers, ranchers, zoos, veterinarians, and owners of pet animals in Oklahoma."[33]

The laboratory has provided notable support for residency and graduate programs of the College of Veterinary Medicine facilitated by the appointments of laboratory staff members in various academic departments of the college.

The American Association of Veterinary Laboratory Diagnosticians is the official accrediting agency for animal disease diagnostic laboratories in the United States. Of approximately 300 laboratories in the nation, 27 have been accredited as full-service laboratories. The first inspection of the Oklahoma laboratory was made in 1978. The site visit report noted: "The planners, architects and engineers should be commended for their outstanding contribution to diagnostic veterinary medicine."[34]

The laboratory was reaccredited in 1983 following another comprehensive appraisal of personnel, procedures, equipment, and facilities. The site visit report proclaimed: "This is a most attractive, functional and well maintained veterinary diagnostic laboratory. We found the building and grounds to be superbly maintained. . . . Although the laboratory was designed in the early 1970s and constructed in the mid-1970s, it remains a model for diagnostic laboratory construction in its security and overall design in general. There has developed in the section of toxicology a petroleum hydrocarbon competency that is probably unexcelled in the United States."[35]

The Oklahoma Animal Disease Diagnostic Laboratory is fulfilling its mission. The Board of Advisors meets faithfully each year and at other times as needed to provide steady support and guidance. Able staff members provide vigilant, accessible, and accountable service for Oklahoma veterinarians and animal owners.

Emergency services have been readily provided 24 hours per day, 365 days per year, since the laboratory opened its doors.

The isolation and identification of the African strain of malignant catarrhal fever virus in 1979 marked the first time that this virus was

The Board of Advisors of the Oklahoma Animal Diagnostic Disease Laboratory meets once a year and more often as necessary. On February 19, 1983, Dan Goodwin from Stillwater, Bill Taggart from Stillwater, Leo Roberts from Ardmore, Paul Muegge from Lamont, Willard Rhynes from Stonewall, Roger Panciera from Stillwater, John Kirkpatrick from Shattuck, Bob Hartin from Edmond, Gene Eskew from Oklahoma City, and Burl Holmes from Oklahoma City are present.

identified in the United States. Increased understanding of the disease that the virus causes has permitted steps to be taken to protect domestic livestock against infection. The Oklahoma laboratory has developed an accurate blood test for the disease that may soon be utilized throughout the United States.

Procedures have been developed for the reliable identification of petroleum hydrocarbons in poisoned cattle. These procedures have distinguished the Oklahoma laboratory as the leader among U.S. veterinary diagnostic laboratories in the investigation of oil/gas field poisoning.

Serology and virology tests for pseudorabies virus in swine have been developed. These tests have allowed Oklahoma to protect itself against devastating outbreaks of pseudorabies in the swine population, such as those that occur regularly in the upper midwest.

Serology tests for leptospirosis have identified infected animals and premises. Protective vaccination programs initiated by practicing veterinarians have lead to a dramatic reduction of *Leptospira hardjo* infections in Oklahoma cattle.

The development of test procedures for cantharidin has allowed the laboratory to identify blister beetle poisoning in horses; this has led to the employment of management practices by horsemen that have helped to reduce the incidence of poisoning.

Since January 26, 1976, when the Oklahoma Animal Diagnostic Disease Laboratory first opened its doors, it has provided service to veterinarians and animal owners in Oklahoma. It continues to make an economic contribution to the state of Oklahoma, to reduce human disease attributable to animals, and to provide support for the College of Veterinary Medicine.

The offering of a uterine biopsy service has led to the accurate assessment of the endometrium of brood mares, which in turn has permitted practicing veterinarians to treat more effectively subfertile mares.

The laboratory's preparedness permitted the ready identification of parvovirus infections in hundreds of Oklahoma dogs in 1979 and 1980 when the disease first made its appearance in Oklahoma. The subsequent development of a serologic test at the laboratory permitted veterinarians and animal owners to monitor the levels of protective antibodies in dogs and devise vaccination programs accordingly.

The weekend identification of anthrax in a cow from Jefferson County in 1979 permitted the immediate quarantine and containment of the disease to a small area; fewer than a dozen cattle died as a result of the disease.

The 1980 establishment of a large stock of emergency antidotes that are available to practitioners 24 hours a day has permitted them to treat poisoned animals quickly and effectively.

The ability of the virology laboratory to isolate and identify bluetongue virus from cattle, sheep, and deer has been a powerful aid to diagnosis and has advanced the general knowledge of disease caused by the virus in Oklahoma and the United States. The establishment of antibody levels for IBR and BVD viruses in 20,000 Oklahoma cattle has served to indicate the widespread incidence of these diseases and has led to the development of protective vaccination programs in the state.

Tests for cat diseases, feline leukemia and feline infectious peritonitis, have indicated that both diseases are widespread in Oklahoma and that protective vaccination may be beneficial.

Oklahoma's parakeet industry has been strengthened through the laboratory's identification of parakeet nestling disease; the laboratory's recent discovery of viral inclusions in tissues of parakeets may contribute to the development of a protective vaccine.

The establishment and steady maintenance of a battery of official U.S. Department of Agriculture tests (pseudorabies, bovine leukemia, anaplasmosis, bluetongue, contagious equine metritis, equine infectious anemia) has promoted the marketing and transport of Oklahoma livestock by making these needed tests readily available for interstate and international health certification.

The laboratory has helped to reduce the threat and incidence of animal diseases that are transmissible to man by identifying in animal tissues a myriad of disease agents that are reported to the State Department of Health and ultimately to practicing physicians. These disease agents have included rabies, brucellosis, tuberculosis, systemic fungi, psittacosis, anthrax, leptospirosis and tularemia.

The laboratory staff has transmitted new knowledge to the scientific community by publication of numerous articles in the scientific literature; a quarterly newsletter is sent to Oklahoma veterinarians and to other U.S. diagnostic laboratories.

January 26, 1986, marked the tenth anniversary of the Oklahoma Animal Disease Diagnostic Laboratory. The state of Oklahoma, Oklahoma State University, and College of Veterinary Medicine are proud of the contribution that the laboratory has made to the economy and welfare of the state and nation.

Endnotes

1. "History and Organization of the Department," author and date unknown. Twenty typewritten onionskin sheets of paper with 1944 as the most recent period covered. Archives, College of Veterinary Medicine.

2. "History and Organization of the Department."

3. "History and Organization of the Department."

4. *Bulletin of the Oklahoma Agricultural and Mechanical College: Veterinary Medicine for 1950-51 with Announcements for 1951-52*, p. 48.

5. President Oliver Willham to Dr. A. W. Monlux, 19 May 1966, Files of Oklahoma Animal Disease Diagnostic Laboratory, Stillwater, Oklahoma.

6. Dr. A. W. Monlux to President Robert Kamm, 2 August 1967, Files of Oklahoma Animal Disease Diagnostic Laboratory.

7. Personal communication between Dr. S. A. Ewing and Dr. Dan E. Goodwin, 2 October 1985.

8. Building and Facilities Committee (John Venable, E. D. Besch, B. L. Glenn, E. W. Jones, D. D. Goetsch, Thomas Monin) to Acting Dean J. Wiley Wolfe, 26 October 1967, Files of Oklahoma Animal Disease Diagnostic Laboratory.

9. Mr. Fred Lowe to Mr. Lewis Munn, 16 December 1968, Files of Oklahoma Animal Disease Diagnostic Laboratory.

10. Mr. Fred Lowe to Congressman Carl Albert, 18 December 1968, Files of Oklahoma Animal Disease Diagnostic Laboratory.

11. Dr. Karl Reinhard to President Robert B. Kamm, 21 November 1968, Files of Oklahoma Animal Disease Diagnostic Laboratory.

12. President Robert B. Kamm to Dr. Karl Reinhard, 6 December 1968, Files of Oklahoma Animal Disease Diagnostic Laboratory.

13. Dr. Karl Reinhard to Dr. J. H. Brashear, 8 January 1969, Files of Oklahoma Animal Disease Diagnostic Laboratory.

14. Senate Bill No. 123; Stipe, First session of the 32nd Oklahoma Legislature, January 21, 1969.

15. "Proposed Veterinary Diagnostic Laboratory, Progress Report," [1971], Files of Oklahoma Animal Disease Diagnostic Laboratory. Members of the planning committee were: Dr. W. E. Brock, dean, College of Veterinary Medicine; Dr. Jay Brashear, state veterinarian; Dr. Don Williams, Ada, Oklahoma; Mr. Wray Finney, Fort Cobb, Oklahoma.

16. Enrolled House Bill No. 1148. Passed the House of Representatives, June 10, 1971. Passed the Senate June 11, 1971. Approved by the Governor, June 24, 1971.

17. "Job Description, Director, Oklahoma Animal Disease Diagnostic Laboratory, 1971," Files of Oklahoma Animal Disease Diagnostic Laboratory.

18. Dan E. Goodwin, "A Look at Selected Veterinary Medical Diagnostic Laboratories, January 1972," Files of Oklahoma Animal Disease Diagnostic Laboratory.

19. A. W. Monlux to Diagnostic Laboratory Coordinating Committee, 3 February 1972, Files of Oklahoma Animal Disease Diagnostic Laboratory.

20. R. J. Panciera, "Report of the Faculty Diagnostic Laboratory Committee Meeting of May 15, 1972," Files of Oklahoma Animal Disease Diagnostic Laboratory.

21. "Report of the Meeting of the Board of Advisors, Oklahoma City, Oklahoma, May 26, 1972," Files of Oklahoma Animal Disease Diagnostic Laboratory. Special guests and participants at the meeting were Representative J. D. Witt of Vinita, and Dr. Frank Hester of Chelsea, president of the Oklahoma Veterinary Medical Association.

22. Dan E. Goodwin, "The Oklahoma Animal Disease Diagnostic Laboratory," *Oklahoma Veterinarian,* vol. 24, no. 2 (April 1972), pp. 25-27; Dan E. Goodwin, "An Update by the Director of the Diagnostic Laboratory," *Oklahoma Cowman,* vol. 12, no. 7 (July 1972), p. 11.

23. "The Case for a State-Federal Animal Disease Diagnostic and Research Laboratory in Oklahoma, 1972," Files of Oklahoma Animal Disease Diagnostic Laboratory.

24. "Address to Oklahoma Wheat Growers by Governor David Hall, December 5, 1972," Files of Oklahoma Animal Disease Diagnostic Laboratory.

25. "Report of the Meeting of the Board of Advisors, Oklahoma City, Oklahoma, January 19, 1973," Files of Oklahoma Animal Disease Diagnostic Laboratory.

26. "Report of the Meeting of the Board of Advisors, Oklahoma City, Oklahoma, June 14, 1973," Files of Oklahoma Animal Disease Diagnostic Laboratory.

27. "Report of Meeting of the Board of Advisors, Stillwater, Oklahoma, May 31, 1974," Files of Oklahoma Animal Disease Diagnostic Laboratory.

28. Oklahoma City *Daily Oklahoman,* 9 January 1974, p. 13.

29. *Memorandum of Understanding Between the Oklahoma State Board of Agriculture and the Board of Regents for Oklahoma State University Concerning the Operation of the Oklahoma Animal Disease Diagnostic Laboratory, [1974],* Files of Oklahoma Animal Disease Diagnostic Laboratory.

30. Plaque honoring Fred D. Lowe: "Grateful recognition and deep gratitude are extended herewith to Fred D. Lowe of McAlester, Oklahoma. His concern for the health and well-being of Oklahoma's livestock industry was translated into effective action when he launched the campaign to create the Oklahoma Animal Disease Diagnostic Laboratory. Out of those

early beginnings has come this laboratory—solidly committed to protect and promote the health and welfare of Oklahomans and their animals. To his memory it is dedicated herewith. 1975"

Plaque honoring J. D. Witt "Grateful recognition and deep gratitude are extended herewith to the late J. D. Witt of Vinita, Oklahoma. His keen foresight and energetic leadership and articulate urgings in the Oklahoma Legislature were responsible for the legislation that created the Oklahoma Animal Disease Diagnostic Laboratory. Firmly rooted in public service, and devoted to improving the lot of all Oklahomans, it stands as a fitting monument to the life and work of J. D. Witt. To his memory it is dedicated herewith. 1975"

31. Oklahoma State Legislature, *Oklahoma Session Laws, 1976, Thirty-fifth Legislature, Second Regular Session, Convened January 6, 1976, Adjourned June 9, 1976. First Extraordinary Session, Convened July 19, 1976, Adjourned July 23, 1976* (St. Paul, MN: West Publishing Company, 1976), p. 352.

32. *A Study of the Programs and Needs of the Oklahoma Animal Disease Diagnostic Laboratory of the Oklahoma State University College of Veterinary Medicine,* (Oklahoma City: Oklahoma State Regents for Higher Education, November 1983), Files of the Oklahoma Animal Disease Diagnostic Laboratory.

33. *A Study of the Programs and Needs of the Oklahoma Animal Disease Diagnostic Laboratory of the Oklahoma State University College of Veterinary Medicine.*

34. "Site visit report, Oklahoma Animal Disease Diagnostic Laboratory, 1978," Files of Oklahoma Animal Disease Diagnostic Laboratory.

35. "Site visit report, Oklahoma Animal Disease Diagnostic Laboratory, 1983," Files of Oklahoma Animal Disease Diagnostic Laboratory.

14 Decade of Hope Continues

From the history of veterinary medicine let veterinarians draw confidence in the invincible strength of their science.

John R. Mohler, V.M.D.

The great year, 1976, had finally arrived. Plans all over the United States had been made for the great celebration. The OSU Bicentennial Committee had been hard at work. A Bicentennial Trust was established for the benefit of the university in which contributors each placed $1.00 to be invested for 100 years. The names of all donors were listed and placed in a time capsule in the center of campus. The capsule also contained other items of historical interest and would be opened in the year 2076.

For the Oklahoma State University family, the bicentennial year started on an agreeable and highly acceptable note. President Kamm designated January 2, 1976, as an extra holiday. In this era of energy crisis, a long weekend would substantially help to conserve energy. It was further decreed that thermostats be set at 68 degrees Fahrenheit.

By the fall of 1975, interest in a proposed teaching hospital for the college was beginning to gain momentum. A group of interested legislators, led by Senator Robert Murphy and Representative Dan Draper, visited the college to survey a proposed site for the hospital on the west side of the campus.

Dean Brock and Dr. Oberst met with the Board of Regents in January 1976 to discuss the building of the new teaching hospital. The regents were anxious to develop a strong case to present to the new legislature that would label the hospital as a non-recurring expense.

Things were now really on the move. Ms. Carol Davis, whose husband was a veterinary medicine student, became the new public information officer for the college. Ms. Davis worked hard to prepare brochures and news releases which helped enormously to inform the whole of Oklahoma of the urgent need for, and the ultimate benefit of, the hospital.

Eventually almost everyone got in the act—dog breeders and lovers, horse owners, cattlemen, wheat farmers, and scores of others! A group of veterinary medicine students met with Governor Boren and presented a statement of support from the student body. On that same day Dr. Brock reported the State Regents for Higher Education had approved $9 million for the construction of the hospital.[1]

Governor Boren budgeted $3 million for the planning phase of the hospital which would have to be approved by the legislature. Fred Frank, professor of architecture at Mississippi State University and part-time faculty member in the veterinary school, was invited to visit the college because of his expertise on hospital design. He was to assist the architects with some of the special needs of a veterinary medical hospital.

The euphoria was now contagious and the administration was already looking ahead to decide what should be done with existing areas that would be vacated. Naturally, a committee was formed!

The hospital planning committee really got down to business. Eventually, along with the architects and time and motion studies by Mr. Frank, an outstanding floor plan was developed. It would be a two-story building with faculty offices and laboratories upstairs. Here at least a

Architects designing the new teaching hospital envisioned a building that eventually was literally turned upside down.

committee really accomplished its objectives and didn't end up with a camel! Lo and behold! It was too good to be true. In the interest of cost and energy savings, and no doubt many other reasons, they "turned the building upside down"! The final plan had the faculty offices in the lower level of a split level facility.

As the legislative session moved toward closure, there were rumblings that there might be a cutback in the appropriations for the teaching hospital, but a united profession showed its dedication. All over the state, veterinarians, students, and their friends conducted an intensive telephone campaign to voice their support of the hospital.

The second college convocation for the graduating seniors was held in the Seretean Center theater with Dr. John Montgomery as guest speaker. After a stirring, eloquent address, he announced, to rousing applause, that the Governor had told him to bring the message, "'You are going to get that teaching hospital.' Then we'll have something really nice to come home to."[2] It was encouragement at a special time as Marguerite Duffy of Charlotte, North Carolina, became the 1000th graduate of the College of Veterinary Medicine.

The Oklahoma state legislature appropriated $2.75 million towards the new teaching hospital, although the Governor had asked for $3 million. The Board of Regents engaged the architectural firm of Jones, Hester, Bates, Reik and Baumeister, Oklahoma City, to prepare the preliminary plans, for which $55,000 was funded in July 1976.

The bicentennial year of 1976 was coming to a close on a resounding note. On Saturday morning, December 1, groundbreaking ceremonies were held for the new teaching hospital. A minor problem evolved in that there was a hard frost the night before! However, "necessity is the mother of invention." There was a top level decision to perform the great event indoors. Enough loose dirt was scraped together to fill several boxes so that a non-traditional, symbolic "dirt turning" was performed by top university, state, and student dignitaries.

Dean Brock presided and gave special recognition to Mr. Ron Ford, past chairman of the Board of Regents, Dr. John Montgomery, Senator Robert Murphy, and Representatives Dan Draper and Joe Manning. President Robert Kamm spoke and gave credit to the many who had "brought us to this day." In particular, he cited the strong support and efforts of former Governor David Hall. The keynote address, given by Governor David Boren, reaffirmed commitment to the hospital and referred to the event as "a milestone in Oklahoma." Following the ceremony, over 200 persons who had braved the slick roads and sub-freezing temperatures joined the dignitaries for a barbecue lunch in the large animal clinic treatment area.

Governor David Boren recommended an additional $2.3 million in his budget for the teaching hospital. In February of 1977, a bid for the

Groundbreaking for the new teaching hospital was a symbolic affair on December 1, 1976. The inclement weather that necessitated the event to be held indoors did not dampen the enthusiasm of dignitaries who performed the "dirt turning."

grading and preparation of the site was received from the Concho Construction Company and approved by the Board of Regents. In March the State Regents for Higher Education allocated $26,869 for this purpose. Very soon a huge hole developed in the ground west of the main veterinary medicine building—ready for the building to begin. It was a time of great expectation, but it was the old story of eternal hope and "wait 'til next year" until sufficient funding could be provided for the building.

In spite of the flurry of activity surrounding the teaching hospital, day-to-day events continued. Dr. John Venable left in mid-January of 1976 to assume the chairmanship of the Department of Anatomy at the College of Veterinary Medicine and Biomedical Sciences, Colorado State University. Dr. Venable was an astute and meticulous administrator. He was succeeded by Dr. G. Pat Mayer as acting head.

Dr. James B. Corcoran, Department of Pathology, retired on June 30, 1976, after forty-two years service to the university and his profession. Dr. Corcoran was truly a gentleman and a scholar.

Dr. Richard E. Corstvet became acting head of the Department of Veterinary Parasitology, Microbiology and Public Health, succeeding Dr. Merwin Frey who left at the end of August 1977.

Unfortunately, a growing institution has to put up with a lot of paper work, and such had been mounting since the activity appraisal system was introduced in 1975. In between filling out all the forms, one had hardly any time for professional duties, let alone read the "O'Colly!"

Dr. James Corcoran joined the Department of Veterinary Pathology in 1957 and directed the clinical pathology laboratory for many years. He was the interim head of the department from 1972-74.

The faculty appraisal system was deemed necessary to provide guidelines and possible justification for promotion, tenure, and retention policies.

The quest by the faculty for academic enrichment and their pursuit of excellence was a very satisfying situation for the college. At the annual Oklahoma Veterinary Medical Association convention in Oklahoma City in February 1976, Dr. Ralph Buckner received the coveted Dr. William F. Irwin Memorial Award presented by the Tulsa Veterinary Medical Association. The award recognizes a member who exemplifies the high professional and social principles held by the late Dr. William Irwin, a Tulsa small animal practitioner.

In 1977, Dr. Louie Stratton became a Diplomate in the American College of Theriogenologists, and Dr. Gerard Rubin was named a Diplomate in the American College of Veterinary Internal Medicine specializing in cardiology. A Diplomate is one who has reached a level of expertise by fulfilling the qualifications and passing the required examinations administered by a specialty board. The American College of Veterinary Pathologists was the first to be established in 1951. Other specialty disciplines include internal medicine, ophthalmology, dermatology, microbiology, veterinary preventive medicine, veterinary radiology, and surgery.

The announcement at the American Veterinary Medical Association Convention in July 1977 that Dr. G. Pat Mayer had been named the recipient of the 34th Annual Borden Award was received with universal acclaim. This prestigious award of a medallion, plaque, and $1000 cash recognizes outstanding research contributing to dairy cattle disease control and the recipient's success in publishing results in official scien-

Dr. Merwin Frey, head of the Department of Veterinary Parasitology, Microbiology and Public Health, also did research on viruses and mycoplasma involved in respiratory diseases and arthritis in cattle and poultry.

tific journals. Dr. Mayer's work on calcium metabolism and parathyroid physiology is regarded as a classical contribution to the world veterinary literature.

Due to a severe illness of several months' duration, Dr. Mayer was not able to attend the convention. The award was received on his behalf by Dr. Robert Marshak, University of Pennsylvania. The plaque and check were brought to Stillwater by a faculty colleague, and on Thursday, July 14, Dean Brock presented them to Dr. Mayer at Stillwater Municipal Hospital. Dr. Mayer died on October 3, 1979.

Improvements in instruction were made possible by grants of $4,700 from the Merck Company Foundation and $5,000 from Schering Corporation in 1976. First-class audiovisual and video educational programs were developed which have been a boom for continuing education.

An electron microscope was installed in the newly completed section of the basement in the middle wing. It became the highlight of the ninth biennial Open House held in 1977.

The College of Veterinary Medicine became the first in the nation in 1977 to purchase a colposcope made possible by a generous grant of $7,700 from Sarkeys Foundation in Norman. The complex medical instrument provides a three-dimensional view of an examination area, magnifies like a microscope and photographs in stereo. Dr. Ralph Buckner and Dr. Jeffie Roszel had submitted the grant proposal. Sarkeys Foundation continued its generous support of the college with an additional grant of $50,000 in 1978 to purchase equipment for the proposed teaching hospital.

Dr. Michael W. Fox, Department of Psychology, Washington University in St. Louis, delivered the third Dr. Lewis H. Moe Lecture on April 15, 1976. Internationally known for his research on animal behavior, Dr. Fox gave an excellent presentation, "Normal and Abnormal Animal Behavior: Ethics and the Veterinarian."

Later in the spring of 1976 Dr. W. Ross Cockrill, former senior officer of the United Nations' Food and Agriculture Organization, Rome, Italy, spoke at the college. In his delightful, Scottish accent, he discussed the world problem of starvation and dealt at length with the water buffalo "which is an excellent worker, an excellent milk animal, and a supreme meat animal."[3]

The American Association of Bovine Practitioners, established in 1964, had made great strides in the meantime and was now a very dynamic organization. In August, District 7 (Oklahoma, Missouri, and Kansas) sponsored a conference on bovine respiratory problems in collaboration with the College of Veterinary Medicine and the OSU Extension Service in Stillwater. Dr. Leland C. Allenstein from Wisconsin, president of the organization, attended and presented a paper on calf diseases. Dr. Harold Miller from Shawnee, class of 1960, was the conference coordinator.

In 1977, Dr. Lloyd C. Faulkner, head, Department of Physiology and Biophysics, Colorado State University, presented the annual Dr. Lewis H. Moe Lecture on "Pets, Inversion, and Iatrogenesis." Dr. Faulkner was a Congressional Science Fellow with Senator Charles Mathias at that time. In his thought-provoking lecture, he stated that the emergence of the age of affluence was creating a situation where, "Pet owners expect that the veterinary priest in his medical temple could correct the ills of irresponsible and uninformed ownership with a miraculous injection, a marvelous pill, a surgical or bioengineering wonder, or a painless dose of lethol."[4]

The ever present need for funds to finance a variety of projects resulted in a joint effort by the student chapter, the dean's office, and the OSU Development Foundation (now the OSU Foundation) in the fall of 1976. A letter from Dean Brock and student chapter officers was mailed to all the college alumni in Oklahoma as a pilot project. The following week, several students assisted by the college director of admissions and student affairs and a representative from the foundation, telephoned each alumnus in the evening to discuss the fund drive. Donations were allocated as follows: 75 percent for general administration by the dean of the College of Veterinary Medicine; 25 percent deposited in the OSU Development Foundation in a newly established Student Support Fund. Interest or dividends from this fund are used for student loans or other purposes. Over the years individual donations have been made to the fund, now called the Student and Alumni Fund.

Mr. and Mrs. James Durham of Okeene, parents of James Edward Durham a third-year student who died in 1976, have graciously presented a $1,000 scholarship to a third-year student for many years.

In an effort to improve communication among the student body and with the faculty and staff, the student chapter launched a newsletter.

The first issue appeared on January 20, 1977. Ron Streeter, student president, was the driving force behind this adventure. He felt that the newsletter, which he referred to in the first issue as a "soon-to-be-great publication" should have a name! The chapter executive board offered a $10.00 prize to the winner of the Newsletter-Naming Contest. It was stated that "All entries should be short and bear in mind good taste and the state pornography laws."[5] The winning entry was SCAVMA Scoop, submitted by Thomas Williams, second-year student. *SCAVMA Scoop: The Student Voice of the College of Veterinary Medicine* has been published regularly just prior to each student meeting. The September 20, 1978, issue carried the added notation, "your 2 cents worth"! In subsequent copies this has varied from 1.74 cents to 7.5 cents worth, before finally stabilizing at 2 cents. It is the responsibility of the president-elect to prepare and publish the newsletter each semester in collaboration with the Office of Student Affairs.

On February 1, 1977, Dr. Robert B. Kamm left the presidency of Oklahoma State University. Dr. Kamm received numerous well deserved accolades for his dedicated service to OSU, the community, and the state. Oklahomans will be grateful to him forever for his astute and wise handling of the changing scene on campus during the late sixties and early seventies. Dr. Kamm also gave his full support to the College of Veterinary Medicine's struggle for better financing and facilities.

Shortly thereafter, the accreditation team of the American Veterinary Medical Association Council on Education arrived on February 21-24. Their report became available in April. The council recommended the existing plans for the construction and equipment of a new teaching hospital and renovation of present clinical areas be implemented and accomplished without delay. Realistic funding for the college needed to be provided at a level that would enable it to meet its objectives and maintain a level of teaching excellence. Added emphasis needed to be placed on the clinical teaching program, and significant stimulus given to encourage interdepartmental effort toward total college goals. The curriculum committee needed to receive clear terms of reference that would charge them to proceed with the development of an integrated teaching program.

The college was granted probational accreditation and given the customary five years to achieve the standards necessary for full accreditation.

Earlier in the year, Dean Brock dropped a real bombshell on the College of Veterinary Medicine when he announced on Friday, September 10, 1976, that he would retire not later than June 30, 1977. President Kamm had appointed a search committee for a new dean, naming Dr. Lester Johnson as chairman.

In anticipation of Dean Brock's intention to retire not later than June 30, a large number of faculty, spouses, and friends gathered at the Stillwater Golf and Country Club on Saturday evening, May 28. Dr. and Mrs. Brock were presented suitable gifts and a check to purchase photographic equipment. Dr. Malle, who presided in his own inimitable manner, also presented Dr. Brock with a black box, which he had built and painted, and was symbolic of a dark room! Dr. Fayne Oberst presented former President Robert Kamm and Dr. Brock with orange and black shovels which were used during the groundbreaking (dirt turning!) ceremony for the new hospital. Since a new dean had not been named, Dr. Brock continued in office.

On July 1, 1977, Dr. Lawrence L. Boger became the 17th president of Oklahoma State University. A native of Indiana, Dr. Boger has degrees from Purdue University and Michigan State University. He had served as dean of the College of Agriculture at Michigan State University where he was currently serving as provost. His main areas of professional interest were agricultural economics and international trade. Dr. Boger was well informed on the needs of veterinary medicine through his close association with the college at Michigan State University.

When the 1977-78 academic year opened in late August, the freshman class had sixty students. State regents, legislators, and university administrators received a lot of pressure from parents of Oklahoma students who were not able to gain admission to the College of Veterinary Medicine. The State Regents for Higher Education, therefore, ruled that only Oklahoma residents would be eligible to apply. All contracts with other states were cancelled, and there was much concern about the loss of revenue from these sources.

One of the main issues to be discussed during the fall semester was the possibility of introducing a comprehensive examination at the end of the second year. This would be a "mini" national board examination covering pre-clinical subjects. The pros and cons were discussed with vigor, emotion, and skepticism. In view of all the obstacles, there was no final decision—"the mountain went into labor and didn't even produce a mouse!"

Finally, Dr. Brock was allowed to retire! He presided over his last veterinary administrative council meeting on November 19, 1977.

Dr. Brock achieved greatness for his work on anaplasmosis, and had greatness thrust upon him as dean of the college which he had accepted very reluctantly. His plans after retirement were to pursue his hobby in the world of photography and to write the history of the college. However, it was not to be! Dr. Brock suffered a heart attack on Sunday, March 5, 1978, and died at Stillwater Municipal Hospital the following morning.

On December 1, 1977, Dr. Patrick Monroe Morgan assumed his duties as dean of the College of Veterinary Medicine. Dr. Morgan received the D.V.M. degree from the University of Georgia. At the time of his appoint-

William Elihu Brock, D.V.M., M.S., Ph.D., D.h.c.
1914-1978

William E. Brock was born in Black-well, Oklahoma, on August 10, 1914. He grew up in Wichita, Kansas, where he attended the public schools. He received the A.B. degree from the University of Wichita and became a graduate student in parasitology at the University of Louisiana. He married the former Alice Lee Massey in Wichita on September 30, 1939, and then moved to Oregon to manage a dairy farm. Two years later he entered the College of Veterinary Medicine, Kansas State University, where he received the D.V.M. degree in 1944.

Dr. Brock returned to Oregon and became engaged in general practice for five years. He moved to Oklahoma and joined the Veterinary Research Station at Pawhuska. In 1954 he came to Stillwater as a member of the Department of Veterinary Parasitology. He received the M.S. degree in nutrition from the College of Agriculture in 1955 and transferred to the Department of Veterinary Pathology in 1956.

Dr. Brock received a grant from the National Institutes of Health in 1958 to commence research in hemophilia in collaboration with the University of Oklahoma Medical School where he received the Ph.D. degree with a major in hematology in 1958.

Dr. Brock and his co-workers continued their research on anaplasmosis culminating in the development of the world's first vaccine against the disease in 1965.

In August 1965 Dr. and Mrs. Brock moved to Guatemala City, Guatemala, where he served as chief of party for the OSU College of Veterinary Medicine to administer the new Agency for International Development contract with the College of Veterinary Medicine and Animal Husbandry of San Carlos University. He also continued his research on anaplas-

OSU PUBLIC INFORMATION

mosis and babesiosis. On the completion of his two-year term of service, Dr. Brock was awarded the honorary degree of Doctor Honoris Causa.

Dr. Brock became acting dean of the College of Veterinary Medicine in May 1969, and in January 1970 he was named dean. He retired on November 30, 1977. Dr. Brock was the author of numerous publications based on his outstanding research work. He was a member of the American Veterinary Medical Association, Oklahoma Veterinary Medical Association, Phi Zeta, Sigma Xi (also 1967-68 lecturer), served as president of the Phi Kappa Phi Chapter at OSU and was a Rotarian for many years.

Dr. Brock died at Stillwater Municipal Hospital on Monday, March 6, 1978.

On May 28, 1980, a brief ceremony was held in which the college library was named the William E. Brock Memorial Library. It was a fitting tribute to a distinguished scholar.

ment, he was chief of preventive medical service for the Oklahoma State Department of Health and a part-time instructor in the college.

Dean Morgan took over at a time of great expectation for a new teaching hospital. Although the "ground had been broken," funds had yet to be provided for the construction of the building.

There were some important personnel changes early in the "Morgan era." Dr. Robert M. Wood, who had worked with Dr. Morgan at the State Department of Health, became a part-time assistant to the dean. Loretta Corley, who had been business manager for Dr. Brock, left with her husband for Mississippi State University. Loretta had worked in the clinical research area for many years. She was an outstanding secretary and organizer. The responsibilities of the business manager of the college were redefined, and Marilyn Wilson was appointed to fill this position.

Dr. E. Wynn Jones, director of research, left for Mississippi State University and a position of vice dean. Dr. Jones had been a consultant to MSU in planning the new College of Veterinary Medicine. Dr. Jones had joined the clinical faculty at OSU in the early 1950s. His contributions to the teaching program and as the pioneer of clinical research were outstanding and deserving of the highest recognition.

The fast moving developments in research related to animal genetics were brought into open forum at the annual Dr. Lewis H. Moe Lecture on February 2. Dr. Deetak Bastia, University of Alabama Medical School, presented a lecture on "The Recombinant DNA in Prospect and Perspective." On reflection, it was a "presentation before its time" and the magnitude of his remarks and prophecy did not strike home until later years.

The 1970-80 decade saw great strides in animal physiology and reproduction. In April 1973 the first laboratory facility in the United States opened for the transfer of fertilized ova from superior cows to less valuable cattle that served as "foster mothers" from pregnancy to birth. New non-surgical flushing techniques greatly simplified the embryo transfer process. Controlled cattle breeding, using prostaglandins, would soon be a reality.

During the 63rd annual Oklahoma Veterinary Medical Association convention in Oklahoma City, February 4-7, 1978, a major step in promoting continuing education was taken. The Oklahoma Academy of Veterinary Practice was officially established to advance the standards of veterinary practice. The first president was Dr. Robert Boss from Edmond, class of 1961. Dr. T. A. Byrd, class of 1953, newly installed president of the Oklahoma Veterinary Medical Association, noted the importance of the academy in his letter to the members, "Continuing Education is a must for all of us, the reasons being self-evident. . . . I would urge each of you to join."[6] In order for a member to remain in

Lynetta Freeman, Genie Thoni, and Sharon Nash, class of 1981, perform during the annual freshman skit.

good standing, a member had to attend a required number of continuing education programs each year.

On Saturday, February 10, OSU alumni leaders met at the College of Veterinary Medicine for the first time during their annual meeting on campus. In spite of severe weather, over 100 county alumni association presidents and other leaders gathered in the auditorium and were welcomed by President Boger, Dean Morgan, and Student Chapter President Terry Lehenbauer. A film on the college by Mark Terpenning was shown to the group, followed by a tour of the college and the Oklahoma Animal Disease Diagnostic Laboratory.

In order to provide a better perspective of the ''state of the college,'' Dean Morgan invited two groups of consultants to visit the college. First, a biosafety team of experts arrived to evaluate if the college had an adequate system for assuring that teaching and experimental procedures did not endanger people, animals, or the environment. They made some interesting suggestions.

Secondly, a committee chaired by Dr. Billy Hooper of Purdue University was selected to review the curriculum, a perennial topic in academia. Previously, the American Veterinary Medical Association Council on Education had recommended that ''the curriculum committee receive clear terms of reference that would charge them to proceed with appropriate modifications of the curriculum to meet the needs of veterinary medicine as a growing and expanding science."[7]

The curriculum consultants visited the college on May 4 and 5 and met with Dean Morgan, the curriculum committee, and individual faculty members. They returned on June 30 and met with the entire faculty for four hours at a retreat at the local Elks Lodge. The session ended with the faculty outlining and agreeing upon a course of action. The consultants' report on July 5 was a re-statement of the faculty's proposed course of action.

Immediate changes in curriculum included increasing the first semester to 18 credit hours, adding a course in laboratory animal medicine to the third year of the curriculum, and moving clinical pathology from the sixth to the fifth semester. Proposals to reduce credit hours in some courses were to be considered, and other disciplines and departments were to be asked to suggest where course credits could be reduced. It was decided the OSU standards for the semester-credit-hour would be followed by faculty in developing their instruction and used by the curriculum committee in considering course modification. To the degree permitted by restructuring the first three years of the curriculum, formal fourth-year courses would be moved back and credits for clinical instruction would be increased to more accurately represent the workload and student effort in clinics.

After these changes were completed, some space would have opened in the first three years, and some material could be moved out of the senior year. All formal non-clinic instruction would be completed by the end of the third year. During this reorganization effort attention would be given to the preprofessional curriculum, and various approaches to scheduling senior clinics could be examined. A system would be selected which would allow year-round operation of all the teaching hospital.

The consultants' report concluded, "The image presented at the faculty retreat was that of a dedicated group willing to be critical, objective, and fair with each other. Individually and collectively they expressed a desire for a high quality professional curriculum and a willingness to work together to achieve that goal."[8]

A high degree of professionalism was shown in the families of graduates, too. The third member of a family received the D.V.M. degree from Oklahoma State University when Vernon Newby graduated in the 1978. His brother Warren was a member of the class of 1966, and his brother Boyd graduated in 1969. The guest speaker at the convocation was Dr. William L. Anderson from Addison, Texas, president of the American Veterinary Medical Association and one of the original participants in the preceptorship program.

July 18 was truly an important day in the history of OSU's youngest college; the great expectations were soon to be fulfilled. Eight bids were received, within the budgetary limits, for the new teaching hospital.

"It was wide smiles and congratulations all around the conference table here Friday afternoon. . . . because the bids received were lower than anticipated." President Boger commented, "I don't know when I've been more pleased. I'm surprised you did not hear me whoopee!"[9]

At their meeting at Langston University on July 28, the Board of Regents accepted a bid from Depco Construction, Inc., Shawnee, Oklahoma, for $7,458,000.00.

In August, the State Regents for Higher Education allotted and allocated extra funding to make a total of $9 million. In September, a notice to "proceed with building" was issued, and by October the dean could proclaim, "It is indeed a real pleasure for me to inform you that the hard work of many is coming to fruition, namely, work has begun on our new teaching hospital."[10]

Endnotes

1. "New Teaching Hospital," *Oklahoma Veterinarian,* vol. 28, no. 4 (October 1976), p. 114.

2. "1976 Graduation Ceremonies: College of Veterinary Medicine Convocation," *Oklahoma Veterinarian,* vol. 28, no. 3 (July 1976), p. 84.

3. *Farm Talk,* 24 November 1976, p. 18, Scrapbook, Archives, College of Veterinary Medicine.

4. "Pets, Inversion and Iatrogenesis," *Oklahoma Veterinarian,* vol. 29, no. 2 (April 1977), pp. 34-39.

5. *Voice of the College of Veterinary Medicine,* vol. 1, no. 1 (January 1977) p. 2.

6. "The President's Letter," *Oklahoma Veterinarian,* vol. 30, no. 2 (April 1978), p. 45.

7. [American Veterinary Medical Association], "Report of Evaluation College of Veterinary Medicine, Oklahoma State University [1977]," p. 43, Archives, College of Veterinary Medicine.

8. "Final Report of Consultants to Dean Morgan and the OSU College of Veterinary Medicine Curriculum Committee, July 5, 1978," Archives, College of Veterinary Medicine.

9. *Stillwater NewsPress,* 30 July 1978, p. 1.

10. "From the Dean's Desk," *Oklahoma Veterinarian,* vol. 30, no. 4 (October 1978), p. 115.

15 Gem of the Decade

There's a beautiful view at the top of the hill if the will be yours to climb.
James M. Beattie

With funding assured and the bid awarded, construction of the new teaching hospital was placed in the capable hands of Dr. Robert M. Wood, full-time assistant to the dean. It would take over two years for the new hospital to be completed, but the intervening time was one of progress for many other areas in the College of Veterinary Medicine.

The financial picture was much brighter than usual during this time. Special funds were authorized for capital improvements through the state system of official agencies during the Oklahoma legislative session. It was the first of four years such appropriations would be made. Of the approximately $23 million that were allocated to the State Regents for Higher Education to be distributed throughout the state higher education system, $1,429,784 was committed to the College of Veterinary Medicine: $673,957 to be spent for the completion of construction of the teaching hospital; $149,385 for the completion of casework in the hospital; and $606,442 for the purchase of moveable hospital equipment.

Until July 1, 1979, the College of Veterinary Medicine had never received direct financing for graduate education. Dean Patrick Morgan and Vice President James Boggs agreed that, henceforth, a sum of money would be allocated from the Office of Academic Affairs and Research for this purpose each year.

The college received the largest private gift in its history when Sarkeys Foundation trustees approved a grant of $195,100. As the result of a college proposal presented on July 1, 1979, funds were received for equipment ($163,000), leverage funding ($20,000), and faculty development fellowships ($12,000). The faculty development fellowships of $3,000 each enabled faculty members to work and study with specialists in their field of interest for varying periods up to one month.

In the spring of 1980, some exciting news was released by the State Regents for Higher Education as the result of a special study to determine the current operational needs of the college. The regents recommended to increase the college's current year's operating budget by $1.3 million. This was approximately double the increase recommended for the college the previous year. It was described by Dean Morgan as "distinct, obvious, and rather dramatic progress."[1]

Even more progress was anticipated when it was revealed in June 1980 that the State Regents for Higher Education had distributed a record $345.8 million, of which the College of Veterinary Medicine would receive $4.4, an increase of $1.1 million over the previous year. The increased availability of funds in the state "coffers" was due to the oil boom. It was predicted to last for a long time—but it didn't! However, for the next few years it enabled Oklahoma to make remarkable, but much needed, strides in higher education. It was also the first time for the college to receive 100 percent of the funding recommended by the State Regents for Higher Education.

Attention focused on veterinary manpower needs once again as the executive summary of the much awaited Little Report was released in August of 1978. The consulting firm, Arthur D. Little, Inc., had been employed by the American Veterinary Medical Association to conduct the study to provide "objective, accurate, and detailed information on the present and future supply of veterinarians, and the demand for them, in the United States."[2]

Based on a state-by-state analysis, the report showed an overall balance nationally for 1977 between the supply of, and demand for, veterinarians in practice, but the report projected a future surplus of about 3,900, assuming twenty-four schools would be in operation by 1985. The report forecast that the demand for veterinarians with post-professional education and training would rise, percentage-wise, more steeply than for veterinarians with only the D.V.M. degree. The report received a mixed reception, especially from academia. Several deans expressed skepticism about the projections and some downright ridiculed the conclusions. It came at a time when colleges had increased student enrollment in order to take advantage of capitation funds. Such increases had been done to excess in several institutions.[3]

In order to receive federal capitation grants, the entering freshman class in 1978 had increased to sixty-nine students. All were legal residents of the state of Oklahoma, however, they were not all Oklahoma born and raised! A considerable percentage of the students had moved

Student and alumni relations became increasingly important to the College of Veterinary Medicine with each passing year. Ms. Marilyn French finds a computer most helpful in keeping up with the ever-present paperwork.

into the state to establish residency. Contrary to general belief, there was no written directive from the Oklahoma Legislature, the State Regents for Higher Education, or the Board of Regents establishing a residency requirement. Not until December 1984 would a new policy be established to permit up to 10 percent of the freshman class to be non-residents.

Several senior students embarked on some interesting missions with the six-week rotations created by the new curriculum. David Wyrick, Harry Wilson, Keith Flanagan, and others became convinced that time off from college did not have to mean time out from learning! They took advantage of this break from class to serve as externs with the Native American Project in Arizona. The externships were a project of the 7000 member Student American Veterinary Medical Association and part of a federal program to upgrade veterinary medical care on Indian reservations. The seniors described their venture as "educationally and culturally stimulating."[4]

Education endeavors were not limited to students though. The Annual Fall Conference of the Society for Theriogenology was held for the first time in Oklahoma at the Hilton Inn West, Oklahoma City, on September 20-22, 1978, with 180 veterinarians and 44 students attending. Dr. Larry Rice was the program chairman, and other college par-

Dr. Donald D. Holmes, class of 1954, returned to Oklahoma State University as the director of Laboratory Animal Services in 1979. The first course in laboratory animal medicine was added to the curriculum in the fall of 1979.

ticipants were Dr. Fayne Oberst, Dr. Louie Stratton, Dr. Duane Garner, and Dr. Fred Hopkins.

The College Alumni Association was growing. At the homecoming banquet on Saturday evening, November 4, Dr. Leroy Coggins, class of 1957, was presented the Distinguished Alumnus of the Year Award by Dr. Roger Panciera, who received the first award in 1974. Dr. Coggins developed the official test for detection of equine infectious anemia which is required by state law since 1975 for all equidae prior to entry into Oklahoma or movement within the state.

In the spring, the college launched a newsletter to be published twice a year. Designed to improve communication with the alumni, the publication was named *Plexus* by Dr. Robert Wood.

The first course in laboratory animal medicine was added to the curriculum in the fall semester of 1979, and Dr. Donald D. Holmes, class of 1954, became the first director of Laboratory Animal Services. He had been chief of the laboratory animal medicine section, Department of Pathology, University of Oklahoma Medical School, since 1974.

Prior to 1966, protection of animals used for instructional purposes and research in the United States was limited to anti-cruelty laws of the various states. Increasingly vocal and politically active humane organizations relentlessly pressed for federal legislation in the 1950s and early

1960s. In 1966, the first Laboratory Animal Welfare Act was passed by Congress, signed by the President, and became effective in 1967. Interestingly, an Oklahoma conservative, Senator A. S. "Mike" Monroney, was a leading advocate of the bill which proponents claimed was designed primarily to curb "petnapping."

The Animal and Plant Health Inspection Service, United States Department of Agriculture, was given responsibility for implementing the Laboratory Animal Welfare Act. The original act was later expanded and in 1971 became the Animal Welfare Act. These regulations prescribe standards for procurement, transportation, caging, husbandry, and veterinary medical care for most species broadly defined as "laboratory animals."

In addition to federal regulations, the Public Health Service adopted what is becoming an increasingly stringent policy on care and use of laboratory animals. Through its various agencies, such as the massive National Institutes of Health, the Public Health Service is the major source of funds for biomedical research. For this reason the policy has the force of law for any institutions aspiring to receive awards. Standards adopted apply to all species and extend to use as well as care of animals maintained for teaching, testing, and research.

Initially scientific and professional organizations strongly resisted the imposition of animal welfare regulations. Most such organizations, however, now recognize their responsibility for animals used in scientific endeavors and the fact that "good science" requires healthy animals, but continued refinement and extension of federal regulations and policies during the coming years can be anticipated.[5]

A highlight of "Veterinary Medicine Week in Oklahoma," was the presentation of the annual Dr. Lewis H. Moe Lecture. A practicing veterinarian from Montana, U.S. Senator John Melcher spoke on Friday evening about the vast opportunities for veterinarians. He discounted the gloom voiced by some in the profession concerning the future. He said: "By and large the fate of our profession will still remain tightly tied to agriculture itself, and it's on that note that I am most hopeful."[6] The grand climax was the tenth biennial Open House on Saturday and Sunday afternoon during which over 3,000 toured the magnificent displays on modern veterinary medicine.

The guest speaker at the convocation for the graduating seniors on May 12 was the Honorable Dan Draper, Speaker of the Oklahoma House of Representatives. He was presented with a construction worker's hard hat as a token of appreciation of his leadership in obtaining the new teaching hospital and promoting higher education.

Dr. James E. Breazile and Dr. Eric I. Williams attended the XXI International Veterinary Congress in Moscow, U.S.S.R., on July 1-7. They had taken private tutoring in Russian, which sounded pretty unusual

U.S. Senator John Melcher from Montana spoke at the annual Lewis Moe lecture in 1979. Also in attendance were Dean Patrick Morgan; Senator John Melcher; Dr. Culver Moe; Dr. Larry Rice, committee chairman, and Dr. Vernon Tharp, president of the American Veterinary Medical Association.

with the Oklahoma accent—well, Missouri-Okie and Welsh-Okie—which no doubt confused the KGB!

In response to the invitation of the dean, the American Veterinary Medical Association Council on Education visited the campus on August 22 and 23, 1979, to evaluate the "state of the college" and to make recommendations accordingly.

The committee paid special attention to the recommendations listed in the 1977 AVMA Council on Education report regarding construction of the teaching hospital, operating funds, clinical teaching program, faculty morale, and of course, the "perennial" curriculum! The report was received later in the year. The committee was encouraged to find the college was progressing toward a solution of its major problems. The determination of the administration, the growing esprit de corps of the faculty, and the supportive posture of the university administration were seen as strong, positive influences. They hoped that the college would continue to evaluate its progress in light of the recommendations made as a result of the last full evaluation visit in 1977. The report of the AVMA Council on Education was encouraging and stated that if present progress would be maintained, full accreditation would probably be reached in the foreseeable future.

The Veterinary Administrative Council turned its attention to a proposal to form guidelines for admission with advanced standing. After considerable enteric hypermotility of words, this astute body finally adopted a policy for persons with doctoral degrees in appropriate disciplines who wished to obtain a Doctor of Veterinary Medicine and who would be potentially valuable resources to veterinary medical education, research, and practice.[7]

The Veterinary Administrative Council also decided that in order for a student to be exempted from a course in the veterinary medical curriculum, a grade of A or B in the course or its equivalent would be required. Hitherto this had been granted if a C grade or better had been achieved, but with a national trend towards grade inflation, it was time to re-evaluate this policy.

The tremendous emphasis on continuing education and advanced training in the 1970s resulted in the founding of several specialty boards and species-oriented societies. This was also the impetus to establish counterpart student chapters, such as the American Association of Equine Practitioners and the American Association of Bovine Practitioners. Other student chapters were initiated later. They were all constituted under the "umbrella" of the Student Chapter American Veterinary Medical Association and not in competition with it. They were also expected to provide speakers for student meetings periodically. In 1979 the college was highly honored to receive the first charter ever granted a student chapter of the American Animal Hospital Association. The new chapter would be a model, carefully followed by the national organization, that would help to determine the fate of student chapters nationwide.

By the end of the year, it was reported that the construction of the new teaching hospital was progressing well, with 70 percent completion—a fitting end to a decade of great anticipation. There was a feeling that the college was finally about to reach out and enjoy the fruits of high endeavor. The dawn of the centennial decade marked the beginning of the most exciting period in the 32-year history of the College of Veterinary Medicine.

Dean Morgan's goals for the college for the next five years were to obtain full academic accreditation, decrease student-faculty ratios to reach the top third of the veterinary schools in the Big 8 region, increase research and graduate education (including residencies) efforts by 100 percent, increase D.V.M. student enrollment, and increase faculty and staff salaries to be in the top third of all colleges of veterinary medicine.

On November 26, 1979, Dr. Brian Sinclair and his wife Sheila from Yorkshire, England, had visited the college and spoken at the student chapter meeting. Because of much public interest, the meeting was held in the Seretean Center Concert Hall. Dr. Sinclair, better known as Tristan Farnon the dare-devil student in James Herriot's best sellers, delighted his audience with a very informative and witty presentation on the background of the books and the filming of "All Creatures Great and Small."

A highlight of any year for the College of Veterinary Medicine was the visit of Dr. Brian Sinclair and his wife Sheila from Yorkshire, England. Dr. Sinclair visited the college in 1979 and again in 1981, spoke to groups on and off campus, and participated in the taping of the series "The Oklahoma Veterinarian." Students Pat Gillis, Tom Puglsey, and Genie and Rob Thoni pose with Dr. and Mrs Sinclair *(center)*.

Dr. Sinclair also spoke at a special meeting of the Tulsa Veterinary Medical Association.

The following year, the 65th Oklahoma Veterinary Medical Association conference, held in Oklahoma City on January 26-28, was a landmark in the profession's public relations program. The Board of Directors voted to sponsor the 41-segment series of the British Broadcasting Corporation Television production of "All Creatures Great and Small," starting in October. The contract called for four complete showings of the entire series between October 1980 and December 31, 1983, for a total fee of $11,030 payable in four equal installments annually. The OVMA Auxiliary pledged $1000 toward the cost of the series. Because each segment ran for fifty minutes, the association was allocated the remainder of the hour to present programs on modern veterinary medicine.

On Thursday evening, October 2, 1980, the first episode of "All Creatures Great and Small" premiered on Oklahoma Educational Television Authority channels in Oklahoma City, Cheyenne, Tulsa, and Eufaula at 9:00 p.m.[8] Immediately following the episode, "The Oklahoma Veterinarian" series was presented. During the late summer and early fall, a group of veterinarians had taped thirteen seven-minute episodes on modern veterinary medicine at the Channel 13 studio in Oklahoma City. The programs were introduced by Dr. Eric Williams, and the coordinator was Dr. Mike Johnston, chairman of the Public Relations Com-

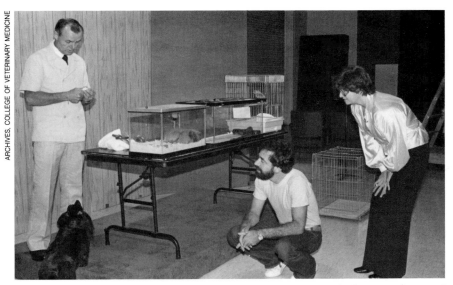

The Oklahoma Veterinary Medical Association sponsored the series, "All Creatures Great and Small," and the College of Veterinary Medicine sponsored "The Oklahoma Veterinarian." Many alumni and faculty were involved in the production. At the OETA studios, Dr. Tony Thomas from Midwest City prepares to tape a program on how to choose a pet.

mittee. When Dr. Brian Sinclair, returned to campus in October 1981, he also recorded three programs for "The Oklahoma Veterinarian."

After a slow start, the series became a very popular family program. In addition to the original programs, another twenty were produced on the OSU campus and on location in collaboration with the OSU Educational Television Services. Dr. Marshall E. Allen, ETS director, and Mr. Billy R. Reinschmiedt, program producer, and their staff of exuberant students, were absolutely delightful to work with and contributed enormously to a highly successful public relations venture for the university, the college, and the veterinary profession. A survey conducted by OETA in 1982 showed that the series was rated fifth out of 128 programs. "The Oklahoma Veterinarian" segments were presented until the OVMA sponsorship contract expired in June 1983.[9]

Another contract of a different kind had the "go ahead." In a letter to Depco Construction, Inc., on April 11, 1980, Bill D. Halley, director of OSU Architectural Services, notified the company to commence construction on the completion of shell space at the teaching hospital on or before April 14, to be completed within 180 consecutive calendar days, namely October 12.

At the Annual Awards Banquet on April 25, Patrick Gillis, president of the student chapter, presented the new college logo to Dean Morgan.

The logo, designed by Gerald Parsons, a second-year student, was the winning entry in a contest sponsored by the student chapter during the spring semester.

The convocation was moved in 1980 to the Seretean Center Concert Hall to accommodate the ever-increasing number of family and friends who attend. The theater has a capacity for only about 600, while the concert hall has about 900 seats. The guest speaker was Dr. Wilford Bailey, associate dean, School of Veterinary Medicine, and former acting president of Auburn University, who gave a very eloquent address on the theme, "Be Diligent."

The State Board of Veterinary Medical Examiners were on campus the following Monday to give the state part of the examination only. The "national board" was given on June 2. This arrangement was not well received due to the necessity to return to the campus and the delay in obtaining the results of the national examination. It was discontinued the following year, and several states now offer the board examinations also in December.[10]

Frenchmen say, "Plus ça change, plus c'est la même chose"—the more things change, the more they stay the same! Such was the case when the summer session arrived. For a trial period of one year, classes were held from 7:30-9:30 a.m. with clinics from 9:30 a.m. until 4:00 p.m. The following year, clinics reverted to the morning schedule with

Pat Gillis *(right)*, president of the Student Chapter, American Veterinary Medical Association, presents the new college logo to Dean Patrick Morgan at the annual awards banquet. The logo was designed by Gerald Parsons *(center)*.

classes in the afternoon—but not for long!

The summer of 1980 was long and hot resulting in the usual departure of the populace to the mountains, but in the world of veterinary medicine, there never seems to be a dull moment. So it was at this time when a mysterious disease crept into the area from east or west, but nobody really knew from where. It was an acute, usually fatal disease of dogs. It was parvovirus which had two syndromes—an intestinal form and one affecting the heart. The first case of the disease in Oklahoma was diagnosed in 1978, and it was now becoming more widespread in the state. Pet owners flocked to have their dogs vaccinated against the disease.[11]

During the American Veterinary Medical Association annual convention in Washington, D.C., in July, the College of Veterinary Medicine and the Oklahoma Veterinary Medical Association co-sponsored a legislative breakfast in appreciation of the efforts by the Oklahoma Congressional delegation in behalf of veterinary medicine. Over eighty attended the breakfast held in Room B338, Rayburn House Office Building. OVMA President Dr. Sam Strahm presided and Dean Patrick Morgan spoke eloquently on behalf of the college. At the college alumni banquet, the following evening, Dean and Mrs. Patrick Morgan, supported by several faculty members and spouses, greeted over 200 alumni and their families.

The 1980-81 academic year opened with the usual all-school picnic and the much anticipated annual freshman skit. The offices of Student Affairs and Admissions were relocated as one unit in the old small animal clinic reception area on the first floor.

The freshman class had seventy students. Why the extra one? In order to receive federal capitation grants the college had to increase freshman student enrollment by five percent. In 1978 the class size had increased to sixty-nine based on the 1976 figure. Now the federal agency, in its infinite attention to minutia, directed that 5 percent of sixty-six should be an increase of four students not three. So seventy students were selected for the class of 1980!

The emphasis on continuing education resulted in the re-establishment of the Conference for Veterinarians on September 5-7. This annual event had been an important link between the college, the alumni, and state practitioners for decades. It was brought about to a large extent by the enthusiasm of the Oklahoma Academy of Veterinary Practice. The main topic was veterinary financial management presented by Dr. Robert Lewis, College of Veterinary Medicine, University of Georgia.

Faculty recruiting had been going well during the past few years, and "the garden was filling up with roses," although there were a few departures. Dr. Alphonso Niec, director of Veterinary Educational

Development and Services, left on November 30, 1978. He was responsible for the Learning Resources Center and audiovisual equipment and preparation. He devised the formula which included an academic profile and a personal profile for the selection of veterinary medicine students that proved to be very beneficial, especially for students who had not been admitted, in preparing for their next application.

Dr. Everett C. Short Jr., became head, Department of Physiological Sciences, on July 1, 1978. He was previously associate dean of veterinary medicine and professor of biochemistry at the University of Minnesota. Dr. Louie Stratton assumed the position of director of research.

Dr. Sidney Ewing returned as head, Department of Veterinary Parasitology, Microbiology and Public Health on January 1, 1979.

Dr. David Dodd left on April 13, 1979, to accept a position with a pharmaceutical company. Dr. Dodd had brought to the college an emphasis on the need for a far better command of the English language and a challenge to students and faculty to improve their academic performance. He instituted a policy in his department of fewer class examinations with questions designed to require the students to express themselves better in writing. It was a refreshing change for correct spelling and good written English to be demanded again in the classroom! Dr. Roger Panciera succeeded him as head of the Department of Veterinary Pathology.

Effective October 1, 1980, Dr. J. Mack Oyler, returned from Virginia

Dr. Louie G. Stratton became the first director of the Boren Veterinary Medical Teaching Hospital.

Administrative changes resulted in Dr. Everett Short Jr. becoming head of the Department of Physiological Sciences on July 1, 1978. A graduate of Colorado State University and University of Minnesota, Dr. Short had been the associate dean in the College of Veterinary Medicine at the University of Minnesota.

Polytechnic Institute and State University, to become the college's first associate dean in charge of academic affairs. Dr. Louie G. Stratton was appointed director of the new teaching hospital to be completed soon. In view of the impending opening of the new hospital and the rigorous administrative duties involved, it was decided a separate administration was needed. Dr. Fayne Oberst continued as head of the Department of Medicine and Surgery.

Other faculty members were in the news also. Dr. Lester Johnson was presented the prestigious Dr. William F. Irwin Award. Dr. Eric I. Williams received the Oklahoma Veterinarian of the Year Award, presented for the first time at the Oklahoma Veterinary Medical Association convention in 1980.

Dr. Sidney Ewing was appointed to the Council, Conference for Research in Animal Diseases. Dr. Ewing served as vice president of the Conference for Research Workers in Animal Diseases in 1983-84, and president, 1984-85. Dr. James Breazile was appointed to a Technical Merit Review Committee for the National Institutes of Health.

Dr. Thomas Thedford took a leave of absence without pay for twelve months to work as a consultant for Winrock International at Morrillton, Arkansas. He spent some time in Haiti setting up a breeding project in milk goats imported for that purpose. He also prepared livestock owners' manuals on goat and sheep diseases and management. Dr. Thedford is presently involved with continuing education via teleconferences.

The year of great fulfillment had finally arrived. For several weeks there was bustling activity everywhere in preparation for the upcoming events.

First, there was the 66th Annual Oklahoma Veterinary Medical Association convention in Tulsa on January 17-20 where several faculty members presented papers. Dr. Louie G. Stratton was installed as president for 1981-82.

Dean Morgan's message to the alumni in the winter issue of *Plexus* was a prose of optimism. The month of February already had the daffodils in bloom as a prelude to the great overtures of splendor that were about to unfold.[12]

Governor George Nigh signed the usual proclamation declaring February 23 through March 1 "Veterinary Medicine Week in Oklahoma." The American Veterinary Medical Association Council on Education team arrived on February 23 and during the next couple of days conducted a thorough study of the college. They had already received stacks of written information several weeks previously.

The annual Dr. Lewis H. Moe Lecture was delivered on Thursday evening by Professor Dr. Mathew Stöber, director of Cattle Clinics, Hannover Veterinary College, Republic of West Germany. He spoke on "Clinical Aspects of Leukemia in Cattle." Professor Dr. Stöber had served as secretary-treasurer of the World Association for Buiatrics (cattle diseases) since 1980 and is regarded as one of Europe's leading authorities on cattle diseases.

Finally it was Friday; the great day had dawned. After many years of planning, replanning, optimism, despair, frustration, but eternal hope, the Boren Veterinary Medical Teaching Hospital was officially dedicated. It was a cool, windy morning when the ceremony commenced at 10:30 a.m. in front of the large animal clinics receiving area where over 500 persons had gathered. Dean Patrick Morgan presided, and Dr. John Montgomery, chairman of the Board of Regents, gave the dedication address. President L. L. Boger responded for Oklahoma State University. U.S. Senator David Boren spoke and performed the ribbon cutting ceremony with a pair of extra large surgical scissors.

Afterwards over 350 guests were bused to the Student Union for a dedication luncheon in the ballroom. Mr. John Link, student chapter president, gave the invocation; Dr. E. T. Dunlap, chancellor of the State Regents for Higher Education; and Mr. Carter Bradley, executive director of the Higher Education Alumni Council for Oklahoma, were the guest speakers. Dr. Jacob Mosier, president-elect of the American Veterinary Medical Association, brought greetings on behalf of the veterinary profession. The guests were given a conducted tour of the hospital in the afternoon. It was the first major new building to be completed on the OSU campus in almost ten years.

The dedication for the Boren Veterinary Medical Teaching Hospital was held in the east parking area outside the large animal clinics where over 500 persons attended. U.S. Senator David Boren *(center)* performs the ribbon cutting ceremony as President Lawrence Boger, Regent John Montgomery, and Dean Patrick Morgan observe.

Years of dreaming were fulfilled when on March 16, 1981, students, clinicians, and staff moved into the Boren Veterinary Medical Teaching Hospital.

Oklahoma State University

The following day it was the students' turn to put on a show as only they can do. On Saturday from 9:00 a.m. to 5:00 p.m. and Sunday afternoon, over 10,000 visitors attended Open House. Guided tours of the hospital and several displays featured the event for which the very appropriate theme was "A New Beginning for an Old Tradition." So ended a truly remarkable week of well-earned celebration.

On March 16 a whole array of clinicians, students, and staff took on the mammoth task of "moving in" from the old clinics to the teaching hospital. But the celebrating was not over.

Monday, March 23, was a blue ribbon day lined with gold. At noon, Dean Patrick Morgan made an announcement to a packed audience of faculty, students, and staff in the auditorium: "I have always regarded ourselves as one family in the College of Veterinary Medicine. Like all families, we share good times and bad times. Today, I am pleased to inform you that we have received word from the AVMA that, for the first time in our history, the college is fully accredited."[13]

Oh! What a beautiful morning. Oh! What a beautiful day!

Endnotes

1. "Report to the Veterinary Medicine Faculty Meeting, Spring, 1980," Archives, College of Veterinary Medicine.

2. Arthur D. Little, Inc., "Summary of U.S. Veterinary Medical Manpower Needs—1978-1990," *Journal of the American Veterinary Medical Association*, vol. 173, no. 4 (15 August 1978), p. 369.

3. Arthur D. Little, Inc., pp. 369-372.

4. "Native American Project," *Oklahoma Veterinarian*, vol. 31, no. 1 (January 1979), pp. 23-24.

5. Author's personal communication with Dr. Donald D. Holmes, October 1985.

6. "College News," *Oklahoma Veterinarian*, vol. 31, no. 2 (April 1979), p. 56.

7. "Guidelines for Admission to Advanced Standing, Approved by Veterinary Administrative Council, September 14, 1979," Archives, College of Veterinary Medicine.

8. "Television Series," *Oklahoma Veterinarian*, vol. 32, no. 3 (October 1980), pp. 131-132.

9. "All Creatures Great and Small," *Oklahoma Veterinarian*, vol. 34, no. 3 (July 1982), p. 77.

10. The Oklahoma Veterinary Practice Act (effective April 19, 1982, as amended): Section 698.9 Licensed veterinarians—Applicants: "Before any applicant is allowed to sit for such examination, he shall submit to the Board sufficient proof that he is of good moral character, is a graduate of a school of veterinary medicine approved by the Board, and such other proof as the Board may require."

11. Oklahoma State University *Daily O'Collegian*, 17 June 1980.

12. "Letter from Dean Morgan," *Plexus*, vol. 3, no. 1 (Winter 1981), p. 1.

13. "College Receives Full Accreditation," *Oklahoma Veterinarian*, vol. 33, no. 2 (April 1981), p. 64.

16 Reach for the Sky

Lend me the stone strength of the past and I will lend you
The wings of the future, for I have them.
Robinson Jeffers, *To the Rock that will be a Cornerstone*

The operation of the teaching hospital was now in full swing and a source of pride and joy to everyone. At the Annual Awards Banquet on April 24, 1981, Dean Patrick Morgan presented Dr. Robert Wood, assistant to the dean, the "Gem of the Decade" plaque for outstanding services to the college and university. Dr. Wood's expertise as a consultant and overseer was invaluable during the construction of the new teaching hospital.

The increased space and facilities in the new teaching hospital and the addition of more clinicians permitted the scheduling of more students in the clinical areas. This was accomplished by assigning students to a special clinic program which included assignments in rural practice, herd health, all-day equine and small animals as well as paraclinical assignments in clinical pathology and parasitology, necropsy, and diagnostic laboratory activities.

These changes released time for expansion of the general clinic courses to include rotations through six main clinic assignments (small animal medicine, small animal surgery, equine medicine and surgery, food animal medicine and surgery, anesthesiology, and radiology). With the special clinics program in effect, the number of on-campus students operating all facets of the clinic program was increased considerably while still maintaining a year-round clinic program. Currently, the general clinics operate from 10:00 a.m. to 5:00 p.m. while the special

Dean Patrick Morgan presents Dr. Robert Wood with a "Gem of the Decade" Award at the 1981 Annual Awards Banquet for outstanding service to the college and university during the construction of the teaching hospital. The plaque was designed, made, and donated by Dr. Dan Woesner of Lawton, class of 1953. A diamond marks the location of Stillwater.

clinics have activities from 8:00 a.m. to 5:00 p.m.

Dr. John Montgomery was guest speaker for the college convocation for the graduating seniors held at the Seretean Center Concert Hall on Saturday afternoon, May 9. However, commencement exercises in Lewis Field had to be cancelled for the first time because of rain. Each college, therefore, held its own ceremony. Dean Patrick Morgan conferred the D.V.M. degrees and presented the diplomas on behalf of President Boger at a gathering of students, parents, and faculty in the Veterinary Medicine Auditorium that evening.

After thirty years of dedicated services, Dr. A. L. Malle retired on June 30, 1981. His lectures were often spiked with humor and good down-to-earth advice on practice economics and professionalism. Dr. Thomas R. Thedford, master of ceremonies, presented Dr. and Mrs. Malle with two leather albums of letters from friends at an appreciation dinner. The Dr. A. L. Malle Emergency Loan Fund for veterinary medicine students was established in his honor, a truly admirable recognition for one who had devoted countless hours as their adviser and teacher.

Late summer brought another first for the college when continuing education was boomed into space—and back again! On Friday, August 21, 1981, a three-hour teleconference on new surgical techniques was

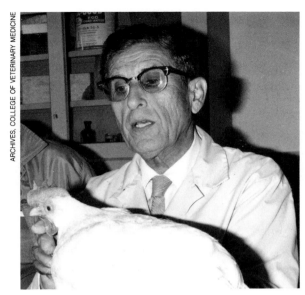

Dr. A. L. Malle retired in 1981 after thirty years of dedicated service. The Dr. A. L. Malle Emergency Loan Fund for students was established in his honor.

presented by the faculty from the new teaching hospital. The OSU Educational Television Service, with the assistance of KTVY Channel 4, Oklahoma City's remote facility, televised the proceedings. It was the first of its kind from any college of veterinary medicine in the world.

Generated signals were transmitted by cable to a portable satellite transmitting facility provided by Public Service Satellite Consortium, which had been brought from Denver and parked outside the teaching hospital. This transportable earth station sent signals to an orbiting satellite 22,300 miles above the earth.

The signals were transmitted from the satellite to portable receiving dishes located at Ardmore, McAlester, Oklahoma City, Tulsa, Woodward, and Stillwater. The receiving dish, parked outside each conference location, sent the video signal via cable to the television sets in the conference room to be observed by those assembled.

A Nexus audio bridge telephone system was provided to connect the area conference centers with the teaching hospital so that the veterinarians could converse with the faculty presenting the program.[1] Over 150 veterinarians participated; 139 presented written reports that the conference was of great educational value. Members of the Board of Regents and the university administration came to the hospital for a first-hand look at a very successful venture.

Teleconferences gave new meaning to Oklahoma State University's land-grant mission to teach, research, and extend to the world. In the 1980s, the College of Veterinary Medicine presented several teleconferences that reached all areas of the United States and Canada. During one such teleconference, Dr. Fayne Oberst *(left)* serves as the moderator while Dr. Ralph Buckner, Dr. Lester Johnson, and Dr. Larry Rice participates in the discussion.

The second satellite video teleconference was boomed across the United States and Canada from the OSU Telecommunications Center on Monday afternoon, February 4, 1984. The three-hour program was presented by the college, OSU Cooperative Extension Service, and the OSU Animal Science Department. Sponsored as part of the nationwide Antibiotic Residue Avoidance Awareness Program, it was funded by the Food Safety Inspection Service of the USDA. Downlinks were located at extension offices in several cities in Oklahoma, while veterinarians and livestock producers in twenty-five other states and two locations in Canada were also able to participate.

Participating veterinarians were able to claim veterinary continuing education credit for one to three hours. The subjects presented were systemic mycoses of small animals with emphasis on histoplasmosis, practical antibiotic residue avoidance, stocker calf receiving programs and equine lameness, nutrition, and young race horse training.

Later in the year, in October 1984, the college and the OSU Cooperative Extension Service presented yet another teleconference. The two-part program on bovine respiratory disease and receiving stocker calves boomed into space on the evenings of October 24 and 30 and were received in thirty-one locations in-state, sixty-six out-of-state, and three in Canada. It was estimated that over 4,000 veterinarians and livestock producers participated. Dr. Thomas Thedford introduced the programs. He was joined by charming, fellow Texan, Dr. Carolynn Taylor MacAllister, who became a full-time extension specialist. Oklahoma State University had undoubtedly become a leader in telecommunication, nationwide and into Canada.

Although capitation grants were no longer available, the college opened the academic year of 1981-82 with a budget increase of over $1 million. Two friends of the college pledged $1,000 per year for three scholarships to establish the Dr. John Wilson Montgomery Scholarship for a black student in the College of Veterinary Medicine or a black student who had successfully completed at least one year in pre-veterinary medicine. The scholarship fund has since become endowed in perpetuity.

On October 5, Governor George Nigh stated in his proposal to the 1982 legislature for a $30 million appropriation for energy, agriculture, and renewable natural resources research that Oklahoma's booming economy was now the virtual envy of the other forty-nine states because of its unprecedented growth and healthy climate. Oklahoma remained the most fully employed, and had a growing per capita income. The Governor emphasized the importance of the "two great comprehensive universities in Oklahoma at O.U. and O.S.U." He recommended an appropriation of $30 million (from surplus funds), $15 million for each university, for research.[2]

At the same time, preliminary budget hearings were in full swing and Dean Morgan issued a memorandum to the department heads and directors on November 10 anticipating salary increases of 12 percent, fringe benefit increases of 16 percent, and increases of 21 percent for new positions. The State Regents for Higher Education had proposed an increase of 25.24 percent for the college for fiscal year 1982-83.

It was announced that $1.7 million had been authorized by the State Regents for Higher Education but not allocated by the legislature. The Veterinary Administrative Council turned its attention to setting priorities on renovations in the Veterinary Medicine building. At a special meeting in December, the following priorities were established: high priority—add two additional classrooms, renovate the library and learning center, consolidate departmental faculty offices and laboratories, provide an air movement system for the gross anatomy laboratory to reduce concentrations of formaldehyde, and get on-line for the chilled water system for the college building and the diagnostic laboratory and steam for the latter. Lesser priorities were set for centralization of laboratory animal resources, teaching laboratories, and an isolation facility. All these would not amount to much unless the most pressing need was taken care of, namely repairing the veterinary medicine building roof! The estimated cost was $111,312. A request to the university administration that this expense be paid from general university funds was not approved. The roof was repaired in the summer of 1984 and the cost prorated for three years from operational funds of the college.

The college was, however, assigned a section of land for teaching and research after a year of negotiations. The university had purchased the land recently from Mr. Jack Downey.

The faculty continued to receive national acclaim. Sarkeys Foundation Fellowships were awarded to Dr. Stanley Newcomer of the Department of Physiological Sciences to study thyrotropin-releasing hormone at the New England Medical Center in Boston; to Dr. James A. Jackson of the Department of Veterinary Parasitology, Microbiology and Public Health to attend a course on mycology research at Emory University Medical School in Atlanta; and to Dr. Lawrence E. Evans, radiologist, to study educational models at the University of California School of Medicine, San Francisco.

Dr. Eric I. Williams received the XII International Veterinary Congress Prize presented annually, for outstanding service toward the international understanding of veterinary medicine at the American Veterinary Medical Association convention in St. Louis. The usual college reception for the alumni held during the convention was well attended.

Dr. Lloyd C. Faulkner assumed his duties as director of research for the college on October 1. A graduate of Colorado State University, he had been engaged in practice in Colorado and served as professor and chairman, Department of Physiology and Biophysics at his alma mater for several years before accepting an appointment as associate dean for research and graduate studies at the University of Missouri College of Veterinary Medicine.

Because Arkansas, which has no veterinary college, is the home of many loyal alumni, a "state of the college" report is presented annually at the Arkansas Veterinary Medical Association Convention. Many of the officers installed at the 1982 convention in Little Rock were graduates of Oklahoma State University. Dr. Raymond Whitehead, class of 1974, succeeded Dr. Ronald Stenseng, class of 1963, as president; and Dr. William R. Roberson, class of 1965, became vice president. Dr. Doyne Hamm, class of 1962, was named Arkansas Veterinarian of the Year.

The need for better communication between the various components of the college and the rest of the campus culminated in the "launching" of a weekly newsletter at the beginning of the 1982 spring semester. It was duly christened Qui, Quid, Ubi? the Latin for who, what, where? Prepared and distributed by the Office of Admissions and Student Affairs each Friday morning, each issue carried the calendar of events for the coming week, accolades for faculty, students, and staff

Dr. Lloyd C. Faulkner became the new director of research for the College of Veterinary Medicine in 1981.

achievements, wisdom for the week, and some good plain gossip! It was soon a roaring success.

The spring semester glided along serenely to a close, bowing out as usual with the senior skit which seemed to maintain its magic attraction if not its theatrical expertise through the years. The new teaching hospital had been in operation for over a year and it was a fitting tribute when the senior class dedicated the *1982 Aesculapius* "to all those whose hard work made the dream of the Veterinary Teaching Hospital and American Veterinary Medical Association accreditation a reality, for it is to their efforts that the hospital stands as a monument."[3]

The college convocation for the graduating seniors, held for the first time in the morning, was highlighted by the presence of Dr. Jacob Mosier, American Veterinary Medical Association president. In his usual dynamic, articulate manner, Dr. Mosier focused his address from the "view" of a member of the graduating class, a member of the faculty, a member of society, and as himself. He remarked, "Pride gives us responsibility, responsibility gives us humility, humility gives us faith, faith gives us hope, and hope leads to success."[4]

The College of Veterinary Medicine and the College of Arts and Sciences conducted joint teaching and research programs for many years. On July 1, 1982, undergraduate programs in physiology, parasitology, and wildlife became the sole responsibility of the College of Arts and Sciences. Four faculty members transferred their appointments from the College of Veterinary Medicine to the College of Arts and Sciences.[5]

Dean Patrick Morgan, reflecting on five years as dean, stated in his message to the alumni: "We face the year 1983 with pride in our past achievements and great optimism that 'the best is yet to be.' Even though the economy of our State is not presently as vibrant as in recent years, we are confident that we can continue to maintain progress towards excellence in teaching, research, and extension."[6] The number of faculty members had increased from 60 to 77 in a few years and very recently six had become Diplomates in their respective specialties.

Dr. James E. Creed, Department of Clinical Sciences, Colorado State University, assumed his position as head of the small animal surgery section. A nationally renowned teacher and surgeon, Dr. Creed was joined by Dr. Kenneth Bartels, a debonair Iowa State University graduate, and Dr. R. Dennis Heald, a quiet, meticulous young man from Auburn University who brought expertise in small animal internal medicine.

Two distinguished veterinarians graciously accepted appointments as adjunct professors in the college, namely, Dr. William J. Kay, director and chief of staff, The Animal Medical Center, New York City, who was board certified in internal medicine, specializing in neurology; and Dr. Werner P. Heuschele, head, Microbiology and Virology Research Department, San Diego Zoo, California. Under the college preceptorship program, senior students would be able to spend six-week assignments in these prestigious institutions.

Yet another accolade was bestowed on a distinguished OSU professor when Dr. Lester Johnson was named the 1983 Oklahoma Veterinarian of the Year at the 68th Annual Convention of the Oklahoma Veterinary Medical Association. After many years of discussion, contemplation, and indepth study, the board of directors of the Oklahoma Veterinary Medical Association appointed an executive secretary. Meg Preston, an ebullient lass from Wisconsin, assumed the position with an office on the third floor of the college building. It was a master stroke

ARCHIVES, COLLEGE OF VETERINARY MEDICINE

Ever present in university activities, the students in the College of Veterinary Medicine have often entered a float in the homecoming parade. Throughout the years from the first class onward, the "spirit" has continued including this float exhibited during the early 1980s.

Dr. Lester Johnson served the College of Veterinary Medicine for thirty years. An outstanding clinician and teacher, he was awarded the Oklahoma Veterinarian of the Year Award by the Oklahoma Veterinary Medical Association in 1983.

of public relations and cooperative effort between the dean and the veterinarians in Oklahoma.

The student chapter continued to develop new projects. Late in the fall of 1981, the student chapter had organized a Southwest Mini Symposium for colleagues from other colleges in the area. It was well attended with representatives from Texas, Louisiana, Missouri, Kansas, and Colorado schools. The organizer was Michael Sealock, fourth-year student and class of 1983.

In the spring of 1983, the student chapter embarked on another adventure when it sponsored the first "Pharmaceuticals Day" on March 11 from 7:00 to 10:00 p.m. at the Ramada Inn. The enterprising coordinator was Tracy D. Rutledge, class of 1984. Over twenty companies displayed their products and gave away door prizes. It was a delightful glimpse into the real world and the event has been held annually ever since.

After several months of negotiations, Oklahoma State University signed a contract with Ross University on the Caribbean island nation of St. Kitts. The contract covered a period of thirty-six weeks during which Ross University School of Veterinary Medicine would send a small number of students for clinical training at the College of Veterinary Medicine, Oklahoma State University. The college would not be granting a degree or any type of academic credit to these students. The income generated by contract fees, which were five to six times more than paid by OSU students, would generate much needed finances for the Department of Medicine and Surgery to hire some instructors. The Department of Pathology also received some of the funds. On April 1, eight students arrived to commence their clinical training.

The skepticism about the caliber of the eight students from Ross University proved ill founded. When they left at the end of the year, having completed their clinical assignments, they all performed admirably in the National Board Examination. The college received a request from the Ross University School of Veterinary Medicine to accept students for clinical training again beginning in July 1984. Although the medicine and surgery faculty members were in favor of accepting more students, the Ross issue was a sensitive one with a lot of misunderstanding in some departments, and the request was denied.

Dr. Lawrence E. Evans, chief of the radiology section, Department of Medicine and Surgery, elected to take early retirement on June 30 and accepted a teaching assignment with Ross University. He had joined the OSU faculty in 1970 and was responsible for the extensive planning on the radiology area for the new teaching hospital.

United States Representative Wes Watkins, Oklahoma District 3, was the guest speaker at the college convocation for the graduating seniors on May 7. The event was moved up to 9:00 a.m. because commencement exercises were held at 11:00 a.m. It was the first time that each college was requested to select a senior student to represent the graduates on the platform. The College of Veterinary Medicine decided that the recipient of the Dean Clarence H. McElroy Award should also receive this honor. John D. Stein represented the graduates.

The college was host to several organizations. For the first time, the Association of Business Officers of the Colleges of Veterinary Medicine in North America met in Oklahoma. The eighth annual meeting was held at Oklahoma State University on October 19-21. Marilyn Wilson, senior financial coordinator in the college and chairman-elect of the association, was the program coordinator.

Undoubtedly the highlight of the season was the arrival of bovine practitioners from all over the United States, Canada, and overseas to attend the 18th Annual Convention of the American Association of Bovine Practitioners in Oklahoma City on November 27-December 1. In spite of wintry weather closing several area airports, over 800 veterinarians and their spouses attended, the grand total being over 1,700 participants. Governor Nigh welcomed the participants with an entertaining

Gaining prominence in the field of veterinary medicine, the College of Veterinary Medicine was host to several organizations that held meetings in Oklahoma. A group of bovine practitioners, attending the American Association of Bovine Practitioners Convention in Oklahoma City, visited the Boren Veterinary Medical Teaching Hospital and the Oklahoma Animal Disease Diagnostic Laboratory. Visitors included *(from left to right)* Dr. Robert Keith from Monroe, Wisconsin, past president; Dr. Harold Amstutz from Purdue University, executive secretary-treasurer; Dr. Neil Anderson from Ontario, Canada, vice president; Dr. Glen Hoffsis from Ohio State University, president; Dr. Ian Baker, president of the British Cattle Veterinary Association; and Dr. Michael Vaughan, president-elect of the British Cattle Veterinary Association.

speech at the opening ceremony. OSU President L. L. Boger presented a sparkling address on the role of Century 21 research plans. Several OSU faculty members participated in the scientific proceedings and local arrangements. A spectator puzzled by the meaning of the letters AABP on a participant's name tag asked what the letters stood for. The AABP member replied that they stood for ''American Association of Beautiful People.''

The Student Chapter AABP at OSU acted as hosts for other students. They arranged a pizza supper before joining the banquet patrons for their entertainment by Indian dancers and the indomitable Baxter Black. The students also took their colleagues on a bus trip to the Boren Veterinary Medical Teaching Hospital followed by a barbecue and a joint meeting with the OSU Student Chapter, AVMA.

A post-convention visit to the OSU campus was also arranged. Dean Morgan welcomed the visitors at a luncheon in the Student Union. The group toured the teaching hospital and the Oklahoma Animal Disease Diagnostic Laboratory. Dr. James Pinsent, Bristol, England, delivered a special lecture on bovine gastroenterology for visitors, students, and faculty members. It was a festive respite at a time when deepening financial woes threatened.

As the fiscal year 1984-85 approached, it became obvious that finances would be tough for academia. The 1980 centennial decade had been greeted with great fanfare and euphoria that the state coffers would be lined with gold, the black gold of the rich oil supply. The sudden torrent of hitherto unknown state wealth was too much to take. Every pork barrel outfit got into the act. So often the electorate is swift to blame greedy, reckless politicians for the state's woes, but when the opportunity arose to put some of the riches away for a rainy day, it was turned down by a vote of the people!

The message was clear that there was a great need to build a broader financial base for the college. During recent years much effort had been made to communicate with alumni, business organizations, and friends to support the college financially. However, quite frequently the question was asked regarding the participation of the faculty—many regarded that charity needed to begin at home. It was with pride that the college could answer with glee that a Faculty Development Fund was already in operation. Private funds would match the financial contributions of faculty members up to a maximum of $20,000.

Once in a while though, a ray of sunshine gleams through the morning air and when it does, how great it is! Such is the case when a true friend comes by to share his success in life. Mr. Claude A. Bradshaw, Stillwater, had been the regional representative for the AVMA group insurance trust for many years and had burned the midnight oil many times to help a student set up a good program. He also spoke regularly to the freshman class and to seniors. In the spring of 1983 he went the extra mile when he established the Claude A. Bradshaw Veterinary Medicine Student Fund with an initial endowment of $10,000—a noble gift from an honorable Christian gentleman.

By November of 1983 the deterioration in the state economy prompted Governor Nigh to convene a special session of the legislature. The state's economy had plunged into a $150 million shortfall in revenue collections and as a result, the college operating budget was reduced approximately $700,000 in December. The year closed with much speculation about the budget for 1984-85. The college anticipated a cut of about 8 percent. Rather than imposing a salary cut, the university administration requested faculty and staff to take two days of their annual leave during Christmas week together with the three days of official holiday and the two weekends. This allowed the university to close for a ten-day period and thus save expenditures on utilities as well.

So the college had to face the all too familiar situation once again of a financial "let down." There was some good news though during the waning hours of the year; the Faculty Development Fund was

A friend of many and especially the College of Veterinary Medicine, Mr. Claude Bradshaw *(seated)* established the Claude A. Bradshaw Veterinary Medicine Student Fund in the spring of 1983. Adrian Grout, manager of Mutual of New York of Oklahoma, Dean Patrick Morgan, and Charles Platt, executive director of the OSU Foundation, were present for the ceremonies.

matched entirely to realize the target amount of $20,000.

The Companion Animal and Equine Giving Plans were also established. Dean Morgan summarized the project: "What more perfect way to show your concern for your client's animal, to demonstrate your care and appreciation for your client than to make a donation to the Companion Animal Fund or the Equine Fund on behalf of the patient that must be euthanatized or succumbs to age, disease, or accident?"[7]

The new year of 1984 brought a report by a biostatistician of his study of the classes of 1980, 1981, 1982, and 1983 to determine whether a student's success could be predicted at admission by any of the parts or combinations of parts of the selection system which had been used by the college admissions committee for several years. Success was defined as satisfactory academic performance and passing National Board Examination scores. Dr. Don Parker, University of Oklahoma Health Science Center, presented conclusions which showed that female students as a group tend not to do as well as males, measures of a student's academic component are the only potential predictors of outcome, and variables such as interview, could not be used in the selection process as a measure of outcome. In general, students ranked low at admission also tended to perform accordingly in the veterinary medicine curriculum and national board scores.

The 69th Annual Convention of the Oklahoma Veterinary Medical Association on January 13 through 16 focused on a recent decision by the OVMA Board of Directors to promote excellence in clinical report writing by veterinary medicine students at OSU. Cash awards of $200, $150, $100 and $50, respectively, were presented to four senior students selected by a special committee who judged the papers. The winning clinical reports were published in subsequent issues of the *Oklahoma Veterinarian*.

Since Student American Veterinary Medical Association, the national organization, was founded in 1971, it has sponsored an annual educational symposium and a national publication, *Intervet*, for over 9000 veterinary medicine students. At the symposium at Texas A and M University in March 1978, C. Steven Hunholz, class of 1980, was elected president of the organization. Joseph H. Carter Jr., class of 1984, was president in 1983-84 and also served as editor of *Intervet* for the 1982-83 academic year.

The ides of March, March 15, appeared as a day of impending disaster for the college just as it had for Caesar. The simmering feud between the dean and some departmental administrators, ignited when the Board of Regents dismissed a tenured faculty member, now boiled over to include sharp differences in administrative philosophy. Several administrators requested that President Boger relieve the dean of his administrative responsibilities.

Amid the gathering gloom and doom, the dean called his staff together one morning and announced that he had resigned. The news brought disbelief and shock. There were requests from many sources for "a delay in execution," for in spite of all the intrigue, the college had a better rapport with those beyond the walls of the ivory tower than had ever existed in the past. The dean's resignation was not accepted by the Board of Regents. Now the old maxim, "If you tangle with the chief you had better not let him escape," was invoked. Departmental administrators returned to teaching and research, and interim department heads were appointed. Dr. Lloyd Faulkner became interim head of the Department of Veterinary Pathology; Dr. Robert Fulton, interim head of the Department of Veterinary Parasitology, Microbiology and Public Health; and Dr. James Breazile, interim head of the Department of Physiological Sciences.

Unfortunately, this unpleasant situation boiled over into the news media and the whole affair became a sordid embarrassment. The dismissed faculty member sought reinstatement, but a federal district court jury found that he had been afforded due process. He appealed to the U.S. Court of Appeals, Tenth Circuit, where the verdict in favor of Okla-

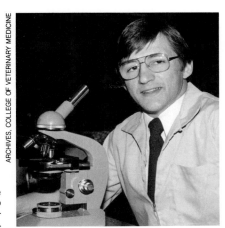

Steve Hunholz, class of 1980, became the first Oklahoma State University student to serve as president of the Student American Veterinary Medical Association.

homa State University was affirmed.

Dean Morgan revealed that a phased plan of action designed to bring stability to the college had been submitted to the university administration. A task force of persons external to OSU would be appointed to evaluate the college's programs, functions, administrative structure, and performance of administrators, including that of the dean. Dr. James H. Boggs, OSU vice president for academic affairs and research, would coordinate this task force authorized by the Board of Regents.

Meantime, the show had to go on and a sense of purpose was again restored by the annual Lewis H. Moe Lecture. The guest speaker was Dr. John R. Gorham, research leader of the USDA/ARS Animal Disease Research Unit, Pullman, Washington, and Professor, Veterinary Microbiology and Pathology, Washington State University, who presented an exceptionally interesting lecture entitled, "Slow Viruses and Slow Virologists." Slow viruses cause veterinary medicine's most challenging diseases including equine infectious anemia, progressive pneumonia, visna in sheep, arthritis and encephalitis of goats, and Aleutian diseases of mink.

The semester stumbled to a close without further event, and it was time again for the Annual Awards Banquet. There appeared to be nothing extraordinary about this happy occasion. Although rumored that most people came each year for the luscious meal topped by the Student Union's incomparable pecan ball dessert, there was the usual good turn-out of students, faculty, and visitors. No longer sponsored by The Upjohn Company, it was co-hosted by several friends of the college. The occasion was graced by the attendance of most of the Board of Regents.[8]

When the banquet was virtually over, Dean Morgan went to the

Patrick M. Morgan, D.V.M., M.P.H., Dr.P.H.

Dr. Patrick Monroe Morgan is a native of Miami, Florida. He attended Dartmouth College and Florida State University. He received the D.V.M. degree from the University of Georgia in 1958, the M.P.H. in 1963, and the Dr.P.H. in 1968 from Tulane University. Dr. Morgan is a Diplomate, American College of Veterinary Preventive Medicine. He married Barbara Hunnius on August 9, 1958.

Dr. Morgan was a part-time associate in private practice at Palos Heights, Illinois, April 1964 to May 1965. He was an assistant professor, Tulane University School of Medicine, Department of Vivarial Science and Research, September 1967 to May 1968; assistant professor and assistant director, National Nutrition Survey for Louisiana, Tulane University School of Public Health and Tropical Medicine, May 1968 to June 1969; assistant dean for Academic Affairs and associate professor, Tulane University School of Public Health and Tropical Medicine, July 1969 to August 1972.

Dr. Morgan served as acting deputy commissioner of Health for Personal Health Services, Oklahoma State Department of Health, December 1972 to January 1974; chief, Preventive Medical Service; director, Division of Veterinary Public Health and State Epidemiologist, Oklahoma State Department of Health, January 1974 to December 1977. He became a visiting professor, OSU College of Veterinary Medicine, Department of Veterinary Parasitology, Microbiology and Public Health, in 1974. He is an adjunct professor, University of Oklahoma College of Public Health.

Dr. Morgan became dean, College of Veterinary Medicine, Oklahoma State University, on December 1, 1977.

Dr. Morgan received the Distin-

ARCHIVES, COLLEGE OF VETERINARY MEDICINE

guished Alumnus Award, University of Georgia College of Veterinary Medicine, in 1983.

Following his resignation as dean on December 31, 1984, he served as Distinguished Visiting Professor, Ross University School of Veterinary Medicine, St. Kitts, West Indies, January through December 1985. He returned to OSU as a regents service professor in the College of Veterinary Medicine on January 1, 1986.

Dr. and Mrs. Morgan have two sons, Mark and Miles.

He is a member of Phi Zeta, Sigma Xi, American Veterinary Medical Association, Oklahoma Veterinary Medical Association, Oklahoma Public Health Association, American Society for Tropical Medicine and Hygiene, and the American Public Health Association. He has published numerous papers on nutrition and public health in veterinary journals.

Students in the class of 1980 observe Dr. Duane Peterson from the anatomy laboratory gallery, better known as "the rack."

podium and read a statement indicating that he had requested the Board of Regents to accept his resignation.

Referring to the proposed task force, Dean Morgan stated: "The Task force desperately needs the opportunity to reach conclusions and solutions beneficial to this College. To do so, I believe it must be free, to the greatest extent possible, of the influences of controversial personalities. In view of these deep personal feelings and the intense desire to see this College obtain preeminence in the field of veterinary medicine, I have concluded that I should do everything possible to help the College obtain this objective. It is for these reasons that I am requesting the President and the Board of Regents to accept my resignation as Academic Dean of the College of Veterinary Medicine effective January 1, 1985. I wish to assure you that as long as I remain in the position of Dean of the College, I will fully discharge the responsibilities of this office and I shall meet the duties and obligations of the office to the fullest extent."[9] The ensuing stillness echoed like the chords of a funeral march.

The sun came up as usual the following Monday morning, and attention turned to the recognition of the graduating seniors. The honeysuckle around the Seretean Center seemed to have an unusual fragrance as the students and their families and friends assembled on Saturday, May 5, for the annual convocation at 9:00 a.m. The Honorable Bernice Shedrick, state senator for Payne and Lincoln Counties, was the guest speaker and spoke eloquently about her commitment to the advancement of higher education in Oklahoma.

The graduating class performed better in the national board examinations than any in the past five years. The class also made a magnanimous commitment to the college. It was announced that they had voted to establish a Faculty Chair Endowment Fund for the college. The class pledged to raise $500,000 for the endowment over the next fifteen years.

The decade, begun as the most exciting and productive in the college history, had reached the mid-point. During the seven years Dr. Patrick Morgan had served as dean, the college made substantial progress. Under the heading, ''Most exciting period in 32-year veterinary medicine college history,'' in the Mid-Point Progress Report, Oklahoma State University Centennial Decade, this progress was well documented. Dr. Morgan's administration was unconventional, sometimes intriguing, but he walked the corridors of power with uncanny perception which reaped a harvest of greatly improved appropriations for the college. The booming oil industry undoubtedly provided a ''luscious pie'' the like of which had rarely been seen before in the state, but such a bonanza could easily have been lost to overzealous and more demanding entrepreneurs from other institutions.

Endnotes

1. ''Historic Satellite Teleconference,'' *Oklahoma Veterinarian,* vol. 33, no. 3 (October 1981), p. 119.

2. *Stillwater NewsPress,* 6 October 1981, p. 6.

3. *1982 Aesculapius,* p. 3, College of Veterinary Medicine Yearbook.

4. ''College of Veterinary Medicine Convocation '82,'' *Oklahoma Veterinarian,* vol. 34, no. 3 (July 1982), p. 86.

5. Dr. Stanley Newcomer, Dr. Calvin Beames, and Dr. Jerry Hurst transferred back to the College of Arts and Sciences. Dr. James Blankemeyer also transferred to the College of Arts and Sciences.

6. ''The Dean Reflects,'' *Plexus,* vol. 5, no. 1 (Winter 1983), p. 1.

7. ''An Open Letter from the Dean,'' *Oklahoma Veterinarian,* vol. 35, no. 4 (October 1983), p. 135.

8. After many years, far longer than at other schools, the company discontinued its patronage and instead hosted a senior student-faculty dinner in March. In recent years, the event has been scheduled in December.

9. ''College News,'' *Oklahoma Veterinarian,* vol. 36, no. 4 (October 1984), p. 156.

17 Ring in the New

Let us then be up and doing
With a heart for any fate;
Still achieving, still pursuing
Learn to labour and to wait.
                    Longfellow, *Psalm of Life*

Faculty, staff, and students awaited the visit of the task force that would soon be on campus. Hopefully, their report would provide guidance and renewed confidence in the future. Dean Patrick Morgan remained dean until his resignation became effective January 1, 1985.

The task force visited the college on July 29 through August 1, 1984. Vice President James Boggs had requested guidance for the university and the college on the main issues of the admissions process; academic standards; role of the faculty and administration in the allocation of resources, recruitment and retainment of quality faculty; the library; ways to improve liaison with basic and clinical sciences; the diagnostic laboratory; and interaction between research and teaching areas.[1]

During their visit, an enormous amount of work was crowded into just over two full working days. Their schedule was so full that it must have been very difficult for them to sort out the real issues and problems from irrelevant minutia. The task force issued its report to President L. L. Boger on September 21. The 17-page document had several interesting recommendations and listed key positive features and characteristics of the college. It acknowledged a deep feeling of loyalty in students, alumni, and faculty; a faculty of overall good quality; superb diagnostic laboratory and teaching hospital; opportunity for growth, particularly in terms of post-D.V.M. programs and research; support from the livestock industries and the Oklahoma Veterinary Medical Association.

The report urged enhancing shared academic governance but left final authority with the dean. It also recommended possible merging of two academic departments; seeking financially favorable student contracts with other states; increasing the number of graduate and other post-DVM students, especially if a reduction in class size was implemented; increasing emphasis on the recruitment and retention of students from minority groups, both at the veterinary and graduate levels; recruiting additional board certified faculty; adapting space within existing walls for badly needed expansion and modernizing of the library and classrooms; increasing utilization of the diagnostic laboratory in teaching and research programs; developing a program of excellence in biotechnology.[2]

The task force strongly urged the appointment of a dean who could successfully represent the college as well as provide effective internal leadership; a strong decisive person, but one committed to the concept of shared academic governance. The dean must be the intellectual leader of the college. The report stated, ''Leadership is the art of stimulating the human resources within the college to concentrate on total organizational goals rather than on individual or subgroup goals,—without the Dean at the head of the line, the faculty will not follow.''[3]

Outside financial support was greatly welcomed. The Merck Company Foundation made a grant of $5,000 to the college to establish a Visiting Scientist Short Course and Lecture Series. On October 18-19 Dr. Roy Pool, class of 1964, returned to his alma mater to conduct several seminars for the faculty and students. Dr. Pool is well known for his ability to correlate basic anatomic and pathologic processes with the clinical situation. On November 29-30 Dr. Oliver J. Ginther, University of Wisconsin, was the guest lecturer. He presented seminars on reproduction in the mare.

Dr. Donald E. Williams from Guymon received the American Association of Bovine Practitioners' Award for excellence in preventive medicine for beef cattle owners at the annual AABP meeting. The award consisted of a $1500 scholarship contributed in the name of the recipient to his/her choice of veterinary college. Dr. Williams requested that the scholarship be presented to the OSU College of Veterinary Medicine. It helped to finance a fellowship which had been established in the OSU Foundation. In November 1985, the same award was presented to Dr. Dee Griffin, also from Guymon, who assigned $750 of the scholarship to the college in honor of Dr. Don E. Williams. It became part of the fellowship which is being used to finance research by Dr. L. J. Perino and his adviser, Dr. Robert Fulton, on the immunomodulation and pharmakinetics of interferons as they relate to the bovine species, especially feedlot cattle.

The 1984 year ended with sadness. Mrs. Ruth Orr, wife of former Dean Harry Orr, died November 15 after a long illness. She was a most gracious lady and a long-time member of the veterinary medicine family. On Tuesday, December 4, Janet Rutledge Smith passed away at Presbyterian Hospital in Oklahoma City. Janet, age 32, was a second-year student.

A really heartwarming accomplishment by a brave alumnus was reported from the slopes of the fearsome Mount Everest. Dr. Carolyn Gunn, class of 1978, was part of the China Everest '84 Expedition, which set out to reach the 29,028-foot summit of Mount Everest from the north, a feat never before accomplished. One of the climbers reached the summit. Dr. Gunn cooked and cared for the nine-man team. When she carried supplies to 23,000 feet, she became one of the few women ever to climb so far up the giant mountain.

Dr. J. Mack Oyler, who had served as associate dean since October 1980, was appointed interim dean effective January 1, 1985, while a search committee, headed by President Boger, finalized the quest for a new dean. There was great anticipation of the announcement of the person who would become the seventh dean of the college. In March the Board of Regents approved the appointment of Dr. Joseph Alexander, an enterprising young Virginian with the dewdrops of youth and vigor on his brow.

The Veterinary Administrative Council focused on "pressing needs" in response to a request for information from the Senate Appropriations Committee. They presented the following needs: Veterinary Medicine Library and Learning Center renovation, classroom renovation, restored faculty positions, new positions, educational and research equipment, research animal facilities, isolation and biocontainment facilities, and laboratory animal facilities. The prospects for implementing any of these were dim in the foreseeable future.

Finances eased temporarily as Vice President Boggs asked the Veterinary Administrative Council to recommend to him the guidelines they would like to implement this year for salary distribution, assuming a 6 percent increase was available for this purpose. They suggested that 4 percent be cost of living and 2 percent be merit. Later it became known that salary increases in the region of 10 percent would be possible from the appropriated funds.

Dr. Isaiah J. Fidler, class of 1963, visited during Veterinary Medicine Week and delivered the Dr. Lewis H. Moe Lecture. Dr. Fidler has had a very distinguished career in cancer research. He is currently chairman of the Department of Cell Biology and head, Division of Interferon Research, University of Texas System Cancer Center, M. D. Anderson

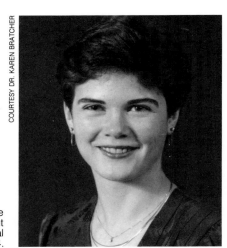

Karen Bratcher, class of 1985, became the first female president of the Student Chapter, American Veterinary Medical Association, in the fall of 1984.

Hospital and Tumor Institute, Houston. Dr. Fidler delivered a brilliant lecture on "The Biological Treatment of Cancer" to a large audience.

Another distinguished scientist came to the campus in April to lead a conference on malignant catarrhal fever. Dr. Walter Plowright, Reading, England, joined research workers from several parts of the United States to discuss this increasingly important cattle disease. Dr. Plowright is one of the world's leading veterinary virologists and is the "father" of tissue culture vaccines against animal diseases. His development of such a vaccine against cattle rinderpest as a result of his research in Nairobi, Kenya, in the 1950s is akin in importance to the Salk vaccine against poliomyelitis in humans. The conference was sponsored by the Oklahoma Animal Disease Diagnostic Laboratory with Dr. Anthony Castro as coordinator. Dr. Plowright also gave a special lecture to the students and faculty on his research leading up to the development of tissue culture vaccines.

Students were making the news. Dr. Marvin Denny, president of the Oklahoma Veterinary Medical Association proposed special membership for the students and that the student chapter appoint a representative to the Board of Directors. The Board of Directors approved a non-voting membership category for the students with automatic free membership on graduation until the end of the year and membership for half fee during the following year. Kevin Gibbs, third-year student, was elected as representative to the Board of Directors.[4]

Karen Bratcher, a vivacious new leader from Altus, became the first female president of student chapter during the fall of 1984. During the 1986 spring semester, Teresa Furr, class of 1987, became the second female president.

John Nick, class of 1985, was named one of the top five senior students at Oklahoma State University. John had served as the first-year class representative and also as president of the student chapter.

To foster good student-faculty relationship, the first Student-Faculty Pentathlon was held at Boomer Lake Park on the evening of April 18. Sponsored by Norden Laboratories, Inc., the pentathlon featured events including scrub suit relay, bat twirl relay, mattress race, pyramid building, and tug-of-war, followed by lots of ice cream.

For the first time, the *Aesculapius* college yearbook was dedicated to a staff member, Mrs. Charlotte Kincaide. It was indeed "a breath of fresh air" when ten years earlier, Mrs. Kincaide came from northeast Oklahoma to undertake the ever-mounting task of admissions coordinator. She had become a "mother" to all the students and was known "for friendly smiles during interviews, for a sympathetic ear and a bottomless candy jar, for cookies during finals, and gentle prodding to help us meet scholarship deadlines" and much more.[5]

The dean's office often gets all sorts of calls daily. In the spring they are mainly about employment opportunities. However, on the day before graduation, a gentleman called and said, "I have a nephew who is seriously looking for a wife and he is interested in the single female graduates in the veterinary medicine class."[6] He requested names and

Mrs. Charlotte Kincaide, admissions coordinator, explains academic requirements for admission during a summer program for Native American students. Mrs. Kincaide was the first staff person to whom the yearbook was dedicated.

addresses but was politely invited to attend the convocation on Saturday morning to see for himself!

Dr. Joseph Alexander, dean-designate, arrived early so that he could be the guest speaker at the college convocation for the senior class on Saturday morning, May 11.

Soon the graduates had left the campus with their treasured roll of parchment to challenge the world beyond. It is always a quiet, nostalgic, almost lonesome feeling to cruise around the campus at this time, but at least there is a place to park! The Veterinary Administrative Council held its monthly meeting and finally approved revised guidelines for academic standards which would be effective for the freshman class in the fall.

Wednesday, May 15, officially brought forth a new era. Dr. Joseph W. Alexander assumed his duties as the seventh dean of the college. With a congenial personality and youthful exuberance, he was also the youngest in the land at age 38. In his acceptance statement to the Board of Regents in March, Dr. Alexander wrote, "I think there is a tremendous potential for OSU to have one of the finest veterinary schools in the nation and I intend to do whatever I can to accomplish that goal."[7]

Dr. Alexander soon set the wheels in motion toward filling some important faculty and administrative positions and urged all departments to prepare a plan of their goals and objectives. Dr. Oyler resumed his duties as associate dean. He played a major role in ensuring a smooth transition of leadership to the new dean.

Dr. Fayne Oberst, who had served as head of the Department of Medicine and Surgery since 1974, had retired on June 30, 1984. Dr. Oberst had devoted many years of loyal service to his profession.

Dr. Lester Johnson also had retired on June 30 after thirty years of dedicated service to the university and the profession. At an appreciation dinner, it was announced that the college had established a Distinguished Visiting Clinician Endowment Fund in the OSU Foundation to which alumni, faculty, and friends made generous donations. The proceeds of the fund will be used to bring nationally and internationally renowned clinicians to share their expertise and experience with the faculty, students, and practitioners. The first OSU Distinguished Visiting Clinician Lecture, honoring Dr. Johnson, was delivered by Dr. I. G. Mayhew from the University of Florida in 1985 at the annual fall Conference for Veterinarians. He gave a brilliant, lucid presentation on "Clinical Anatomy and Neurological Examination of Large Animals." A plaque was placed in a place of honor in the teaching hospital.[8]

Dr. Bertis L. Glenn, professor of veterinary pathology, had retired on February 1 after over thirty years of outstanding service to the college in the field of clinical pathology. In latter years, the 1952 alumnus had become a motorcycle enthusiast.

Joseph W. Alexander, D.V.M., M.S.

Dr. Joseph William Alexander received the B.S. degree in animal science from the University of Arizona in 1969, the D.V.M. degree from Colorado State University in 1973, and became an intern in medicine and surgery, followed by a residency in surgery at Cornell University, 1973-76. He spent the next year in private practice in Cheshire, Connecticut, and then moved to the University of Tennessee as an assistant professor in surgery, becoming director of clinical services in 1979. He received the M.S. degree in educational administration and supervision from the University of Tennessee during this time. He was appointed coordinator of surgical services at Virginia-Maryland Regional College of Veterinary Medicine in 1981 and served as acting chairman, division of agricultural and urban practice, 1982-83. He became chairman of the division and director of the veterinary medical teaching hospital in 1983.

Dr. Alexander has been a Diplomate, American College of Veterinary Surgeons, since 1979. He is a member of Phi Zeta, Phi Kappa Phi, American Veterinary Medical Association, American Association of Veterinary Clinicians, American Animal Hospital Association, Virginia Veterinary Medical Association, Veterinary Orthopedic Society, the American Association for the Advancement of Science, and the Oklahoma Veterinary Medical Association (ex-officio member, Board of Directors). He has published over fifty articles, contributed seven book chapters, and has written two books on veterinary orthopedic surgery.

Dr. Alexander has presented numerous papers at state and national meetings and was the editor of the *Journal of Veterinary Orthopedics*. He serves on the editorial review board for the *Journal of the American Animal Hospital Association.*

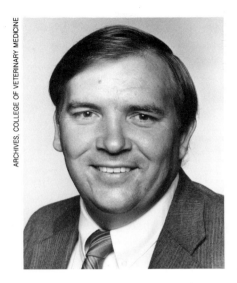

ARCHIVES, COLLEGE OF VETERINARY MEDICINE

Dr. Alexander received the Norden Distinguished Teacher Award in 1981 and the College Teaching Excellence Award, Virginia Polytechnic Institute and State University, in 1983.

Dr. Alexander has devoted much of his time to community service. He was president of the Blacksburg Breakfast Lions Club, chairman of the Special Olympics Board of Directors, and a member of the Montgomery County Humane Society Board of Directors, the University Methodist Church Student Foundation Board of Directors, and the Administrative Board of the Methodist Church. Dr. Alexander is a member of the Stillwater Chamber of Commerce, Oklahoma Cattlemen's Association, and the Cimarron Valley Kennel Club.

Dr. Alexander became dean of the College of Veterinary Medicine on May 15, 1985.

Dr. Alexander and his wife, Merry, have two daughters, Amy Sue and Laura Lynn.

Dr. Bertis L. Glenn, class of 1962, received a Ph.D. from the University of Oklahoma in 1961. A Diplomate, American College of Veterinary Pathologists, he conducted extensive research on photosensitivity diseases.

Dr. Andrew W. Monlux retired on June 30. A true academician who demanded excellence in the classroom, Dr. Monlux believed that faculty and students should always present themselves in a professional manner. Unfortunately, his request for support in this respect from his administrative colleagues and faculty was not always forthcoming.

The college was honored to welcome some very distinguished visitors during the summer. Dr. Christiaan Barnard, the pioneer of human heart transplants, toured the Teaching Hospital and visited the Department of Animal Science herds. Dr. Barnard was a consultant at Baptist Memorial Hospital, Oklahoma City. He had a special interest in cattle and raised a herd of Simmental cattle on his ranch near Johannesburg, South Africa.

A few weeks later, Dean Alexander welcomed back to the campus the son and daughter of Dr. Lowery L. Lewis, dean of the veterinary medical school founded in 1914. Mr. Samuel Lewis from Dallas and Mrs. Ruth Lewis Baber from Tulsa were accompanied by her son Harvey Baber.

The close working relationship between the college and the College of Agriculture was exemplified when Dr. Earl VanEaton left in August to accept an appointment in another university. Dean Alexander presented him a gift in appreciation of his outstanding service in the pre-veterinary program.

Manpower needs still remained an important issue. The August 15 issue of the *Journal of the American Veterinary Medical Association* included the results of a recent veterinary manpower study, "Synopsis of U.S. Veterinary Medical Manpower Study: Demand and Supply from 1980 to 2000." In order to deal with trends and changes in the context of the profession's goals, the Executive Board at its April 1983 meeting authorized the Office of Economics to conduct the study which found the supply and demand of veterinary manpower indicated a continuing

Dr. J. Mack Oyler, class of 1953, reviews plans for a proposed new library and learning center. Dr. Oyler became the first associate dean in October 1981 and served as interim dean in 1985.

surplus of private practitioners on a national level to the year 2000. The surplus would affect veterinarians in various geographic divisions of the country to different degrees.

The report stated, "These findings suggest a need for practitioners to adapt to new economic circumstances in their own self-interest. . . . Efficient practice management and effective outreach to clients will be important in making necessary adaptations. . . . Ways to facilitate midcareer transitions as veterinarians' employment opportunities and professional interests change should be demonstrated."[9]

The month of August was unusually cool, but as soon as the semester opened the sweltering heat returned. The increased emphasis on continuing education brought surgery enthusiasts to an intensive short course on "External Fixation of Long Bone Fractures of Dogs" on Friday, September 13, followed, bright and early, on Saturday morning, by a "wet lab" (hands-on experience) at the Teaching Hospital. A sumptuous lunch ended an outstanding meeting for which the participants earned ten hours of continuing education credit.

Arriving with the new freshman class in the fall of 1985 was Mike Sheets of Tahlequah, a two-time NCAA Wrestling Champion, 1983 Outstanding NCAA Wrestler, four-time All American, three-time Big 8 Champion, 1984 Male Athlete of the Year, 1984 *Amateur Wrestling News* "Wrestler of the Year," 1986 Canadian Cup Champion, and Academic

Oklahoma State University

All Big 8 Wrestling Team. Outstanding athletes were not new to the college. Ron Boyer was a regular starter at tight tend for the OSU Cowboys in 1974. Harold Rinker, class of 1958, also played for the Cowboys. Dr. John Hammond, class of 1970, had played quarterback for the University of Oklahoma while pursuing his pre-veterinary studies. Michelle Belanger, class of 1986, was a two-time All American and member of the Southwestern Oklahoma State University NAIA Championship Basketball Team in 1982.

Each fall the College of Agriculture has hosted a "football Saturday morning" when the joint House and Senate Agricultural Committee held a meeting on the OSU campus. This year, for the first time, Dean Charles Browning graciously asked the College of Veterinary Medicine to co-host this auspicious event on Saturday morning, October 5. Following a program in the College of Agriculture the group boarded vans for transport to the Boren Veterinary Medical Teaching Hospital where Dean Alexander was the host. Several faculty members made 10-minute presentations on their current research projects.

The ever increasing cost of college education, especially professional training, is becoming an enormous financial burden on the students. The announcement by the trustees of the Dr. Joseph E. Salsbury Foundation that each of the twenty-seven colleges of veterinary medicine in the United States had been endowed $100,000 for senior veterinary stu-

Dean Joseph Alexander expresses appreciation from the College of Veterinary Medicine to Dr. Earl VanEaton, College of Agriculture, who served as an advisor to preveterinary medicine students for many years.

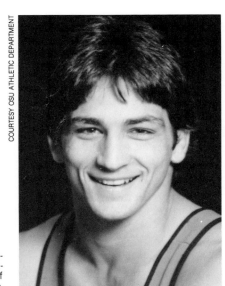

Mike Sheets, an OSU wrestler from Tahlequah, is one of the many outstanding athletes who have attended the College of
Veterinary Medicine.

dent scholarships was most welcome. Proceeds from the endowment
would be administered by each college for this purpose. The OSU College of Veterinary Medicine's convocation and awards committee was
assigned the responsibility of selecting the scholarship recipients based
on the demonstration of superior scholarship, initiative, perseverance,
potential for leadership, and financial need. The first scholarships of
$2,000 each were presented to Martin Furr and Paul Robertson.

Christmas also came a little early for the college when great tidings
were received from the American Veterinary Medical Association that
the Council on Education had voted to continue the college on full
accreditation status until the next scheduled evaluation in 1988.[10]

Ring out the old, ring in the new. The Alexandrian era had begun!
Time alone will evaluate progress in the ensuing years.

Endnotes

1. The task force members were: Dr. Robert B. Wilson, Washington State University, chairman; Dr. J. T. Vaughan, Auburn University; Dr. Paul Landis, Norfolk, Virginia; Dr. Russell
   Frey, Kansas State University; and Dr. Farrell Robinson, Purdue University.

2. "Task Force Report to President Boger on Veterinary Medicine, Oklahoma State University, 21 September 1984," Archives, College of Veterinary Medicine.

3. "Task Force Report to President Boger on Veterinary Medicine."

4. "The President's Letter," *Oklahoma Veterinarian,* vol. 37, no. 3 (July 1985), p. 74.

5. *1985 Aesculapius,* p. 2, College of Veterinary Medicine Yearbook.

6. "Special Request," *Oklahoma Veterinarian,* vol. 37, no. 3 (July 1985), p. 87.

7. "Dr. Joseph W. Alexander Named Dean," *Oklahoma Veterinarian,* vol. 37, no. 2 (April 1985), p. 58.

8. The inscription on the plaque reads, "Established in honor of Lester Johnson, A.S., B.S., D.V.M., Professor, Medicine and Surgery, and Head, Equine Section, who retired on June 30, 1984 after 30 years' dedicated service to the College of Veterinary Medicine, Oklahoma State University. He was universally acclaimed as an outstanding teacher, an astute clinician, and the epitome of professional and personal ethics."

9. J. Karl Wise and John E. Kushman, "Synopsis of U.S. Veterinary Medical Manpower Study: Demand and Supply from 1980 to 2000," *Journal of the American Veterinary Medical Association,* vol. 187, no. 4 (15 August 1985), p. 361.

10. Dr. R. Leland West, American Veterinary Medical Association director, Division of Scientific Activities to Dean Alexander, 12 December 1985, Archives, College of Veterinary Medicine. Dean Alexander and Dr. J. Mack Oyler had appeared before the Council on Education in Chicago on Monday, November 18, to present a progress report on the college.

18 The Future is Now

And I said to the man who stood at the gate of the year: "Give me a light that I may tread safely into the unknown." And he replied: "Go out into the darkness and put your hand into the hand of God. That shall be to you better than light and safer than a known way." So I went forth, and finding the Hand of God, trod gladly into the night. And He led me towards the hills and the breaking of day in the lone East.

Minnie Louise Haskins

In the fall of 1985, Dean Alexander wrote a position paper for the OSU Board of Regents in which he expressed his aspirations for the college.

"Since opening its doors in 1948, the College of Veterinary Medicine at Oklahoma State University has had a reputation for providing excellent service to the citizens of Oklahoma and of producing outstanding general private practitioners. While it is very important that the college continues to provide needed clinical and diagnostic service for Oklahoma, the time has come to set priorities and directions that will allow the school to attract outstanding scholars, to keep its most productive faculty members, to prepare professional students for the challenges of the 21st century, and to build a strong national reputation.

"We must continually strive for improvement in the quality and efficiency of our academic program. After all, the Wizard of Oz was able to give the scarecrow a diploma, but not a brain. It is our responsibility to provide for our students, the faculty, staff, equipment, and facilities to assure the quality of the educational process.

"While it is impossible to predict the future, we must attempt to meet the needs of society and move toward preparing our graduates in such

Achievements of the future will build on the firm foundation laid by the dedication of faculty, students, and staff of the past. In 1985, retiring professors Dr. Duane Peterson, Dr. Paul Barto, Dr. Jonathan Friend, and Dr. Ralph Buckner pose with Dr. Dianne Nail, class of 1965, and Dr. Nick Nail, class of 1962, president of the Oklahoma Veterinary Medical Association.

The first graduating class in the School of Veterinary Medicine was all men, but increasing interest in the veterinary profession by women is exemplified by these two sisters in the class of 1986, Cynthia Newnam and Beverly Newnam Fritzler.

a manner that they can contribute to societal demands and be competitive in the market place.

"The challenge for the remainder of this century and the first part of the next would appear to be how to produce enough veterinarians to fill the needs of society for professional services other than patient care that are best provided by persons with the educational background and problem solving skills obtained by a veterinary education. If we continue to operate as we have been, we will be able to produce an adequate supply to meet the needs of the primary patient care sector; however, we must also react to the need to have an adequate supply to place 15 to 20 percent of the profession in non-patient care areas of professional service. They must also be given the proper level of support and have an environment that will allow them to meet the institutional goals and objectives expected of them.

"Another important group that will help to protect faculty time and add to the overall resources of the college are individuals engaged in post-D.V.M. training programs. Graduate students in the basic sciences and interns and residents in the teaching hospital are individuals who will contribute significantly to all of the college's goals and objectives. These people are the educators of the future and are needed if the educa-

Teleconferencing capabilities have expanded the classroom to the world, increasing the potential of instruction in the College of Veterinary Medicine. Dr. Thomas R. Thedford, extension veterinarian, Dean Joseph Alexander, and Dr. J. Mack Oyler, associate dean, look to the future and the receiving dish for satellite mediated continuing education programs. The dish was made possible by donations.

tional process is to progress. Many of today's young scholars will need to seek opportunities to apply their professional knowledge and skills in industry, government, international agriculture, teaching, and other areas of professional activity outside the general practice area.

"The aforementioned opportunities will demand post-doctoral education and training, and research is the engine that drives these two important areas. Thus, if we are to give young Oklahoma veterinary students the edge over their contemporaries around the nation, we must have active research and post-D.V.M. training programs in both the basic and clinical sciences.

"While teaching and service remain high priorities in the College of Veterinary Medicine, the time has come to look toward greater emphasis in the area of research and creative activities. In a veterinary medical college, research and creative activities may take many forms. It may be basic research in the laboratory; it may be clinical investigation on cases which are effectively experimental in nature; or it may be speculation and reflection on a scientific or clinical problem. In all the areas of teaching, service, and research, the faculty has an obligation to demonstrate scholarship and to communicate to their students and to the profession their interpretation of the truth and to share their ideas, discoveries and thoughts with others in the profession.

"As I talked with my colleagues around the country about accepting the dean's position at Oklahoma State University, they all had a simi-

ARCHIVES, COLLEGE OF VETERINARY MEDICINE

The saints of Darrowby *(left to right)*, heroes in James Herriot's books, Dr. Donald Sinclair (Siegfried Farnon), Dr. J. Alfred Wight (James Herriot), and Dr. Brian Sinclair (Tristan Farnon) are three veterinarians whose lives have provided encouragement to youngsters who will grow up to be veterinarians of the future.

Veterinary Medicine Budget
Total Expenditures

1948-49	$ 110,023.00	1967-68	845,087.74
1949-50	162,453.00	1968-69	959,804.63
1950-51	179,492.49	1969-70	1,048,008.16
1951-52	201,320.63	1970-71	1,196,638.41
1952-53	181,670.68	1971-72	1,320,122.71
1953-54	210,004.32	1972-73	1,400,096.76
1954-55	256,731.41	1973-74	1,561,536.31
1955-56	270,642,08	1974-75	2,778,579.07
1956-57	307,038.66	1975-76	3,521,725.52
1957-58	328,886.99	1976-77	3,048,891.07
1958-59	391,415.61	1977-78	3,433,977.86
1959-60	420,863.62	1978-79	3,750,730.44
1960-61	414,192.60	1979-80	4,264,202.86
1961-62	503,894.43	1980-81	5,345,395.54
1962-63	519,883.86	1981-82	6,589,551.90
1963-64	542,515.65	1982-83	8,006,044.17
1964-65	671,964.98	1983-84	7,366,032.00
1965-66	704,299.65	1984-85	7,551,078.00
1966-67	771,388.61		

FALL 1984 PLEXUS

The sorrel filly with her surrogate mother, OSU's first successful equine embryo transfer performed by Dr. Gregor Morgan, is indicative of the research achievements of the future.

Oklahoma State University

lar notion—that there was a great, but to a large extent unrealized, potential in the College of Veterinary Medicine. The college is most fortunate to have (1) a dedicated faculty and staff that have remained through good and bad times; (2) an ideal location for potential clinical cases; (3) an outstanding teaching hospital and diagnostic laboratory; and (4) a supportive and enthusiastic university administration. The need now is for additional faculty, equipment, and financial support to allow the college to realize its full potential, to achieve a strong national reputation, while maintaining its present dedication to the needs of Oklahoma, and to allow us to prepare our students for the needs of today and the future. With appropriate support, the college can move ahead toward becoming one of the nation's finest.

"Walt Disney made the statement, 'If you can dream it, you can do it'; however, dreams only become realities through hard work and dedication to one's goals and objectives. Goals are nothing more than dreams with a deadline and we have many goals for the College of Veterinary Medicine. During the past few years, higher education has and will continue into the foreseeable future, to face its most challenging times. This does not mean we cannot continue to move ahead to build a stronger, more productive college and a stronger profession. However, it will not happen just because we want it to, but will require the support and dedicated efforts of all our faculty, staff, students, alumni, and the citizens of this great state. We must act now if we expect a better tomorrow. One of my favorite quotes comes from T. E. Lawrence and helps to capture my feelings about the future:

> 'All men dream, but not equally.
> Those who dream by night
>   in the dusty recesses of their minds
> Awake to find that it was vanity;
> But the dreamers of the day are dangerous men,
> That they may act their dreams
>   with open eyes to make it possible.'

"The past is only prologue—the future is now."

Appendices

Appendix 1

Graduates of the College of Veterinary Medicine

CLASS OF 1951

Jack S. Ambrose	Hope, AR	Hubert M. Goins	Green Forest, AR
Martin Y. Andres	Anadarko	Raymond E. Henry	Ralston
Sam H. Best	Wagoner	Jorge A. Lanza	Aguirre, PR
Jack L. Bostwick	Ardmore	Roderick Parker	Knightstown, IN
Leonard B. Carpenter	Bridgeport	Thomas A. Ritchie	Bixby
William C. Carter	Sayre	William E. Ryan	Oklahoma City
James E. Cook	Miami	Doyce D. Smith	Cherokee
J. O. DeFoe	Enid	James O. Tucker	Drumright
Alvin H. Dowdy	Perkins	Leo J. Voskuhl	Marshall
William L. Garner	Tulsa	Austin W. Weedn	Elk City
S. C. Gartman	Shawnee	L. E. Wilcoxson	Sayre
King S. Gibson	Fayetteville, AR	Glenn D. Willis	Olustee
M. Weldon Glenn	Stillwater	C. Mark Wilson	Broken Arrow

CLASS OF 1952

Harold E. Adams	Ardmore	Bertis L. Glenn	Stillwater
Frank S. Beloncik	Schenectady, NY	Curtis N. Harder	Oklahoma City
Frank R. Benton	Tucson, AZ	James D. Hatton	Dewey
Edward L. Blevins	Enid	Arthur K. High	Warwick
Jay H. Brashear	Ochelata	Finis E. Hilton	Tulsa
William C. Burnett	New Albany, MS	Mervin V. Hinderliter	Waynoka
Mark L. Carter	Ponca City	Charles L. Hobbs	Hennessey
William J. Chandler	Tulsa	Harold H. Howell	Meeker
Glen G. Clefisch	Spencer, SD	W. S. Hutchison	Waynoka
Henry O. Denney	Pocasset	Harold D. Ivie	Tulsa
Joe M. Dixon	Owasso	Allen T. Kimmell	Cherokee
Charles E. Doyle	Oklahoma City	Robert H. Leonard	Oklahoma City
J. Frank England	Columbia, MO	Willard E. Rhynes	Houston, TX
John Foley	Stillwater	William A. Semple	Caddo
Fred J. Fullerton	Little Rock, AR	Robert E. Simpson	Glendale, AZ

Lloyd C. Skow	Cocolalla, ID	Lawrence H. Valentine	Idabel
Don C. Thompson	Bristow	Joseph C. Wiley	Fairview
Claude A. Tigert	Stillwater	Raymond D. Young	Hollis

CLASS OF 1953

Warren L. Alberty	Mounds	Frederick T. Lynd	Siloam Springs, AR
Ivan D. Alexander	McQueen	Samuel K. Morrison	Marshall, AR
C. W. Brown	Bixby	J. Mack Oyler	Locust Grove
T. A. Byrd	Oklahoma City	Alvin Pailet	New Orleans, LA
Louis E. Carlin	Tulsa	Roger J. Panciera	Westerly, RI
Carl D. Cason	Porter	William A. Potts	Mt. Olive, NC
David E. Clymer	Oklahoma City	Willard M. Pounds	New Orleans, LA
Robert D. Conrad	Hugo	Leland D. Schwartz	Perry
James P. Devine	Tulsa	Ronald H. Swayze	Tulsa
John M. Gambardella	New Haven, CT	John H. Venable	Oklahoma City
Frank W. Hester	Chelsea	John A. Walker	Wewoka
Morris L. Hill	Deep Run, NC	Ivan R. Wilcox	Weleetka
Kenneth W. Huffman	Medford	Robert E. Williams	Elk City
Leonard J. Kimray	Roosevelt	Daniel A. Woesner	Lawton
Clyde A. Kirkbride	Malvern, AR	Anton V. Yanda	Yukon

CLASS OF 1954

Ira P. Antin	Bronx, NY	Robert M. Kenney	Cranston, RI
James R. Atkins	Guymon	Loris D. Lauener	Jennings
Elmer A. Barce	Brockton, MA	Ray L. Lessert	Ponca City
William R. Barrowman	Norman	Wade N. Lyon	Geary
Joseph E. Bruce	DeQuincy, LA	Maurice W. Markham	Locust Grove
Jasper D. Carter	Skipwith, VA	G. Pat Mayer	Coalgate
Wallace R. Carter	Skipwith, VA	Carlos D. Mayes	Tahlequah
James E. Christy	Wellston	James E. McLaurin	Elaine, AR
George L. Clement	Wilburton, AR	Richard R. Orr	Lawton
Marvin E. Dreisbach	Cheyenne, WY	Donald F. Patterson	Houston, TX
Paul W. Edmundson	Shawnee	Carlton E. Porter	Long Beach, CA
James B. Foley	New York, NY	Sanford M. Schor	North Bergen, NJ
Charles R. Hales	Oxford, KS		
Hugh K. Henderson	Wagoner	Jack N. Southall	Nowata
James V. Hendrix	Cane Hill, AR	Edmond E. Staley	New Mexico
Dewey G. Hobson	Tulsa	Kenneth K. Stinson	Des Plaines, IL
Donald D. Holmes	Mannford	Carl E. Wasson	Harrison, AR
Kenneth K. Keahey	Garber		

CLASS OF 1955

John L. Azlin	Heavener	Robert S. Hudson	Sulphur
Harrison A. Brown	West Bridgewater, MA	Bryan O. Hutchens	Tulsa
		Fred L. Hutton	Grainola
James E. Carpenter	Ada	June D. Iben	Monaca, PA
William J. Carson	Balboa, CZ	John M. King	Boston, MA
Gwyn Chapin	Tucson, AZ	Harold Kopit	Lynbrook, NY
James C. Cooper	Claremore	Merlin D. Kunkel	Oklahoma City
John C. Day	Ft. Smith, AR	Glenn R. Orr	Arnett
Frederick Feibel	Meriden, CT	Philip T. Parker	Knightstown, IN
Leo W. Ford	Pawhuska	Robert G. Reim	Hillsdale
C. Perry Freeman	Elk City	Ted M. Richardson	Sallisaw
Dan E. Goodwin	Durham	Lewis R. Stiles	Broken Bow
Charles E. Harmon	Broken Arrow	Louie G. Stratton	Cookson
Douglas M. Hawkins	Tulsa	James R. Taylor	Stillwater
Jack G. Hill	St. Attica, IN	George T. Vickers	Ingalls, AR
Donald L. Hohmann	Lone Wolf	Richard C. White	Summit, MS

CLASS OF 1956

George W. Bierbower	Masontown, PA	Milton O. Carlin	Tulsa
Alfred M. Bradley	Edmond	Ted L. Cline	Claremore
Donald R. Callicott	Lawton	Clarence L. Coley	Ponca City

Max A. Cress	Florence, KS	Coyne C. Miller	Natchez, MS
John N. Eischen	Okarche	James C. Price	Shepherdstown, WV
James E. Ferneau	Joplin, MO		
Joe Flanagan	Sayre	I. Q. Sewell	Texola
Carl O. Gedon	Alpine, NJ	Oren A. Sills	Henryetta
James O. Harrod	Vick, AR	Martin A. Spindel	New Orleans, LA
Everett J. Hickock	Pond Creek	Robert D. Stephenson	Perryton, TX
Arlon D. Hill	Farmington, NM	David W. Swicegood	Muskogee
Leslie N. Johnston	Wilmington, NC	J. Pat Tripp	Waurika
Herbert A. Justus	Hendersonville, NC	Jesse G. Walker	Kenefic
		Donald R. Walton	Newton, MA
Paul C. Long	Oklahoma City	Jackson E. Wiley	Whitetail, MT
Max E. McElroy	Jennings	Melvin J. Worth	Garber
Thomas E. Messler	Tulsa	Charles H. Wulz	Hunter

CLASS OF 1957

Norman K. Adams	Perrysville, IN	Ralph K. Jenner Jr.	Hugo
Harvey L. Arnold	Farris	Anton A. Kammerlocher	Mooreland
William G. Askew	Cordell	William W. Leatherwood	Oklahoma City
Franklin D. Baker	Poteau	Michael H. Morrison	Stillwater
Bert D. Briscoe	Edmond	Carroll D. Olson	Edmond
Lester F. Cardey	Alva	Calvin M. Poole	Stillwater
Stedman H. Carr	Burgaw, NC	Joseph C. Potucek	Michigan City, IN
James L. Clark	Pawhuska	Theodore T. Reeder	Bison
Leroy Coggins	Thomasville, NC	James B. Roberts	Booneville, AR
Warren E. Decker	Thomas	Betty Benton Self	Odessa, TX
Jerry V. Dunaway	Sand Springs	Leon C. Self	Albion
William A. Endacott	Tulsa	George W. Sherrick	Connellsville, PA
Jack C. Gregory	Carmen	Louis D. Stubbs	DeQueen, AR
Ernest I. Hart	Clayton, MA	Gus W. Thornton	Bartlesville
James F. Hughey	Gastonia, NC	Warren J. Ward	Ponca City
Jerry A. Humphrey	Sand Springs	John L. Weeks	Clinton, NC

CLASS OF 1958

Abdul A. J. Al-Hummadi	Hillah, Iraq	George A. Lester	Mountain Park
Jerry M. Bonham	Cordell	William R. McCallon	Wynnewood
Tommy J. Byrd	Hollis	Elmer E. McCrary	Watonga
Sam Forrest Cheesman	Colorado Springs, CO	Kermit W. Minton	Sulphur
John H. Collins	Drumright	Thornal D. O'Quinn Jr.	Lillington, NC
Clement V. Cottom Jr.	Mounds	John C. Peckham	Eufaula
Donald R. Crockett	Grove	Jack W. Peterson	Vernon Center, MN
John W. Davis Jr.	Harrisburg, NC		
Murtadha H. El Hashimi	Howiider, Iraq	Harold B. Rinker	Clayton, NM
Lawrence H. Erwin	Tulsa	Alfred A. Robinson	Newton, NC
Rex R. Every	Piedmont	John M. Rust	Ardmore
Robert L. Godby	Oak Hill, WV	David L. Seaman	Edmond
Louis W. Heavner Jr.	Stillwater	James G. Sewell	Perry
Buddie C. Hickey	Muskogee	Robert M. Spragg	Blacksville, WV
Joe B. Jolliffe	Knob Fork, WV	Wayne E. Stout	Henryetta
Paul L. Kunneman	Kingfisher	Lloyd C. Weldon	Stillwater
Thomas R. Lathan	Monroe, NC	Charles E. Wyatt	Oklahoma City
Robert L. Lawrence	Tulsa		

CLASS OF 1959

E. Ray Baird	Hinton	Robert H. Gengler	Perry
John H. Barton	Charlotte, NC	Claude G. Gillette Jr.	Stuttgart, AR
Byron W. Behring	Enid	William J. Guinan	Muskogee
Alton C. Caplinger	McAlester	Robert L. Hartin	Madill
Nedra A. Carpenter	Weirton, WV	J. Fred Johnson	Marlington, WV
Willis L. Chatham	Scottsdale, AZ	Harold B. Kimble	Morgantown, WV
Rodney V. Clark	Perkins	Robert S. Laves	Oklahoma City
John D. Colvert	Ardmore	Jack D. Miller	Galesburg, IL
Russell L. Donathan	Henryetta	Boyd D. Mills	Ury
John B. Dunaway	Miami	Thomas G. Mooney	Shawnee

Katharine L. Morrison — Gladewater, TX
Lester G. Naito — Waialua, HI
Albert M. Pearson — Fairview
Judson H. Pierce Jr. — Perry
Clay M. Posey — Tulsa
William H. Pratt — Tulsa
Richard S. Reese — Reese, NC
Alfred W. Renfroe — Fort Towson
Kenneth L. Royse — Elk City
William D. Taylor — Woodford

Robert S. Titus Jr. — Frederick
Michael G. Walsh Jr. — Southern Pines, NC
Wayne E. Weber — Stillwater
James R. Wells Jr. — Durant
Robert A. J. Whitney — Enid
Jack E. Williamson — Hammon
Paul L. Winsor — Perry
Frederick J. Woodall — Delhi

CLASS OF 1960

Gerald L. Appelgate — Tulsa
James E. Boyd — New Bern, NC
Cyril M. Brown — Jet
Rodye E. Butler — Rippon, WV
Michael Canaan — Tel Aviv, Israel
William F. Carter — Ponca City
James A. Countryman — Hooker
Ralph E. Doutey — Yale
James J. Eischen — Okarche
John J. Fletcher — Platteville, WI
Kent J. Fletcher — Platteville, WI
John M. Harper Jr. — Madill
David K. Haviland — Indianapolis, IN
Charles L. Heaton — Capron
LaVelle A. Holley — Ashton, IL
J. Harry James — Jefferson
Kenneth G. Keenum — Hazelwood, NC
William E. Knighten — Ashville, NC
Marvin R. Leighton — Clayton, NM

Larry D. Major — Kingfisher
Henry W. Mappes — Norman
Harold V. Miller — Hennessey
Culver D. Moe — Stillwater
Don R. Morrow — Ada
Thomas M. Mowdy — Freeport, NY
William D. Munson — Claremore
Benny B. Norman — Shawnee
Kenneth B. Redmond — Clinton
William A. Ridenour — Tunnelton, WV
Milton C. Schulze — Chelsea
Frank A. Serra — Westerly, RI
James A. Shmidl — Kildare
Ernest L. Stair Jr. — Faxon
William C. Terry — Tishomingo
Billy H. White — Whiteville, NC
Raymond G. White — Newton, WV
Howard L. Whitmore — Dallas, WI

CLASS OF 1961

Richard L. Blake — Enid
Robert L. Boss — Pawnee
David E. Breshears — Pine Bluff, AR
Jess L. Brewer — Enid
Donald M. Campbell — Binger
Frank W. Crider Jr. — Ada
Phillip W. Day — Oklahoma City
Marvin L. Denny Jr. — Tulsa
Richard E. Dillman — Balboa, CZ
Brian H. Espe — Palatine, IL
Robert C. Fischel — Roslyn, PA
Donald D. Ford — Wann
Jerry R. Gillespie — Gothenburg, NB
James G. Graham — Tulsa
Gerald A. Hegreberg — Burlington, ND
J. Frederick Hensley — Lewisburg, WV
Michael J. House — Bethel, NC
William E. Johnston — Beckley, WV

Daniel R. Jones — Kellyville
William E. Kyser — Waurika
Garland M. Lasater — Enid
Ronald D. Lockwood — Salem, SD
Andrew D. Mach — Vinita
Phillip R. Major — Omega
William S. McDowell — Alva
Michael N. Podolin — Stratford, NJ
Richard L. Rissler — Charlestown, WV
Robert D. Stewart — Morgantown, WV
William J. Strube — Idabel
Russell J. Tate — Blowing Rock, NC
John E. Terrall — Vinita
Anthony C. Thomas — Shawnee
James R. VanBeckum — Wauwatosa, WI
Claude B. Vanzant — Muskogee

CLASS OF 1962

James L. Arrington — Stillwater
Arlis D. Boothe — Nettie, WV
Anthony B. Carter — Ponca City
Wylie A. Dunn — Conway, AR
Lester R. Dupler — Cache
Donald A. Ensey Jr. — Boswell
Janet Y. Grantham — Gage
Roy W. Griffith — Hartshorne
Doyne Hamm — Mt. Judea, AR
Truman L. Hudson — Duncan
Joseph W. Inscoe — Newton, NC

Dwayne L. Jeffries — Ringwood
Thomas E. Jueschke — Tonkawa
Emil J. Kasik Jr. — Richland, NE
Michael A. Lucas — Blackwell
James M. McCallis — DeWitt, AR
David G. Mitchell — Tulsa
Donald A. Muncy — Tulsa
Nicholas A. Nail — Vinita
Louis W. Nightengale — Homestead
Robert D. Perkins — Shawnee
Michael M. Richie — Benton, LA

Richard D. Roth — Casselton, ND
Edward L. Schenk — Chickasha
Dale L. Schomp — Taloga
Roy B. Smith — Hingham, MA
Alton K. Spencer Jr. — Creswell, NC

William D. Tolbert — Hinton
Robert J. Van Patter — Hot Springs, AR
Edgar E. Wallop — Washington, DC
Jerry A. Wilson — Charlestown, WV

CLASS OF 1963

Stanley C. Acree — Maud
Jack C. Allen — Okmulgee
Dellalene M. Baker — Denison, TX
Zane G. Bowles — Hiddenite, NC
J. C. Bryson — Collinsville
Louis T. Burch — Little Rock, AR
Joseph F. Chabot — Whitinsville, MA
Robert R. Dahlgren — Alliance, NE
James R. Dear — Baskin, LA
Frederick G. Ferguson — Green Bay, WI
Isaiah J. Fidler — Jerusalem, Israel
Eugene Fingerlin Jr. — Tulsa
Edwin D. Fisher — Cushing
Wayne C. Franks — Philo, IL
Gaylord H. French Jr. — Draper, NC
Gary B. Gibbons — Lakota, ND
Elmer D. Giddeon — Drumright
Robert L. Hardy — Tarboro, NC
Wylie S. Hough Jr. — Ardmore
Franklin A. Humphreys — Bachelor, LA
Clinton N. Jewett — Little Rock, AR

Demarious L. Keller — Austin, TX
Jerry Z. Kendrick — Fairmont, WV
Thomas G. Loafmann — Prague
Donald G. Luther — Elk City
George B. Meyer Jr. — Viola, AR
Charles A. Montgomery Jr. — Tulsa
Jack R. Nightengale — Fairview
Lewis D. Roach — Texhoma
Don S. Robertson — King, NC
William R. Robertson — Boswell
Ned M. Ross — Burlington, NC
Lee G. Simmons Jr. — Jones
Daniel P. Solomon — Osage, WV
Ronald A. Stenseng — Fayetteville, AR
James H. Stone — Lawton
Bruce G. Stinger — Tulsa
Elden D. Svec — Rogers, NE
Donald H. Vrbka — Shelby, NE
Charles C. Warner Jr. — Charleston, WV
John D. Wehling — Minco

CLASS OF 1964

Marvin M. Adams — Oklahoma City
Richard E. Allen — North Little Rock, AR
Benny H. Baker — Checotah
Terry L. Beals — Greenfield
Richard J. Boatsman — Edmond
James H. Brandt — Tulsa
Richard G. Burchinal — Morgantown, WV
John I. Freeman — Lincolnton, NC
James F. Gehring — Wheatley, AR
Robert D. Hall — Hot Springs, AR
Lemuel G. Halterman — Moorefield, WV
Joseph S. Hayden — Tulsa
James C. McCoy — Ravenswood, WV
Deorsey E. McGruder Jr. — Muskogee
Vicki L. Mannschreck — Tulsa
Keith O. Martin — Elmore City

Gloyd R. Miller — Webbers Falls
Tran-Quang Minh — Saigon, Vietnam
Wayne L. Moore — Stillwater
Clarence M. Moreton — Fort Smith, AR
Laurin L. Patton — Ada
Lowell A. Pease — Portsmouth, NH
Roy R. Pool Jr. — Raleigh, NC
Billy J. Robinson — Winnsboro, LA
James M. Santino — Shawnee
Charles R. Seagren — Wausa, NE
Kenneth J. Sims — Medford
Janice M. Smith — Denton, TX
Lewis R. Smith — Canton
Daniel B. Stroup — Waco, NC
Larry J. Swango — Welch
Dale O. Turner — Renick, WV
Gordon H. Voss — Goltry
Sandra B. Wilson — Dublin, TX

CLASS OF 1965

Darrell C. Allison — Woodward
Richard E. Bailey — Tulsa
Lloyd D. Barker — Snyder
Dorland C. Bennett — Hennessey
Barney J. Bertrand — Sulphur, LA
Talmage T. Brown Jr. — Raleigh, NC
Joseph F. Buxton — Nowata
Thomas A. Carter — Stillwater
William M. Carter — Crossett, AR
Thomas E. Coffin — Waukomis
Don G. Crow — Wheeling, WV
Richard E. Dahlem — Medford
Joe R. Davis — Marked Tree, AR
John C. Doyle — Erick

Jerry P. Durham — Fayetteville, AR
Larry W. Edwards — Elk City
Ronald T. Ford — Wann
Paul O. Frith Jr. — Little Rock, AR
Ronald G. Geisert — Ogallala, NE
Jack V. Hill — Clinton, NC
Jackie W. Horton — Winters, TX
Jerry E. Jacobs — Okmulgee
Joel K. Jensen — Asheville, NC
John G. Kirkpatrick — Shattuck
William R. Lance — Lindsay
Duane R. Lemburg — Dannebrog, NE
Wade Markham — Locust Grove
Barbara A. McAbee — Wilmington, NC

Billy J. McDougal	Valiant	Dianne M. Wall	Houston, TX
Starling Miller Jr.	Chickasha	Carl E. Ward	Claremore
Rex M. Olson	Waynoka	Roger G. Wells	Tulsa
Richard C. Patterson	Sanford, NC	Thomas J. Welsh	Collinsville
Johnnie R. Remer	Spiro	Delbert L. Whitenack	Mooreland
William R. Roberson	Dardanelle, AR	John R. Wyant	Lawton
James R. Rocconi	Lake Village, AR	John Q. Young	El Reno
Ronald L. Solow	Tulsa	James M. Zyskowski	Tulsa

CLASS OF 1966

Philip F. Alm	Casselton, ND	Stephen M. Jones	Hot Springs, AR
Andy B. Baker	Wellington, KS	Travis W. Jones	Texarkana, AR
Bill F. Barnum	Texhoma	Silvija A. Liepnieks	Lincoln, NE
Kay J. Bose	Orleans, NE	James N. Livingston	Cache
Marvin W. Buck	Stillwater	Bruce H. Mammeli	Stanley
William B. Core	Core, WV	Ernest S. Martin	Trenton, ND
Joel B. Cox	Owasso	Stauffer Miller	Inwood
Shirley T. Currin	Oxford, NC	Jerry A. Mitchell	Hennessey
Jefferson G. Edwards	Newark, AR	Warren K. Newby	Caney, KS
Edward A. Fell	Pine Bluff, AR	Joe F. Nickell	Alva
Robert W. Fulton	Blackwell	Lewis W. Partridge	Gould, AR
Gerry L. Grant	Marked Tree, AR	Betty L. Reddick	Fairfax
William A. Grantham	Portland, AR	Robert J. Roberson	McAlester
Nolan L. Gross	Moore	Ronald Q. Roberts	Tulsa
Ronald N. Guthrie	Burns Flat	William C. Russell	Tulsa
John W. Hahn	Bartlesville	Jack L. Taylor	Sayre
Donald G. Harrington	Perryville, AR	Vernie R. Walker	Welch
Stephen R. Holmes	Fairview	John R. Webster	Stoneville, NC
Danny A. Hudson	Cramerton, NC	Dale L. Wendlandt	Braggs
Terry A. Jackson	Kenesaw, NE	Harold L. Williams	Delaware

CLASS OF 1967

Arden L. Anderson	Fremont, NE	Roger A. Howland	Marquette, NE
Robert J. Arko	Pryor	Gene B. Hubbard	Mandan, ND
Rodger D. Atkins	Jenks	Nicholas T. Jewell	Springdale, AR
Don W. Beavers	Chattanooga	Dick D. Kirby	Colcord
Robert H. Burns Jr.	Sutton, WV	Charles F. Kirkland	Henderson, NC
Stephen R. Cobb	Gibsonville, NC	William S. Kolar	Prague
Donald D. Connally	Stratford	James H. McGee	Schulter
Rueben R. Cowles Jr.	Statesville, NC	James B. Mortimer	Owasso
Hollis U. Cox	Lamar	Larry M. Murphy	Cherokee
Kenneth J. Davis	Cherokee	James P. Patton	Coalgate
Paul R. DuBois	Cameron	James W. Provo Jr.	Raleigh, NC
Merlin E. Ekstrom	Bowbells, ND	Phillip N. Richardson	Pocasset
David B. Fields	Huntsville, AR	Samuel S. Rubin	Sallisaw
Judd I. Giezentanner	Ponca City	Dennis E. Savell	Baton Rouge, LA
Herschell D. Giles	Carnegie	Joe H. Smith	Idabel
Charles W. Gray	Clinton	Resley F. Soirez	Erath, LA
Clarence B. Hackett	Baton Rouge, LA	Kenneth R. Sperling	Oklahoma City
Ernest C. Harland	Goodwell	Randy W. Thayer	Bunkie, LA
Kester W. Hawthorne	Baton Rouge, LA	Edwin T. Thorne	Oklahoma City
Wilber A. Haynes	Seiling	Benjamin S. Turner	Pink Hill, NC
Toby R. Hoover	Jay	James W. Waymack	Cabot, AR
William E. Hornbuckle	Perry		

CLASS OF 1968

Donald R. Biles	Madill	Earl G. Frie	Broken Arrow
E. Wayne Boland	Beulan, ND	Roy P. Garrison	Bartlesville
Michael F. Bounds	Chapel Hill, NC	William K. Gibbs	Reidsville, NC
Charles C. Callahan	Hobart	Jeanne L. Green	Oilton
Samuel J. Combs	Thomas	William D. Grossman	Chouteau
Danny D. Denham	Kellyville	John A. Hamil	Riverside, IL
William H. Foster	Turpin	Keith A. Hand	Ames
James C. Freeny	Caddo	Johnny D. Hoskins	Midwest City

John S. Howarth	Cave Springs, AR	Richard W. Schafer	Tulsa
Kenneth O. Isom	Edmond	Richard L. Shafer	Newkirk
Hershel G. Jaggars	Chouteau	Arch E. Sheets	Muskogee
Richard E. Killough	Indian Trail, NC	Eugene F. Simon	Conway, AR
Thomas R. Latta	Fort Supply	Willard T. Sodowsky Jr.	Fairview
Richard A. Mauldin	Hollis	Harold R. Spalding	Dewey
Michael T. McCreight	Oklahoma City	Charles E. Starkey	Malvern, AR
Lawrence D. McGill	Waverly, NE	James A. Summers	Ozark, AR
Roger A. McMillan Jr.	Mena, AR	Bill C. Swafford	Broken Arrow
Daniel L. Merkey	Cordell	George E. Taylor	Clinton
Gerald D. O'Mealey	Tonkawa	George M. Thomas	Ninnekah
David J. Parks	Union Grove, NC	Vernon R. Thornton	Copan
Henry C. Randazzo	St. Martinville, LA	James R. Walcott	Altus
H. Ellen Rayl	Jonesville, LA	Charles G. Warren	Robersonville, NC
Eddie J. Richey	Pawhuska		
Adrienne E. Ruby	Muskogee	Gary L. White	Stratford

CLASS OF 1969

Jimmie U. Baldwin	Stillwater	David E. Marx	DeRidder, LA
John D. Beal	Muskogee	John W. Miller	Muskogee
Albert B. Blanton Jr.	Shelby, NC	Ronald L. Mills	McCloud
Jim F. Bonham	Cordell	William R. Moore	Ruston, LA
Ray E. Burd	Okmulgee	Boyd C. Newby	Copan
Kenneth L. Byrd	Ft. Towson	Eugene O'Neal Jr.	Wister
John S. Chitwood	Poteau	Nancy B. Pate	Fayetteville, NC
Jeannette F. Clark	Oklahoma City	Thomas E. Phelps	Ponca City
James M. Cockrill	Little Rock, AR	Robert W. Poteet	Plainview, AR
William F. Cody II	Tulsa	James S. Ruster	Stillwater
Neil J. Corneil	Nardin	John K. Sexton	Walnut Ridge, AR
Georg Ann Davenport	Oklahoma City		
Charlotte S. Detch	Lewisburg, WV	Richard V. Shawley	Enid
Max E. Ficken	Marshall	James E. Shearer	Ft. Smith, AR
Roger L. Foote	Baton Rouge, LA	John K. Skeeles	Alexandria, LA
John A. Goedeken	Naponee, NE	Richard M. Stedman	David
Donald H. Heise	Sayre	James G. Taylor	Imboden, AR
Charles A. Holmberg	Erick	Gary G. Wallis	Rogers, AR
David A. Long	Lawton	Lee Roy Ward	Pencil Bluff, AR
Mike D. Lorenz	Enid	Gerald F. Weinand	Guthrie
Alan N. Maddox	Black Mountain, NC		

CLASS OF 1970

Michael L. Andrews	Stillwater	John M. McDaniel	Texhoma
Robert J. Bahr	Ft. Smith, AR	Eric A. Munson	Glenfield, ND
Cleta S. Bailey	Bartlesville	Marvin B. Newlin	Mebane, NC
Robert E. Barros	Lindsay	Larry L. Nolen	Burbank
Jack W. Butler	Tulsa	Lawayne T. Nusz	Okeene
Bill R. Clay	Liberty Mounds	Thomas C. Randolph Jr.	Sallisaw
Donald P. Dicharry	Baton Rouge, LA	James O. Richardson Jr.	Stokedale, NC
Larry D. Endersby	Woodward	Coleman L. Scott	Sapulpa
Frederick M. Enright	Baton Rouge, LA	Larry D. Shaw	El Reno
Susan F. Faulkner	Lewisburg, WV	David N. Shell	Tulsa
Donnie L. Gardner	Lone Grove	Thomas H. Shroyer	Eufaula
John P. Hammond	Stillwater	Bruce A. Simmons	Hickory, NC
Howard W. Haney	Ardmore	Charles B. Smith	Warren, AR
Richard D. Hanschu	Nowata	David C. Smith	Jet
Babette S. Humphrey	Mannington, WV	James H. Smith Jr.	Birdeye, AR
W. Joe Humphrey	Sallisaw	Jon M. Southerland	Rush Springs
Ronny E. Kiehn	Cordell	Gary W. Still	Wright City
David R. Kinkaid	Ponca City	Lyndon H. Tate	Keota
Cheryl P. Knoblock	Chicago, IL	O'Hara O. Tyler	Clayton
Stanley D. Kosanke	Cordell	Philip C. Ulmer	Miami
Maxwell A. Lea Jr.	Baton Rouge, LA	Ted L. Wiggins	Paris, AR
John M. LeBus	New Orleans, LA	Arthur G. Wills	Glen Morgan, WV
William P. McClees Jr.	Oriental, NC		

CLASS OF 1971

Malcom N. Allison	Woodward
George P. Badley	Shidler
Donald G. Battin	Green Forest, AR
Julia T. Blue	Romney, WV
Thomas M. Bowles	Henryetta
Carl D. Brown	Hickory
Tommy C. Brown	Perryville, AR
Phillip R. Chitwood	Poteau
Jim C. Chockley	Beaver
Sybil F. Christian	Kinder, LA
Sam M. Crosby Jr.	Frederick
Alvon P. Crosslin	Tahlequah
Gary L. Detrich	Midwest City
Thomas C. Eubanks	N. Little Rock, AR
William E. Ferrell	Leedey
George W. Flynt III	Winston-Salem, NC
John T. Gage	Tulsa
Douglas G. Gast	New Orleans, LA
Kenneth E. Gunkel	Eldorado
Robert D. Hall	Oklahoma City
Charles S. Hatfield	Southwest City, MO
James B. Hensley	Pauls Valley

Dicky J. Hodges	Boise City
Glenn D. Huckabee	Oklahoma City
Charles S. Jackson	Edenton, NC
Richard E. Keeton	El Dorado, AR
Larry A. Kerr	Burton, WV
Carl P. McCoy	Ripley, WV
Cliff R. McDonald	Atoka
Lawrence F. McTague	Ardmore
Larry L. Minter	Oklahoma City
John L. Myers	Tulsa
Anna B. Parker	Alma, AR
James B. Ralston	El Dorado, AR
James L. Reynolds	Stillwater
Jon C. Rogers	Sapulpa
John F. Scott	Broken Arrow
Richard H. Shepherd	Lake Providence, LA
Jimmie L. Shipman	Guthrie
Marcia L. Short	Mt. Ida, AR
Kenneth W. Sizelove	Laverne
John P. Thilsted Jr.	Alva
John R. Weisner	Greensboro, NC
Eugene M. Williams	Ft. Smith, AR
Charles W. Wills	Ralston
Timothy J. Woody	Greenwood, AR

CLASS OF 1972

Jimmy W. Antle	Mannford
Richard M. Baker	Guymon
G. Patrick Belford	Broken Arrow
Deborah K. Briggs	Ashville, NC
Rebecca J. Burdette	Charleston, WV
Gary T. Burger	Hartshorne
Bobby R. Clements	Imboden, AR
Anthony W. Confer	Hot Springs, AR
Danny L. Dillon	Kernersville, NC
Kenneth L. Doyle	Stilwell
Robert W. Dugan	Oklahoma City
James R. Ekart	Tulsa
William B. Fairchild	Sunshine, LA
Larry E. Franks	Waldo, AR
George A. French	Madill
Emile C. Frisard	New Orleans, LA
William H. Gooldy	Pryor Creek
Robert C. Green	Vinita
John B. Hays	Oklahoma City
Jerry B. Hedges	Mutual
Fred A. Hines	Oklahoma City
E. Clay Hodgin III	Greensboro, NC
Joe M. Howell	Morrison
Kay K. Husen	Oklahoma City
Glenn A. Hutchinson	Springfield, LA

John A. M. Johnston	Comanche
Terence O. Jones	Pawnee
Philip L. Linnemann	Oklahoma City
John E. McGuire	Tulsa
Ben H. McKinley	Lookout
Jeffery D. McMaster	Okolona, AR
Virgil E. McWilliams	Stillwater
Larry O. Mayberry	Pauls Valley
Lonnie D. Moore	Waynoka
Sammy F. Moore	Lawton
Kenneth G. Neuens	Bismarck, ND
Ronald W. Nida	Perry
Thomas Pastor	New Orleans, LA
Leslie J. Pshigoda	Shattuck
John O. Regnier	Kenton
John B. Renfro	Cary, NC
Kenton E. Riddle	Tulsa
Charles M. Steeds	Oklahoma City
Walter W. Tabor	Baton Rouge, LA
Bobby J. Ward	Pencil Bluff, AR
Richard C. Wilson	Fairview
George M. Woods	Poteau
Gary W. Woulfe	Stillwater
Charles W. Yount	Gering, NE

CLASS OF 1973

Randy L. Ashley	Haileyville
Mary E. Baribeau	Huntington, WV
David E. Billins	Hampton, AR
William W. Branscum	Mason
Richard T. Bredlow	England, AR
Elizabeth A. Cochran	Bradley, AR
James R. Crawford	Winston-Salem, NC
C. Ned Demorest	Tulsa

Gary W. France	Rogers, AR
Charles R. Freeman	Sentinel
Gerald L. Gibson	Hardesty
John L. Guerra	Wilburton
Robert M. Gwin	Oklahoma City
Hartford R. Hamilton Jr.	Lonoke, AR
Kenneth W. Hill	Hickory, NC
Alvin L. Howell	Panama
Billy J. Johnson	Claremore

Jesse W. Johnson | Magnolia, AR
George H. Kendall | Guthrie
Michael D. Krieger | Hobart
Diana G. Loeffler | Oklahoma City
Joseph A. Luebker | Stuttgart, AR
James J. Lumbers | Del City
Edward A. Mahaffey | Winston-Salem, NC

Kristan K. Meyerer | Baton Rouge, LA
Roger L. Mims | Oklahoma City
E. Anne Morris | Oklahoma City
Gary D. Nida | Perry
Kenneth E. O'Hanlon | Marietta
Burl R. Phifer Jr. | Savanna

Charles W. Qualls Jr. | Oklahoma City
Jerry D. Roll | Vinita
Charles M. Savell | Baton Rouge, LA
Robert A. Sperle | Napolean, ND
James A. Stiles | Ponca City
B. Britton Stringer | Jena
Richard A. Tallent | Ft. Smith, AR
Richard S. Templeton | Enid
Craig A. Tigert | Oklahoma City
Charles L. Watterson | Miami
James E. Weidman | Tulsa
Bernard L. Wiedemann | Yukon
Dwight L. Witcher | Little Rock, AR

CLASS OF 1974

Kenneth G. Bell | Perkins
David F. Brown | Russellville, AR
Lafe M. Burnett | Pawhuska
James W. Carpenter | Malverne, NY
Ewell L. Center | Miami
Stephen A. Chambers | Enid
Linda K. Clark | Claremore
Brenda R. Corbin | Mount Olive, NC
David D. Davis | Hatfield, AR
Ronald K. Fallon | Huntington, WV
Larry E. Freeman | Ahoskie, NC
Keith B. Gilliam | Oklahoma City
Gary L. Glisan | Waynoka
Darryl K. Guthrie | Burns Flat
Charles W. Harms | Dover, AR
David S. Haworth | Okeene
Michael R. Hurt | Princeton, WV
Lonnie G. Jay | Elk City
Gary O. Kinder | Charleston, WV
Paul G. Klinger | Ponca City
Bruce N. Kunkle | Grand Island, NE
Ralph C. Lockhart | Charleston, WV
Eileen M. McGoey | New Orleans, LA
Phillip R. McKinney | Sand Springs

William M. Martin | Ponca City
Richard D. Mitchell | Greensboro, NC
Robert W. Moak | Baton Rouge, LA
Ronald W. Mollett | Elk City
David R. Myers | Tulsa
Paul C. Peterson | Norman
Rick K. Pickard | Woodward
Ronald D. Powell | El Reno
Cecil M. Purdy | Altus
John R. Rector | Wilson
Kenneth L. Reynolds | Tulsa
Mark D. Rose | Whitesboro
Larry R. Salyer | Shidler
Bill W. Schaefer | Marshall
Gary E. Schieber | Newkirk
Trenton R. Schoeb | Cherokee
William G. Smith | Jet
Joe L. Smothers | Lawton
Patrick F. Thistlethwaite | Washington, LA
Stephen H. Walker | Wewoka
Ronald R. Wallis | Claremore
D. Raymond Whitehead | Taylor, AR
Julie C. Wiedemann | Covington, LA

CLASS OF 1975

Glenn F. Anderson | Broken Arrow
Brenda C. Bright | Hope, AR
Thomas L. Bright | Hope, AR
Delia M. Burchfield | McGrew, NE
Gary K. Burns | Geary
Vickie Stonestreet Burns | Elkview, WV
Jerry M. Cates | Okmulgee
James D. Conklin | Tulsa
Donald B. Conkling | Elmhurst, IL
Gene J. Courtright | Bogalusa, LA
Timothy C. Eaker | Oklahoma City
Katherine M. Ellis | Oklahoma City
Marvin L. Ellis | Guthrie
Ted A. Eudy | Hugo
Theodore A. Falconer | Stigler
James R. Faw | Oklahoma City
Stacy B. Fry | Bethany
Eugene A. Garcia III | New Orleans, LA
James F. Glassford | Raleigh, NC
D. Dee Griffin | Vamoosa
John D. Hackett | McAlester
Ann H. Hatley | Hubener, AR

J. David Helms | Okmulgee
Dennis C. Henson | Sweetwater
Anita L. Hinshaw | Springdale, AR
Robert A. Hughes | Tulsa
Ernest M. Hunter | Shenandoah Junction, WV
George H. Jackson | Oklahoma City
Robert B. Jensen | Ridgefield, CT
Edward E. Jorden | Enid
Gary J. Kiehn | Cordell
Timothy F. Lafferty | Enid
Jimmie O. Lloyd | Tulsa
Jesus A. Lopez | Altus
Bruce W. Martin | Gravette, AR
John D. Minson | Perry
Elliott K. Nelson | Ryden, ND
R. Benton Netherton | Miami
Larry J. Nieman | Edmond
Gene A. Niles | Perkins
Arthur W. O'Brien | N. Little Rock, AR
Larry J. Peters | Pryor

Milton E. Pollard — Tulsa
Alan K. Potter — Cleveland
James R. Powell — Bartlesville
Gordon D. Rahmes — Sanford, NC
K. Patrick Rains — Danville, VA

Clare S. Seagren — Princeton, WV
Stephen P. Sullivan — Greensboro, NC
Jonathan B. Turner — Holdenville
Larry D. Wilson — Harrah
Sharon Wilson — Perry

CLASS OF 1976

Shirley R. Ahern — Stillwater
Thomas P. Albright — Pauls Valley
Larry J. Allen — Garber
Billy M. Burkett — Provencal, LA
Fred W. Bush — Helena, AR
Frank O. Denney — Vinita
Frances M. Doepel — Ponca City
Marguerite F. Duffy — Charlotte, NC
James F. Goodman — Sulphur
William E. Guthrie Jr. — Burns Flat
Bonnie C. Harding — Magnet Cove, AR
Roger W. Harlin — Oklahoma City
Michael D. Haworth — Okeene
H. David Haynes — Tulsa
Ronald G. Helvey — Colony
Paul J. Hoopes Jr. — Muskogee
John D. Howard — Pryor
Daniel E. Jones — Bent Mountain, VA
Timothy L. Jones — Potters Hill, NC
Charles Kelsey Jr. — Lawton
David Kerr — Broken Arrow
Stephen A. Letzig — Blackwell
Fenton R. Lipscomb — New Orleans, LA
John D. Long — Cordell
Nelson B. McKinney — Durant
Tom P. McLarty — Hitchcock
Frederick G. McNeill — Mulhall
John R. Marshall — Ponca City
Mark J. Matli — Watonga

Tommy J. Melton — Yellville, AR
Paul D. Minnick — Claremore
Michael P. Mohler — Batesville, AR
Loyd A. Nall — N. Little Rock, AR
Timothy M. Neer — Tulsa
Lee A. Nickels — Oklahoma City
Jerry D. Pack — Edmond
Lyndsay G. Phillips Jr. — Tulsa
Robert A. Purvis — Sayre
Brian E. Renegar — Bunch
Lawrence P. Ruhr — Tulsa
Ronald R. Schurter — Morrison
Gary J. Seagren — Wausa, NE
David G. Sparks — Rosston
James D. Sprague — Coalgate
Kenneth L. Stelzer — Guymon
David L. Sturgeon — Cordell
Tim M. Synar — Muskogee
Michael D. Thames — Ft. Smith, AR
Myrna C. Thomas — Charleston, WV
David W. Vest — Siloam Springs, AR
Roger D. Vocque — Poteau
Steven L. Vonderfecht — Gothenburg, NE
G. Gary Walker — Stillwater
Kent P. Walker — Lafayette, LA
John W. Whittaker — Fairfax
William R. Wooden — Tulsa
David C. Zoltner — Oklahoma City

CLASS OF 1977

Alvin L. Baumwart — Clinton
Elton R. Cleveland — Magazine, AR
John E. Collins — Marietta
Max C. Combs — Oklahoma City
Marion P. Copley — Stillwater
Robert M. Cross — Oklahoma City
Richard F. Cullison — Wellston
Joseph M. Day — Orlando
Tom L. Dayton — Pond Creek
Marlys P. Easton — Stillwater
Charles D. Eisenhour — El Reno
Robert P. Evans — Perkins
Bradley C. Floyd — Oklahoma City
Kathryn S. Fuller — Keyser, WV
Teresa G. Fulp — Raleigh, NC
David K. Ganzel — South Gate, CA
Rudy D. Garrison — Vian
Andrew C. Gladden — Gurdon, AR
Brian E. Gordon — Mulhall
Rodney R. Hall — Stonewall
Debbie W. Hasse — Minco
Jan M. Hasse — Charleston, WV
Dickie D. Herbel — Hooker
Marie E. Hogsett — Oklahoma City
Gary D. Holden — Collinsville

Michael L. Huggins — Winston-Salem, NC
Carney B. Jackson — Morgantown, WV
Gloria B. Janovetz — Midwest City
John D. Johnson — Russellville, AR
Roger P. Johnson — Oklahoma City
William D. Kirkpatrick — Forgan
Randall H. McBride — Del City
Carlos D. Mayes — Tahlequah
Caren L. Miller — Weirton, WV
Robert B. Moeller — Fremont, NE
James D. Mort — Foster, RI
Daniel A. Murphy — Keyser, WV
Elizabeth M. Murphy — Stillwater
William R. Noble — Stillwater
Frederick W. Reuter — El Reno
Thomas A. Richardson — West Memphis, AR
Jacob B. Roth — Woodmere, NY
Thomas G. Sartain — Tulsa
Theodore A. Schupbach — Tulsa
Dennis N. Seymore — Little Rock, AR
Ronnie K. Simon — Oklahoma City
James R. Stewart — Ponca City
Sharon J. Strain — Wetumka

David G. Tanner — Morrillton, AR
Jimmy D. Thurman — Okmulgee
Dennis R. Tooley — Maysville
John R. Tye — Muskogee
Ronald D. Tyler — Purcell
Judith E. Vaeth — Covington

Karen J. Vargas — Oklahoma City
Carl F. Willis — Altus
Gary L. Wolf — Salina
Rickey J. Wolfe — Oklahoma City
Larry L. Woods — Wayne
William P. Yonushonis — Raleigh, NC

CLASS OF 1978

Paul L. Aldridge — Tulsa
Jimmy A. Bentley — Rush Springs
David L. Bone — Temple
Robert A. Bower — Shawnee
Ronald L. Boyer — Oklahoma City
Michael A. Breider — Fessenden, ND
Gary D. Brown — Ponca City
Randy J. Burgess — Heavener
Margaret L. Clark — Wellston
Zola B. Cobb — Hunter
Annette K. Cowell — Raleigh, NC
Rick L. Cowell — Kingfisher
Daniel G. Danner — Tulsa
Elizabeth Lee Denney — Cushing
Robert W. Fields — Red Oak
Nicholas R. Finn — Greenbrier, AR
J. Keith Flanagan — Texhoma
Curtis J. Fried — Selfridge, ND
Marilyn J. Gardner — Winston-Salem, NC
Marshall E. Goodenberger — Trenton, NE
Lyndon J. Graf — Cordell
Floyd G. Graham — Muskogee
Carolyn Gunn — Tulsa
John C. Haliburton — Stillwater
Richard M. Halvorson — Rugby, ND
Roger D. Holley — Broken Bow
Kenneth R. Hoodenpyle — Vinita
Guy L. Humphrey — Miami
Candace A. Jacobs — Lincoln, NE

Michael R. Kollar — Edmond
William C. Lankford — Holdenville
Kenneth R. Leach — Orlando
Ronald E. Lenington — Sallisaw
Johnny R. McCabe — Wilburton
Kimsey W. McCulloch — Saginaw, MI
Robert E. McKinney — Ames
Brian E. McNeil — Perry
Linda J. Mason — Depew
Vernon L. Newby — Copan
R. Scott Nicholson — Tulsa
Barbara L. Nicks — Elkin, NC
James E. Posey — Yukon
Howard L. Pue — Tulsa
Sharon E. Reamer — Okmulgee
Dexter U. Reavis — Welch
Warren G. Resell — Petersburg, ND
B. Riddick Ricks — Conway, NC
James W. Robertson — Laverne
Donald A. Rone — Bentonville, AR
Martin E. Roth — Perry
Donald K. Russell — Maysville
David L. Sabala — Tulsa
Andreas M. Senske — Tulsa
Orval L. Stadheim — Reeder, ND
James E. Stock — Kingfisher
Gary W. Stone — Shawnee
Cecil H. Tangner Jr. — Oklahoma City
Frederick F. Vernon — Blanc, NC
Thomas W. Vickers — Batesville, AR
Gene E. Yost — Kingfisher

CLASS OF 1979

B. Francine Allee — Elk City
Timothy M. Ashley — Grandfield
Margaret S. Barry — Wagoner
Charles P. Beall — Broken Arrow
William T. Blankenship — Gentry, AR
Philip D. Boone — Tulsa
Michael D. Bradley — Miami
Ernestina S. Buchanan — Lawton
Cynthia B. Buhl — Tulsa
James L. Curl — Golva, ND
Marlyn D. Curtis — Carney
Robert M. Davis — Wilburton
Michael E. Diesen — Highland, IL
Connie B. Edwards — Orlando
Jimmy M. Fuchs — Elk City
Larry K. Gaines — Duncan
Stuart W. George — Bartlesville
Danny J. Glover — Marlow
Jim H. Guthery — Broken Bow
Patrick J. Haley — Los Alamitos, CA
Donald K. Hamilton — Albemarle, NC
Craig T. Hanson — Scranton, ND
Carolyn S. Hays — Grove

Roger A. Henneke — Drummond
Bradford W. Hildabrand — Hunter
Harold W. Howell — Chandler
Christine E. Hunt — Raleigh, NC
Dale Kaufman — St. Vincent, AR
Larry M. Kysar — Waynoka
John G. Lasarsky — Tulsa
Terry W. Lehenbauer — Ames
Gary L. Lenaburg — Lookeba
Carol E. Long — Fremont, NE
Jimmy R. Lucas — Winston-Salem, NC
Mike D. McGuire — Cheyenne
Brian K. McKinley — Marlow
Ladd Oldfield — Burbank
Arlyn T. Omtvedt — Norman
Jon W. Owen — Fargo, ND
Roger D. Parker — Welch
Tommy N. Pool — Lawton
Carl L. Propp — Adair
Michael E. Sanders — Erick
Ronnie D. Sarratt — Ringling
Eva M. Sartin — Chattanooga
Larry A. Schuler — Tuttle

Steven L. Schwandt   Mulhall
Steven L. Seidenberger   Vinita
Sandra Sherman   Oklahoma City
Rebecca S. Snyder   Roca, NE
James B. Sprouse   Oklahoma City
Gregory B. Stanbery   Boone, NC
Clarence S. Steward   Shawnee
Michael L. Steward   Shawnee
Ronald J. Streeter   Ponca City

Terry F. Sutterfield   Morrilton, AR
Michael D. Talkington   Newcastle
Dennis R. Unruh   Waynoka
Thomas B. Williams   Tulsa
Harry W. Wilson   Winston-Salem, NC

Joel L. Wilson   Seminole
David W. Wyrick   El Reno
Howard M. Zent   Mott, ND

CLASS OF 1980

Glynda K. Ashley   Haileyville
M. Sue Barrett   Reydon
David M. Blount   N. Little Rock, AR
William W. Brinkley   Lawton
Mike L. Bunning   Snyder
Roger D. Cahill   Ord, NE
Brian S. Carroll   Weleetka
O. Mark Carter   Holdenville
Kelley A. Chace   North Platte, NE
Gary W. Chandler   Broken Arrow
William E. Clymer   Antlers
Virginia S. Copland   Duncan
Jeffrey F. Ellis   Tulsa
Tony K. Epperson   Holdenville
B. Michael Flynn   Oklahoma City
Patricia T. Franks   Fayetteville, AR
Douglas L. Fulnechek   Duke
Sandra E. Gilbert   Wynnewood
Frances L. Gramlich   Oklahoma City
Paul G. Greenlee   Sudbury, MA
Terry D. Hargis   Tulsa
James E. Haught Jr.   Sapulpa
Eddie P. Horn   Cordell
George A. Horn Jr.   Seminole
Susan G. Hossenlopp   Bartlesville
Mark D. Hubbard   Elk City
Larry S. Hudman   Poteau
C. Steven Hunholz   Midwest City
Sherri L. Huntress   Oklahoma City
Catherine A. Jewell   Tulsa
Janis L. Johnson   Tulsa
Charlie E. Jones Jr.   Amber

Ronald R. Laughlin   El Reno
Fred D. Lehman   Balko
Joel D. Lenz   Enid
Randy K. Lewis   Maysville
Leldon W. Locke   Tishomingo
Terry R. Lohmann   Alva
Nancy F. McCurley   Muskogee
Randall S. Miller   Tulsa
Michael P. Moore   Phoenix, AZ
LeMac G. Morris   Haileyville
Robert G. Morris   Pryor
Lynn E. Norman   Granite
Kevin C. O'Hair   Shattuck
Gregg M. Ohmann   Oklahoma City
Dwight A. Olson   Enid
Larry D. Powers   Tulsa
Charles D. Reavis Jr.   Claremore
Thomas R. Reece   Tipton
Lowrey L. Rhodes Jr.   Stillwater
R. Bruce Rosier   Waurika
M. Allison Shassere   West Memphis, AR
Larry D. Shipman   Cleveland
Gordon F. Simpson   Purcell
Michael W. Voss   Checotah
Edward A. Wagner   Tulsa
Steven R. Weir   Catoosa
Michael J. Wiley   Hardesty
John L. Williams   Tulsa
Steven K. Wilson   Tulsa
Larry D. Wyckoff   Pond Creek
David H. Zeman   Minot, ND
Paul E. Zimmer   Edmond

CLASS OF 1981

Bob D. Ables   Sulphur
Kevin R. Allen   Altus
Mikel L. Athon   Ponca City
Lawrence R. Barrett   Kellyville
John L. Bartholomew Jr.   Norman
Julie C. Belden   Stillwater
Kim B. Bigbie   Ringling
Thomas S. Cannon   New Berlin, WI
David J. Cason   Okay
H. Ashton Cloninger   Lawton
Michael G. Courtney   Oklahoma City
Gary W. Cox   Sallisaw
Thomas K. Cox   Watonga
Judith A. Davis   Chickasha
Renee H. DeGidts   Colcord
Dennis E. Dugger   Oklahoma City
Patrick J. Finley   Tulsa
Kathleen A. Freeman   Tulsa

Lynetta J. Freeman   Eldorado
Mary A. Gaughan   Oklahoma City
Kenneth A. Gianetti   Perkins
John P. Gillis   Barrington, IL
William D. Glover   Purcell
Dee M. Gragg   Edmond
Larry W. Hamilton   Mustang
William P. Jackson   Ardmore
James S. Jenkins   Wetumka
James R. Jorgensen   Yankton, SD
Mark J. Kopit   Anaheim, CA
Michael R. Lappin   Edmond
Judith A. Larson   Tulsa
Jeffrey J. Livingstone   Okmulgee
Rocky McKelvey   Lawton
Denis Matousek   Hennessey
Margaret C. Meade   Atwood
Stephen R. Meyerdirk   Bartlesville

Sharon L. Nash	Keota	Susan C. Tankersley	Cameron
Rick L. Neilson	Altus	Larry D. Thompson	Oklahoma City
Frederic W. Northern	Tulsa	Betsey B. Thoni	Muskogee
Deena G. Oakley	Enid	Robert P. Thoni	Midwest City
Kenneth M. Olivier	Jones	Jeffery L. Tidwell	Empire
Thomas W. Pugsley	Oklahoma City	Kent N. Torbeck	Oklahoma City
Edward S. Richardson	La Puente, CA	Paul L. Welch	Tulsa
Patricia A. Skavlen	Bartlesville	Stuart W. White	Ardmore
Phillip R. Steinert	Marshall	Alvin W. Williams	Capron
Kerry A. Steward	Stillwater	Marvin L. Wollard	New Orleans, LA
Thomas S. Taggart	Edmond	Paul B. Young	Tulsa

CLASS OF 1982

Gregory J. Bennett	Vinita	David H. Migliaccio	Chester, NJ
Lynne C. Bennett	Tulsa	Marcinda Mitchell	Sallisaw
Victor R. Boyer	Fairland	Mike R. Mitchell	Sallisaw
Craig M. Bullock	Oklahoma City	Ronnie L. Nye	Ninnekah
Jamie S. Burner-Schrag	Woodland Hills, CA	Melissa D. Orr	Kingfisher
		Paula J. Paetz	Tulsa
Theresa M. Casey	Guthrie	David L. Panciera	Stillwater
Gary L. Chace	Guthrie	Alfonso Paredes Jr.	Oklahoma City
Larry P. Chambers	Beggs	Gerald W. Parsons	Holdenville
Daniel R. Christian	Oklahoma City	Tony L. Pickard	Hooker
David L. Combs	Thomas	David A. Powers	Ardmore
Danny R. Cox	Springer	Burt A. Pritchett	China Lake, CA
Catherine F. Cranmore	Ardmore	Diana G. Procter	Oklahoma City
C. W. Dicketts	Allen	Deborah A. Rames	Norman
Cassie L. Duffer	Ada	Gerald L. Rayburn	Lawton
Patrick L. Edmonds	Morris	Frank Roberts	Shawnee
Mark I. Elwell	Fairview	James E. Rose	Ringling
Linda S. Engberg	Oklahoma City	Stephanie A. Rosin	Oklahoma City
Michael L. Fox	Guymon	Charles E. Sanders	Erick
Lavinia K. Frank	Norman	Paul M. Schmitz	Tulsa
Vicki L. Funkhouser	Hobart	Glen J. Schoenhals	Shattuck
James L. Hackworth	Tulsa	Mark D. Setser	Tulsa
Howard B. Hopps III	Oklahoma City	Mark H. Shackelford	Tulsa
John C. Hunt	Chickasha	Lawrence D. Shamis	Great Neck, NY
George A. Jacoby	Hugo	Robert A. Shoup	McAlester
Stephen R. Jarman	Oklahoma City	Sandford C. Smith	Oklahoma City
Robin L. Johnson	Tulsa	John R. Sohl	Tulsa
Michael S. Jones	Goodwell	Edmond C. Staley	Alamogordo, NM
Kim E. Knowles	Enid	Elsa B. Stephens	Oklahoma City
Dale H. Kosted	Enid	Margaret A. Thompson	Tulsa
Gary J. Kubat	Oklahoma City	Michael L. Tripp	Guymon
James F. Kuhn	Glencoe	Gregory A. Turner	Cordell
John E. Link	Choctaw	James L. Walker	Kingfisher
Stephen B. McAuliff	Wagoner	Christopher F. Wilson	Fairland

CLASS OF 1983

April L. Altman	Stillwater	Warren E. Deal	Tonkawa
Patricia M. Auge	St. Paul, MN	Ronald R. Eby	Adair
Frank W. Austin	Tulsa	Kevin C. Ehlers	Stillwater
Catherine S. Auten	Tulsa	Gary J. Eskew	Moore
David M. Barnett	El Reno	Debra D. Evans	Moore
Keith M. Betzen	Hereford, TX	Deborah S. Fimple	Oklahoma City
Glenn E. Bullock	Yukon	Roxann M. Gleichman	Wilburton
Stanley S. Carroll	Roswell, NM	Lisa D. Good	Ponca City
Cindy G. Carter	Gore	Jean A. Graff	Crescent
Daniel W. Cason	Okay	David K. Henderson	Stigler
John W. Civic	Cranston, RI	Stephen R. Hopkins	Oklahoma City
Frank J. Corrado IV	Dover, DE	Terry L. Jantzen	Ringwood
John A. Cowart	Cameron	Kit Kampschmidt	Ardmore
Perry F. Crenshaw	Hodgen	Elizabeth N. King	Lawton
Rebecca J. Darland	Vinita	Kenneth D. Kirlin	Tulsa
Greg A. Daubney	Bixby	Deborah A. Krueger	Talala

Danny P. Lankford	Vinita	Jonathan L. Shepherd	Norman
Carol J. Lockhart	Northville, MI	M. Barbarita Smith	Tulsa
Ellen J. Magid	Chickasha	Stanley E. Smith	Tulsa
Carolyn McLemore	Comanche	John D. Stein	Cherokee
deShawn Merrell	Seminole	Bob G. Story	Perkins
Eddie L. Moore	Leedey	Jan Stratton	Cookson
Richard D. Oberst	Stillwater	Susan M. Thiel	Tulsa
David J. Orton	Oologah	Ronnie D. Thomason	Morrison
Beverly A. Osteen	Oklahoma City	Jean P. Thompson	Ponca City
David R. Parks	Edmond	Terrence G. Turner	Pawnee
H. Keith Parrish	Lawton	David L. Von Tungeln	El Reno
Dianna G. Pugsley	Cleveland	Kenneth A. Waldrup	El Dorado, AR
P. Richard Reid	Nowata	Betsy G. Walker	Martin, TN
Deborah S. Reitter	Manchester, MO	Janet S. Weaver	Tulsa
Michael L. Richey	Yukon	Bradley R. Weeks	Tecumseh
Marcella S. Roan	Oklahoma City	Kristine V. Wells	Ponca City
Jeffrey S. Sample	Miami	Michael S. Williams	Tulsa
Martha G. Schoenhals	Tulsa	Randy D. Winn	Jones
Michael C. Sealock	Duncan	Jerry M. Woodall	Gerty
Tad H. K. Shadid	Oklahoma City		

CLASS OF 1984

Mary Ann Allen	Muskogee	Judy K. Lewis	Broken Arrow
Gordon A. Andrews	Batavia, NY	Randall A. Lovell	Weatherford
Keith A. Bailey	Tulsa	Charlotte Means	Tulsa
Frederick E. Brown	Morristown, NJ	Nancy J. Middleton	Peace Dale, RI
James W. Butler	Lawton	David M. Murphy	Tulsa
Anne M. Buxton	Tulsa	Paul R. Newman	El Reno
Joseph H. Carter Jr.	Moore	Joseph K. Noble	Oklahoma City
John R. Chancey	Nowata	Stanley Pope Jr.	Boswell
Robert D. Chaplin	Perkins	Brian E. Pribil	Hennessey
Robert M. Cole	Woodward	Kathy R. Rayner	Enid
Donna K. Cook	Pond Creek	Katherine A. Reiss	Oklahoma City
Margaret L. Darcy	Kingston, RI	Jonathon C. Remer	Spiro
Paul W. Dean	Claremore	Ronald W. Richardson	Kiowa
Alan D. Donnell	Weatherford	Mark S. Roberson	Pryor
Mary Ann N. Doyle	Ponca City	Dawn M. Roberts	Lawton
Kit C. Farwell	Norman	Gerald M. Roundtree	Madill
James D. Fikes	Adair	Tracy D. Rutledge	Woodward
Leslie W. Fikes	Lawton	Charles H. Schor	Livingston, NJ
Steven J. Gatlin	Tulsa	Thomas L. Sifers	Del City
Robert M. Gibbens	Norman	Argus G. Smith	Lawton
Patrick D. Grogan	Garber	Kenneth R. Smith	Batesville, AR
D. Greg Hall	Norman	Michael T. Staton Sr.	Oklahoma City
Thomas D. Harbour III	Norman	Randolph D. Stokes	Locust Grove
Burke L. Healey	Davis	Diane L. Thompson	Stillwater
David W. Henderson	Bartlesville	Janice M. Thornbrugh	Tulsa
Nancy C. Johnson	Tryon	Thomas E. VanGundy	Norman
Kathleen A. Kennedy	Laverne	Becky L. Brewer Walker	Tulsa
David A. Kleck	Claremore	Marianne M. Williams	Tulsa
Michael W. Knight	Mead	Deborah L. Wysocki	Lawton
Alan F. Knox	Tulsa	Joyce C. Yauk	Buffalo
Dawn M. Lawson	Montclair, CA	Douglas B. Young	Perkins
Gregory W. Lawson	Ontario, CA	Karen M. Zagorsky	Oklahoma City

CLASS OF 1985

Kenneth L. Abrams	Cranston, RI	Diana L. Carper	S. Charleston, OH
M. Gayle Arbaugh	Pauls Valley		
Karen J. Bachle	Oklahoma City	Bert B. Chesney	Wewoka
David A. Beckstrom	Tulsa	Heather A. Cobb	Bethany
Melvin D. Bowers	Terlton	Linda P. Coenen	Fresno, CA
Andrew B. Broaddus	Ponca City	Colette P. Crotty	Tulsa
Randal E. Burris	Oklahoma City	Wesley A. Dill	Spencer
Gregory A. Campbell	Harrah	Michael J. Dodd	El Reno
Joyce G. Campbell	Enid	Kathryn S. Dunaway	Jay

Carey L. Floyd	Ada	Julia M. O'Carroll	Vinita
L. Kay Ford	Oklahoma City	W. Bruce Omohundro	Ada
Gordon R. Gathright	Fort Supply	F. Kelley Ray	Edmond
Mary L. Gray	Amorita	James L. Rebele	Claremore
Marjorie E. Gross	Oklahoma City	John M. Revere	Rush Springs
Melinda J. Hawkins	Oklahoma City	Judith A. Roberds	Dewey
James T. Hays III	Laverne	Jeffrey J. Sarchet	Hooker
Leslie J. Henshaw	Bartlesville	Tommy D. Shelton	Miami
David W. Hille	Dallas, TX	Stuart A. Sherrell	Tulsa
Donivan F. Hudgins	Stilwell	Jill H. Shults	Oklahoma City
Steven C. Hurlbert	Miami	Kelly W. Smith	Welch
David L. Hutto	Bartlesville	Kimothy L. Smith	Altus
Stanley K. Johnson	Grove	Ronald S. Smith	Chester
Fawn King	Enid	Gary J. Spodnick	Duncan
Charlotte A. Krugler	Rosemont, PA	Kenneth W. Spradley	Cameron
Michael D. Major	Watonga	John C. Summar	Fort Gibson
Carl G. Manske	Shattuck	Delana D. Taylor	Spiro
Richard L. Marrinson	Tulsa	Edward G. Taylor	Perkins
Nita K. McNeill	Mustang	Harry E. Traylor II	Oklahoma City
L. Douglas Meador	Erick	Sharon M. Tripp	Lawton
James H. Meinkoth	Tulsa	Randel W. Walker	Stuart
Alfred L. Million	Oklahoma City	J. David Wolfe	Tulsa
Susan L. Moore	Tulsa	Eric D. Wynn	Checotah
Mary E. Morgan	Moore	Laurie S. Zelby	Norman
John T. Nick	Scottsdale, AZ	Judy W. Zinn	Chouteau

CLASS OF 1986

Delwin D. Allen	Reed	Thomas J. Loafman	Ardmore
Kevin J. Anderson	Durham	Monte C. McMeans	Marietta
Susan E. Basler	Stillwater	James M. McQuade	Tonkawa
Michelle L. Belanger	Weatherford	Boyd D. Mills	Durant
James R. Bixler	Oklahoma City	Cynthia L. Newnam	Shawnee
Denise I. Bounous	Valdese, NC	Michael D. Nichols	Choctaw
William R. Boyd	Sand Springs	Robert I. Norris	Norman
Karen M. Bratcher	Altus	Kenneth C. Powell	Pryor
Calvin B. Carpenter	Beggs	Richard C. Prather	Elk City
James A. Carpenter	Chickasha	Scott L. Price	Duncan
Roy A. Carroll	Roswell, NM	Michael R. Pruitt	Hobart
Danny R. Cary	Jenks	Joseph J. Quinn III	Oklahoma City
Clay A. Clark	Bartlesville	James D. Rankin	Sand Springs
Leslie E. Cole	Cushing	Brian P. Rean	Guthrie
Diane L. Delbridge	Oklahoma City	Sandra L. Reisbeck	Stillwater
Gretchen L. Foster	Meers	Grant B. Rezabek	Buffalo Valley
Beverly N. Fritzler	Shawnee	Jerry R. Roberson	Adair
Keith D. Fuchs	Elk City	Roddy R. Roberts	Tulsa
Martin O. Furr	Prue	Paul M. Robertson	Oklahoma City
Carl D. Gragg Jr.	Morris	Roger D. Schwartz	State College, PA
Benjamin L. Haning	Norman	Kathleen E. Scott	Moore
Kevin E. Hawthorne	Beggs	Susan L. Scott	Tulsa
Jeffrey A. Hicks	Ardmore	Patricia I. Simpson	Joppa, MD
Kim V. Hombs	Tulsa	Damon C. Smith	Catoosa
Jeffery S. Horner	Miami	Tamara K. Soupene	Yukon
David S. Hudson	Clovis, NM	Barbara E. Starr	New York, NY
Pamela M. Hughes	Edmond	Howard H. Stevens	Tulsa
Debra A. Jackson	Broken Bow	Ritchie D. Stover	Pryor
Rebecca C. Jestes	Pawnee	Susanne B. Trent	Hooker
James D. Jordan	Stillwater	Philip W. Tripp	Guymon
Richard D. Keeton	Fairview	Dewey L. Waide	Oilton
Todd L. Kopit	Anaheim, CA	Linda M. Westall	Oklahoma City
Mel A. Kress	Owasso	Timothy A. Wilkins	McLoud
Judith R. Kyle	Oklahoma City	Bradley K. Williams	Ardmore
James P. Lee	Lawton	Wayne R. Wolfenkoehler	Moore
Marilyn K. Lieb	Ralston, NB		

Deans of the College of Veterinary Medicine

Clarence H. McElroy	1948-53
Harry W. Orr	1953-56
Duane R. Peterson*	1956
Glenn C. Holm	1956-67
J. Wiley Wolfe*	1967-68
Karl R. Reinhard	1968-69
William E. Brock	1969-77
Patrick M. Morgan	1977-84
J. Mack Oyler*	1985
Joseph W. Alexander	1985-

*Interim Dean

Faculty of the College of Veterinary Medicine

Stanley C. Acree	1965-67	Talmage T. Brown	1975-78
Joseph W. Alexander	1985-	Ralph G. Buckner	1956-86
Daniel C. Anderson	1974-79	George E. Burrows	1978-
Ian L. Anderson	1968-70	C. R. Butler	1961-63
Judy A. Armstrong	1974-75	Raymond L. Butler	1946-51
Clarke E. Atkins	1980-82	P. T. Cardeilhac	1954-55,1963-68
Robert R. Badertscher II	1979-83	Anthony E. Castro	1978-85
Robert J. Bahr	1984-	John S. Chitwood	1975-76, 1977-84
Elton R. Baird	1961-63	Albert N. Christiansen	1951-52
Charles Baldwin	1985-	David M. Clark	1985-
Jerry D. Barak	1951-52	Linda K. Clark	1974-75
Charlie N. Barron	1949-53	Bill R. Clay	1970-77
Selwyn J. Barron	1977-79,1980-	Deborah Claypool	1984-
Kenneth E. Bartels	1982-	Thomas B. Cleland	1959-60
Paul B. Barto	1955-86	Russell M. Coco	1941-45
Calvin G. Beames	1963-82	Harry W. Colvin	1956-57
David M. Bedell	1972-74	R. B. Conaway	1953
J. Don Bell	1967-69	Anthony W. Confer	1981-
Luigi B. Belli	1968-69	James E. Cook	1951-52
E. A. Benbrook	1915-17	Nelson R. Cooley	1953-56
Ernest R. Benner	1964-66	Robert W. Coppock	1977-80
D. V. Benson	1947-48	James B. Corcoran	1956-76
Gillett Berger	1954-55	Lane D. Corley	1974-78
Everett D. Besch	1956-68	Richard E. Corstvet	1966-81
James Blankemeyer	1979-82	Richard L. Cowell	1985-
Albert B. Blanton	1969-70	Victor S. Cox Jr.	1965-67
Bruce S. Blauch	1958-65	Arthur Craigmill	1977-80
Edward L. Blevins	1952-58	James E. Creed	1982-84
Julia T. Blue	1974-77	Malcolm H. Crump	1958-59
M. Joseph Bojrab	1966-69,1972-73	Richard R. Dahlgren	1963-66
Mary H. Bowles	1975-	Ragnar N. Danielson	1936-40
Byron G. Boysen	1978-79	Georg Ann Davenport	1969-72
William J. Bracken	1956-57	Lyle A. David	1970-71
James E. Breazile	1963-67,1978-	Lionel J. Dawson	1982-
William E. Brock	1954-78	Joseph P. Desch	1980-83
C. P. Brose	1947-48	Claude Desjardins	1969-72

Lorna Dewes	1974-75	E. Wynn Jones	1954-78
David C. Dodd	1975-79	Eugene M. Jones	1965-86
William C. Edwards	1969-	LaVerne M. Jones	1981-
Frankee P. Eliot	1967-69,1972-73	Helen E. Jordan	1969-
Theodore E. Eliot Jr.	1967-73	Margaret Juliana	1977-78
Edwin W. Ellett	1956-58	Robert A. Kainer	1953-55
Katherine M. Ellis	1977-78	G. B. Klaus	1965-67
Ray W. Ely	1984-	Ira O. Kliewer	1954-77
Robert L. Emerson	1946-47	Franklin R. Knotts	1949-53
Brian H. Espe	1982-83	A. Alan Kocan	1974-
Lawrence E. Evans	1970-83	Katherine M. Kocan	1974-
Barbara Everhart	1958-59	Marilyn Kostolich	1985-
Larry L. Ewing	1963-72	Wendell H. Krull	1948-64
Sidney A. Ewing	1960-65,68-72, 1979-	John J. Lammerding	1978-80
		Harold Laubauch	1976-77
Floron C. Faires Jr.	1965-68	J. M. LeBus	1970-71
Lloyd C. Faulkner	1981-	Bruce A. Lessley	1975-
Joseph P. Fontenot	1954-55	Lowery L. Lewis	1896-1922
Donald D. Ford	1964-65	James N. Livingston	1967-68
J. Carl Fox	1978-	Dan H. Lochner	1982-85
Patricia Franks	1980-83	Frank K. Lochner	1981-
Kathleen P. Freeman	1982-83	Patricia J. Luttgen	1976-78
Larry E. Freeman	1974-78	Charles G. MacAllister	1979-
James C. Freeny	1968-74	Kathrine MacNeil	1974-80
Martin R. Frey	1959-63	Duncan W. MacVean	1974-81
Merwin L. Frey	1973-77	Albert L. Malle	1953-81
Jonathan D. Friend	1949-86	A. E. Marshall	1966-67
Duane L. Garner	1972-85	G. Pat Mayer	1956-58,1973-79
Lynn L. Gee	1955-64	C. Sidney McCain	1981-
Bertis L. Glenn	1953-85	G. David McCarroll	1975-81
Dennis D. Goetsch	1957-69	Leslie E. McDonald	1954-69
Gerald D. Goetsch	1948-53	Clarence H. McElroy	1910-14, 1918-53
Dan E. Goodwin	1971-	Chester F. Meinecke	1956-60
Lea Gordon	1974-77	Mushtaq A. Memon	1982-84
James G. Graham	1961-66	L. D. Meyer	1953-54
Bruce W. Gray	1969-72	Harold V. Miller	1979-81
Robert A. Green	1970-74	Lewis H. Moe	1928-66
Alexander Greenfield	1968-69	Thomas Monin	1966-
D. Dee Griffin	1978-81	Andrew W. Monlux	1956-85
Charles J. Hardin	1949-52	Ward W. Moore	1954-55
Karl S. Harmon	1942-45	Gregor L. Morgan	1981-
Edward E. Harnden	1923-49	Patrick M. Morgan	1974-
Grace E. Clause-Hassler	1927-28	Sandra Gilbert Morgan	1982-
F. S. Hathaway	1916-17	Maurice C. Morrissette	1954-67
R. Dennis Heald	1982-	Rebecca J. Morton	1975-
Charles D. Heinze	1958-61	Derek A. Mosier	1985
Perrian R. Henry	1953-54	Clifton N. Murphy	1952-56
Glenn C. Holm	1956-67	Nicholas A. Nail	1964-65
Donald D. Holmes	1959-62, 1979-86	J. E. Nance	1917-18
Stephen R. Holmes	1968-69	Sharon L. Nash	1981-
John T. Homer	1974-	Thomas M. Neal	1969-74
John P. Hoover	1983-	T. Mark Neer	1979-82
Fred M. Hopkins	1975-79	Stanley W. Newcomer	1950-57,1963-83
Paul E. Howard	1980-82	Alphonsus P. Niec	1975-79
James C. Hruska	1961-64	Theodore Nobel	1980-81
Kenneth W. Huffman	1956-57	Ben B. Norman	1962-64
Donald A. Hulse	1975-77	Jerry W. Northington	1976-77
Jerry G. Hurst	1965-82	Ruby Mae Northup	1927-28
James A. Jackson	1968-86	Fayne H. Oberst	1974-84
Edmund E. Jeffers	1945-47	William D. O'Mara	1950-52
David B. Jennings	1968-78	Harry W. Orr	1919-56
Billy J. Johnson	1979-	Richard J. Orts	1973-79
Eileen Johnson	1984-	Bennie I. Osburn	1964-69
Lester Johnson	1954-84	Charlotte L. Ownby	1974-
Thurston L. Johnson	1941-58	J. Mack Oyler	1968-69,73-75, 1980

Roger J. Panciera	1956-	George E. Short	1950-55
Clark S. Patton	1970-78	W. P. Shuler	1912-17
Charles C. Pearson	1954-77	B. T. Simms Jr.	1951-53
Roger C. Penwick	1983-	Steven H. Slusher	1978-
Duane R. Peterson	1948-86	Hubert C. Smith	1941-43
Thomas P. Piekunka	1964-65	Joseph E. Smith	1966-69
Roy R. Poole	1968-69	Kent D. Smith	1984-
Leon N. D. Potgieter	1975-78	Robert A. Smith	1977-
Felix D. Prater	1979-84	W. Thomas Sodowsky	1973-75
Thomas Pugsley	1982-83	Richard Spall	1973-74
C. Max Purdy	1983-86	George H. Stabenfeldt	1962-68
Marshall R. Putnam	1979-83	Ernest L. Stair	1975-
Charles W. Qualls	1982-	Theodore E. Staley	1965-
Art J. Quinn	1975-	W. A. Starin	1909-10
Thomas C. Randolph Jr.	1970-76	F. O. Steele	1947-48
Joseph R. Raught	1966-67	A. J. Steiner	1918-19
Charles Redmond	1979-81	Louie G. Stratton	1973-
Herbert W. Reuber	1957-62	Carolynn Taylor-	1982-
Willard E. Rhynes	1972-74	MacAllister	
Lawrence E. Rice	1976-	Newton B. Tennille	1948-73
Walter M. Rice	1949-65	Thomas R. Thedford	1965-
L. P. Richardson	1963-67	William D. Thompson	1965-67
Eddie J. Richey	1974-77	Donald M. Trotter	1948-54
L. J. Ritter	1912-14	Ronald D. Tyler	1978-
W. S. Robbins	1910-11	Duane E. Ullrey	1954-55
E. V. Robinette	1914-15	James R. VanBeckum	1964-65
Lester L. Rolf	1974-	Claude B. Vanzant	1961-62
Charles R. Root	1983-85	John H. Venable	1954-76
Jeffie F. Roszel	1972-	Robert D. Walker	1974-77
Gerard J. Rubin	1969-79	Billy C. Ward	1969-73
Robert Rubin	1949-53	C. Kenneth Whitehair	1947-55
Miguel A. Ruiz	1969-70	Delbert L. Whitenack	1975-
James P. Rupp	1966-71	R. O. Whittenton	1913-14
James F. Rusher	1964-65	Eric I. Williams	1961-
Anne C. Rusoff	1980-85	Jeanne Williams	1974-77
Subbiah S. Sangiah	1981-	Frances E. Willison	1928-44
James Sartin	1977-79	Jerry A. Wilson	1962-64
David A. Schoneweis	1958-64	J. Wiley Wolfe	1949-73
Wesley G. Schroeder	1965-66	Robert M. Wood	1978-81
D. F. Schwartz	1948-50	James C. Wright	1981-85
Richard V. Shawley	1973-	W. R. Wright	1905-09
Everett C. Short	1979-	Mark A. Zimmer	1982-85

Agriculture Faculty Who Taught Veterinary Medicine Courses

Duane A. Benton	Dept of Biochemistry
Doyle Chambers	Dept of Animal Science (formerly Animal Husbandry)
Richard R. Frahm	Dept of Animal Science
Edward A. Grula	Dept of Microbiology (formerly Bacteriology)
LaVell M. Henderson	Department of Biochemistry
Ronald R. Johnson	Dept of Animal Science
Roger E. Koeppe	Dept of Biochemistry
Michael E. Mason	Dept of Biochemistry
Earl D. Mitchell Jr.	Dept of Biochemistry
Stanley Musgrave	Dept of Animal Science (formerly Dairy Dept)
Arnold B. Nelson	Dept of Animal Science
Eldon C. Nelson	Dept of Biochemistry
George V. O'Dell Jr.	Dept of Biochemistry
Allen D. Tillman	Dept of Animal Science
George Waller	Dept of Biochemistry
Laken G. Warnock	Dept of Biochemistry
Joe V. Whiteman	Dept of Animal Science
William E. Wilson	Dept of Biochemistry

Staff with Ten or More Years of Service

Vera Brown	Veterinary Parasitology, Microbiology and Public Health	1975-86
Eugene Bucke	Veterinary Pathology	1961-72
Ruth Ann Flowers	Veterinary Parasitology, Microbiology and Public Health	1973-
Gladys Grant	Veterinary Parasitology, Microbiology and Public Health	1965-85
Lois V. Greiner	Dean's Office	1952-68
Charlotte Gruhlkey	Medicine and Surgery	1963-84
Ruth Hume	Veterinary Parasitology, Microbiology and Public Health	1965-84
Charlotte A. Kincaide	Dean's Office	1972-
Aaron Kint	Physical Plant	1969-79
J. Clydene Klinger	Medicine and Surgery	1962-74
Fred Lawson	Veterinary Pathology	1966-82
Everett LeGate	Physical Plant	1964-
Wanda Maddux	Medicine and Surgery	1975-
Benetta Martin	Veterinary Parasitology, Microbiology and Public Health	1971-81
Marilyn Moffat	Medicine and Surgery	1975-
Marie Payne	Veterinary Parasitology, Microbiology and Public Health	1975-
Vinita Pill	Physiological Sciences	1964-85
Kathleen Purdum-Smith	Veterinary Pathology	1967-86
Jean Robbins	Medicine and Surgery	1952-85
James Rupp	Veterinary Pathology	1965-

Appendix 6

OSU Faculty Council Representatives

1953-57	Duane R. Peterson	1971-72	Jonathan D. Friend
1957-60	Lester Johnson	1972-75	Bertis L. Glenn
1960-63	Everett D. Besch	1975-78	Lester Johnson
1963-66	Dennis D. Goetsch	1978-81	Ralph G. Buckner
1967-69	Paul B. Barto	1981-84	John S. Chitwood
1969-72	Eric I. Williams	1984-86	George E. Burrows
	Chairman, 1971-72	1986-	Richard V. Shawley

Appendix 7

Norden Distinguished Teacher Award

The Norden Distinguished Teacher Award is presented annually to a faculty member who is selected for teaching ability, character, and leadership. The recipient must have been a member of the college faculty for three years and engaged primarily in teaching.

1963	Wendell H. Krull	1976	William C. Edwards
1964	Duane R. Peterson	1977	Lester Johnson
1965	Lester Johnson	1978	Albert L. Malle
1966	Paul B. Barto	1979	Duane R. Peterson
1967	Roger J. Panciera	1980	Thomas R. Thedford
1968	Ralph G. Buckner	1981	Jonathan D. Friend
1969	Eric I. Williams	1982	Thomas Monin
1970	Sidney A. Ewing	1983	Robert A. Smith
1971	Jonathan D. Friend	1984	Eugene M. Jones
1972	James B. Corcoran	1985	James E. Breazile
1973	John H. Venable	1986	Roger J. Panciera
1974	Ralph G. Buckner		

Appendix 8

College Yearbook Dedications

1957	Harry W. Orr
1958	Duane R. Peterson
1959	Lester Johnson
1960	E. Wynn Jones
1961	Lewis H. Moe
1962	Wendell H. Krull
1963	Ralph G. Buckner
1964	Newton B. Tennille
1965	Eric I. Williams
1966	Roger J. Panciera
1967	James E. Breazile
1968	M. C. Morrissette
1969	Albert L. Malle
1970	Sidney A. Ewing
1971	Thomas Monin
1972	Eric I. Williams
1973	Billy C. Ward
1974	Ralph G. Buckner
1975	Roger J. Panciera
1976	Thomas C. Randolph Jr.
1977	Louie G. Stratton
1978	Patricia J. Luttgen
1979	Albert L. Malle
1980	Lester Johnson
1981	Thomas Thedford
1982	. . . to all those whose hard work made the dream of the Veterinary Teaching Hospital and AVMA accreditation a reality, for it is to their efforts that the hospital stands as a monument.
1983	Joseph P. Desch
1984	Duane R. Peterson and Jonathan D. Friend
1985	Charlotte A. Kincaide
1986	Robert J. Bahr

Appendix 9

Presidents of the Student Chapter, AVMA

	FALL	SPRING
1948	Sam H. Best	Sam H. Best
1949		J. O. Lane
1949-50	M. Weldon Glenn	James O. Defoe
1950-51	Roderick Parker	Sam K. Morrison
1951-52	Lawrence H. Valentine	Robert H. Leonard
1952-53	R. E. Williams	Paul W. Edmundson
1953-54	Kenneth K. Keahey	P. Ted Parker
1954-55	Donald L. Hohmann	Herbert A. Justus
1955-56	James Ferneau	James B. Roberts
1956-57	William G. Askew	Robert L. Godby
1957-58	Ed McCrary	W. Lee Chatham
1958-59	Albert Pearson	R. Gene White
1959-60	Gerald L. Appelgate	Anthony C. Thomas
1960-61	Jerry R. Gillespie	Edward L. Schenk
1961-62	Doyne Hamm	Edwin D. Fisher
1962-63	James R. Dear	C. Monroe Moreton
1963-64	Larry J. Swango	Billy J. McDougal
1964-65	Joe R. Davis	Vernie R. Walker
1965-66	Ronald Q. Roberts	Stephen R. Cobb
1966-67	Philip N. Richardson	Vernon R. Thornton
1967-68	Richard E. Killough	Donald H. Heise
1968-69	John S. Chitwood	Bill R. Clay
1969-70	Coleman L. Scott	Timothy J. Woody
1970-71	Leslie J. Pshigoda	John B. Renfro
1971-72	Lonnie D. Moore	Charles R. Freeman
1972-73	Michael R. Hurt	Ronald R. Wallis
1973-74	J. Bruce Turner	Elliott K. Nelson
1974-75	Joe Melton	Lawrence P. Ruhr
1975-76	James D. Mort	Elton R. Cleveland
1976-77	Kenneth R. Leach	J. Keith Flanagan
1977-78	Ronald J. Streeter	Terry W. Lehenbauer
1978-79	James E. Haught Jr.	Douglas F. Fulnechek
1979-80	Robert P. Thoni	J. Patrick Gillis
1980-81	G. Jeff Schoenhals	John E. Link
1981-82	Stephen R. Hopkins	Ronald R. Eby
1982-83	Randall A. Lovell	Patrick D. Grogan
1983-84	John T. Nick	David L. Hutto
1984-85	Karen M. Bratcher	Robert I. Norris
1985-86	Mark R. Kimsey	Teresa E. Furr
1986-87	Brant A. Schneider	Bill E. Oxford

Dean McElroy Award

The Dr. Clarence H. McElroy Award is presented to the outstanding member of the senior class. Selected by a vote of classmates and faculty of the senior class, the recipient must demonstrate excellent scholarship and professional ability. Named in memory of Dr. McElroy, who was the first dean of the college, the award was originally $50.00, but in 1986 was increased to $500.00 through an endowment which was established by Dr. Austin Weedn in honor of Dr. Duane R. Peterson.

1954	Paul W. Edmundson	1971	Lawrence F. McTague
1955	Robert S. Hudson	1972	Kenneth G. Neuens
1956	Donald R. Callicott	1973	Hartford R. Hamilton
1957	Gus W. Thornton	1974	Bill W. Schaefer
1958	Robert M. Spragg	1975	David Helms
1959	Robert S. Laves	1976	Steven L. Vonderfecht
1960	Raymond Gene White	1977	Thomas A. Richardson
1961	James R. VanBeckum	1978	J. Keith Flanagan
1962	Doyne Hamm	1979	Michael J. Diesen
1963	Fred G. Ferguson		Terry W. Lehenbauer
1964	Larry J. Swango	1980	Bruce Rosier
1965	Joe R. Davis	1981	Michael Lappin
1966	Danny A. Hudson	1982	John E. Link
1967	William E. Hornbuckle	1983	John D. Stein
1968	Vernon R. Thornton	1984	Thomas E. VanGundy
1969	Michael D. Lorenz	1985	Kenneth L. Abrams
1970	Larry L. Nolen	1986	Michael D. Nichols

Dean Orr Award

The Dean Harry W. Orr Award is made annually to a third-year veterinary medicine student who has demonstrated high academic achievement and unusual professional growth in pre-clinical training.

1958	Robert S. Laves	1973	Brenda Rowe Corbin
1959	Frank A. Serra	1974	Glenn F. Anderson
1960	Donald D. Ford	1975	John W. Whittaker
1961	Doyne Hamm	1976	Judith Johnson Vaeth
1962	Fredrick G. Ferguson	1977	Curtis J. Fried
1963	Larry J. Swango	1978	Terry W. Lehenbauer
1964	William R. Roberson	1979	Steven R. Weir
1965	Stephen M. Jones	1980	Michael R. Lappin
1966	Charles F. Kirkland	1981	Melissa D. Orr
1967	Eddie Joe Richey	1982	Perry F. Crenshaw
1968	Mike D. Lorenz		Warren E. Deal
1969	Larry Lee Nolen	1983	Thomas E. VanGundy
1970	Julia T. Blue	1984	Michael D. Major
	John R. Weisner	1985	Rebecca C. Jestes
1971	James R. Ekart	1986	Joy Huska
1972	Elizabeth Ann Cochran		

Appendix 12

SCAVMA Auxiliary Presidents

	FALL	SPRING
1957-58	Mary Heavner	Joyce Colvert
1958-59	Peggy Chatham	Drew Terry
1959-60	Norma Moe	Viola Mack
1960-61	Sandra Brashears	Joy Schomp
1961-62	Cassie Spencer	Bobby Gibbons
1962-63	Ann Jewett	Pat Seagren
1963-64	Lora Swango	Donna Kirkpatrick
1964-65	Sandra Olson	Judy Alm
1965-66	Lenetta Grantham	Sue Patton
1966-67	Laurel Anderson	Kay Killough
1967-68	Carol Thornton	Kathleen Chitwood
1968-69	Mona Stedman	Nancy Kiehn
1969-70	Susan Nusz	Donnie Eubanks
1970-71	Ginny Flynt	Carolyn Kendall
1971-72	Kat Dillon	Jerrie McKinley
1972-73	Melinda Watterson	Diane Freeman
1973-74	Nancy Whitehead	Sandra Pollard
1974-75	Kathy Rains	Brenda Renegar
1975-76	Ginger Lipscomb	Linda Cleveland
1976-77	Suzanne Thurman	Monica Rone
1977-78	Linda Lenington	Carol Davis
1978-79	Pam Epperson	Vanessa Hunholz
1979-80	Donna Sanders	Donna Sanders
1980-81	Cindy Rose	Cheryl Winn
1981-82	Cheryl Winn	Carey Pribil
1982-83	Jana Healey	Dana Cole
1983-84	Robin Nick	Suzanne McQuade
1984-85	Tina Smith	Sharon Fall
1985-86	Kim Hefley	Anna Schick
1986-87	Anna Schick	

*Beginning in January 1986, SCAVMA Auxiliary presidents will serve a full year, January through December.

Appendix 13

Lillie Grossman Award

The Lillie Grossman Award is presented by the AVMA Auxiliary to the outstanding senior spouse at the Annual Awards Banquet. The award is a beautiful engraved silver bowl and is named in honor of Lillie Grossman.

1968	Kay Killough	1980	Linda Shipman
1969	Kathleen Chitwood	1981	Janet White
1970	Nancy Kiehn		Special Award to
1971	Donnie Eubanks		Jeannine Gillis
1972	Jerrie McKinley	1982	Donna Sanders
1973	Carolyn Kendall	1983	Cheryl Winn
1974	Susan Thistlethwaite	1984	Carey Pribil
1975	Kathy Rains		Special Award to Jana
1976	Jane Bush		Healey
1977	Linda Cleveland	1985	Robin Nick
1978	Jan Flanagan	1986	Suzanne McQuade
1979	Carol Davis		

Dissertations

DEPARTMENT OF VETERINARY PARASITOLOGY, MICROBIOLOGY AND PUBLIC HEALTH

E. R. Beilfuss	1957	The Life History of *Phyllodistomum lohrenzi* (Loewen, 1935) (Trematoda: Gorgoderinae)
R. J. Tonn	1959	Morphological and Experimental Studies on *Otodectes cynotis* (Hering, 1838)
E. D. Besch	1963	Studies of the Biology of *Cooperia punctata* (V. Linstow, 1907) Ransom, 1907, (Nematoda: Trichostrongylidae) in the Domestic Rabbit, *Oryctolagus cuniculus*
S. A. Ewing	1964	Recognition of a Canine Rickettsiosis in Oklahoma and its Differentiation from Babesiosis
C. S. Hayat	1972	Pathogenesis of two Isolates of *Ehrlichia canis* in dogs
L. D. Corley	1975	Local Immunoprophylaxis in Enteric Colibacillosis
B. W. Starks	1975	Biology of the Infectious Agent of Feline Infectious Peritonitis
H. E. Laubach	1977	The Relationship of Phospholipase B to Infectious Agents
J. A. Jackson	1978	A Study of the Membrane Nictitans and Genitalium of the Canine with Reference to Lymphofollicular Hyperplasia and its Etiology
H. K. Cheruiyot	1978	The Distribution and Factors Influencing the Establishment of *Fasciola hepatica* Linnaeus 1758, in Native Oklahoma Cattle
R. D. Walker	1978	A Study of the Bovine Pulmonary Response to *Pasteurella haemolytica*. I. Pulmonary Macrophage Response. II. Specificity of Immunoglobulins Isolated from the Bovine Lung
K. M. Kocan	1979	A Study of *Anaplasma marginale* Theiler in Selected Ixodid Ticks
M. Y. Yue	1980	Studies of the Life Cycle and Epidemiology of *Pterygodermatites nycticebi* (Monnig, 1921) Quentin, 1969 from *Leontopithecus rosalia, Pithecia pithecia, Pithecia monachus,* and *Callimico goeldii* in the Oklahoma City Zoo
S. Abdul-Hamed	*1983*	*Studies on the Effects of Host Dietary Factors on the Host-Parasite Relationship Between Hetereakis gallinarum* (Nematoda: Heterakidae) and the Chicken
K. K. McKenzie	1984	A Study of the Transmission of Canine Leishmaniasis by the Tick, *Rhipicephalus sanguineus* (Latreille), and Ultrastructural Comparison of the Promastigotes
M. J. Gentry	1984	The Role of Capsular Material of *Pasteurella haemolytica,* Type 1, in Bovine Pneumonic Pasteurellosis
P. Charanasomboon	1985	A Comparison of Flurometric Assay (FIAX) With Two Other Serological Tests in Experimental and Natural Bluetongue Virus Infected Sheep
J. S. Afolabi	1985	Vectors of Newly Endemic Canine Dirofilariasis in Stillwater, Oklahoma
A. O. Adibi	1985	Particulate Antigens of *Trypanosoma cruzi* and Four Leishmania spp.: Study of Binding Specificities of Monoclonal and Polyclonal Antibodies

DEPARTMENT OF VETERINARY PATHOLOGY

J. C. Hruska	1965	A Study of the Cryogenic Preservation and *in vitro* Cultivation of Anaplasma
J. N. Livingston	1971	Characterization of Feline Porphyria: Features and Selected Enzyme Assays
H. D. Giles	1972	Studies in Canine Nephrites
R. E. Schmidt	1973	Effects of Aflatoxin on Pregnant Hamsters and Hamster Fetuses
J. F. Roszel	1975	Cells in Canine Mammary Gland Fluids Associated with Parturition, Pseudocyesis and Tumor
T. E. Palmer	1978	The Demonstration and Identification of Acid Mucopolysaccharides in Canine Mammary Tumors: A Histological and Histochemical Study
R. W. Coppock	1982	Evaluation of Succinyldicholine as an Agent of Euthanasia: Determination of the Rate of Change of Arterial Blood Oxygen and Carbon Dioxide Following Administration of a Lethal Dose of Succinyldicholine

DEPARTMENT OF PHYSIOLOGICAL SCIENCES

C. F. Meinecke	1952	The Effects of Exogenous Testosterone on Spermatogenesis of Bulls
A. W. Jaussi	1960	Some Effects of ACTH on Metabolism and Blood Cells in the Chicken
D. D. Goetsch	1961	Some Metabolic Effects of Glucocorticoids in Cattle and Rats
L. C. Ellis	1961	Some Aspects of Steroid Metabolism and Conjugation in Mammals
R. W. Heninger	1961	Studies on Thyroxine and Tricodothyronine in the Chicken
M. O. Hutchins	1964	The Metabolism and Excretion of Thyroxine and Tridothyronine in Chickens
M. C. Morrissette	1964	Effects of Progestins on Reproduction in Swine and Rats
N. S. Jocobsen	1965	Lipid Metabolism in Female *Ascaris lumbricoides* During Starvation
G. D. Bottoms	1966	Some Metabolic Effects of Corticosterone in Different Tissues of the Rat and the Subcellular Distribution of (3H) Corticosterone in These Tissues
B. G. Harris	1967	Fatty Acid Synthesis From Propionate in *Ascaris lumbricoides*
J. G. Hurst	1967	Role of the Hypothalamus in the Control of Thyrotropin Production by Anterior Pituitary of Chickens
J. G. Hurst	1967	Some Effects of Hypophysectomy on Thyroid Function in Chickens
W. D. Thompson	1967	A Study of the Effects of Direct Pyramidal Stimulation on Some Lumbar Spinal Motonewon Populations in the Dog
G. H. Stabenfeldt	1968	Studies on Progesterone Levels in the Peripheral Blood of Cows During the Estrous Cycle
E. L. Atkins	1968	Some Temporal Relationships Between the Anterior Pituitary, Corpora Lutea and Endometrium of Nulliparous Gilts During the Estrous Cycle

R. C. Mills	1968	Progesterone Synthesis by the Perfused Bovine Ovary of Early and Late Pregnancy
K. L. Jones	1969	*In Vitro* Enzymatic Activity and Metabolic Studies with Caprine and Brain Homogenates
J. M. Oyler	1969	Utilization of Glucose and Volatile Fatty Acids by Canine and Caprine Brain
D. P. Jennings	1969	Rubrospinal Influences on Selected Alpha Motoneuron Populations of the Dog
R. W. Williams	1969	Effect of Cofactors and Lateotropic on the Biosynthesis of Progesterone by Porcine Luteal Tissue
W. E. Rhynes	1971	The Effect of High Ambient Temperature on Adrenal Cortical and Testicular Endocrine Function in Hereford Bulls
D. E. Goodwin	1972	The Effect of Growth Hormone on Testosterone Secretion in Perfused Rabbit Testes
L. G. Stratton	1972	Inhibition of Spermatogenesis in Rabbits with Testosterone Filled Polydimethylisiloxane Implants
J. A. Holt	1972	Acute Effects of Removing Components of the Entire Gravid Uterus, on Systemic Plasma Concentrations and Ovarian Output of 20 OH-Progesterone and Progesterone in 21-Day Pregnant Rabbits
R. D. Zachariasen	1972	A Functional Interrelationship of the Cortical and Medullary Tissues of the Avian Adrenal
R. F. Clegg	1973	The Effects of Aging on Testicular Function in the Rabbit: A Biochemical, Hormonal and Spermatogenic Study
D. J. Noble	1973	Early Effects of Experimental Cryptochidism Upon Rat Testis Metabolism
H. D. Cole	1975	Reduction of Enterotoxin Reactivity by Brush Border Membranes and Enterotoxin-Induced Alteration of Brush Border Chemistry
J. E. Peterson	1976	Metabolism of Testosterone Following Continuous Infusion of (3H) Testosterone: Effect of Orchiectomy and Testicular Atrophy
J. T. Haskins	1976	Response of Supraoptic Neuroendocrine Cells to Linear Changes of Plasma Osmolality in Unanesthetized Sheep
I. L. Anderson	1977	Porcine Malignant Hyperthermia: Studies on Isolated Muscular Sheep
M. J. Donahue	1977	Permeability Characteristics and Ion Selectivity in the Basal Lamella of *Ascaris suum*
J. M. Merz	1977	Short-circuit Current and Solute Fluxes Across the Gut Epithelium of *Ascaris suum*
N. S. Latman	1977	Pituitary Stimulation of Parathyroid Hormone Secretion
B. C. Bruot	1978	The Influence of the Pineal Peptide Arginine Vasotoxin on Reproductive Adenohypophyseal Hormones
J. L. Sartin	1978	Regulation of Synthesis and Secretion of Pineal Hormonal Principles
L. J. Myers III	1981	Responsiveness of Supraoptic Neuroendocrine Cells to Sequential Oxytocin and Vasopressin Evoking Stimuli

L. L. Zinn	1982	The Effects of Cadmium and Naphthalene on Osmoreregulatory Transport in the Opercular Epithelium of the Channel Catfish, *Ictalurus punctatus*
J. M. Gutierrez	1984	Isolation Partial Characterization, and Pathologic Effects of a Myotoxin From Bothrops Asper Venom
H. J. Mass	1984	A Study of the Treatment of Metabolic Acidosis in Dogs
R. J. Gamble	1984	Effect of Drug Derivatives on the Electrical Characteristics of the Isolated Gut Epithelium of *Ascaris suum*

Bibliography

BOOKS

Adams, Francis. *The Genuine Works of Hippocrates*. Baltimore, MD: The Williams and Wilkins Company, 1946.

Bartlett, John. *Familiar Quotations,* 13th ed. Boston: Little, Brown and Company, 1955.

Bierer, B. W. *A Short History of Veterinary Medicine in America*. East Lansing: Michigan State University Press, 1955.

Brubacher, John S. and Willis Rudy. *Higher Education in Transition: A History of American Colleges and Universities, 1636-1976,* 3rd edition. New York: Harper and Row, 1976.

Cunningham, Robert E. *Stillwater, Where Oklahoma Began*. Stillwater, OK: Arts and Humanities Council of Stillwater, Oklahoma, Inc., 1969.

Farrington, Benjamin. *Greek Science*. Harmondsworth, Middlesex, England: Penguin Books, Ltd., 1944.

Gill, Jerry Leon. *The Great Adventure: Oklahoma State University and International Education*. Stillwater: Oklahoma State University Press, 1978.

Green, Robert Montraville. *A Translation of Galen's Hygiene*. Springfield, IL: Charles C. Thomas, 1951.

Kirk, K. *Index of Diagnosis,* 4th ed. Baltimore, MD: Williams and Wilkins Company, 1953.

Leonard, Ellis P. *A Cornell Heritage: Veterinary Medicine 1868-1908*. Ithaca: New York State College of Veterinary Medicine, 1979.

Lyons, Albert S., and Petrucelli, R. Joseph II. *Medicine, An Illustrated History*. New York: Harry N. Abrams, Inc., 1978.

McKenzie, A. E. E. *The Major Achievements of Science*. Cambridge, MA: Cambridge University Press, 1960.

Pattison, Iain. *The British Veterinary Profession 1791-1948*. London: J. A. Allen & Company Limited, 1984.

Schouten, J. *The Rod and Serpent of Asklepios*. Amsterdam, The Netherlands: Elsevier Publishing Company, 1967.

Schwabe, Calvin W. *Cattle, Priests and Progress in Medicine*. Minneapolis: University of Minnesota Press, 1978.

Smithcors, J. F. *Evolution of the Veterinary Art*. Kansas City: Veterinary Medicine Publishing Co., 1957.

Smithcors, J. F. *The American Veterinary Profession.* Ames: Iowa State University Press, 1963.

Smithcors, J. F. *The Veterinarian in America, 1625-1975.* Santa Barbara, CA: American Veterinary Publications, Inc., 1975.

Steuer, Robert O., and Saunders, J. B. de C. M. *Ancient Egyptian and Cnidian Medicine.* Berkeley and Los Angeles: University of California Press, 1958.

COLLECTIONS

Archives, College of Veterinary Medicine, Oklahoma State University, Stillwater, Oklahoma:

"Analysis of Accreditation Reports of 1958, 1962, and 1968 Concerning Veterinary Medicine Facilities."

Author interview with Mr. Bill Abbott, College of Veterinary Medicine, 30 June 1983.

Author interview with Mrs. Ruth Lewis Baber, Tulsa, 19 July 1985.

Author interview with Mr. Paul Barto, College of Veterinary Medicine, 20 May 1983.

Author interview with Mrs. A. H. Blankenship, Stillwater, 13 September 1984.

Author interview with Mrs. Harry W. Boyce, 9 May 1984.

Author interview with Dr. Ralph G. Buckner, College of Veterinary Medicine, 27 May 1983.

Author interview with Dr. James Corcoran, Stillwater, 10 January 1983.

Author interview with Dr. Max A. Cress, College of Veterinary Medicine, 8 June 1984.

Author interview with Dr. Jonathan D. Friend, College of Veterinary Medicine, 12 May 1983.

Author interview with Dr. Bryan Glass, College of Veterinary Medicine, 25 August 1983.

Author interview with Dr. Raymond E. Henry and Dr. Duane R. Peterson, College of Veterinary Medicine, 15 August 1984.

Author interview with Dr. Donald D. Holmes, College of Veterinary Medicine, 23 May 1983.

Author interview with Dr. Lester Johnson, College of Veterinary Medicine, 24 May 1983.

Author interview with Dr. Albert L. Malle, College of Veterinary Medicine, 7 January 1983.

Author interview with Dr. Leslie E. McDonald, Stillwater, 29 July 1985.

Author interview with Dr. J. Mack Oyler, College of Veterinary Medicine, 24 May 1983.

Author interview with Mrs. Grace Peebles, College of Veterinary Medicine, 17 May 1983.

Author interview with Ms. Kathleen Purdum, College of Veterinary Medicine, 25 May 1983.

Author interview with Dr. Louie G. Stratton, College of Veterinary Medicine, 4 June 1984.

Author interview with Dr. Newton B. Tennille, Stillwater, 17 May 1983.

Author interview with Dr. James O. Tucker, College of Veterinary Medicine, 25 May 1983.

Author interview with Dr. Delbert L. Whitenack, College of Veterinary Medicine, 30 June 1983.

Author interview with Mrs. Lois Greiner, 9 December 1982.

"AVMA Council on Education Site Visit Report, January 1963."

[AVMA]. "Report on Evaluation College of Veterinary Medicine, Oklahoma State University," [1981].

[AVMA]. "Report of Evaluation College of Veterinary Medicine, Oklahoma State University, [1977]."

"AVMA Council on Education Accrediation Policies and Procedures, August 1985."

"AVMA Council on Education Report, January 1969."

College of Veterinary Medicine. "Report to the AVMA Council on Education, November 18, 1985."

"College of Veterinary Medicine: Self Study 1975."

Contract Between the United States of America and Oklahoma State University, 1965.

Dr. J. C. Evans with Dr. Dan Goodwin, 18 January 1973.

Dr. S. A. Ewing with Dr. D. Goodwin, 2 October 1985.

"Final Report of Consultants to Dean Morgan and the OSU College of Veterinary Medicine Curriculum Committee, 5 July 1978."

Final Report Contract No. LA-282 Between the Agency for International Development and the Oklahoma State University, 1965-1971 for Assistance to the Regional College of Veterinary Medicine and Animal Science at San Carlos University, Guatemala. September 1972.

"Guidelines for Admission to Advanced Standing, Approved by Veterinary Administrative Council, September 14, 1979."

"History and Organization of the Department."

G. C. Holm to Oliver S. Willham, 22 February 1964.

Dean C. H. McElroy to Dr. Henry Bennett.

"Missions, Goals, and Objectives: College of Veterinary Medicine, Oklahoma State University, 18 April 1973; revised 6 November 1973."

Oklahoma State Regents for Higher Education, *The Third Biennial Report of the Oklahoma State Regents for Higher Education, Period Ending June 30, 1946.*

H. W. Orr to C. H. McElroy, 21 March 1934.

Dr. Harry Orr to Dr. M. A. Nash, 19 November 1954.

Dr. Harry Orr to J. L. Sanderson, 22 June 1953.

G. Poppenseik to R. B. Kamm, 1968.

"Remarks by Dean Morgan at the College Convocation, May 10, 1980."

"Report to AVMA Council on Education from the College of Veterinary Medicine, Oklahoma State University, November 1969."

"Report to the AVMA Council on Education, November 18, 1985."

"Report of the Committee on Biotechnology to Dean Alexander, January 31, 1986."

"Report to the Veterinary Medicine Faculty Meeting, Spring, 1980."

"Report of a Visit to Oklahoma State University, Stillwater, Oklahoma, April 5, 6, 7, 1976, for the Commission on Institutions of Higher Education of the North Central Association of Colleges and Schcols."

Scrapbooks of Newspaper Clippings, Archives, College of Veterinary Medicine, Stillwater, Oklahoma.

B. T. Simms to C. H. McElroy, 6 March 1951.

Study of the College of Veterinary Medicine, Oklahoma State University. Prepared by Larry K. Hayes. Oklahoma City: Oklahoma State Regents for Higher Education, September 1970.

Tape-recorded message received from Dr. June Iben, June 1984.

Tape-recorded message received from Dr. George Short, May 1984.

"Task Force Report to President Boger on Veterinary Medicine, Oklahoma State University, 21 September 1984."

Veterinary Administrative Council Minutes, 1969-1986.

R. Leland West to J. W. Alexander, 12 December 1985.

C. K. Whitehair to E. I. Williams, February 1986.

Whitehair, C. K., W. S. Newcomer, and W. H. Krull. *A Proposal to the Graduate Council, Graduate School, Oklahoma Agricultural and Mechanical College: A Program for Advanced Degrees in Veterinary Medical Science in the School of Veterinary Medicine.* [Stillwater:] No publisher, 1954.

Personnel file of Wendell Krull, Business Office, College of Veterinary Medicine, Oklahoma State University, Stillwater, Oklahoma:

G. C. Holm to O. S. Willham, 14 June 1962.

W. H. Krull to C. H. McElroy, 21 October 1947.

W. H. Krull to C. H. McElroy, 12 April 1948.

W. H. Krull to C. H. McElroy, 9 June 1948.

W. H. Krull to C. H. McElroy, 22 June 1948.

W. H. Krull to C. H. McElroy, 16 July 1948.

C. H. McElroy to W. H. Krull, 17 March 1947.

C. H. McElroy to W. H. Krull, 18 October 1947.

C. H. McElroy to W. H. Krull, 20 July 1948.

R. O. Whittenton, S. Scroggs, and C. H. McElroy to W. H. Krull, 2 June 1948.

W. R. Williams to B. J. McDougal, 13 April 1964.

Files of Oklahoma Animal Disease Diagnostic Laboratory, Stillwater, Oklahoma:

"Address to Oklahoma Wheat Growers by Governor David Hall, December 5, 1972."

Building and Facilities Committee (J. Venable, E. D. Besch, B. L. Glenn, E. W. Jones, D. D. Goetsch, T. Monin) to J. W. Wolfe, 26 October 1967.

"The Case for a State-Federal Animal Disease Diagnostic and Research Laboratory in Oklahoma, 1972."

Goodwin, D. E. "A Look at Selected Veterinary Medical Diagnostic Laboratories, January 1972."

"Job Description, Director, Oklahoma Animal Disease Diagnostic Laboratory, 1971."

R. B. Kamm to K. Reinhard, 6 December 1968.

Fred Lowe to Congressman Carl Albert, 18 December 1968.

Fred Lowe to Lewis Munn, 16 December 1968.

Memorandum of Understanding between the Oklahoma State Board of Agriculture and the Board of Regents for Oklahoma State University Concerning the Operation of the Oklahoma Animal Disease Diagnostic Laboratory, [1974].

A. W. Monlux to Diagnostic Laboratory Coordinating Committee, 3 February 1972.

A. W. Monlux to R. B. Kamm, 2 August 1967.

"Notes made following the visit with Governor David Hall, December 21, 1972."

Panciera, R. J. "Report of the Faculty Diagnostic Laboratory Committee Meeting of May 15, 1972.

"Proposed Veterinary Diagnostic Laboratory, Progress Report, [1971]."

K. Reinhard to J. H. Brashear, 8 January 1969.

K. Reinhard to R. B. Kamm, 21 November 1968.

"Report of the Meeting of the Board of Advisors, Oklahoma City, Oklahoma, May 26, 1972."

"Report of the Meeting of the Board of Advisors, Oklahoma City, Oklahoma, June 14, 1973."

"Report of the Meeting of the Board of Advisors, Oklahoma City, Oklahoma, May 31, 1974."

"Report of the Meeting of the Board of Advisors, Oklahoma City, Oklahoma, January 19, 1973."

A Study of the Programs and Needs of the Oklahoma Animal Disease Diagnostic Laboratory of the Oklahoma State University College of Veterinary Medicine. Oklahoma City: Oklahoma State Regents for Higher Education, November 1983.

Oliver Willham to A. W. Monlux, 19 May 1966.

"Site Visit Report, Oklahoma Animal Disease Diagnostic Laboratory, 1978."

"Site Visit Report, Oklahoma Animal Disease Diagnostic Laboratory, 1983."

A Study of the Programs and Needs of the Oklahoma Animal Disease Diagnostic Laboratory of the Oklahoma State University College of Veterinary Medicine. Oklahoma City: Oklahoma State Regents for Higher Education, November 1983.

Special Collections, Edmon Low Library, Oklahoma State University, Stillwater, Oklahoma:

Board of Regents Minutes, 1 December 1956.

Correspondence File in Admission Office, College of Veterinary Medicine, Office of Coordinator of Admissions, Stillwater, Oklahoma:

E. C. Godbold to J. J. Hudson, August 1973.

W. E. Brock to L. H. Nygaard, 23 July 1976.

GOVERNMENT DOCUMENTS

Marks, Larry. *100 Years of Animal Health, 1884-1984.*Washington, DC: U.S. Government Printing Office, 1984.

Martin, Robert A., compiler. *The Statutes of Oklahoma, 1890,* Guthrie, OK: State Capital Printing Company, 1891.

U.S. Department of Commerce, Bureau of Health Personnel. *Student Financial Aid Guidelines, Book I. Health Professions Programs, Document No. HRP-0902568.* Hyattsville, Maryland: National Technical Information Service, 1980.

U.S. Congress. *Statutes at Large of the United States of America, from December 1885 to March 1887 and Recent Treaties, Postal Conventions, and Executive Proclamations.* Vol. 24. Washington, DC: Government Printing Office, 1887.

U.S. Congress. *The Statutes at Large of the United States of America from March 1913 to March 1915. Part 1, Vol. 38.* Washington, DC: no publisher, 1915.

Oklahoma State Legislature. *Oklahoma Statutes 1981 Comprising All Laws of a General and Permanent Nature Including Laws and Amendments Passed by the First Regular Session and First Extraordinary Session of the Thirty-eighth Legislature, 1981. Vol. 2.* St. Paul, MN: West Publishing Company, 1981.

Oklahoma State Legislature. *Oklahoma Session Laws, 1976, Thirty-fifth Legislature, Second Regular Session, Convened January 6, 1976, Adjourned June 9, 1976. First Extraordinary Session, Convened July 19, 1976, Adjourned July 23, 1976.* St Paul, MN: West Publishing Company, 1976.

JOURNALS AND ARTICLES

Arthur D. Little, Inc., "Summary of U.S. Veterinary Medical Manpower Needs–1978-1990." *Journal of the American Veterinary Medical Association,* vol. 173 (August 15, 1978), pp. 369-372.

"The George Sarton Medal." *Isis,* vol. 47 (1956), pp. 31-34.

Goodwin, Dan E. "An Update by the Director of the Diagnostic Laboratory." *Oklahoma Cowman,* vol. 12, no. 7 (July 1972), pp. 11, 20.

Krull, W. H. "Philosophy of Graduate Degrees." *Biologist,* vol. 39 (1956-57), pp. 40-41.

Miller, Everett B. "Nonacademic Influences on the Education of the Veterinarian in the United States, 1887-1921." *Journal of the American Veterinary Medical Association,* vol. 175 (November 15, 1979), pp. 1106-1110.

Miller, Everett B. "Private Veterinary Colleges in the United States, 1852-1927." *Journal of the American Veterinary Medical Association,* vol. 178 (March 15, 1981), pp. 583-591.

Oklahoma Veterinarian, vols. 1-38.

"U.S. Accredits VM School." *A. and M. College News,* vol. 4, no. 1 (15 April 1951), p. 1.

Weedn, Austin W. "A. and M.'s Newest School." *Oklahoma A. and M. College Magazine,* vol. 21, no. 7 (March 1950), pp. 12-13.

Williams, W. L. "Veterinary Education in America." *Veterinary Journal,* vol. 62 (November 1906), pp. 667-687.

Wise, J. Karl and John E. Kushman. "Synopsis of U.S. Veterinary Medical Manpower Study: Demand and Supply from 1980 to 2000," *Journal of the American Veterinary Medical Association,* vol. 187, no. 4 (15 August 1985), p. 361.

RESEARCH PUBLICATIONS

Baumel, J., J. E. Breazile, H. Evans, and A. King, editors. *Nomina Anatomica Avium.* London: Academic Press, 1979.

Beames Jr., C. G., H. H. Bailey, C. O. Rock, and L. M. Schanbacher. "Movement of Sterols and Glycerides Across the Intestine of Ascaris." *47th Annual Meeting American Society of Parasitologists* (1972).

Beames Jr, C. G. "Movement of Sugars Across the Mid-gut of the Parasitic Roundworm *Ascaris lumbricoides suum.*" *Federation Proceedings,* vol. 28 (1969), p. 651.

Bottone, E. J., J. M. Janda, M. R. Motyl, G. L. Archer, N. M. Sullivan, T. D. Wilkins, K. M. Sosnowski, T. M. Kerkering, and A. A. Kocan. "Gastrointestinal Tract Specimens." In *Interpretive Medical Microbiology.* Edited by H. P. Dalton and H. C. Nottebart Jr. New York: Churchill Livingston, 1986.

Breazile, J. E., editor. *Textbook of Veterinary Physiology.* Philadelphia: Lea and Febiger, 1971.

Breazile, J. E. "Nervous Tissue." In *Veterinary Histology,* Chapter 6. Edited by H. D. Dellmann and E. M. Brown. Philadelphia: Lea and Febiger, 1976.

Brock, W. E., C. C. Pearson, I. O. Kliewer, E. W. Jones. "The Relation of Treatment to Hemotological Changes in Anaplasmosis." *Proceedings of the U.S. Livestock Sanitation Association* (October 1959), pp. 61-67.

Brock, W. E., I. O. Kliewer, E. W. Jones, C. C. Pearson. "Vaccine Studies in Bovine Anaplasmosis." *Proceedings of the 5th Pan American Congress on Veterinary Medical Zootechnic,* vol. 1 (1968), pp. 260-263.

Brock, W. E., R. G. Buckner, J. W. Hampton, and R. M. Bird. "Canine Hemophilia: Establishment of a New Colony." *Archives of Pathology,* vol. 76 (1963), p. 464.

Brock, W. E., B. B. Norman, I. O. Kliewer, E. W. Jones. "Autoantibody Studies in Bovine Anaplasmosis." *American Journal of Veterinary Research,* vol. 26 (1965), pp. 250-253.

Brock, W. E., I. O. Kliewer, C. C. Pearson. "A Vaccine for Anaplasmosis." *Oklahoma State University Agricultural Experiment Station Technical Bulletin,* no. T-116 (June 1965).

Buckner, R. G. and S. A. Ewing. "Experimental Treatment of Canine Ehrlichiosis and Haemobartonellosis." *Journal of the American Veterinary Medical Association,* vol. 150, no. 12 (1967), pp. 1524-1530.

Buckner, R. G. *Hemophilia A, Hemophilia B. Spontaneous Animal Models of Human Diseases.* Vol. 1. New York: Academic Press, 1979.

Burrows, G. E., W. C. Edwards, and R. J. Tyrl. "Toxic Plants of Oklahoma." *Oklahoma Veterinarian.* The column is a regular feature of volumes 35-38.

Confer, A. W., R. J. Panciera, and R. W. Fulton. "Effect of Vaccination with Live or Killed Pasteurella Haemolytica on Resistance to Experimental Bovine Pneumonic Pasteurellosis." *American Journal of Veterinary Research,* vol. 46 (1985), pp. 342-347.

Corstvet, R. E., R. J. Panciera, H. B. Rinker, B. L. Starks, and C. Howard. "Survey of Tracheas of Feedlot Cattle for Hemophilus Somnus and Other Selected Bacteria." *Journal of the American Veterinary Medical Association,* vol. 163 (1973), pp. 870-873.

Deftos, L. J., G. P. Mayer, J. F. Habener, and J. T. Potts Jr. "Radio-Immunoassay for Bovine Calcitonin." *Journal of Laboratory & Clinical Medicine,* vol. 79, no. 3 (1972), pp. 480-490.

Ewing, S. A. and R. G. Bucker. "Manifestations of Babesiosis, Ehrlichiosis, and Combined Infections in the Dog." *American Journal of Veterinary Research,* vol. 26, no. 113 (1965), pp. 815-828.

Ewing, S. A. "Observations on Leukocytic Inclusion Bodies from Dogs Infected with *Babesia canis.*" *Journal of the American Veterinary Medical Association,* vol. 143, no. 5 (1963), pp. 503-506.

Ewing, S. A. Correspondence. (Recognition of Ehrlichia infection in dogs). *Journal of the American Veterinary Medical Association,* vol. 144, no. 1 (1964), p. 4.

Ewing, S. A. "Canine Ehrlichiosis." *Advances in Veterinary Science and Comparative Medicine,* vol. 13 (1969), pp. 331-353.

Garner, D. L., and E. S. E. Hafez. "Spermatozoa." In *Reproduction in Farm Animals,* 4th ed., Chapter 9, pp. 167-188. Edited by E. S. E. Hafez. Philadelphia: Lea and Febiger, 1979.

Garner, D. L., and M. P. Easton. "Immunofluorescent Acrosin in Mammalian Spermatozoa." *Journal of Experimental Zoology,* vol. 200 (1977), pp. 157-162.

Glenn, B. L., A. A. Kocan, and E. F. Blouin. "Cytauxzoonosis in Bobcats." *Journal of the American Veterinary Medical Association,* vol. 183, no. 11 (1983), pp. 1155-1158.

Glenn, B. L., A. W. Monlux, and R. J. Panciera. "A Hepatogenous Photosensitivity Disease of Cattle: I. Experimental Production and Clinical Aspects of the Disease." *Pathologia Veterinaria,* vol. 1 (1964), pp. 469-484.

Glenn, B. L. "Feline porphyria. An Animal Model for Human Disease." *Comparative Pathology Bulletin,* vol. 2 (1970), pp. 2-3.

Glenn, B. L., R. J. Panciera, and A. W. Monlux. "A Hepatogenous Photosensitivity Disease of Cattle: II. Histopathology and Pathogenesis of the Hepatic Lesions." *Pathologia Veterinaria,* vol. 2 (1965), pp. 49-67.

Hampton, J. W., R. G. Buckner, C. G. Gunn, L. R. Miller, and J. S. Mayes. "Canine Hemophilia in Beagles: Genetics, Site of Factor VIII Synthesis, and Attempts at Experimental Therapy." *Proceedings of the VII Congress of the World Federation of Haemophilia, May 17-20, 1971, Tehran, Iran.*

Jones, E. W., L. Johnson, and C. D. Heinze. "Anesthesia in the Horse—a Rapid Induction Technique." *Journal of the American Veterinary Medical Association,* vol. 137, no. 2 (15 July 1960), pp. 119-122.

Jones, E. W., K. A. Vasko, D. Hamm, and R. W. Griffith. "Equine General Anesthesia—Use of Halothane for Maintenance." *Journal of the American Veterinary Medical Association,* vol. 140, no. 2 (1962), pp. 148-153.

Jones, E. W., T. E. Nelson, I. L. Anderson, D. D. Kerr, and T. K. Burnap. "Malignant Hyperthermia of Swine." *Journal of Anesthia,* vol. 36, no. 1 (1972), pp. 42-51.

Jordan, H. E., and E. E. Byrd. "The Life Cycle of *Brachycoelium mesocorchium* Byrd, 1937 (Trematoda: Digenea: Brachycoeliinae)." *Zeitschrift fur Parasitenkunde,* vol. 29 (1967), p. 61.

Jordan, H. E. and S. A. Ewing. "Concepts of Gastrointestinal Parasitism and Strategies for Designing Corrective Control Programs." In *Veterinary Gastroenterology.* Edited by Neil O. Anderson. Philadelphia: Lea and Febiger, 1980.

Jordan, H. E., N. A. Cole, and S. A. Ewing. "Influence of *Ostertagia ostertagi* and *Cooperia* Infections on the Energetic Efficiency of Steers Fed a Concentrate Ration." *American Journal of Veterinary Research,* vol. 38 (1977), p. 1157.

Kerr, D. D., E. W. Jones, T. E. Nelson, and E. E. Gatz. "Treatment of Malignant Hyperthermia in Swine." *Anesthesia and Analgesia,* vol. 52 (September/October 1973), p. 734.

Kocan, A. A., A. E. Castro, B. Espe, R. T. Doyle, and S. K. Olsen. "Inapparent Bluetongue in Free-Ranging White-Tailed Deer." *Journal of the American Veterinary Medical Association,* vol. 181, no. 11 (1982), pp. 1415-1416.

Kocan, A. A., B. L. Glenn, T. R. Thedford, R. T. Doyle, K. Waldrup, G. Kubat, and M. G. Shaw. "Effects of Chemical Immobilization on Hematologic and Serum Chemical Values in Captive White-Tailed Deer," *Journal of the American Veterinary Medical Association,* vol. 179, no. 11 (1981), pp. 1153-1156.

Kocan, K. M., S. P. Morzaria, A. D. Irvin, W. P. Voigt, J. Kiarie. "Demonstration of Colonies of *Cowdria ruminantium* in Midgut Epithelial Cells of *Amblyomma variegatum* (Abstr)." *American Journal of Veterinary Research* (in press).

Kocan, K. M. "Development of *Anaplasma marginale* in Ixodid Ticks: Coordinated Development of a Rickettsial Organism and its Tick Host." *Morphology, Physiology, and Behavioral Ecology of Ticks.* Edited by J. Sauer and J. A. Hair. England: Harwood, Inc., in press 1985.

Kowalczyk, D. and G. P. Mayer. "Cation Concentration in Skeletal Muscle of Paretic and Nonparetic Cows." *American Journal of Veterinary Research,* vol. 33, no. 4 (1972), pp. 751-757.

Lessley, B. A., A. W. Confer, D. A. Mosier, M. J. Gentry, J. A. Durham, and J. A. Rummage. "Saline-Extracted Antigens of *Pasteurella haemolytica:* Separation by Chromatofocusing, Preliminary Characterization, and Evaluation of Immunogenicity." *Veterinary Immunology and Immunopathology.* (in press).

MacVean, D. W., A. W. Monlux, P. S. Anderson, S. L. Silberg, and J. F. Roszel. "Frequency of Tumors in a Defined Population." *Veterinary Pathology,* vol. 15 (1978), pp. 700-715.

Mayer, G. P. "A Rational Basis for the Prevention of Parturient Paresis." *Oklahoma Veterinarian,* vol. 24, no. 1 (January 1972), pp. 2-11.

McKee, P. A., R. T. Coussons, R. G. Buckner, G. R. Williams, and J. W. Hampton. "Effects of the Spleen on Canine Factor VIII Levels." *Journal of Laboratory and Clinical Medicine,* vol. 75 (1970), pp. 391-401.

Monlux, A. W., J. F. Roszel, D. W. MacVean, and T. E. Palmer. "Classification of Epithelial Canine Mammary Tumors in a Defined Population." *Veterinary Pathology,* vol. 14 (1977), pp. 194-217.

Monlux, A. W., B. L. Glenn, R. J. Panciera, and J. B. Corcoran. "Bovine Hepatogenous Photosensitivity Associated With the Feeding of Alfalfa Hay." *Journal of the American Veterinary Medical Association,* vol. 142 (1963), pp. 989-994.

Morris, R. G., H. E. Jordan, W. G. Luce, T. C. Coburn, and L. V. Maxwell. "Prevalence of Gastrointestinal Parasitism in Oklahoma Swine." *American Journal of Veterinary Research,* vol. 45 (1984), pp. 2421-2423.

Nelson, T. E., E. W. Jones, and I. L. Anderson. "Porcine Malignant Hyperthermia: An Animal Model of Human Disease." *American Journal of Pathology,* vol. 84, no. 1 (1976), pp. 197-199.

Newcomer, W. S. "Accumulation of Radioiodine in Thyroids of Chicks of the Obese Strain with Hereditary Thyroidities and of Their Parental Strain." *General and Comparative Endocrinology,* vol. 21 (October 1973), pp. 322-330.

Newcomer, W. S., F. F. Huang. "Thyroid Rleasing Hormone in Chicks." *Endocrinology,* vol. 95 (July 1974), pp. 318-320.

Ownby, C. L., W. M. Woods, and G. V. Odell. "Antiserum to Myotoxin from Prairie Rattlesnake *(Crotalus viridis viridis)* Venom." *Toxicon,* vol. 17 (1979), pp. 373-380.

Ownby, C. L., G. V. Odell, W. M. Woods, and T. R. Colberg. "Ability of Antiserum to Myotoxin a from Prairie Rattlesnake *(Crotalus viridis viridis)* Venom to Neutralize Local Myotoxicity and Lethal Effects of Myotoxin a and Homologous Crude Venom." *Toxicon,* vol. 21 (1983), pp. 35-45.

Ownby, L., T. R. Colberg, and G. V. Odell. "In Vivo Ability of Antimyotixon a Serum Plus Polyvalent (Crotalidae) Antivenom to Neutralize Prairie Rattlesnake *(Crotalus viridis viridis)* Venom." *Toxicon,* vol. 24 (1985), pp. 197-200.

Ownby, C. L., G. V. Odell, and T. R. Colberg. "In Vivo Test of the Ability of Antiserum to Myotoxin a from Prairie Rattlesnake *(Crotalus viridis viridis)* Venom to Neutralize Local Myonecrosis Induced by Myotoxin a and Homologous Crude Venom." *Toxicon,* vol. 22 (1984), pp. 99-10.

Panciera, R. J., R. W. Thomassen, and F. M. Garner. "Cryptosporidial Infection in a Calf." *Veterinary Pathology,* vol. 8 (1971), pp. 479-484.

Panciera, R. J. "Oak poisoning in cattle." In *Effects of Poisonous Plants on Livestock.* Edited by Richard F. Keeler, Kent R. VanKampen, and Lynn F. James. New York: Academic Press, 1978.

Panciera, R. J., R. R. Dahlgren, and H. B. Rinker. "Observations on Septicemia of Cattle Caused by a Haemophilus-like Organism." *Pathologia Veterinaria,* vol. 5 (1968), pp. 212-226.

Panciera, R. J. and R. E. Corstvet. "A Model for Pasteurella Haemolytica and Pasteurella Multocida-Induced Pneumonia in Calves." *American Journal of Veterinary Research,* vol. 45 (1984), pp. 2532-2537.

Panciera, R. J., R. E. Corstvet, A. W. Confer, and C. N. Gresham. "Bovine Pneumonic Pasteurellosis: Effect of Vaccination with Live Pasteurella Species." *American Journal of Veterinary Research,* vol. 45 (1984), pp. 2538-2542.

Panciera, R. J., L. Johnson, and B. I. Osburn. "A Disease of Cattle Grazing Hairy Vetch." *Journal of the American Veterinary Medical Association,* vol. 148 (1966), pp. 804-808.

Peterson, D. R. "Nerve Block of the Eye and Associated Structures." *Journal of the American Animal Hospital Association,* vol. 68, no. 888 (March 1951), pp. 145-148.

Peterson, D. R. "Bovine Emphysema Caused by the Plant Perilla Frutescens." Presented at the Symposium on Acute Bovine Pulmonary Emphysema, Laramie, Wyoming, August 1965.

Rosenberg, Steven A., Michael T. Lotze, Linda M. Muul, Susan Leitman, Alfred E. Chang, Stephen E. Ettinghausen, Yvedt L. Matory, John M. Skibber, Eitan Shiloni, John T. Vetto, Claudia A. Seipp, Colleen Simpson, and Cheryl M. Reichert. "Observations on the Systemic Administration of Autologous Lymphokine-Activated Killer Cells and Recombinant Interleukin-2 to Patients with Metastatic Cancer." *New England Journal of Medicine,* vol. 313 (5 December 1985), pp. 1485-1492.

Schoeb, T. R., and R. J. Panciera. "Blister Beetle Poisoning in Horses." *Journal of the American Veterinary Medical Association,* vol. 173 (1978), pp. 75-77.

Staley, T. E., E. W. Jones, and L. D. Corley. "Attachment and Penetration of *Escherichia coli* into the Intestinal Epithelium of the Ileum of Newborn Pigs." *American Journal of Pathology,* vol. 56 (1969), p. 371.

Staley, T. E., L. D. Corley, and E. W. Jones. "Early Pathogenesis of Colitis in Neonatal Pigs Monocontaminated with *Escherichia coli*. Fine Structural Changes in the Colonic Epithelium." *American Journal of Digestive Diseases,* vol. 15 (1970), p. 923.

Staley, T. E., E. W. Jones, and J. A. Smith-Staley. "The Effect of *Escherichia coli* Enterotoxins on the Small Intestine With or Without Mucosal Contact." *American Journal of Digestive Diseases,* vol. 18 (1973), p. 751.

Staley, T. E., E. W. Jones, and A. E. Marshall. "The Jejunal Absorptive Intestinal Cell of the Newborn Pig. An Electron Microscopic Study." *Anatomical Record,* vol. 161 (1968), p. 497.

Staley, T. E., E. W. Jones, and L. D. Corley. "The Fine Structure of the Duodenal Absorptive Cell in the Newborn Pig Before and After Feeding of Colostrum." *American Journal of Veterinary Research,* vol. 30 (1969), p. 567.

Stratton, L. G., R. E. Corstvet, and J. E. Brown. "Isolation of *Klebsiella pneumoniae* from the Urogenital Tract of Experimentally Infected Mares." *Journal of Reproduction and Fertility Supplement,* vol. 27 (1979), pp. 317-320.

Stratton, L. G., R. E. Corstvet, and J. E. Brown. "Isolation of *Klebsiella pneumoniae* from Mares, Stallions and Sawdust Bedding Located on One Ranch." *Journal of Equine Medicine and Surgery,* vol. 3 (1979), pp. 250-261.

Thompson, C. M., C. K. Whitehair, R. W. MacVicar, and J. C. Hiller. "Observations on Artificially Raising Healthy Swine." *Oklahoma Agricultural Experiment Station M-P27,* (June 1952).

Venable, J. H. and S. A. Ewing. "Fine-Structure of *Haemobartonella canis* (Kikuth, 1928) (Rickettsiales: Bartonellaceae) and Relation of the Parasite to its Host Erythrocyte." *Journal of Parasitology,* vol. 54, no. 2 (1968), pp. 259-268.

Williams, Eric I., Donald Williams, Dennis Goetsch, and Paul O. Frith. "Surgical Technique for Removal of the Forestomachs of Calves." *American Journal of Veterinary Research,* vol. 27, no. 121 (November 1966), pp. 1777-1779.

UNIVERSITY AND VETERINARY MEDICINE PUBLICATIONS

Aesculapius, College of Veterinary Medicine Yearbook, 1973-current.

Caduceus, College of Veterinary Medicine Yearbook, 1957-1972.

Gilmore, Francis Richard. "A Historical Study of the Oklahoma Agricultural Experiment Station." Doctor of Education dissertation, Oklahoma State University, 1967.

Lewis, L. L. *Oklahoma Agricultural Experiment Station Bulletin No. 53: Common Parasites of Domestic Animals* (June 1902).

Oklahoma A. and M. College Catalog and Announcements, 1891-1957.

Oklahoma Agricultural Experiment Station Eleventh Annual Report 1901-02.

Oklahoma Agricultural Experiment Station Biennial Report, 1946-1948, part 1, July 1, 1946, to June 30, 1948.

Oklahoma State University Catalog, 1958-current.

Oklahoma State University Faculty Handbook, Appendix D.

Oklahoma Veterinary Bulletin, vol. 1, nos. 2, 3, 4 (January, March, May 1950).

Plexus, 1979-current.

Qui, Quid, Ubi?, 1982-current.

SCAVMA Scoop: The Student Voice of the College of Veterinary Medicine, 1977-1985.

Veterinary Bulletin, vol. 1, no. 1 (November 1949).

Index

A

Accreditation of veterinary school, 47-49, 52. *See also* American Veterinary Medical Association.

Adams, Kenneth, 147.

Addis Ababa University College, 63.

Administrative Council. *See* Veterinary Administrative Council.

Aesculapius: ancient god, 5; symbol of veterinary medicine, 7; Veterinary Medicine Building front door, 151; yearbook, 83, 209, 225.

Affirmative action, 148-149.

Agency for International Development, 52, 63, 113-115, 127, 132, 152.

Agricultural Experiment Station, 22, 25-27, 29-30, 37, 87, 102, 111, 114.

Albert, Carl, 160, 162.

Alexander, Joseph W., 111, 223, 226, 228, 230.

All Sports Club-Dorm Trophy, 44.

Allen, Marshall E., 195.

Allenstein, Leland C., 179.

American Animal Hospital Association, 193.

American Association of Bovine Practitioners, 122, 179, 193, 212-213, 222.

American Association of Equine Practitioners, 193.

American Association of Veterinary Laboratory Diagnosticians, 167.

American College of Theriogenologists, 177.

American College of Veterinary Internal Medicine, 177.

American College of Veterinary Pathologists, 177.

American Indians: early veterinary history, 18.

American Veterinary College: first successful U.S. veterinary school, 19.

American Veterinary Medical Association, 19, 23, 28, 31, 34, 42, 49, 52, 58, 73, 84, 93, 121, 127, 130-132, 134, 136, 140, 142, 146, 177, 180, 184, 185, 188, 192, 197, 200, 202, 208-209, 228, 231.

American Veterinary Medical Association Auxiliary, 122.

Anaplasmosis. *See* Diseases: animal.

Anaplaz,® 99.

Anderson, Jack, 150.

Anderson, William L., 185.

Anesthesia inhalation, 103.

Animal tumor registry, 108.

Annex, 61.

Annual Awards Banquet, 85-86, 123, 140, 141, 195, 203, 217.

Anthrax. *See* Diseases: animal.

Apsyrtus: Greek, father of veterinary medicine, 9.

Aristotle: Greek philosopher, 4, 10.

Arkansas Veterinary Medical Association, 90, 208

Armistead, William W., 84, 134.

Arrington, Jim, 82.

Asklepios. *See* Aesculapius.

Auxiliary to the Student Chapter, AVMA, 45, 67, 149.

Moe, Lewis H., 33, 39, 52, 95, 98, 121, 153, 157; lecture, 153, 178-179, 183 191, 200, 217, 223.
Monk, John, 82.
Monlux, Andrew W., 68, 108, 121, 145, 158, 161, 228.
Monlux, William, 121.
Monogastric calf, 110.
Monroney, A. S., 191.
Montgomery, John, 149, 175, 200, 204; scholarship, 207.
Morgan, Patrick Monroe, 181, 183-185, 187, 193, 195, 197, 200, 202-204, 207, 209, 213, 215, 217, 220, 221.
Morrill Hall, 29.
Morrill, Justin, 20.
Morris (Mark L.) Foundation, 82.
Morrissette, M., 94.
Morton, Rebecca, 165.
Mosier, Jacob, 200, 209.
Munn, Lewis, 160.
Murphy, Clifton, 63, 64.
Murphy, Marvin, 45.
Murphy, Robert, 163, 165, 173, 175.

N

Nail, Nicholas, 90.
Nash, M. A., 58.
National Academy of Science, 107.
National Animal Disease Center, 109.
National Board Examinations, 49, 51, 90, 212, 215, 220.
National Cancer Institute, 108.
National Institutes of Health, 86-88, 91, 94-95, 105, 137, 149, 191, 199.
National Science Foundation, 87, 95, 107.
New York College of Veterinary Surgeons: early U.S. veterinary school, 19.
Newby, Boyd, 185.
Newby, Vernon, 185.
Newby, Warren, 185.
Newcomer, W. Stanley, 71, 74, 94, 106, 208.
Nick, John, 225.
Niec, Alphonso, 197.
Nigh, George, 200, 207, 212, 214.
Nightengale, Lewis, 90.
Nixon, Richard, 152.
Norden Laboratories, 225.
North Central Association, 154-155.
Northup, R. M., 33.

O

Oberst, Fayne H., 146, 173, 190, 199, 226.
Odell, George V., 108.
Oklahoma Academy of Veterinary Practice, 183.

Oklahoma Animal Disease Diagnostic Laboratory, 136, 140, 156, 157-171, 184, 207, 213, 221, 222, 224.
Oklahoma Board of Agriculture, 29, 37, 46, 160-161, 164-165.
Oklahoma Cattlemen's Association, 123, 161.
Oklahoma City Zoo, 107.
Oklahoma Cowman, 162.
Oklahoma Department of Agriculture, 31, 121, 162, 163, 166.
Oklahoma Department of Wildlife Conservation, 109.
Oklahoma Farm Bureau, 160.
Oklahoma legislation: diagnostic laboratory, 160-165; Eighth Legislature, 30; First Legislative Assembly, 25; funding livestock disease research, 98; match NIH grant, 87; name change, 82; Oklahoma Veterinary Practice Act, 132; teaching hospital, 175-177.
Oklahoma State Board of Veterinary Medical Examiners. *See* State Board of Medical Examiners.
Oklahoma State Department of Health, 122, 170, 183.
Oklahoma State Regents for Higher Education. *See* State Regents for Higher Education.
Oklahoma Veterinary Educational Supply, Inc., 153.
Oklahoma Veterinary Medical Association, 31, 33, 35, 43, 61, 122-123, 132, 135, 153, 177, 183, 194-195, 197, 199-200, 205, 210, 216-217, 219, 222, 224, 233; award, 199, 210; journal, 43, 122, 162, 216.
Oklahoma Veterinary Medical Association Auxiliary, 151, 194.
Old Central, 26.
Open House, 89, 94, 149, 178, 191, 202.
Orr, Harry William, 30, 33, 39, 57-60, 68-70, 74, 79, 158.
Orr, Ruth, 223.
Osage County Cattlemen's Association, 98, 99.
Ownby, Charlotte L., 108.
Oyler, J. Mack, 198, 223, 226.

P

Pan American Agricultural Institute, 118.
Panciera, Roger J., 105, 107, 125, 190, 198.
Parker, Don, 215.
Parsons, Gerald, 196.
Pathology Diagnostic Laboratory, 60.
Pawhuska station, 98, 100
Pearson, Charles C., 98-99.

176, 186-189, 200, 207.
Steed, Tom, 115, 123, 162.
Steele, James H., 122.
Stein, John D., 212.
Stenseng, Ronald, 208.
Stephens County Veterinary Students
Scholarship Trust, 134.
Stiles, George W., 35.
Stipe, Gene, 160.
Stober, Mathew, 200.
Stover, G. A., 71.
Strahm, Sam, 197.
Stratton, Addie, 88.
Stratton, Louie, 54, 177, 190, 198-200.
Streeter, Ron, 180.
Stringer, Bruce, 66.
Student and Alumni Fund, 179
Student American Veterinary Medical
Association, 189, 216
Student Chapter, AABP, 213
Student Chapter, AVMA, 42, 45, 49, 67,
88, 130, 135, 152-153, 179-180, 193,
196, 200, 202, 211, 213, 224-225.
Student Union, 49, 85, 200, 213, 217.
Student Veterinary Society. See Student
Chapter, AVMA.

T

Tavernor, Derek, 130.
Taylor-MacAllister, Carolynn, 207.
Teaching hospital. See Boren Veterinary
Medical Teaching Hospital.
Technical Cooperation Administration. See
Agency for International Development.
Teleconference, 204, 206-207.
Temporary Frame #9 (TF-9), 39, 42,
58-60.
Tennille, Newton B., 45-46, 81, 84, 141.
Terpenning, Mark, 184.
Thedford, Thomas R., 109, 152, 199, 204,
207.
Theta Pond, 49.
Thornton, Gus, 82.
Thyroid function in birds, 107.
Tillman, Allen, 94, 118.
Trotter, Donald M., 40-41, 54-55, 140.
Truman, Harry S, 52.
Tucker, James, 41.
Tulsa Veterinary Medical Association, 177,
194.
Turner, Roy J., 62.

U

U.S. Atomic Energy Commission, 85.
U.S. Civil Service Commission:
employment practices, 23, 49.
U.S. Department of Agriculture, 21, 29-
30, 35, 109, 170, 191, 206, 217.

U.S. Department of Health, Education,
and Welfare, 135, 147.
U.S. International Agricultural Programs,
140.
U.S. Legislation: Allied Health Professional
Personnel Training Act of 1966, 123;
Civil Rights Act of 1964, 147; Family
Education Rights and Privacy Act of
1974, 153; fund NIH grant, 87; Hatch
Act, 22, 27; Laboratory Animal Welfare
Act, 191; Meat Inspection Act of 1906,
29; Morrill Act, 21, 25; Public Health
Service Act 1970, 137; Smith-Hughes
Act, 22, 29; Smith-Lever Act, 22, 29;
U.S. Public Health Service, 191;
Veterinary Education Facilities Act of
1966, 123; Veterinary Medical Education
Act, 123.
United States Veterinary Medical
Association. See American Veterinary
Medical Association.
United Nations' Food and Agriculture
Organization, 179.
University Center for Molecular Genetics,
110.
University of San Carlos, 100, 114-120.
The Upjohn Company, 217; class trip, 88.

V

VanEaton, Earl, 228.
Vegetius: Roman veterinary author, 9.
Venable, John H., 87, 132, 139, 176;
plan, 150.
Venezuelan equine encephalomyelitis,
139.
Vesalius, Andreas: Roman anatomist, 10.
Vetceteras, 154.
Veterinary Administrative Council, 125,
127, 129, 140, 147, 150-151, 153, 181,
192-193, 207, 223, 226.
Veterinary College of London:
establishment, 13.
Veterinary Corps: component U.S. Army
Medical Department, 31.
Veterinary Council. See Veterinary
Administrative Council.
Veterinary education: early U.S., 18-23.
Veterinary Medical Alumni Association,
135, 149, 190, 208-209.
Veterinary Medicine Building, 46, 57, 60,
80, 82, 85-87, 92-94, 204, 207.
Veterinary: origin of term, 9.
Veterinary Research Institute, 37, 48, 87,
98, 102.
Veterinary Smoker, 44.
Villagran, Ernesto, 119.

W

Walker, E. R., 99.
Water follies, 86.
Watkins, Wes, 109, 212.
Wayland, Francis, 20.
Weedn, Austin W., 43, 55.
Wells, Milton, 118.
White, Andrew D., 21.
Whitehair, C. Kenneth, 74, 102.
Whitehead, Raymond, 208.
Whitenack, Delbert L., 64, 165.
Whittenton, R. O., 29, 72.
Wight, James Alfred, 143.
Wilber, Philip, 80.
Wilcox, Ray, 44.
Willham, Oliver S., 52, 60, 63, 82, 86, 93, 115, 127, 158.
Williams, Donald E., 222.
Williams, Eric, 95, 118-119, 122, 139, 145, 148, 191, 194, 199, 208.
Williams Hall, 27, 33.
Williams, Teresa D., 88.
Williams, Thomas, 180.
Williams, Walter L., 20.

Willis, Bill, 163.
Wilson, Harry, 189.
Wilson, Marilyn, 183, 212.
Wilson, Mark, 42.
Winters, Leo, 89.
Witt, J. D., 161, 163-165.
Wolfe, J. Wiley, 52, 121, 129, 141-142, 145-146, 159.
Wolfe, Virginia C., 141.
Women's Auxiliary to the Student Chapter. *See* Auxiliary to the Student Chapter, American Veterinary Medical Association.

Wood, Robert M., 183, 190, 203.
Wood, Terry, 135.
Woolley, Walter, 162.
World War I: effect on veterinary medicine, 30, 34.
World War II: effect on veterinary medicine, 34-35, 37.
Wyrick, David, 189

Z

Zoltner, David C., 153.

A History of the Oklahoma State University College of Veterinary Medicine

is a specially designed volume of the Centennial Histories Series.

The text was composed on a personal computer, transmitted by telecommunications to the OSU mainframe computer, and typeset by a computerized typesetting system. Three typefaces were used in the composition. The text is composed in 10 point Melliza with 2 points extra leading added for legibility. Chapter headings are 24 point Omega. All supplemental information contained in the endnotes, charts, picture captions, appendices, bibliography, and index are set in either 8 or 9 point Triumvirate Lite.

The book is printed on a high-quality, coated paper to ensure faithful reproduction of historical photographs and documents. Smyth-sewn and bound with a durable coated nonwoven cover material, the cover is stamped with flat black foil.

The Centennial Histories Committee expresses sincere appreciation to the progressive men and women of the past and present who created and recorded the dynamic, moving history of Oklahoma State University, the story of a land-grant university fulfilling its mission to teach, to research, and to extend itself to the community and the world.